CW00546439

FROM
SICKLES
TO CIRCLES

FROM
SICKLES
TO CIRCLES

BRITAIN AND IRELAND AT THE
TIME OF STONEHENGE

Edited by Alex Gibson and
Alison Sheridan

TEMPUS

The contributors dedicate this book to Emeritus Professor
Derek Douglas Alexander Simpson to mark his retirement

First published 2004

Tempus Publishing Ltd
The Mill, Brimscombe Port
Stroud, Gloucestershire GL5 2QG
www.tempus-publishing.com

© Alex Gibson and Alison Sheridan, 2004

The right of Alex Gibson and Alison Sheridan to be identified as the Authors
of this work has been asserted by them in accordance with the
Copyrights, Designs and Patents Act 1988.

All rights reserved. No part of this book may be reprinted
or reproduced or utilised in any form or by any electronic,
mechanical or other means, now known or hereafter invented,
including photocopying and recording, or in any information
storage or retrieval system, without the permission in writing
from the Publishers.

British Library Cataloguing in Publication Data.
A catalogue record for this book is available from the British Library.

ISBN 0 7524 2902 7

Typesetting and origination by Tempus Publishing.
Printed and bound in Great Britain.

CONTENTS

LIST OF TABLES

LIST OF CONTRIBUTORS

P. Ashmore
  Historic cotland
  Longmore House
  Salisbury Place
  Edinburgh
A.L. Brindley
  Archaeologisch-biolo-
  gisch Instituut
  Universiteit van
  Groningen
  Poststraat 6
  Groningen
  Netherlands
C. Burgess
  64, Avenue Bonneval
  Pacha
  Coussac Bonneval
  F-87500
  France
H.A.W. Burl
  2 Woodland Road
  Northfield
  Birmingham
H. Case
  Pitt's Cottage
  147 Thame Road
  Wanborough
  Oxon
J.G. Evans
  15 Fairleigh Road
  Cardiff
A. Gibson
  Dept Archaeological
  Sciences
  University of Bradford
  Bradford
J. Harding
  Dept of Archaeology
  University of

Newcastle
  Newcastle Upon
  Tyne
B. Hartwell
  Dept of Archaeology
  Queen's University of
  Belfast
  Belfast
F. Healy
  School of Archaeology
  and History
  University of Wales
  Cardiff
  Cardiff
A.S. Henshall
  4/2 West Grange
  Gardens
  Edinburgh
I. Kinnes
  26 Grand Cour
  Rue de l'Eglise
  F-14470 Courseulles
  France
R. Loveday
  Dept. Archaeology
  University of Leicester
  Leicester
R. McHugh
  Dept of Archaeology
  Queen's University of
  Belfast
D. McLaren
  Dept. Archaeoloy
  National Museums of
  Scotland
  Chambers Street
  Edinburgh
T.G. Manby
  43 Meadow Drive

Market Weighton
  York
J.V.S. Megaw
  Dept Archaeology
  University of Glasgow
  Glasgow
E. Murphy
  Dept of Archaeology
  Queen's University of
  Belfast
E. Nelis
  Dept of Archaeology
  Queen's University of
  Belfast
W. O'Brien
  Dept. Archaeology
  University of Ireland,
  Galway
  Galway
  Republic of Ireland
A. Ritchie
  50/1 Spylaw Road
  Edinburgh
G. Ritchie
  50/1 Spylaw Road
  Edinburgh
J.A. Sheridan
  Dept. Archaeology
  National Museums of
  Scotland
  Chambers Street
  Edinburgh
G. Varndell
  Prehistoric and Early
  Europe
  British Museum
  Great Russell Street
  London

INTRODUCTION

This collection of essays on the Neolithic and Bronze Age in Britain and Ireland is offered to Professor Derek Simpson to mark his retirement from the Chair of Archaeology at the Queen's University of Belfast.

As its title suggests, the book covers a variety of topics that reflect the diversity of Derek's own contribution to our understanding of the fourth to first millenia BC. The contributors range from old partners in crime to young ex-students, with a host of colleagues, research students and friends in between; and the papers range from reminiscences of halcyon fieldwork days, through reflections on monuments, artefacts and practices, to considerations of chronology and environment. Kites are flown; misconceptions are set right; new information and new interpretations are presented. What unites these disparate papers is the affection with which they are presented to Derek.

Derek, the contributors to this volume – and a large number of others who, for various reasons, were unable to contribute to this volume, but join us in thanking you for your teaching, kindness, good humour and, above all, friendship over the decades – wish you a long, happy and productive retirement with the good health to enjoy it.

Alex Gibson and Alison Sheridan

Preface
Derek Simpson: A Personal Appreciation

These essays are dedicated to a great friend and an inspirational teacher, Professor Derek Simpson.

Derek studied archaeology at Edinburgh under Stuart Piggott and Richard Atkinson, two scholars who heavily influenced British and Irish archaeology in their long and distinguished careers. As a student under these two archaeological giants, Derek dug at Stonehenge *(1)*. He then returned to Wiltshire and took up a post at Devizes Museum which held then, as it does now, one of the richest collections of Neolithic and Bronze Age artefacts in Britain. *The Catalogue* (Annable & Simpson 1964) that resulted from these years remains, 40 years later, an essential reference book for students of the period.

A lectureship at Leicester University followed Devizes and there, with Charles Thomas, John Wacher, Vincent Megaw and Stanley Thomas, Derek helped build a strong and respected department. Throughout this period (including Devizes) Derek continued to compile an artefact and fieldwork portfolio, encompassing sites such as Overton Hill, Pitnacree, Croft Moraig, Kaimes, Seamer Moor, Raigmore and Skendleby. And of course Northton, one of the few Beaker settlements not just to produce artefacts in abundance, but also the 'Holy Grail' of many prehistorians, a rarity of rarities, not just one house plan, but two. It was the Beaker connection that lured the present writer away from Newcastle and the inspirational George Jobey to the English Midlands ('The Deep South' as George described it). After graduation, I spent some of the summer digging with George Jobey at the Green Knowe platform settlement in Peeblesshire. This was firstly for two weeks helping to supervise on the first year training excavation and then for two weeks with the expert trowellers of George's Adult Education class who supervised me! On the last night at the end of the dig and before an early start hitch-hiking to Fife, we were in a pub in West Linton. As we prepared to leave at closing time (OK, substantially after closing time) George warmly shook my hand, wished me luck and said 'you'll get on with Derek'.

As always, George was quite correct. In those days the then Department at Leicester was an incredibly sociable one and the sociability of particularly Derek ('Simpso') and John Wacher ensured that I was made welcome and enjoyed my postgraduate years. Ann Woods, also one of the socialites, taught

1 The undergraduate Simpson (standing and clean shaven) during the Stonehenge excavations in 1958 with Stuart Piggott and Richard Atkinson. Unfortunately we are not told exactly what is gripping the attention of the group. Is it some fascinatingly complex detail of stratigraphy or is Atkinson demonstrating exactly how much cigarette ash is needed to ensure an acceptable radiocarbon date? *From the cover of The Archaeological Newsetter, 6 (No. 7), 1958*

me much about ceramic technology while Derek guided the main thesis. Trips with Derek to Orkney and the Netherlands, and field trips to Francis Pryor's excavations at Fengate and to Wessex, widened my archaeological horizons at home and abroad. The student-teacher relationship developed into friendship. Derek and Nancy extended this friendship to my parents and the last photograph I have of my father was taken in Derek and Nancy's lounge following my graduation ceremony and about three months before his unexpected death. My mother still sees more of Derek and Nancy than I now do.

After graduation and a short spell at the Instituut voor Prae- en Protohistorie at the University of Amsterdam I returned to Leicester to work for Derek as a research assistant on the ceramic assemblage from Northton – a daunting task. It all looked the same. But it was a wonderful assemblage to work on and I suspect that it will continue to be worked on and reworked by future generations. Derek and I worked closely and I learned a lot – not just about pottery but also about the movies of John Ford and Sam Peckinpah! There were Bronze Age Studies Group meetings in Derbyshire, Aberdeen, Devon, Burgundy and Brittany. The Breton trip, enjoyable though it was, ended in gastroenteritis for Derek and myself and a book for Aubrey Burl (my recollection of the course of events differs in some minor detail from Aubrey's – see Burl, this volume – but we won't fall out over it) *(2)*. There was a trans-European trip to Austria to return the small finds from the Leicester contribution to the Dürrnberg excavations: excellent companionship but no book (Burl wasn't there).

2 Aubrey Burl and Derek enjoying *un verre du cidre* in the *crêperie* within the *Cromlech du Ménec, Carnac.* I sense a book hatching

In 1986 Jane and I were married and Derek did us the great honour of agreeing to be my Best Man. One of the most memorable wedding photographs we have is of Derek starting to read what he thought was a telegram but which turned out to be Jane's Barclaycard bill. It had been inadvertently scooped up with the rest of the post and Derek had the discretion not to read it! But *Schadenfreude* followed. *Schadenfreude* has been loosely translated as 'the feeling you get when you watch your mother-in-law drive off a cliff in your brand new Jaguar'. Derek was appointed to the Chair of Archaeology at the Queen's University of Belfast. We were sorry to lose Derek (it was certainly Queen's gain) but delighted for his career… and I got all his teaching. Unfortunately with the tragic death of Stanley Thomas, Vincent Megaw's departure to Australia, the financial uncertainties emanating from the then University Grants Committee and Derek's departure, the Department at Leicester was in a downward spiral. Other resignations followed and John Wacher and I departed two years after Derek. It was left to Graeme Barker to halt the flow and effect a restoration.

A (Southern) Irish colleague has described Derek's appointment to Queen's as 'a breath of fresh air for Irish archaeology'. Certainly Derek has not been idle in the Chair and has made his contribution to the archaeology of the Island, not just in an advisory capacity through the numerous committees that solicited his expertise, but also in terms of his fieldwork and research. Derek and I collaborated at Lyles Hill, and then there was Balleygalley and Dun Ruadh which prompted a review of possible Irish henges (Condit & Simpson 1998 and see O'Brien, this volume).

Unfortunately, ill health struck Derek in the years before his retirement. I remember visiting him in hospital after his heart surgery. Derek was weak and in pain but the old spark of humour was still there. Derek was surprised to see me (neither Nancy nor I had told him I was coming) but he just looked, smiled and said in his comically exaggerated *Whisky Galore* Scots accent 'Aye! Ye'll hae come tae look at ma library'. I hadn't, Derek, I already knew what was there!

Thankfully Derek made a full recovery and, though now retired, he continues to work on British and Irish prehistory with his research team at Queen's. During his years in Ireland, Derek attracted a new generation of research students, some of whom have contributed to this volume.

Derek, the contributors to this volume wish you a long, happy and productive retirement. We thank you for your teaching, wisdom and, above all, friendship.

Alex Gibson
Ilkley, May 2004

BIBLIOGRAPHY

Annable, K. & Simpson, D.D.A., 1964 *Guide Catalogue of the Neolithic and Bronze Age Collections in Devizes Museum*. Devizes: Wiltshire Archaeological and Natural History Society.
Condit, T. & Simpson, D.D.A., 1998 *Irish Hengiform Enclosures and Related Monuments*. In Gibson A. & Simpson D. (eds), 1998, *Prehistoric Ritual and Religion. Essays in Honour of Aubrey Burl*. 45-61. Stroud: Alan Sutton.

1

BANKS AND BRAES: NOTES FOR A FILM-BUFF FELLOW [1]

J.V.S. MEGAW

To be included in the present company might seem a little curious for someone who last wrote on topics appropriate to the present volume almost 25 years ago (Megaw 1976; 1979). But seniority, if only in years, has to have some advantages – that is, over and above free travel within the area of Strathclyde Passenger Transport.

In the 1950s Derek Simpson and I were students together in the halcyon days of the Department of Prehistoric Archaeology – as it was then – at the University of Edinburgh. Derek's exceptional access – as it then was – to a car meant we had the ability at weekends to follow a gipsy existence digging on sites more renowned for their exposed position than for the frequency of finds or features – any finds, any features. We were resuscitated by the late great George Jobey with hot toddies in his 'field office', a ramshackle caravan, after a sodden day on a 'wog site'; we marvelled at Brian Hope Taylor's exposition of the minimalist stratigraphy at Yeavering; with Richard Atkinson, Stuart Piggott and J.F.S. Stone we shook the April snow off our parkas as we worked our way through an alphabet soup of structural features at Stonehenge. The car – more accurately, Derek's father's car – also enabled us to travel occasionally to the bright lights of downtown Glasgow in order to catch the latest Hollywood blockbusters, courtesy, if memory serves me right, of an uncle of Derek's, who was a regional manager with Twentieth Century Fox. Later, much later, when I returned after a decade in Australia to the University of Leicester there was Derek Simpson again, for another decade before I was once more pulled Down Under, a loyal colleague as well as an old friend. The chief joint product of those years was the publication with a group of others, mostly also graduates of Edinburgh, of the *Introduction to British Prehistory* (Megaw & Simpson 1979), a description of what was then known of the archaeology of the British Isles and Ireland from the end of the Palaeolithic to the Claudian Invasion. A key feature of this book was the line drawings rivalling those of Stuart Piggott, drawings executed by another fellow student at Edinburgh, Morna McCusbic. We were castigated by several of our peers for the generally 'old-fashioned', theory-light approach which was followed – it must be said, much in the style that Derek Simpson has always preferred. Notwithstanding, the 'idiots' guide', as it came to be known, conceived as Derek himself put it, 'by idiots for idiots', went through no fewer than six reprints. Indeed, it was merely circumstances only partly within our control that prevented a completely revised edition appearing in the early 1990s.

Another decade and Derek was to be seen in his Chair at Queen's University Belfast – my father's university rather than that of either of my two archaeological uncles – and now he is, if anything, more productive than he was when, as I too have found, he discovered that being a university professor is simply a one-way ticket to the committee room. The following notes, then, are just that and are offered simply in homage and with affection to Derek Simpson, Fellow of two Antiquarian Societies and one whose catholic interests may not unfairly be compared to those of an even more widely travelled English antiquary, Joseph Banks (1743-1820).[2]

Banks was also a Fellow of the Society of Antiquaries of London, being elected in 1766 exactly 200 years before Derek and the present writer received the same honour. In neither case could we claim that our admission quite lived up to that depicted by Thomas Rowlandson in 1782 *(3)*. Banks' interests were, to say the least, all embracing. A precursor again of Derek the barrow digger, Banks records in his journal of a visit in 1767 to the West Country that it should be possible to settle the question of whether or not such structures were 'the common place of interment of the slain in a Battle' by 'Opening one or more of them, by which alone it can be determined for what use they were erected' (Perceval 1899). In 1780 Banks went on to open three barrows located

3 Thomas Rowlandson (1750-1827), 'The Reception of a New Member in the Society of Antiquarians'. Watercolour over pencil. Signed lower left and dated '1782' on the mount. *Photo courtesy of the Society of Antiquaries of London*

4 Thomas Rowlandson, 'An Antiquarian', etching and aquatint, 1789. Published by William Holland for his exhibition hall of satirical drawings. *Photo courtesy of the Society of Antiquaries of London*

on his estate at Revesby in Lincolnshire; barrows previously described by William Stukeley. Banks however was much disappointed when he failed to find any traces which could be associated with ancient druids.[3] Not all his contemporaries spoke – or wrote – flatteringly of the Squire of Revesby. James Boswell thought he resembled 'an elephant quite placid and gentle, allowing you to get upon his back or play with his proboscis' (quoted in Fara 2003, 47) but Banks was certainly a larger-than-life character. It comes as no surprise that this child of the Age of Enlightenment should have evinced an early and more than passing interest in Egyptology – of which Derek's early enthusiasms once more have a resonance: Derek who in his youth used to sign his letters with an *ankh*. Banks, instrumental in assisting the often troubled days that surrounded the establishment of the British Museum – *plus ça change* – may be found discussing the Rosetta Stone (Gascoigne 1994) and commenting on a mummified ibis which Banks regarded 'exhibit[ed] some of the products of a civilized life from a Nation whose Customs and Arts are little known'.[4] It is not hard to appreciate how, then as now, the antiquarian was rapidly being inducted into the hall of the readily lampooned *(4)*.

Banks' lifelong interest in his native fens needs little further elaboration here; his watching briefs which were to net him so many antiquities are frequently recorded in his copious correspondence. On 23 August 1788 Banks, writing to John Lloyd of Ruthin, comments: 'The Scouring out of the Witham here has produced a most Extraordinary lot of Danish [more likely, prehistoric] & Roman Antiquities. If I had you here to ride about, & assist to Collect them for the various hands into which they may have fallen, I think they would make a most Curious Collection. I got last year above 20 articles, many of them Quite unique, and this year a larger Quantity of River has been Cleard [sic] out, but my harvest has not begun' (Chambers 2000, no. 32). What could Banks have done with a metal detector!

One story concerning this 'curious collection' is well known but, like all the best stories, it is worth repeating not least for the minor additions which it is possible to make to the original published accounts. In 1768 a bronze object was dredged from the River Witham at Tattershall Ferry not far from Revesby Abbey. First published by a Dr George Pearson (1796, esp. 395 and pl. xi) in the *Philosophical Transactions* of the Royal Society – of which Banks was to become President ten years later – it was subsequently republished in that pioneering collection of British Iron Age art, *Horae Ferales* (Kemble *et al.* 1863, 171 and pl. xiii:2). While long recognised for what it most certainly is – or was – the Tattershall Ferry 'Celtic war trumpet' or *carnyx* has been the subject of much modern discussion (Piggott 1959; Megaw 1968, 349-50; 2001, esp. 100-1 and fig. 3; Hunter 2001). The basic document however remains a contemporary pen-and-wash drawing, probably the work of J.C. Nattes, which it seems likely had been commissioned by Banks and which is now in the Lincoln Central Library of the Lincolnshire County Council *(5)*.[5] The additional annotations strongly suggest that the drawing was intended for publication as the sheet is captioned top right 'Tab. 8' while at the bottom of

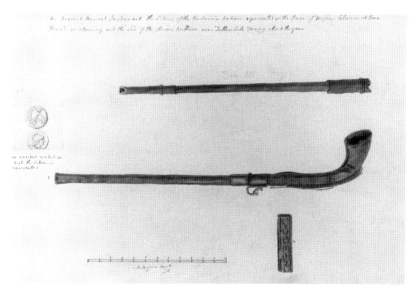

5 J.C. Nattes (1765-1822). Tattershall Ferry, River Witham, Lincs. Carnyx. Watercolour over pencil. *Photo courtesy of the Education and Cultural Services Directorate, Lincolnshire County Council*

6 Denarius of D. Iunius Brutus Albinus. Maximum diameter 17mm. *Photo courtesy of the National Museums of Scotland*

the sheet a drawing of the obverse and reverse of a Roman Republican coin has been pasted on labelled 'Fig. 2' with the added pencilled note 'To be / engravd [sic]'; the coin is further captioned: 'an ancient medal / on which the Lituus is represented'. Above the left margin of the drawing is the main description: 'An Ancient Musical Instrument the Lituus of the Barbarian Nations represented on the Base of Trajans Column at Rome / Found in clearing out the bed of the River Witham near Tattershall Ferry about the year [omitted]'. It is typical of Banks the numismatist that he should have cited a Roman coin – one might fancy one from his own extensive collection. As illustrated, the coin is a denarius of Decimus Iunius Brutus Albinus struck in Rome in 48 BC to mark Caesar's victories in Gaul 58-52 BC. (Crawford 1974, no. 450.1; Hunter 2001, 93, Table 2 and fig. 8) *(6)*. As to the question of where is the actual surviving fragments of the 'lituus', one of the very few surviving Iron Age musical instruments, Pearson sums up the total loss which followed on their discovery: Banks' 'zeal for science induced him to sacrifice them to chemical analysis' (Pearson 1796, 405) – in other words, the bronze was melted down.

It is time to move north to the Western Isles and beyond, the object of many early visitors (Bray 1996, esp. chap. 6). In 1772 Banks, having fallen out with the Admiralty, decided not to join James Cook on his second voyage of discovery, but to mount his own small group of enquiring minds, including Daniel Solander, botanist on Cook's first voyage of 1768 -71, Joseph Zoffany, the painter, and no fewer than three other draftsmen including John Frederick Miller, employed later with his father by Banks to complete the scientific illustrations from the *Endeavour* (for notes on Banks' scientific illustrators see Lysaght 1959, 259-65). The route to Iceland ran via the Hebrides and the Faroes and then west, returning via the Orkneys (Rauschenberg 1973), and amongst Banks' most spectacular 'observations' on the outward voyage was a visit to Staffa and the first published description of

7 John Frederick Miller (*fl.* 1768-80). The Stones of Stenness. Watercolour over pencil. Signed and dated 1775, lower right. Recto a note reading: 'Based on his pen and ink sketch of the stones of Stennis, 1772, known then as the Circle of Loda'. British Library Add. MS 15511 ff. 7-8. *Photo courtesy of the British Library*

8 The Stones of Stenness, Orkney. *Crown Copyright: Royal Commission on the Ancient and Historical Monuments of Scotland*

the Cave of Fhinn, Fingal's Cave, as published by that untrustworthy fellow antiquary, Thomas Pennant (1773; 1790). On the return trip from Iceland, Banks and his party were much interested in the archaeology of Orkney, with visits that included Skara Brae and the Stones of Stenness. In his journal for 16 October Banks notes in an eighteenth-century form of texting: 'See old lead works copper walk to Circles of Stone temples of Sun and Moon Druidical Places of Judgement bridges whether or no coeval with circles Tumuli.' One of Banks' servants, James Roberts, is more expansive and his journal for 18 October reads: '...went this morning with Mr Miller and [John] Cleveley [two of the team of artists] and Mr Walden [a marine surveyor] to a place called Stenhouse to assist them in measuring some Stones which stand a little distant from each other in the shape of a half moon, some of them were twenty feet high, six feet wide and about a foot and a half thick.' *(7-8)*.

Again, as chance would have it, Derek Simpson and I, together with a party of staff and students from the Universities of Leiden and Leicester, visited Stenness and Skara Brae almost two centuries to the day later (Lysaght 1974) and Derek incorporated his impressions in one of his contributions to the *Introduction to British Prehistory* (Simpson 1979, esp. 159-66). While Banks, for all the time he and his party spent measuring and drawing the monuments of Orkney, clearly was not to be divorced from the druidomania of the period (Piggott 1985; Green 1997; Ross 1999), we now know better. Stenness is among the most northerly of the 900 henge monuments recorded by Derek's close friend, Aubrey Burl (1976, esp. 99-102) and radiocarbon estimations following excavations in 1973-4 establish an age for Stenness of *c*.3000 BC. However, the theory that the builders of stone circles may have utilised astronomical observations and standard units of measurement (Ruggles 1999) may well have first been put forward by Banks (Lysaght 1974, 231-3).

The Links of Skaill lie some 10km north west of Stenness and close by the Neolithic village of Skara Brae, first excavated by Vere Gordon Childe between 1927 and 1931 who, provocative as ever, designated the site 'Pictish' (Childe 1931; see more recently Clarke & Sharples 1985; Clarke 2003). In his journal for 18 October 1772 Banks briefly alludes to 'Burying places in the Links... coffins of Slate 4-3 2.4 sides & top no bottom'; Roberts again is more expansive: 'Mr Banks, Dr Solander, with the rest of the Gentlemen, and Servants, and many of the Natives with Spades went to a place call'd Sandwick, where we open'd two Ancient Tombs, or Tumuli, in each of them was found the Bones of a man, and woman... the man was laid with his feet nearly up to his Chin... The draftsmen made drawings of both the Tombs.' (Lysaght 1972).

Also part of the party was the Reverend George Low living at the time at Stromness who describes how one of the skeletons was associated with a 'bag of some very Coarse Vegetable stuff... containing the Bones of a Younger person' (Low 1775), a fact recorded in a surviving contemporary sketch *(9)*. Otherwise unassociated short cist burials are a not uncommon feature of the

9 Links of Skaill, Orkney. Crouched burial with bag of bones (bottom left). Verso detail showing bag. Pencil drawing, artist unknown. *British Library Add. MS 15509*

Western and Northern Islands and the difficulties of ascribing any firm dating to them have been well argued (Hedges 1981). While our honorand's research into the earlier prehistory of the Hebrides is also well-known (Simpson 1976), what is not so well-known is that both he and the present writer have also added their mite to what one might categorise, following a comment by Stuart Piggott at the end of an undergraduate essay, as 'non-light on un-problems' or, more generously, a good example of speculative archaeology (Megaw & Simpson 1961).

Certainly, here is where faction and fiction blend into each other, even as, when viewed from afar, the profile of the islands blends into the all-surrounding sea. In 1956, Derek and I found ourselves excavating a wheel-house at Sollas on North Uist, part of a team of Edinburgh students led by

Richard Atkinson, as the much delayed final publication describes it, 'one of the earliest large-scale rescue projects in Scottish archaeology... in advance of the proposed "rocket range" on the west coast' (Campbell 1991, esp. 118).[6] In fact, this fall-out from the darkest days of the Cold War was, like the perceived threats that were seen as requiring a new defensive system for Britain, totally unnecessary but not before Compton Mackenzie (1958) had immortalised the Sollas excavations in *Rockets Galore*, his less than entirely successful attempt to reprise the enormous popularity of his earlier novel and subsequent Ealing Films comedy, *Whisky Galore*. Be that as it may, it transpired that there was a short cist located just below Newton House, excavation headquarters for the Edinburgh team; discovered by the owner in 1955, there were signs of further cists in the immediate vicinity. Since no other short cist had been recorded as having been excavated in recent times, after-hours each day – excepting of course on the Sabbath – we undertook the total excavation of the cist which transpired to contain the otherwise unassociated but well-preserved bones of a young female adult, lying on her right side in a fully flexed position

10 Newton, North Uist. Crouched cist burial (scale of inches)

(10). Undeterred by the absence of dating evidence for any short cists previously discovered in the region, we undertook an examination of the material culture of the second millennium and later prehistory of the Outer Isles as it was then known. We relied not only on the literature available but also on examination of the scant pottery finds associated with other cist burials in the Outer Isles located in the then National Museum of Antiquities of Scotland (Megaw & Simpson 1961, esp. 66-72). We concluded that there might be an argument for a continuous pottery – and burial – tradition from the Neolithic through, but not into, the Iron Age and the period represented by the Sollas wheelhouse.

Inexplicably, with one exception, this pioneering work has remained uncited in the more recent literature dealing with the archaeology of the Western Isles. It is missing from Ian Armit's first overview of the pottery sequence as beginning in the mid-first millennium BC (Armit 1992, esp. 142-4) as well as from, for example, the debates centred on Euan MacKie's excavations at Dun Ardtrek on Skye (MacKie 2000) and, perhaps most devastating for these, the sins of our young age, Patrick Topping passed it by in his re-examination of the prehistoric pottery of the Western Isles where he suggests, in the light of the C14 evidence, that typologies based on form and decoration are over-simplistic (Topping 1987). However, more recently, Armit, prior to a more extensive review of wheelhouses and 'wheelhouse pottery', does mention the Newton cist – if only to underscore how uncertain is the whole question of Bronze Age (or possibly not Bronze Age) cists in the Hebrides (Armit 1996, 96 and chap. 8, esp. 151-20).

Ah well, it was fun while it lasted; Banks, that son of the enlightenment whose curiosity knew no bounds, would I think have approved. Why, even when, at the conclusion of the Sollas excavations, I was being ferried by one of the locals to Benbecula to catch the flight back to the mainland, the skull and one femur of the cist burial secreted in my rucksack, I was continuing to collect material for my first published article – on the folklore of death in North Uist (Megaw 1957). Could it all have been the whisky talking?[7]

FOOTNOTES

[1] These notes draw on material used for another Festschrift: q.v. Megaw 2001.

[2] Surprisingly, there remains to date no modern full-scale biography of Banks. Relevant here are: Smith 1911; Cameron 1952; Lysaght 1980; Carter 1988; Gascoigne 1994; Fara 2003; Thomas 2003. The last is described by its author, a prolific and often provocative anthropologist, as using Cook's 'life as [his] lens, for a new look at those formative encounters that in one man's experience produced connections' across the world. Banks is here, portrayed very much as a bit-player. For a sketch of Banks as archaeologist see Megaw 2001; further specific sources are referred to below.

3 'Account of excavations near Revesby' Oct. 1780: Welcome Institute for the History of Medicine MS 5215/2. Derek also has excavated barrows in Lincolnshire but alas once more without recovering evidence of druidical practices: Evans & Simpson 1991.

4 'Notes on a mummified ibis found in Egypt *c.*1804': Sutro Library, San Francisco Or 1:2-3 – cited by Gascoigne 1994, 189. The 'cabinet of curiosities', that precursor of the modern museum, lived on in the Belfast of my youth. Pride of place in the family collections, maintained in their younger days by my uncles, two of whom were destined to be archaeologists, was given to a mummified ibis, a trophy of New Kingdom Egypt obtained by one of my military ancestors on the Grand Tour. For the record, the ibis now reposes in the Ulster Museum.

5 Lincoln Central Library MS Banks f.317.

6 It came as some surprise for the present writer, at the time in his third undergraduate year at Edinburgh, to read that he is credited with having been the Assistant Director on the Sollas excavations.

7 We cannot tell a lie – much of the background for our joint 1963 paper was collected at Newton House which was also the region's main licensed premises. In answer to our questions, for the price of a wee dram, a new – possibly very new – story concerned with death and burial would be offered; no wonder that Edinburgh University's renowned School of Scottish Studies should have introduced the 'whisky allowance' for researchers in the field.

BIBLIOGRAPHY

Armit, I., 1992 *The Later Prehistory of the Western Isles of Scotland*. BAR British Series 221. Oxford: British Archaeological Reports.

Armit, I., 1996 *The Archaeology of Skye and the Western Isles*. Edinburgh: Edinburgh University Press.

Bray, E., 1996 *The Discovery of the Hebrides: Voyages to the Western Isles 1745-1883*. Edinburgh: Birlinn (revised edition).

Burl, A., 1976 *The Stone Circles of the British Isles*. New Haven & London: Yale University Press.

Cameron, H.C., 1952 *Sir Joseph Banks, K.B., P.R.S.: The Autocrat of Philosophers*. London: Batchworth Press.

Campbell, E., 1991 Excavations of a wheelhouse and other Iron Age structures at Sollas, North Uist, by R.J.C. Atkinson in 1957. *Proceedings of the Society of Antiquaries of Scotland*, 121, 117-73.

Carter, H.B., 1988 *Sir Joseph Banks 1743-1820*. London: British Museum (Natural History).

Chambers, N. (ed.), 2000 *The Letters of Sir Joseph Banks: A Selection, 1768-1820*. London: Imperial College Press.

Childe, V.G., 1931 *Skara Brae: A Pictish Village*. London: Keegan Paul, Trench & Tubner.

Clarke, D.V., 2003 Once upon a time Skara Brae was unique. In Armit, I., Murphy, E., Nelis, E. & Simpson, D.D.A. (eds), *Neolithic Settlement in Ireland and Western Britain*, 84-92. Oxford: Oxbow.

Clarke, D.V. & Sharples, N., 1985 Settlements and subsistence in the third millennium BC. In Renfrew, A.C. (ed.) *The Prehistory of Orkney*. 54-82. Edinburgh: Edinburgh University Press.

Crawford, M., 1974 *Roman Republican Coinage*. London: Cambridge University Press.

Evans, J.D. & Simpson, D.D.A., 1991 Giants Hills 2 long barrow, Skendleby, Lincolnshire. *Archaeologia*, 109, 1-45.

Fara, P., 2003 *Sex, Botany and Empire: The Story of Carl Linnaeus and Joseph Banks*. Cambridge: Icon Books.

Gascoigne, J., 1994 *Joseph Banks and the English Enlightenment: Useful Knowledge and Polite Culture*. Cambridge: Cambridge University Press.

Green, M.J., 1997 *Exploring the World of the Druids*. London: Thames & Hudson.

Hedges, J.W., 1981 Short cists recently excavated at Lower Ellibister and other locations in Orkney. *Proceedings of the Society of Antiquaries of Scotland*, 110, 44-71.

Hunter, F.S., 2001 The carnyx in Iron Age Europe. *Antiquaries' Journal*, 81, 77-108.

Kemble, J.M., Latham, R.G. & Franks, A.W. (eds), 1863 *Horae Ferales or Studies of the Archaeology of the Northern Nations*. London: Lovell Reeve.

Low, G., 1775 Extract of a Letter from the Reverend Mr. George Low, to Mr. Paton, of Edinburgh. Communicated by Mr Gough. Read at the Society of Antiquaries, March 12, 19, 1773, *Archaeologia* 3, 276.

Lysaght, A.M., 1959 Some Eighteenth-Century Bird Paintings in the Library of Sir Joseph Banks (1743-1820). *Bulletin of the British Museum (Natural History): Historical Series*. 1, 253-371.

Lysaght, A.M., 197 Note on a grave excavated by Joseph Banks and George Low at Skaill in 1772. *Proceedings of the Society of Antiquaries of Scotland*, 104, 1971-72, 285-9.

Lysaght, A.M., 1974 Joseph Banks at Skara Brae and Stennis, Orkney, 1772. *Royal Society Notes and Records*, 28, 221-34.

Lysaght, A.M., (commentary by) 1980 *The Journal of Joseph Banks in the 'Endeavour'*. Guilford: Genesis Publications.

Mackenzie, C., 1958 *Rockets Galore*. London: Chatto & Windus.

MacKie, E., 2000 Excavations at Dun Ardtrek, Skye, in 1964 and 1965. *Proceedings of the Society of Antiquaries of Scotland*, 130, 301-411.

Megaw, J.V.S., 1957 Folklore and tradition on North Uist. *Folk-Lore*, 68, 483-8.

Megaw, J.V.S., 1979 The Later Bronze Age (1400 b.c. – 500 BC). In Megaw, J.V.S. & Simpson, D.D.A. (eds), 242-343.

Megaw, J.V.S., 1968 Problems and non-problems in palaeo-organology: A musical miscellany. In Coles, J.M. & Simpson, D.D.A. (eds), *Studies in Ancient Europe. Essays Presented to Stuart Piggott*, 333-58. Leicester: Leicester University Press.

Megaw, J.V.S., 1976 Gwithian, Cornwall: Some notes on the evidence for Neolithic and Bronze Age settlement. In Burgess, C.B. & Miket, R. (eds), *Settlement and Economy in the Third and Second Millennia BC*, 51-79. BAR British Series 33. Oxford: British Archaeological Reports.

Megaw, J.V.S., 2001 'Your Obedient and Humble Servant': Notes for an Antipodean antiquary. In Anderson, A., Lilley, I. & O'Connor, S. (eds), *Histories of Old Ages: Essays in Honour of Rhys Jones*, 95-110. Canberra: Pandanus Books, Australian National University.

Megaw, J.V.S. & Simpson, D.D.A., 1961 A short cist burial on North Uist and some notes on the prehistory of the Outer Isles in the second millennium BC. *Proceedings of the Society of Antiquaries of Scotland*, 94 (1960-1), 62-78.

Megaw, J.V.S. & Simpson, D.D.A. (eds), 1979 *Introduction to British Prehistory*. Leicester: Leicester University Press.

Pearson, G., 1796 Observations on some ancient metallic arms and utensils, with experiments to determine their composition. *Philosophical Transactions of the Royal Society*, 86, 395-451.

Pennant, T., 1773/1790 *A Tour of Scotland and a Voyage to the Hebrides MDCCXII, 1-2*. London: Benjamin White.

Perceval, S.G. (ed.) 1899 Joseph Banks: Journal of an excursion to Eastbury and Bristol... in May and June 1767. *Proceedings of the Bristol Naturalists' Society*, 9, 6-37.

Piggott, S., 1959 The *carnyx* in Early Iron Age Britain. *Antiquaries' Journal*, 39, 19-32.

Piggott, S., 1985 *The Druids*. London: Thames and Hudson (revised edition).

Rauschenberg, R.A., 1973 The Journals of Joseph Banks' voyage up Great Britain's west coast to Iceland and to the Orkney Isles, July to October, 1772. *Proceedings of the American Philosophical Society*, 117, 186-226.

Ross, A., 1999 *Druids and Druidism*. Stroud: Tempus.

Ruggles, C., 1999 *Astronomy in Prehistoric Britain and Ireland*. New Haven and London: Yale University Press.

Simpson, D.D.A., 1979 The Later Neolithic (*c*.2500-1700 BC). In Simpson, D.D.A. & Megaw, J.V.S. (eds), 130-77.

Simpson, D.D.A., 1976 The Later Neolithic and Beaker settlement site at Northton, Isle of Harris. In Burgess, C.B. & Miket, R. (eds), *Settlement and Economy in the Third and Second Millennia BC*, 221-31. BAR British Series 33. Oxford: British Archaeological Reports.

Smith, E., 1911 *Life of Sir Joseph Banks*. London: John Lane, The Bodley Head.

Thomas, N., 2003 *Discoveries: The Voyages of Captain Cook*. London: Allen Lane.

Topping, P.G., 1987 Typology and chronology in the later prehistoric assemblages of the Western Isles. *Proceedings of the Society of Antiquaries of Scotland*, 117, 67-84.

2

From Madhouse to Megaliths

Aubrey Burl

It was in 1964 at the university in Leicester that I first met Derek Simpson. His cell, optimistically called a study, was in a block of decrepit buildings locally known as the 'loony bin'. They had been 'temporary' hospital wards for shell-shocked soldiers in the First World War. Subsequently they were annexed by the Wyggeston Grammar School for Boys and later still some became part of the city's new University College. It was there that I met my supervisor for a projected MA in archaeology. 'Loony bin' or not the Pinteresque discussion was certainly disjointed.

'What topic have you chosen?' I was asked. Confidently I replied, 'Beakers'. Having read about the murderous invasions of those warrior-folk, their appropriation of native women and the building of Stonehenge they seemed a good choice. But not to my would-be tutor. David Clarke at Cambridge was already researching them. A tempting alternative was Rinyo-Clacton pottery, Skara Brae and the challenge of mystical carved stone balls, but that also was impossible. Isla McInnes at Edinburgh had claimed it. When I hesitantly proposed the study of prehistoric illnesses and mortality rates my perhaps-to-be supervisor uncompromisingly rejected it as a subject beyond his competence. That exhausted my shortlist.

Cricket saved me. In August my club had been on tour in Oxfordshire and one morning I visited the Rollright Stones, haunt of witches and scene of a pitchfork murder. Tentatively, almost without hope, I muttered, 'Stone circles?' 'Excellent,' enthused my unpredictable supervisor. 'No one has tackled them. Mind you,' he warned, 'there must be almost two hundred.' (Multiply by six!)

That unexpectedly eager consent – which committed me to decades of exhausting fieldwork and just as exhausting plodding through unindexed journals of long-abandoned and forgotten archaeological societies – was not disinterested altruism on my tutor's part. Unknown to me – and unexplained – was that next year he was joining Stuart Piggott to excavate Croft Moraig stone circle in Perthshire. Scottish canniness murmured that the megalithic innocent in front of him might provide insights into those unexplored mysteries of the past. Despite his unashamed self-interest I remain uncertain whether it is gratitude for his response or astonishment at my gullibility that dominates. The certainty is that the somersaulting discussion took me to sites not only in England, Scotland, Wales and Ireland but also to Brittany. And it is in memory of those fulfilling overseas excursions that revealed unrecorded cross-`channel links that this contribution to Derek's Festschrift is gratefully written. It concerns Britain, Brittany and Cyclopean prehistorians.

Every piece from the past should be scrutinised, not selected aspects. It is vital, as John Aubrey pleaded, to 'revive the Memories and Memorials of [people] since dead and gonne', those abandoned, almost forgotten relics of centuries ago. Too many have been overlooked. Megalithic anomalies do exist. Archaeology has complacently contrived to ignore them. 'Death', observed Aubrey ruefully, 'comes even to Stones and Names' (Hunter 1975, 166).

Even today there is an almost obstinate refusal to admit any human connection between the stone monuments of Brittany and Britain even though other foreign links are accepted. Mesolithic groups splashed their hunter-gathering ways through the puddles and deepening swamps of the incipient English Channel. Immigrations in antiquity are unquestioned: Beaker infiltrations and Belgic intrusions are undisputed yet not one Breton builder has been allowed to reach these shores. Even an association between the architecturally similar passage-tombs of Brittany and Ireland is denied. Lonely voices have cried in the wilderness, arguing that the people who constructed the monumental tombs of Newgrange, Knowth, Dowth and other passage-tombs in the Boyne Valley of Ireland were immigrants from the *département* of Morbihan, 'the little sea', in southern Brittany. The Irish archaeologist, Michael Herity, believed it. 'The group that set off for Anglesey and the Boyne may have gathered in sheltered harbours inside the Gulf [of Morbihan]... In this small area are massed many of the finest of the ornamented Breton tombs... It certainly serves to link the *Golfe de Morbihan* and the Boyne Valley much more closely' (Herity 1974, 200). Such cries from outerspace occasionally reached the Establishment. That fervent Breton and austere archaeologist P.R. Giot reviewed Herity's book and its heretical conclusions. He was unequivocal. 'May I be permitted to say that I don't believe in a word of this lovely picture', (Giot 1975, 232–3).

But which of them was nearer the truth? Those who know the literature also know the perverse archaeological ambivalence between what is agreed about foreign artefacts and what is ignored about foreign architecture. Since the nineteenth century it has been accepted that there were cultural contacts between Bronze Age Wessex and Brittany. The axes, daggers, ornaments of gold, amber, jet and faience in round barrows near Stonehenge are like those of the warrior graves in northern Brittany. As Derek Simpson himself has written, in the Early Bronze Age 'southern Britain and Brittany presented a single cultural province' (Megaw & Simpson 1979, 223).

Despite this unarguable evidence of cross-Channel contacts – obviously not the handiwork of extra-terrestrials or troglodytes from the Lower Earth – there has been no recognition of the equally strong fact that Breton architectural styles influenced the design of ritual sites in Britain, in particular the alien shapes of rectangles and horseshoes. Even when demonstrated, this has been ignored. The rejection is puzzling. It is not as though the claimed continental associations were restricted to unheard-of sites. To the contrary, 'Made in Brittany' is metaphorically engraved on the sarsens of Stonehenge, a site quite well known to archaeologists. Avebury can be added: and Arminghall in Norfolk, Croft Moraig in central Scotland, King Arthur's Hall on Bodmin Moor, even the 'stone circle' of Machrie Moor I, Arran.

Stonehenge is seminal to this argument and for years it has been a companion of Derek and myself. It was the subject of a Birmingham Day School in 1984, Richard Atkinson describing its construction, Douglas Heggie its astronomy, and this writer talking about death and burial on Salisbury Plain. The speakers were introduced by the best of chairmen, Derek Simpson, who informed the large audience in detail of our qualifications, explaining why we were being imposed on them. His introductions were a highlight in themselves. Stonehenge, however, did once fail us. At a weekend course at Knuston Hall Derek spoke about Stonehenge and I followed with a description of Avebury, telling the group that next day we would go to Avebury but not Stonehenge because of time. All but one of the participants enjoyed the occasion. The exception grumbled that she had spent the entire afternoon at Avebury looking for but never finding the Heel Stone. That was some years before I first explored the great stone monuments of Brittany, slowly recognising how similar some were to parts of Stonehenge. The long-accepted, virginal British ancestry for Stonehenge did not account for its 'foreign' rectangle of the Four Stations, nor its three outlandish horseshoes of stones, nor its Breton carvings of axes, a dagger and anthropomorphic figurines. Elements of Stonehenge were replicas of the architecture and art of megalithic Brittany (Burl 1976).

I state this confidently. I spent years visiting Brittany and Derek Simpson was partly responsible. In late September 1981 he, Alex Gibson and I went to a disorganised conference at Rennes, on the way planning to see Barnenez, then the Carnac sites. We failed.

We never did find Barnenez, even though that monstrously long and high cairn must have been conspicuously silhouetted on the skyline. From Morlaix we drove to Plouézoc'h, and then northwards… to nowhere; just empty lanes. We were two miles from Barnenez but never arrived. There were no sign-posts to it in those uncommercial days, and no literature, even French, in any Maison de la Presse. Frustratedly, I grumbled, 'Why isn't there a guidebook?' Derek and Alex instantly, magnanimously, advised me to write one!

Barnenez and the conference were not the only disappointments. Learning that it was my birthday that week Derek generously offered to buy me a splendid meal. We ate it in a lorry drivers' caff near Quimper. Despite that, I did begin the preparation of a 'Guide' and I have been grateful to Derek and Alex ever since. We found obscure but significant sites on empty moors or along unmapped tracks, and those monuments illuminated the individuality of Breton architecture (Burl 1985). I was greatly assisted by the copy kindly sent me by Alexander and Archie Thom of their punctilious surveys and plans of the Carnac sites (Thom & Thom 1977).

In the centuries when gold, copper, tin and flint were being exported across the Channel from Ireland and Cornwall, materials scarce in many parts of western

	GREAT ELLIPSES
e.	Twelve Apostles
g.	Pobull Fhinn
h.	Loch a Phobuill
I.	Achnagoul
	HORSESHOES (Fer-aux-Chevaux)
a.	East Down
c.	Lugg
d.	Carn Beg
f.	Machrie Moor I
i.	Latheronwheel
j.	Broubster
k.	Achavanich
m.	Haerstanes
n.	Cowiemuir
o.	Croft Moraig
r.	Arminghall
s.	Avebury (North)
t.	Stonehenge (II, III)
	RECTANGLES
b.	King Arthur's Hall
p.	Fortingall (NE, NW)
u.	Stonehenge. (Four Stations)
	UNCERTAIN
q.	Hethpool

Table 1 'Breton' sites in Britain and Ireland

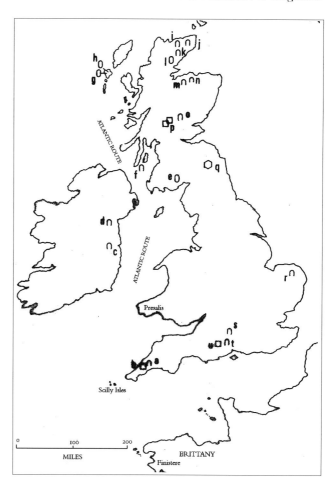

11 'Breton' megalithic settings in Britain and Ireland. Horseshoe settings (inverted U), greater ellipses (0), rectangles (square) and 'Breton' site of uncertain form (hexagon). Note their proximity to the coast

Europe, incomers from Brittany, traders or merchants, apparently raised distinctive sites around the coasts of Britain and Ireland *(11 and Table 1)*. Seagoing had for generations been part of a Breton way of life. Mesolithic hunter-gatherers fished off the Morbihan coast. Carvings that may represent boats exist in Neolithic *dolmens-aux-couloir* and later *allées-couvertes*. 'Perhaps these alleged ships were ceremonial vessels carrying away the souls of the dead' (Giot 1960, 52; Patton 1993, 87-9; Shee Twohig 1981, 114). Centuries later the Iron Age Veneti of southern Brittany were experienced mariners whose heavy, leather-sailed vessels rode the Atlantic waves. It was that 'Atlantic Route', protected from the turbulence of the ocean itself, that early voyagers followed, northwards between Britain and Ireland and then between the Outer Hebrides and the Scottish mainland. It was a long-known, much travelled seaway.

There was no sudden irruption of overseas sightseers when the sarsens of Stonehenge were erected. Contacts between Brittany and Britain had existed for centuries before that megalithic astonishment and continued for centuries afterwards, from the earliest of New Stone Age tombs to Early Bronze Age stones in arrangements unlike anything known in these islands, over a thousand years of cross-Channel interaction. At the onset of the Neolithic there were stylistic affinities between the single-celled Severn-Cotswold tombs of the Marlborough Downs and the *dolmens à couloir avec chambre simple* of Brittany. (Daniel 1950, 155-6; Powell 1969, 259-60). A thousand years later in the Late Neolithic there was a comparable similarity between the long-chambered Breton *allées-couvertes* and a monument inside Avebury that John Aubrey described.

'One of the Monuments in the Street like that above Holy-head… is converted into a Pigstye or Cow-house – as is to be seen in the Rode'. On Anglesey Aubrey had seen the megalithic tomb of Trefignath, 'of great rough Stones about 20 in number and about 30 paces…' (Aubrey 1982, 798-9). That long-sided tomb was unlike those around Avebury with their short, single cells but did resemble Avebury's elongated tomb on the 'crosse-street'… that runnes East and West' (Aubrey, 1980, 41). With no covering mound five close-set upright slabs formed the southern side of a megalithic burial-place. It was different from those on the Marlborough Downs but almost identical to the *allées-couvertes* of Brittany whose exposed side-slabs were not concealed under a barrow.

Stonehenge is even more revealing of Breton influences. It is an amalgam of a circle, a rectangle and two, perhaps three, horseshoe settings. Yet there has been no debate about the reasons for the oblong of the Four Stations around the circle and the horseshoes of sarsens and bluestones inside the ring. Horseshoes were uncommon in Britain and Ireland. So were rectangles. In Brittany they jostle. Infrequent in Morbihan, where horseshoes dominate, elsewhere they exist in Ile-et-Vilaine and the Côtes du Nord. In Finistère, the *département* closest to Britain, there were almost a dozen, the now-lost granite quadrilaterals of Parc ar Varret, and Lanvéoc on the Crozon peninsula, uprooted in the nineteenth century but planned and sketched before their destruction. There were oblongs at Ty-ar-c'Huré, Leuré and Landaoudec, even a polygon at Kermorvan near the fishing-port of Conquet, and a rectangle on Ushant in the Atlantic. All of them contained astronomical alignments. 'Tous obéissant, sans aucun exception, à la loi mégalithique d'orientation' (Pontois 1929, 106, 116, 117, 250).

In Britain, however, only two quadrilaterals are certainly known, both in southern England. There may be two more in central Scotland. Five years after the 1965 excavation at Croft Moraig Derek, Marius Cook and I went to investigate the perplexing Fortingall stones four miles east of Croft Moraig on the northern shore of lovely Loch Tay. Stuart Piggott visited the dig and had a vinicultural altercation with a barman over the genealogy of a bottle dubiously labelled 'vintage' port. The Fortingall settings were supposed to be the remains of two four-posters but, like the port, their parentage was questionable. Genuine four-posters, originating in central Scotland, were recognised as regional monuments by Fred Coles, 'originally four stones, as in so many other Perthshire groups' (Coles, F.R. 1908, 126-7). They were given their distinctive title by Coles' namesake, John, when Derek and he were excavating at Pitnacree and hurling their landlady's malodorous mince sandwiches over roadside hedges. Noticing the paradox of calling four stones arranged in sub-oblongs 'stone circles', Coles wrote, 'two of these "four-posters" have recently been examined' (Coles & Simpson, 1965, 43). A true four-poster is not a rectangle. Its stones stand on the circumference of a circle. Fortingall was different. Its oblongs possessed the singular trait of being composed not of four but eight stones, four tall at the corners, four lower in each side, reminiscent of the 'high-and-low' stones of King Arthur's Hall. The sites were outsize, more than double the area of an average four-poster, and they were rectangular, the NE square, the NW oblong.

They had possible astronomical alignments, the sides of the NE site perhaps directed towards the minor summer moonset, a diagonal arranged east–west. The NW's sides were orientated on the minor summer moonrise, a diagonal on the major summer moonset. It is conjecture. Even with the plans of the Thoms, made before the 1970 investigation, the deductions are possible rather than probable (Burl 1988, 9-11; 166-73; Thom *et al.* 1980, 336-7).

Of the two proven English sites one on Bodmin Moor, King Arthur's Hall, is an earth-banked rectangle arranged north-south, internally lined with alternating stones of low flat-topped slabs and higher lean pillars like the parapet of a battlement. The oblong and the cardinal orientation are critical. Combinations of rectangles and horseshoe settings hardly exist in Britain. But less than six miles from King Arthur's Hall there is a massive D-shaped horseshoe of low stones on East Moor. Not many miles to the east there was another paired rectangle and horseshoe at Stonehenge. Its sarsen pillars, the Four Stations, formed the corners of a long oblong inside Stonehenge's earthen bank. It was almost perfect, the sharp corners creating a nearly exact parallelogram whose long sides were aligned SE–NW.

'Aligned' is correct. The Four Stations were astronomical. In 1846 the Revd Edward Duke, who introduced the term 'Stations', noticed that the short sides pointed north-eastwards to the midsummer sunrise (Duke 1846, 144). In 1906 Sir Norman Lockyer deduced that a rectangle was designed so that its NE–SW diagonal 'would mark the sunset place in the first week in May', the festival of Beltane (Lockyer 1906, 93). Sixty years later Gerald Hawkins, using the novelty of a computer, demonstrated that the SE–NW sides of the rectangle were aligned on the most northerly setting of the moon (Hawkins 1966, 134). Three celestial coincidences are unlikely. There is no comparable rectangle in Britain or Ireland but there is a remarkable correlation with the lateral and diagonal alignments in the Crucuno quadrilateral west of Carnac. Its long sides lie neatly east–west towards the equinoctial sunsets and the NE–SW diagonal is in line with the midwinter sunset (Burl 2000, 339-40).

Even more compelling evidence of Breton influence are the megalithic horseshoes. They are plentiful in Brittany. But despite the hundreds of stone circles and ovals in Britain and Ireland horseshoe shapes are unusual. At Avebury, as well as his *allée-couverte*, John Aubrey may have recorded one, a Breton *fers à cheval*. Its surviving sarsens are traditionally identified as the remains of a 'North Circle' but a resistivity survey appeared to confirm a U-shaped setting. Of the two reliable observers before its disruption, John Aubrey and William Stukeley, Stukeley thought it had been a concentric circle (Stukeley 1743, 23). He was mistaken. A geophysical survey in 1989 discovered no traces of an inner ring but did detect depressions and anomalies which, with the two surviving standing and one fallen stone, indicated a horseshoe setting. Aubrey actually planned it as one (Aubrey 1980, 44-5). The resistivity survey cautiously concluded that 'it is at least possible that Aubrey's version in this area may yet turn out to be the most accurate of all' (Ucko *et al.* 1991, 221, 227). There is independent astronomical support. The axis from the centre of the mouth to the apex of the setting is due north, an orientation often found in Brittany. It can be no more than conjecture. Short of finding a Breton vase-support or other Middle Neolithic *Chasséen* ware at Avebury the interpretation is just a tempting possibility, nothing more. But if it had been an earlier Breton *allée-couverte* that Aubrey had drawn at Avebury then the misinterpreted North 'Circle' may well have been a *fer-à-cheval* from Brittany.

There are at least 16 *fers à cheval* in Brittany, the farthest apart being the dilapidated Kergonan on Ile-aux-Moines in the Gulf of Morbihan, and Tossen-Keler on the north coast. There are others in Morbihan including the pair on the former hill, now island, of Er-Lannic. As well as their shape they have stones graded in height and an astronomical axis, often towards a cardinal point or to a solar alignment.

Unaware of those informative Breton sites no authority except William Stukeley wondered why Stonehenge contained that unexpected trilithon horseshoe. Sensibly, he thought that its mouth acted as an entrance to the sacred cell (Stukeley 1740, 21). For the following three centuries others were bleakly unimaginative about its origins, reporting but not enquiring: John Smith, 'originally an Ellipsis, or oval' (Smith 1771, 56); Sir Richard Colt Hoare, 'a large oval' (Hoare 1812, 147); William Long, 'in horse-shoe form' (Long 1876, 59); Herbert Stone, 'in horseshoe style' (Stone 1924, 9); Robert Cunnington, 'the form of a horseshoe' (Cunnington 1935, 13); Richard. Atkinson, 'set in a horseshoe' (Atkinson 1956, 27; 1979, 40). None asked why. Even the encyclopaedic *Stonehenge in its Landscape* of 1995 shrugged, 'a horseshoe' (Cleal *et al.* 1995, 29).

Paradoxically, in 1840 the Revd Robert Weaver, a congregational minister, who believed that Stonehenge had been built by Phoenicians, was closest to the truth. The trilithon and bluestone settings represented 'two-thirds of a large oval, and a concomitant small oval' (Weaver 1840, 101). In contrast to those

SITE	LOCALITY	MATERIAL	EARTHWORK?	MILES FROM COAST
Achavanich	Caithness	Stone	Yes	5
Arminghall	Norfolk	Stone	Yes	20
Avebury (N)	Wiltshire	Stone	Yes	48
Broubster	Caithness	Stone	No	6
Carn Beg	Co. Louth	Stone	Yes	2
Cowiemuir	Moray Firth	Earth	No	2
Croft Moraig	Perthshire	Stone	Yes	30
Haerstanes	Moray Firth	Stone	No	4
King Arthur's Hall	Bodmin Moor	Stone	Yes	12
Latheronwheel	Caithness	Stone	No	1
Lugg	Co. Dublin	Timber	Yes	5
Machrie Moor I	Arran	Stone	No	2
Stonehenge II	Wiltshire	Stone	Yes	31
Stonehenge II	Wiltshire	Bluestone	Yes	31
Stonehenge III	Wiltshire	Bluestone	Yes	31
Stonehenge III	Wiltshire	Sarsen	Yes	31

(An average distance from the sea of just over 12 miles, less than one-eighth of the national mean of 90 miles)

Table 2 Horseshoe settings in Britain and Ireland

uncurious scholars the amateur investigator was perceptive. Such open-ended settings do seem truncated versions of the spacious ellipses around Carnac. Huge ovals such as Ménec West contained solar alignments along their axis. By 'cutting' such enclosures in half a horseshoe would be formed with a mouth facing the foresight of a tall pillar at the curved apex. Tellingly, comparably immense ovals also exist along the west coast of Britain: the Twelve Apostles near Dumfries; Loch a Phobuill and Pobull Fhinn on the island of North Uist (Burl 1995, 124, 152-3); and in Caithness at Achnagoul (Myatt 2003, 23-5). They are all near the sea *(Table 2)*.

It is significant that the horseshoes in Britain and Ireland also are coastal, often near a bay or river-mouth as though set up by seafarers *(Table 1)*. There is a fine example in Caithness at Achavanich, 'field of the holy man', by Loch Stemster five miles from Lybster Bay and only six north of Achnagoul. Originally 54 tall stones formed an embanked setting 69m long with a 26m- wide mouth at the SSE. The setting has a characteristic Breton 'high-and-low' trait with taller stones on its eastern side (Myatt 2003, 24-5; Dryden 1872, 530-1; Thom *et al.* 1990, II, 288-9). Astronomically it is aligned NNW towards the most northerly setting of the winter moon. Like other horseshoes it was composed of local material. Another horseshoe, this time inside a stone circle, exists at Croft Moraig, one of the farthest from the sea of these foreign sites. Robert Burns saw it in 1787, 'the Druid's Temple… say prayers in it' (Gillies 1938, 140). The ruinous Hethpool in Northumberland could be added to the list. It was interpreted as a gigantic horseshoe 61m by 27m wide or the remains of two circles. It is 12 miles from Budle Bay and its size is in accord with large *fers à cheval* in Morbihan such as Kergonan and the Champ de la Croix. It merits consideration (Burl 1995, 71).

Of Stonehenge's three horseshoe settings, the first, a concentric of bluestones, of Atkinson's Phase II is debatable. Two are later and certain, a slighter one of 19 bluestones inside another of five sarsen trilithons, lintelled pairs of ten tall, closely-set pillars. That horseshoe is graded in height up to the apex of the Great Trilithon and the midwinter sunset. It is most persuasively explained as an innovation from overseas.

E.H. Stone did stress the enigmatic architecture of Stonehenge but only as a negative. 'In Britain Stonehenge is unique. We have no earlier structure in the same style from which its evolution may be traced, and the design has never been repeated… It has no ancestors and no descendants' (Stone 1924, 33). He was mistaken. Barclay remarked that trilithons were unknown elsewhere in Britain but 'examples are to be met with abroad' (Barclay 1895, 35-8). So are megalithic horseshoes and rectangles.

With so few horseshoes and rectangles for the 121,400 square miles of Britain and Ireland but more than 1,300 stone circles, statistics demonstrate how atypical the horseshoes and rectangle of Stonehenge were if created by natives. Conversely, there are numerous U-shaped settings and rectangles in Brittany, a *département* of 10,500 square miles, a twelfth the size of Britain and Ireland. Comparative densities to the square mile of rectangles and horseshoes in these islands and Brittany greatly favour the latter, making it plausible that the plan of Stonehenge was influenced by the Breton geometry and astronomy of the rectangle and the monumentality of the horseshoe. Its indisputably representational Breton carvings, perhaps of a dagger, axes and rectangles, quite different from the abstract designs of Britain and Ireland, simply increase proof of connections with Brittany. Archaeologically, such associations are well attested. 'Links are demonstrable between southern Britain, Brittany and central Europe in the Early Bronze Age', (Megaw & Simpson 1979, 227).

What remains unclear is the reason for these incursions from Brittany. Were the incomers driven, as Childe speculated, by religious fervour? 'Like Celtic missionaries the megalithic saints would have sailed to the coasts of Scotland, Ireland and the remoter isles inspired by equally unworldly motives', (Childe 1958, 129). Or were they homeless people seeking land? Or merchants as the misinterpreted 'circle' of Machrie Moor I suggests, one of a medley of stone settings, stylistically different, crowded together on an island staging-post like traders assembling at a market-place (Burl 2000, 87-102)? That could have been true at settlements like Avebury but unlikely at ritual sites such as Stonehenge.

In conclusion the writer can offer relief to those afflicted with wishful thinking and uncritical faith in make-believe. As early as 1976 I was doubtful about the notorious epic of human transportation of the Stonehenge bluestones from the Preseli mountains of south-west Wales by Beaker heroes (Burl 1976, 308-9). Research revealed that the 'evidence' for the feat was a collection of ancient mistakes and modern ignorance. Counter-arguments were given in *Great Stone Circles* (Burl 1999, 107-23), a volume of essays dedicated to Derek Simpson for his profound influence on my archaeological thinking. I could be wrong.

It is arguable that Breton seamen, having sailed from Ushant to Scilly, went on to Cornwall's Padstow Bay near Bodmin Moor. Enterprising explorers then ventured 50 miles northwards to south-west Wales and the harbour of Milford Haven. The landmark of the Preselis guided them, mountains that on a clear day are visible from the Wicklow Mountains in eastern Ireland; from Snowdon in North Wales; and from Dunkery Beacon in north-east Exmoor. To those daring crews such a magical range may have seemed the embodiment of powerful stone, potent material ideal for a Breton sanctuary on Salisbury Plain.

They sullied the earthwork of the first Stonehenge, uprooting its central wooden structure, setting up a double *fer-à-cheval* of bluestones, two horseshoes, one inside the other, with the sandstone pillar of the future Altar Stone erected like a phallic statement at their mouth.

It is a commendable theory with one enormous benefit. The undertaking would occur at the right time unlike the favoured candidates for the unlikely feat, the Wessex/Middle Rhine Beaker people (Clarke 1970, 107; Pitts 2000, 211-12). Dates establish that those copper and gold prospectors were exploring Ireland two centuries too late for the Stonehenge bluestones. Nor were there native rivals. Unlike those Beaker wraiths beloved by romantics, Breton crews around 2700 BC could have been the daredevils of that petrological triumph, rafting tons of stones across treacherous tides and sandbanks, heading like homing-pigeons through an uncharted tangle of rivers, hills and forests to Salisbury Plain. It is persuasive. The chronology is perfect. It explains why geologists have discovered no trace of doleritic deposits in Wiltshire and although the theory contains no comforting ley line it does have sex in accord with current thinking about prehistoric societies and stone circles. There is one discordant note. It is wrong, a fantasia of phantom Beakers bearing disembodied bluestones across the waves and woodlands of a wished-for wonderland.

'We speak from facts, not theory', stated Colt Hoare. 'Such is the motto I adopt, and to the text I shall most strictly adhere' (Hoare 1812, 7). I am at one with Hoare and Giot. I do not believe in one shipwrecked raft or forest-flustered sledge of this geological escapism. But those who do wish to adopt it will have to accept that Stonehenge is partly a production from Brittany. As John Aubrey sighed, 'Thus the height of Antiquity ends in Fable; and the depth of ignorance discends to Credulity' (Hunter 1975, 167).

In 1996, in celebration of my seventieth birthday, Derek and Alex were the joint editors of a Festschrift for me, an unexpected honour and one for which I shall be forever grateful. It now gives me unreserved satisfaction to return that gift with this modest but affectionate contribution to an archaeologist and friend with whom I have enjoyed such a long, pleasurable and rewarding association. There is a postscript from the 'loony bin'. If my long–ago suggestion of a Beaker thesis had been accepted I might have become one more unthinking adherent of the fairy story of Beaker supermen. Instead, an enthusiastic supervisor turned me towards the scepticism demanded in the study of stone circles. Thank you, Derek. And thank you, Croft Moraig.

BIBLIOGRAPHY

Atkinson, R.J.C., 1956 *Stonehenge*. London: Hamish Hamilton.

Atkinson, R.J.C., 1979 *Stonehenge. Archaeology and Interpretation*. Harmondsworth: Penguin.

Aubrey, J., 1980 *Monumenta Britannica, I*. Milborne Port: Dorset Publishing Company.

Aubrey, J., 1982 *Monumenta Britannica, II*. Milborne Port: Dorset Publishing Company.

Barclay, E., 1895 *Stonehenge and its Earthworks*. London: Nutt.

Burl, A., 1976 *The Stone Circles of the British Isles*. London: Yale University Press.

Burl, A., 1985 *Megalithic Brittany: A Guide to over 350 Ancient Sites and Monuments*. London: Thames & Hudson.

Burl, A., 1988 *Four-Posters: Bronze Age Stone Circles of Western Europe*. BAR British Series 195. Oxford: British Archaeological Reports.

Burl, A., 1995 *A Guide to the Stone Circles of Britain, Ireland and Brittany*. London: Yale University Press.

Burl, A., 1999 *Great Stone Circles: Fables, Fictions, Facts*. London: Yale University Press.

Burl, A., 2000 *The Stone Circles of Britain, Ireland and Brittany*. London: Yale University Press.

Childe, V.G., 1958 *The Prehistory of European Society*. Harmondsworth: Penguin.

Clarke, D.L., 1970 *The Beaker Pottery of Great Britain and Ireland*. Cambridge: Cambridge University Press.

Cleal, R.M.J., Walker, K.E. & Montague, R., 1995 *Stonehenge in its Landscape: Twentieth-century Excavations*. London: English Heritage.

Coles, F.R., 1908 Stone circles surveyed in Perthshire. NE Section. *Proceedings of the Society of Antiquaries of Scotland*, 42 (1907-8), 95-162.

Coles, J.M. & Simpson, D.D.A., 1965 The excavation of a Neolithic round barrow at Pitnacree, Perthshire, Scotland. *Proceedings of the Prehistoric Society*, 31, 34-57.

Cunnington, R.H., 1935 *Stonehenge and its Date*. London: Methuen.

Daniel, G., 1950 *The Chamber Tombs of England and Wales*. Cambridge: Cambridge University Press.

Dryden, Sir H., 1872 Letter to the editor of the *John O' Groats Journal*, September 21, 1871. In Fergusson, J. *Rude Stone Monuments in all Countries: Their Age and Uses*. London: John Murray, 527-32.

Duke, Revd E., 1846 *The Druidical Temples of the County of Wilts*. London: Russell Smith.

Gillies, Revd W.A., 1938 *In Famed Breadalbane*. Perth: Munro Press.

Giot, P.R., 1960 *Brittany*. London: Thames & Hudson.

Giot, P.R., 1975 Michael Herity, *Irish Passage-Graves*, a Review. *Antiquity*, 49, 232-3.

Hawkins, G.S. with White, J.B., 1966 *Stonehenge Decoded*. London: Souvenir Press.

Herity, M., 1974 *Irish Passage Graves. Neolithic Tomb-Builders in Ireland and Britain, 2500 BC*. Dublin: Irish University Press.

Hoare, Sir R.C., 1812 *The Ancient History of South Wiltshire*. London: William Miller.

Hunter, M., 1975 *John Aubrey and the Realm of Learning*. London: Duckworth.

Lockyer, Sir N., 1906 *Stonehenge and Other British Stone Monuments Astronomically Considered*. London: Macmillan.

Long, W., 1876 Stonehenge and its barrows, *Wiltshire Archaeological Journal*, 16, 1-244.

Megaw, J.V.S. & Simpson, D.D.A., 1979 *An Introduction to British Prehistory*. Leicester: Leicester University Press.

Myatt, L., 2003 The standing stones of Caithness. Unpublished guide. Halkirk: L. Myatt.

Patton, M., 1993 *Statements in Stone. Monuments and Society in Neolithic Brittany*. London: Routledge.

Pitts, M., 2000 *Hengeworld*. London: Century Press.

Pontois, B. le 1929 *La Finistère Préhistorique*. Paris: Librarie Émile Nourry.

Powell, T.G.E., 1969 The Neolithic in the west of Europe and megalithic sepulture: some points and problems. In Powell, T.G.E., Corcoran, J.X.W.P., Lynch, F. & Scott, J.G., *Megalithic Enquiries in the West of Britain*, 247-72. Liverpool: Liverpool University Press.

Shee Twohig, E., 1981 *The Megalithic Art of Western Europe*. Oxford: Oxford University Press.

Smith, J., 1771 *Choir Gaur; the Grand Orrery of the Ancient Druids, commonly called Stonehenge*. Salisbury: J. Smith.

Stone, E.H., 1924 *The Stones of Stonehenge*. London: Robert Scott.

Stukeley, W., 1740 *Stonehenge a Temple Restor'd to the British Druids*. London: Innys & Manby.

Stukeley, W., 1743 *Abury, a Temple of the British Druids, with Some Others Described*. London: Innys, Manby Dod & Brindley.

Thom, A. & A.S., 1977 *La Géométrie des Alignements de Carnac (Suivi de Plans Comparatifs)*. Rennes: Université de Rennes.

Thom, A. & A.S. & Burl, A., 1980 *Megalithic Rings. Plans and Data for 229 Monuments in Britain*. BAR British Series 81. Oxford: British Archaeological Reports.

Thom, A. & A.S. & Burl, A., 1990 *Stone Rows and Standing Stones, II*. BAR International Series S560. Oxford: British Archaeological Reports.

Ucko, P.J., Hunter, M., Clark, A.J. & David, A., 1991 *Avebury Reconsidered. From the 1660s to the 1990s*. London: Unwin Hyman.

Weaver, Revd R., 1840 *Monumenta Antiqua*. London: J.B. Nichols & Son.

3
Destructions, Re-erections and Re-creations

J.N. Graham Ritchie

Introduction

The toppling of two of the stones of the stone circle known as the Standing Stones of Stenness in Orkney in 1814 caused consternation in the county. The circumstances surrounding the re-erection of one of them in August 1906, after the monument, along with Maes Howe and the Ring of Brodgar, was taken into guardianship of the Office of Works (the predecessor of Historic Scotland) are less well known. This guardianship agreement can be seen as a first part of the conservation process that was eventually to prepare two areas of Orkney, known as the Heart of Neolithic Orkney, as worthy of inscription onto the World Heritage List in 1999, but this was a long way off (Historic Scotland nd). The prehistoric aspects of the Stones of Stenness and the Ring of Brodgar are well known (Ritchie 1976; Renfrew 1979, 39-43; Ritchie 1988). The approaches involved in the re-erection of stones in the early twentieth century have not previously been explored and are, in times before the advent of heavy hydraulic machinery, early examples of experimental archae-ology in Scotland. The circumstances surrounding the re-erection of standing stones and stone circles may be of interest in conservation matters generally.

The Stones of Stenness and the Ring of Brodgar

The henge monuments and stone circles known as the Stones of Stenness and the Ring of Brodgar are situated on opposing promontories that separate the two major lochs of mainland Orkney, the lochs of Stenness and Harray. The Stones of Stenness are situated on a flat expanse, only a little above high tide level of the Loch of Stenness, a salt-water loch with an entrance to the sea at the Bridge of Waithe. There were originally 12 stones and a diameter of 30m (the numbering of the stones follows that of the excavation report, Ritchie 1976). The Ring of Brodgar (with originally 60 stones and a diameter of 104m) is on more elevated ground over 10m OD and is visible on the skyline between the lochs from all around. Both circles have surrounding rock-cut ditches, in the case of Stenness probably with only one causeway left uncut, and in that of Brodgar there are certainly two. There was evidence of an external bank at Stenness almost completely removed by ploughing and only a thin clayey band surviving (Ritchie 1976, 12) (now partly landscaped by Historic Scotland to enhance the impression of bank and ditch, with the original surviving bank protected by a permeable layer). An illustration of Stenness that has not previously been used in archaeological discussion is that of Thomas Stanley of 1789 (West 1975), which shows a 'mud wall' *(12)*. Stanley annotates the drawing: 'The Mud wall is scarcely traceable, and the Plan here has been laid down by me perhaps too strongly as indicative of the temple having been a Circle & not a Crescent', but given the excavated

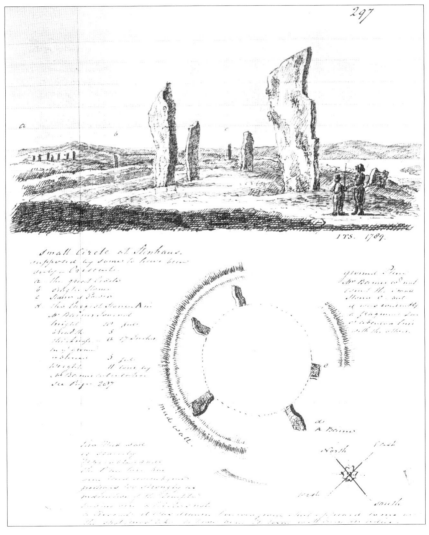

12 Stones of Stenness, Orkney. Sketch and plan by John Thomas Stanley, 1789.
Copyright National Library of Iceland, Reykjavik

remains of a clayey band the description of a mud wall at a period before the extensive ploughing of the site is suggestive. (Stanley shows Stones 2 and 3 in the foreground, with Stones 5 and 6 at centre and the Stone of Odin behind.) At Brodgar the evidence for an external bank was also ambiguous, but again a lens of clayey soil may represent the last vestiges of a bank (Renfrew 1979, 41). Both circles are thus set within classic henge monuments. Both had been much denuded by ploughing, and Renfrew quotes Thomas's account of 1852 to the effect that 'the Ring of Brogar has no sanctity with these barbarous depredations, as the broken and scarified turf will witness' (1979, 43). To the north of the Stones of Stenness stood a single standing stone, the Stone of Odin. It had an important role in Orcadian folk tradition for it had a hole through it, and lovers plighted their troth by passing their hands through the hole (Marwick in Ritchie 1976, 28–34). In December 1814 the tenant farmer, Captain W. MacKay, broke the Stone of Odin into pieces and began to topple and break up the Stones of Stenness. Stone 5 was felled and the adjacent Stone 6 broken into pieces. Popular opinion was outraged, and action was taken against MacKay in the Sheriff Court and he agreed to stop the destruction. He claimed that he was removing the stones to strengthen the fields, and he was clearly perceived as an improving farmer and was removing impediments to the agricultural practices of the day. He may well have been seeking stone for building, but Stallybrass's report (see below) also makes mention of blast-holes. MacKay might well have succeeded in destroying the circle had not the Stone of Odin a special place in Orcadian traditional life.

There is no evidence about how MacKay's men pulled the stones down, but it seems likely that they dug out one side of the packing in the stone-hole and then, presumably with tackle and horse-power toppled the stone to the inside of the circle. The stone-hole of Stone 6 showed the shaft that had been dug into one side of it to facilitate the operation. The stone was then systematically broken up, possibly with explosives. There is no record of any pieces surviving or being used for other purposes, as vividly reported for the Stone of Odin by Ernest Marwick (in Ritchie 1976, 31). That Stone 5 was intact after it was felled shows the resilience of the stone chosen for the circle, as it was 5.5m in length and weighed between 9 and 10 tons. The circle remained in this sorry state throughout the nineteenth century with the ditch largely silted up and the whole area part of a cultivated field – there is a photograph of what appear to be cabbages covering the site.

There was renewed interest in the sites in the early twentieth century, and the Society for the Protection of Ancient Monuments commissioned a report on the major monuments (Stallybrass 1906, in the Archives of Scotland file quoted below): 'As the stones were brought down by vandalism and their history is a record I see no reason why re-erection should be objected to in this case. In regard to the central cromlech, it is too far broken for anything to be done, but the prostrate stone, measuring 18ft by 5ft 3in by 1ft 6in,

13 Stones of Stenness, Orkney. The re-erection of Stone 5 in 1906. *Crown Copyright: Royal Commission on the Ancient and Historical Monuments of Scotland*

I recommend be raised. It has only one flaw running down the face of the stone, so that elaborate cradling would be unnecessary, and suitable tackle for the purpose can, I find, be obtained in Stromness. A hole should be dug to receive it immediately at its foot and at a depth calculated from the former ground line, which can be detected on it. ... Flaws, and the blast-holes made by the farmer in the prostrate stone, should be mended as above directed'. The interest of the Society was brought to the attention of the Office of Works and the sites were taken into guardianship in April 1906. The Office of Works lost no time in putting the work of restoration into place, 'to take advantage of the best part of the summer', (Archives of Scotland MW/1/586 2302/2A). The *Orkney Herald* of 5 September 1906 records the work of preservation and re-erection. 'During the past few weeks workmen have been engaged under the superintendence of Mr Myres, R.I.B.A., of Edinburgh, in preserving the Standing Stones of Brogar and Stenness. All cracks in the stones have been cleaned and filled with cement and mastic. Sockets and stumps which had become covered over have been exposed. Where necessary, the foundations of the stones have been made up and returfed. ... The Stenness Circle has also been carefully treated, and the largest stone, which has lain prostrate since 1814, has been raised to a horizontal position, cradled, and set up in the exact position of its original socket, which was found. Before being re-erected, a document recording the circumstances was written by Mr Myres, and signed by Mr J.W. Cursiter, F.S.A. Scot., as representing the Department of Woods and Forests, placed in a bottle, and deposited in the cement in the foundation.' The photographs of the newly-erected stone are of particular interest as they show that with timber, ropes and tackle eight men could raise the stone, presumably without previous experience *(13)*. Such massive baulks of timber might have been available to Neolithic Orcadians as driftwood. The photograph shows clearly what can be achieved with limited resources and a small team. Also interesting is the record trail that the Office of Works papers offer for this site in terms of both conservation supervision and public understanding. A report logged 22 May 1907 records the raising of Stone 5, the discovery of its original stone-hole and the importance of local involvement in the re-erection with the approval of the antiquary Mr J.W. Cursiter. Cursiter felt that a small bronze plaque should be attached to one side of the stone stating that it had been re-erected. There were indeed blast-holes bored into the stone (identified by Anne Brundle, Orkney Museums), and it clearly had a very lucky escape. At that time discussions were underway to ensure that the site was not wholly under cultivation, but it was in a field of oats, and there is correspondence about the appropriate sum that might be paid to the tenant in compensation for leaving an area including the ditch and the outer bank unploughed. This record trail has been described in a little detail not just as an anecdotal exercise, but to show that the understanding of any site is not merely an experiential moment of understanding, but may involve a good deal of background research.

An unusual feature recorded in the course of the excavation of the circle was the discovery of a pair of stone-holes, from which the stones appeared to have been extracted in antiquity, but elements of the careful horizontal packing remained (Ritchie 1976, 14).

In 1991 the exciting discovery was made of what is probably the stone-hole of the Stone of Odin some 60m NNW of the Stones of Stenness; the stone appeared to have been extracted by pulling it to the eastern side of the hole, but the horizontal packing of the western side remained in position (Richards 1992). The width of the packing seems to tally well with the width of the stone recorded by Stanley in 1789 on what is probably the most reliable depiction (Ritchie 1976, 55). It is one of a pair of stone-holes, but as the other stone is not recorded in the many early illustrations of the site, it was presumably removed many centuries ago.

In 1978 examination of a stone-hole at Deepdale on the south side of the Loch of Stenness where the farmer had removed one of a pair of stones, which had become loosened by ploughing, showed that a fragment of the base remained very close to one side of the hole, and it was assumed that it had been introduced into the hole from the opposite side and then levered upright against the edge of the hole (Burton 1978). This is an interesting contrast to Stenness and Brodgar, where the stones appear to be central to the holes.

CALANAIS AND CLAVA

At Calanais, Lewis, Western Isles, it was likely that there was a missing stone at the east end of the east row, and in 1980 Margaret Ponting probed the peat to try to identify a likely position. Excavation showed that this was indeed the case and the stone was fully revealed (Stone 33A). In 1982 it was set upright in its original stone-hole and on the correct orientation, raised into position within a scaffolding tripod with a ratchet jack and a team of four workmen (Ashmore 1983; 1995; 2002, 34, 50; Ponting & Ponting 1984, 11, 23, which shows the packing stones at the base; Roy 1999, 175-6). The tip of Stone 19 was identified in a field-wall and was put back on the stone in 1978 (Ponting & Ponting 1984, 8-9; Roy 1999, 176). The full tale of the re-erection of Callanish VIII / Bernera Bridge is told by Roy (1999, 180-3); suffice it to say that it was originally re-erected in the wrong spot, but, after archaeological excavation, the original stone-hole was identified and a stone of about 4 tons was repositioned in the same way as that of Stone 33A of the principal site.

Other well-known circles have been tinkered with in the past. Some of the upright stones in the Balnuaran of Clava, Inverness-shire[1], monuments have been re-erected: '... these have recently been put up on end in their original positions by the proprietor, Mr Davidson of Cantray, who has erected all the fallen blocks of the three larger cairns, and otherwise cleared off the obscuring brushwood and removed the turf round them, so as to expose them in their present state completely to view, (Jolly 1882, 303). The re-erected stones are identified in Henshall & Ritchie (2001, 204-5, 208-9) and Fraser had spotted that one of the stones at least was re-erected upside down. Only five of the stones surrounding the cairn at Corrimony, Inverness-shire, appear to be *in situ* (Henshall & Ritchie 2001, 214). Jolly was critical about what could happen to stones which were wrongly re-erected, 'such errors make one question the wisdom of tampering in any way with these monuments, which it would be wiser, for many reasons, to leave in their present dilapidated condition' (1882, 313). At Clava, tree-planting in late Victorian times created the grove within which we see the monuments today (Bradley 2000, 15).

BALBIRNIE AND BALFARG

In 1970-1 the writer undertook the excavation of a stone circle and cairn in Balbirnie Park, Fife, within the precinct of Glenrothes New Town (Ritchie 1974) in advance of a road-widening operation, although the eventual road scheme, many years after the excavation, would not have involved the destruction of the site. It was not an easy site to disentangle, much disturbed by tree roots and by earlier explorations, but the circle of ten stones could be planned with some confidence including several impressive monoliths. It may be noted that the Grooved Ware sherds from stone-hole no. 10 (McInnes in Ritchie 1974, 15-17) can now be seen to join, and Henshall (in Mercer 1981, 132-3, 165) has suggested that other sherds from the site might be Grooved Ware. Several cists were found beneath the cairn of stones, one beneath a large sandstone capstone. The facilities to move this intact could not be made available, and the workmen were instructed (not by the excavator) to break it up using mells. Destruction on a nineteenth-century scale; fortunately the slab was not decorated on the underside. During a visit by members of Glenrothes Development Corporation, which had bought Balbirnie Park in 1969, the question was raised of what should become of the stones. The Department of the Environment had no thought of re-erecting them; this was a purely rescue excavation. The Corporation members were appalled and instructed their Planning Department to see what could be done. Aspects of antiquity are important to 'New' towns and Glenrothes did not intend to see a prehistoric circle disappear. The excavation plans were provided, the Department of the Environment made no objections, and the stones were lifted by crane on to a flatbed trailer and trundled to a new location in Balbirnie Park about 125m

14 Balbirnie Stone Circle, Fife, in the course of re-erection. *Crown Copyright: Royal Commission on the Ancient and Historical Monuments of Scotland*

15 Balbirnie Stone Circle, Fife, settled into its new site. *Crown Copyright: Royal Commission on the Ancient and Historical Monuments of Scotland*

south-east of the original position *(14)*. One of the cists had a decorated side-slab, and the Glenrothes Town Artist, David Harding, was asked to create a stone that could be used in the recreated stone circle (illustrated by Burl 1979, 16); the original is now in the collections of the National Museums of Scotland. The circle remained in the sylvan setting of the Park *(15)* until a new road and houses encroached on it, and it now looks a rather quaint garden feature. But it remains a positive statement from a New Town about the antiquity of its patch.

Increasingly archaeologists are being encouraged to record an experiential approach to the practice of excavation. The discovery of the deposit of two galvanised pails at Balbirnie deserves to be recorded in greater detail than in the 'official account' (Ritchie 1974, 3). Excavation of the disturbed cairn material to the west of Stone 1 revealed a pit and, as the surface was carefully trowelled down, the tops of two circular metal objects were revealed. To an excavator schooled in European Prehistory, Late Bronze Age buckets were an exciting possibility, though the metal was rather dull. Little by little the realisation that they were comparatively modern galvanised pails became apparent, though one was prettily encased in wickerwork. The circumstances of the deposition only became clear when the Balfours of Balbirnie, still at Balbirnie House, visited the site with an elderly aunt. 'Oh the pails', she said, 'I was out with one of the gardeners and we dug a hole and popped them in.'

16 Balfarg Henge, Fife; re-erecting one of the standing stones. *Copyright Roger Mercer*

Many excavations involve the ghastliness of destruction, the raising of unrealistic hopes of discovery, and the re-creation of something rather different, and Balbirnie had it all.

The expansion of Glenrothes necessitated the excavation of the area of a henge monument identified on aerial photographs and associated with two standing stones (Atkinson 1950, 58-9). Full-scale excavation was undertaken by Roger Mercer in 1977-8, including the removal of the standing stones and an examination of the stone-holes (1981). The stones were enveloped in straw as a precaution against wintry weather as the Development Corporation mulled over their plans for the site. Vandals, however, set the straw alight. Never before, perhaps, has the reinstatement of a standing stone been so meticulously recorded. 'The straw was, however, set on fire on 22 April [1979] by young persons who were seen running from the site. The fire brigade was called; water was used to put out the fire, resulting in the rapid cooling of the stones causing hairline fractures to appear.' Advice was sought and the conservation firm Renofors (UK) Ltd was approached. The stone was monitored in the succeeding months and fell into three large pieces and some 40 smaller fragments. The larger pieces were connected with stainless steel bars bonded with epoxy resins, '... the 40 or so smaller pieces were then fitted into place like a complex jigsaw puzzle with no picture to follow. The cracks were pointed with Renofors Mineros material to match the weathered stone exposed faces.' (Report of Glenrothes Development Corporation, Department of Architecture, Planning and Quantity Surveying, 29 January 1980). It was estimated that the reconstituted stone weighed about 6.75 tons. The stones were re-erected on 11 December 1979 *(16)*. The ditch of the henge was partly dug out to create a public open space and play area with a circle of houses round about, with an unusual street-name – The Henge. An important landscape has been created and the stones have a vital part to play in adding a sense of history to the townscape. Glenrothes also commissioned a 'henge' as a piece of modern sculpture.

A further programme of excavation in advance of development at Balfarg Riding School was undertaken between 1983 and 1985, which added yet more information about Neolithic and Bronze Age activity in the area (Barclay & Russell-White 1993). Among the extensive remains were the post-holes of two structures, interpreted as mortuary enclosures of mid-third millennium date. Such sites are unusual and a reconstruction has been created to give an impression of scale and to remind the visitor of the importance of timber in prehistoric contexts.

Balbirnie, Balfarg and Balfarg Riding School have largely by chance illustrated the incremental possibilities of the public presentation of archaeology in Scotland in the 1970s and 1980s. Re-erection and re-creation has a large part to play. The little stone circle of Balbirnie was in such a sorry state that no consideration of its preservation was originally contemplated; the local authority took the lead. At Balfarg too the original excavation was envisaged as providing a *tabula rasa* for development. The notion of preserving the space came later and it still offers one of the best impressions of the scale of such an earthwork. There is now an archaeological heritage trail with detailed information panels at the three sites and an accessible guidebook (Barclay nd).

MAROONED MEGALITHS

Many megaliths are now marooned within modern developments: Sandy Road, Scone, Perthshire, stones at St Madoes, Perthshire, in the flowerbed of a primary school (RCAHMS 1994, 34), and the ring-cairn at Aviemore, Inverness-shire. But modern creations also attempt to generate a sense of history within new developments. A number of cist burials were discovered in the course of the housing development at Aberdour Road East, Dunfermline, Fife, in 1972 (Close-Brooks *et al.* 1972). Scottish Special Housing Association decided to mark the spot and a stone with a plaque was 'surrounded by a semi-circular pattern of railway sleepers, interspersed with evergreen and deciduous shrubs… Sycamores and holly are to be planted around these sleepers to form an enclosed space', (SSHA press release). At a tree-planting ceremony in 1975 with children from the local school Professor Stuart Piggott explained that it was not *his* far-off relations that were being remembered, for these were in the far south of England, but those of the people of this part of Fife. New monuments can be important in making an area feel distinct. Some stones have been moved for great distances and put to new uses. A cupmarked stone from the crater at the top of the barrow at Strathallan, Perthshire, was found in 1957, left by the explorers of that time, and removed 'to a place of safety' after the excavations of 1978-9. It is now a feature in the *Land Gallery: a Vanished World* in the Museum of Scottish Country Life, Wester Kittochside, Lanarkshire (Barclay 1983, 189-90, 199, pl. 15c).

RE-CREATION AT CAIRNPAPPLE

Cairnpapple, West Lothian, is a creation now more than half a century old and is a monument that must confuse as many visitors as it informs. The henge monument, circle of uprights, and two-period cairn, excavated by Stuart Piggott in 1947-8 (Piggott 1948), has been re-evaluated by Gordon Barclay (1999 and references therein; also Barclay & Grove 1998) The sequence is not our concern here, but it was considered of such importance that the Ministry of Works took the site into guardianship and set about presenting it to the public. In order to simulate the central cairn a concrete dome was erected over the Beaker grave and a cist with a Food Vessel, and the dome is entered through a hatch and down a steep ladder (following a pattern that had been pioneered on cairns in Orkney). A later enlargement of the cairn is represented by a low plinth of rubble set within the surviving kerb-stones. Part of the importance of the site is the sequence of events for which the evidence is represented by the pits dug into the subsoil. How could such features be shown to the public? A series of pits that once held uprights are preserved as shallow stone-lined depressions with red gravel at the bottom. A number of pits, some of which had deposits of cremated bone, were found under the cairn material of the enlarged cairn, and these are indicated by deep stone-revetted hollows in the reconstructed cairn with greyish gravel at the base. A group of undated burials is shown as elongated hollows with silver-white gravel at the base. The visitor is bound to be puzzled by the presentation. Archaeological opinion is divided as to whether the pits within the henge bank and ditch contained timber or stone uprights, but it seemed to the present writer on a recent visit to Cairnpapple that there were ample elongated stones on the site to make a stumpy stone circle perfectly likely (and Piggott was after all one of the few excavators at the time with a specific interest in timber circles). Whatever the case, Cairnpapple is important as a ground-breaking attempt to present a multi-period site to the public; it is an archaeological creation in its own right.

STRICHEN AND LOCAL INVOLVEMENT

Local involvement in re-creating a stone circle is most tellingly illustrated by work at Strichen, Aberdeenshire. In 1978 the Community Council sought

17 Strichen Stone Circle, Aberdeenshire; moving a stone by people-power. *Copyright Philip Abramson and Iain Hampsher-Monk*

18 Strichen Stone Circle, Aberdeenshire; the restored circle, with the ruins of Strichen House in the background. *Copyright Philip Abramson and Iain Hampsher-Monk*

help to re-erect stones of a recumbent stone circle that had been toppled by earth-moving machinery in 1965 and dumped a little distance away. Unwilling to see part of local heritage lost, approaches were made to Aubrey Burl, an expert on such circles, and an excavation was organised under the direction of Hampsher-Monk and Abramson with a view to re-erecting the stones (Hampsher-Monk & Abramson 1982). It was discovered that this was not the first time that the stones had been removed, for in the early nineteenth century the tenant farmer had felled most of them, only to be instructed by the land owner Lord Lovat to put them up again. The restored circle was not set up in the same position as before, but to the south side of the recumbent circleand flankers. Thom knew that the circle had been re-erected (1967, 142; Ferguson 1988, 66), but he did not know about the change of position. Excavation revealed the positions of the original stone-holes and with ropes, a wooden trackway and people-power the stones were dragged into position and set up *(17)*. The sense of place is returning *(18)*.

As a result of local interest, one of the most recent re-creations is that of the recumbent stone circle at Tomnaverie, Aberdeenshire, where fallen monoliths have been righted after careful excavation, and the vista from the site to Lochnagar can again be seen across the recumbent circle framed by the flanking stones (Bradley *et al.* 2002).

Local involvement resisted the removal and re-erection of the stone setting known as Leys of Marlee, Essendy, Perthshire, where the surviving stones on either side of a minor road were considered to be a hazard to traffic as two of the stones had been knocked over in accidents. The Blairgowrie, Rattray and District Civic Trust gathered a petition to make a plea that if work could be undertaken to demonstrate the antiquity of the stones they should be left in their original positions and the fallen stones re-erected. Archaeological examination revealed little, but confirmed the likely antiquity of the site, and two fallen stones were duly re-erected (Gibson 1988).

Such exercises have a vital part to play in our understanding of how stones may have been moved and put up in prehistoric times. Abramson has recorded (in litt) that even quite small stones of about one ton required many hands to drag them over pine rollers to the correct position, and that without a covering of dry straw to provide a slippery surface for the stone to be dragged along the rollers were ineffectual. He showed that a series of surges was the best method of moving the stones, as this gave time for the labourers to rest and for the timber trackway to be reconstituted in front of the stone.

ALEXANDER THOM

Such study shows the importance of conservation records of objects and sites. In conversation with the present writer Professor Alexander Thom bemoaned the fact that one could not rely on the current layout of a monument for study

19 Moncreiffe Stone Circle, Perthshire, in the course of excavation, with the Director, Dr M.E.C. Stewart, at the centre of the circle, before it was relocated. *Crown Copyright: Royal Commission on the Ancient and Historical Monuments of Scotland*

as there appeared to be constant unrecorded intervention. He makes allusion to this in several of his publications. 'It must, however, be remarked that where 're-erection' has been done by unqualified people the result is the lowering of the value of the site. I must make a plea for every stone to be left where it lies until a survey has been completed – and by 'survey' I do not mean the kind of plan that appears in many reports' (Thom 1967, v). This is why the consistent record of his own work in NMRS is so important (Ferguson 1988). He makes a plea for preservation and recording. 'In this century, to the author's knowledge, aerodromes, roads, reservoirs, housing, quarries, agriculture, and forestry have all taken their toll, and the pace of destruction is quickening. One well-meaning individual took a stone into his garden "to preserve it"'. Another menhir was cut up by a mason to make lintels; farmers have removed large outliers; and so the list goes on. The author makes a plea for the position of every stone near a site, however insignificant looking, to be recorded exactly, before the information it may hold is lost for ever' (Thom 1971, 116). Thom's despair is greatest when it comes to re-location of monuments. At Moncreiffe House, Perthshire, a stone circle was excavated and re-located in advance of motorway building *(19)* (Stewart 1985). 'The intention was to remove this circle and to re-erect it elsewhere as has been done with another circle near Inverness [Stoneyfield; Simpson 1996, 54-5]. To see how completely useless such a procedure really is, one only has to picture what will happen when all record of the re-erection is lost and investigators take the re-erected circle as genuine' (Thom & Thom 1978, 176). It is important to have sympathy with the spirit of this view. Thom's approach may well have been shaped by personal experience. It is remembered within the Royal Commission that many years ago Thom wrote to the Secretary to draw attention to a circle in Dumfriesshire where his system of measurements and shapes worked wonderfully; Kenneth Steer, then Secretary of the Commission, wrote back to say that the circle had been entirely created in the eighteenth century (the correspondence has not survived). The circle in question was at Friar's Carse, Dunscore, and was erected as a landscape feature by a noted antiquarian Robert Riddell, owner of the estate, and at one time a friend of Robert Burns. The description of the visit of the Dumfriesshire and Galloway Natural History and Antiquarian Society to Friar's Carse in 1947 is relevant to our theme. 'Another of his [Riddell's] imitations was a Bronze Age stone circle which he erected on a knoll a short way up the river. It is now a most realistic affair, correct in lay-out and so weathered as to take in anyone. It should be a warning to all antiquaries' (Field Meeting 1947, 185). It is fair to say that this revelation did not dent Thom's confidence in his results. The fashion for modern stone circles is outlined by Rob Roy (1999) along with suggestions as to how to build them and a gazetteer of their locations worldwide.

MODERN MEGALITHS AND MEGALITHS AS SYMBOLS

New standing stones too are being erected, including that of Caithness stone set up by Billy Connolly in his Aberdeenshire estate at Candacraig; it is inscribed and will not thus be confusing from an archaeological point of view (*The Times*, 13 July 2003). Standing stones are very symbolic, perhaps best known in Scottish literature in *The Pirate* with the Stones of Stenness, Orkney, where this paper began (Scott 1822) and at Blawearie in the Mearns in *Sunset Song* (Grassic Gibbon 1932), and the Stones of Stenness form the cover and poster for the Van Morrison album, *The Philosopher's Stone*. The standing stone at Highpark farm near Campbeltown is surely the inspiration of Sir Paul McCartney's symphonic poem *Standing Stone*. The booklet that accompanies the CD has atmospheric photographs by Linda McCartney and paintings by McCartney himself; '[T]here are many things that we love that we can't explain. But it seems that everyone I know has some deep feeling for these standing stones, even if they are a complete mystery' (McCartney 1997). The monuments of the past have a role in the art of today, as Ashmore demonstrated in his presentation of the art inspired by Calanais/Callanish (Ashmore 1995; 2002). The exhibition in Stornoway, in 1995, brought together artists, musicians and writers who took Calanais/Callanish as their theme for contemporary painting, photography and much more (An Lanntair 1995). Re-creation is not just a matter of re-erection.

Many re-erections and re-locations take place after the archaeological work has been done and, while an archaeologist may be present, the professional input on the final positioning of a stone swinging from a hydraulic crane is limited. The best that is possible is to leave as full a record of the event in the local Sites and Monuments Record and the National Monuments Record of Scotland. The Conservation Record is now *de rigeur* for artefacts in museums, and with monuments in State care, but for some other monuments such information may be more difficult to track down, if it exists. 'Best Practice' in stone conservation in graveyards demands a careful statement of condition and treatment, as exemplified by Historic Scotland's *Guide for Practitioners* (Maxwell *et al.* 2001, 99-118). The data about re-erections on a site like the Ring of Brodgar can be worked out (Ritchie 1988), but Thom's plea for the ready availability of that record of change, and that it be not lost, is important. Thom & Thom record Le Rouzic's practice at Carnac in marking re-erected stones with a plug of red cement (1978, 3). The Moncrieffe photograph, however, also illustrates how misleading plans of circles at present-day ground level may be as to the size of the original stones.

STANDING STONES

For obvious reasons archaeologists have been unwilling to excavate the stone-holes of standing stones, mindful perhaps of the traditional fate of the barber-surgeon at Avebury (Smith 1965, 177-80). There are several cases where stones have been re-erected and the original holes have been examined. In 1860 Sir James Young Simpson excavated around the standing stone known as the Loth

20 Loth Stone, East Lothian, excavations of Sir James Young Simpson, 1860, recorded by James Drummond. *Crown Copyright: Royal Commission on the Ancient and Historical Monuments of Scotland*

Stone situated in a field on Cairndinnis Farm near Traprain Law, East Lothian (a mythical ruler Loth is said to be the origin of the name Lothian). The work was recorded in a pencil and chalk drawing by James Drummond *(20)*. Although it was still standing in 1913 (RCAHMS 1924, 99, no. 149), it had fallen by the 1940s and it was brought to the attention of the Office of Works on behalf of Lord Traprain in December 1944, who felt that the fallen stone was a hazard to agricultural machinery. The discussions surrounding the question of re-erection touch on a number of issues relevant to our theme. James Richardson, the Inspector of Ancient Monuments, was against re-erection in other than the original position. The advice was sought of Stuart Piggott, Abercromby Professor of Archaeology in the University of Edinburgh, and representing archaeology on the Ancient Monuments Board for Scotland. Piggott felt that there was no objection to the re-erection of the stone so long as the archaeological potential of the area of the stone-hole was examined. He cited work by W.F. Grimes at St Nicholas, Glamorgan, where a stone had been moved in advance of road-widening and trenches examined to discover whether it was a single stone or had been part of a 'cromlech' (Grimes 1934). Piggott offered to direct the work but was in fact too committed to do so. In the end it was decided to re-erect the stone near a hedgerow, where it would not be a hazard to the plough, some 47m north of the original position. The work was undertaken under the direction of J.R.C. Hamilton, Office of Works, in December 1948 and the stone-hole examined with care. On the south-east side of the stone-hole a sloping ramp was found about 0.8m wide

21 Orwell Standing Stones, Kinross-shire; east standing stone in the course of excavation. *Crown Copyright: Royal Commission on the Ancient and Historical Monuments of Scotland*

22 Orwell Standing Stones, Kinross-shire; east standing stone: a closer view showing the cremation deposit in the stone-hole. *Crown Copyright: Royal Commission on the Ancient and Historical Monuments of Scotland*

and 1m in length, which Hamilton thought to have been an original feature. He thought that it had originally been packed with stones disturbed by Simpson's excavation, and had been inadequately backfilled, and that this had weakened the stability of the stone. The suggestion that the surrounding area be examined was met by the excavation of four narrow trenches (0.6m by 4.6m) at the four cardinal points of the compass converging on the stone-hole to check for surrounding features. Hamilton's typescript report is in Archives of Scotland DD/27/328 along with the protracted correspondence (copy of the report in NMRS). Today one might think that the stances of Richardson and Piggott were both correct in part. Simpson also excavated round the base of the Catstane, Midlothian (discussed by Rutherford & Ritchie 1974 and re-excavated by Cowie 1978).

At Orwell, Kinross-shire, a pair of standing stones was excavated in 1972 (Ritchie 1974, 8-9), but the burial deposit in the east stone-hole has not previously been illustrated *(21-22)*. The more westerly of the pair had fallen and the intention was to re-erect it and to protect both by setting their bases in concrete plinths. The fallen stone had barely any recognisable socket, but the upright stone was set in a hole about 0.8m deep. Within the south-west side of the more easterly stone there was a two-tiered cremation deposit. The complexity of the deposit is of some interest as the state of preservation was good. The lower represented more than one individual, one possibly male and the other two possibly female, as well as fragments of a small dog and of pig. This was covered by a small slab, and the upper deposit, partly enclosed by small upright slabs, the tips just visible in the photograph, was that of an adult male over 30 (Denston in Ritchie 1974, 27-8). Deposits of cremated bone and cists in the vicinity show that this has been a place for burial for some time (*NSA*, 9 (Kinross), 59). Small deposits of cremated bone were found within a stone-hole at Ballymeanoch, Mid Argyll, and were contemporary with the erection of the stone. Sadly in this case the stone could not be pieced together and re-erected (Barber 1978). Although it is conceivable that part of the stone-hole could have been dug out in antiquity, it is more likely that the cremation deposits were part of the rituals of erection. Pairs of stones occur throughout Britain and Ireland (Burl 1993, 181-202), with concentrations in Scotland in Argyll and Perthshire, and Orwell is presumably an outlier of the latter group. Rows of three stones are found in Argyll and its islands (Burl 1993, 149, 172-3), and excavation at Ardnacross, Mull, where there are two lines of three, discovered charcoal in one stone-hole that gave a radiocarbon date of 1260-89 cal BC (OxA-3880), but nothing of note was found in the others (Martlew & Ruggles 1996, 125-8). It is remarkable how many sockets are on examination 'ill-defined', as at Peterhead, Blackford, Perthshire (*Discovery and Excavation in Scotland 1990*, 44), yet the myth perpetuated by many tourist guides that standing stones are 'a third again'/'half again' into the ground remains unshakeable.

One stone that was unusually deeply embedded in proportion to its height was that on the summit of a Neolithic round barrow at Pitnacree, Perthshire; here a thin slab of schist about 1.6m in height and 0.2m thick was set in a pit dug into the top of the mound to a depth of 0.6m and chocked round with stones at its base. At the bottom of the hole there were the scattered cremated remains of a female and quantities of charcoal that provided a radiocarbon determination in the later third millennium BC (Coles & Simpson 1965, 38); more recently the cremated bone itself has produced a radiocarbon date of 2340-1950 cal BC (at 2σ, GrA-21744: Sheridan pers. comm.).

There are also tantalising reports of discoveries at stones for which there is now no surviving evidence. One of my favourite pairs of stones is at Carse, Mid Argyll (cover of Ritchie 1997; RCAHMS 1988, 131, no. 204). In 1864 'fragments of Bronze Plates found at the base of a Standing Stone on the estate of Carse' were presented to the Society of Antiquaries of Scotland, but sadly they have not survived. They are described as showing 'traces of small projecting embossed ornaments of Vandyke pattern, and knobs, etc.' What can they have been? Even today survival in the public domain can be a matter of chance.

Derek Simpson's excavation at Kintraw, Argyll, between 1959 and 1960, examined a massive cairn and a small cairn with a tall standing stone in between, some 4.25m in height (1967). The cairns were interesting structurally, the larger (14.6m in diameter and 2.4m in height) with large kerb-stones and a 'false portal' arrangement on the south–west and the smaller, an example of a class now thought of as kerb cairns, with a box-like cist just within the kerb, but the finds were few and the excavation 'physically

23 Kintraw, Argyll, the prone stone with the lighter colour showing how little was below ground, with the kerb-cairn behind. *Copyright Mike Brooks and Trevor Cowie*

exhausting' over the two seasons. The stones all had to be removed and then put back. Little could Derek Simpson have expected that it was the standing stone that would generate an inordinate literature in the following years because of Alexander Thom's interpretation of its position in archaeoastronomical terms (summarised in RCAHMS 1988, 64, no.63, n 4; Ruggles 1999, 25-9). The stone fell to the ground in March 1979 after an unusually hard winter with a combination of severe frosts and heavy rain. Clearly a stone of such interest ought to be re-erected, and this was undertaken later that year *(23-24)*, but the shallow stone-hole revealed little. *(23)* shows clearly that it had stood in the ground to a depth of no more than a metre (Cowie 1980).

A rousing story of erection rather than re-erection is told about the impressive pillar some 3.4m in height that stands on a knoll to the east of Taynuilt village, Lorn, Argyll. The stone, which may indeed have been a fallen monolith, lay prone on a ridge known as Barra na Caber, some 1.6km to the north-west of its present location, 'till the glorious news of Trafalgar reached' the workers at the Bonawe furnace. 'The iron-workers at the Lorn furnace, then in full blast at that place, marched in a body to Barra na Caber, mounted the four ton block on wooden rollers, and dragged it a mile eastward to a prominent knoll called Cnoc Aingeal (knoll of the fire), and there raised it – the first monument to Lord Nelson in the British Isles' (Thomson 1927, 230-1; RCAHMS 1974, no. 121, 63-4). This spontaneous act is of interest as it offers

24 Kintraw, Argyll, the stone in the course of re-erection, with the large cairn on the right. *Copyright Mike Brooks amd Trevor Cowie*

one clear impetus to the erection of stones among many other possibilities, even in prehistoric times. Angus Smith muses: 'The stone was set up in the evening, in the old way; no writing, no sign, but that inanimate and illegible one. Curious that the people did not consider that no man knew for what purpose it was first set up, and so infer that their purpose too would soon also be forgotten; but the stone is of great value as showing the old spirit and habit remaining to this century' (Smith 1885, 74). An inscribed slate plaque fixed to the stone now records the event.

CONCLUSION

My purpose has been to demonstrate the importance of record-keeping when stones are moved or re-erected and to stress the need to check on any previous history of intervention. I have also explored the ways that stones can remind us of the past, even in modern places like Glenrothes (perhaps with a little on-site interpretation). A short paper such as this cannot include all the examples known or suspected, but I hope those described are representative. Certainly standing stones and stone circles can be experienced in their settings in myriad ways, but archaeological study demands a careful examination of any earlier records as well. Standing stones and stone circles exert a fascination in the Scottish landscape over the millennia and we should certainly try to retain as many as possible in their original locations.

ACKNOWLEDGEMENTS

Many friends and colleagues helped in the preparation of this essay in remembering examples of re-erection, providing references, as well as the clarification of events: Patrick Ashmore, Gordon Barclay, Anne Brundle, Aubrey Burl, Trevor Cowie, Margaret and Ron Curtis, Sally Foster, Iain Fraser, Steven Gordon, Mark Hall, Audrey Henshall, Kristina Johansson, R.K. Leslie of The Orkney Library, Roger Mercer, Andrew Nicholson, Olwyn Owen, Matthew Ritchie, Ian Shepherd, Alison Sheridan, Jack Stevenson, Jim Wilson. I am particularly grateful to Philip Abramson and Iain Hampsher-Monk for permission to use previously unpublished photographs of the excavation of Strichen, and to Roger Mercer and Trevor Cowie for photographs from Balfarg and Kintraw. Douglas A. Speirs and Lisa Wood of Fife Council Archaeological and Law and Administration Services provided valuable information about Balfarg. The National Library of Iceland provided the illustration from the Stanley papers. Anna Ritchie helped with memories of Balbirnie and Orwell as well as with many improvements to the final text.

FOOTNOTE

[1] The original, pre-1974 county names are used here as they offer greater geographical precision than the more recent Local Authority Areas.

BIBLIOGRAPHY

An Lanntair 1995 *Calanais*. Stornoway: An Lanntair.

Ashmore, P., 1983 Callanish: making a stone stand again. In Magnusson, M. (ed.), *Echoes in Stone: 100 Years of Ancient Monuments in Scotland*, 41-4. Edinburgh: Scottish Development Department.

Ashmore, P.J., 1995 *Calanais*. Stornoway: Urras nan Tursachan.

Ashmore, P.J. 2002 *Calanais*. Edinburgh: Historic Scotland.

Atkinson, R.J.C., 1950 Four new henge monuments in Scotland and Northumberland. *Proceedings of the Society of Antiquaries of Scotland*, 84 (1949-50), 57-66.

Barber, J.W., 1978 The excavation of the holed-stone at Ballymeanoch, Kilmartin, Argyll. *Proceedings of the Society of Antiquaries of Scotland*, 109 (1977-8), 104-11.

Barclay, G.J., 1983 Sites of the third millennium BC to the first millennium AD at North Mains, Strathallan, Perthshire. *Proceedings of the Society of Antiquaries of Scotland*, 113, 122-281.

Barclay, G.J., 1999 Cairnpapple Revisited: 1948-1998. *Proceedings of the Prehistoric Society*, 65, 17-46.

Barclay, G.J., not dated *Balfarg: The Prehistoric Ceremonial Complex*. Glenrothes: Fife Regional Council.

Barclay, G.J. & Grove, D., 1998 *Cairnpapple Hill*. Edinburgh: Historic Scotland.

Barclay, G.J. & Russell-White, C.J. (eds), 1993 Excavations in the ceremonial complex of the fourth millennium BC at Balfarg/Balbirnie, Glenrothes, Fife. *Proceedings of the Society of Antiquaries of Scotland*, 123, 43-210.

Bradley, R., 2000 *The Good Stones: a New Investigation of the Clava Cairns*. Society of Antiquaries of Scotland Monograph Series 17. Edinburgh: Society of Antiquaries of Scotland.

Bradley, R., Ball, C., Croft, A. & Phillips, T., 2002 The stone circles of northeast Scotland in the light of excavation. *Antiquity*, 76, 840-8.

Burl, A., 1979 *Rings of Stone*. London: Frances Lincoln/Weidenfeld & Nicolson.

Burl, A., 1993 *From Carnac to Callanish*. New Haven & London: Yale University Press.

Burton, J., 1978 Excavation of a standing stone site at Deepdale, Stromness, Orkney. *Proceedings of the Society of Antiquaries of Scotland*, 109 (1977-8), 357-60.

Close-Brooks, J., Norgate, M. & Ritchie, J.N.G., 1972 A Bronze Age cemetery at Aberdour Road, Dunfermline, Fife. *Proceedings of the Society of Antiquaries of Scotland*, 104 (1971-72), 121-36.

Coles, J.M. & Simpson, D.D.A., 1965 The excavation of a Neolithic round barrow at Pitnacree, Perthshire, Scotland. *Proceedings of the Prehistoric Society*, 31, 34-57.

Cowie, T.G., 1978 Excavations at the Catstane, Midlothian, 1977. *Proceedings of the Society of Antiquaries of Scotland*, 109, (1977-8), 166-201.

Cowie, T.G., 1980 Excavations at Kintraw, Argyll, 1979. *Glasgow Archaeological Journal*, 7, 27-31.

Ferguson, L.A., 1988 Catalogue of the Alexander Thom archive held in the National Monuments Record of Scotland. In Ruggles, C.L.N. (ed.) *Records in Stone: Papers in Memory of Alexander Thom*, 31-131. Cambridge: Cambridge University Press.

Field Meeting 26 July 1947 *Transactions of the Dumfriesshire and Galloway Natural History and Antiquarian Society*, 3 ser, 25 (1946-7), 182-6.

Gibson, A., 1988 *The Essendy Road Stones*. Blairgowrie: Blairgowrie, Rattray and District Civic Trust.

Grassic Gibbon, L., 1932 *Sunset Song*. London: Jarrolds.

Grimes, W.F., 1934 The Cottrell Park Standing Stone, St Nicholas, Glamorgan. *Transactions of the Cardiff Naturalists' Society*, 67, 104-9.

Hampsher-Monk, I. & Abramson, P., 1982 Strichen. *Current Archaeology*, 84, 16-199.

Henshall, A.S. & Ritchie J.N.G., 2001 *The Chambered Cairns of the Central Highlands*. Edinburgh: Edinburgh University Press.

Historic Scotland, not dated *Nomination of the Heart of Neolithic Orkney for Inclusion in the World Heritage List*. Edinburgh: Historic Scotland.

Jolly, W., 1882 On cup-marked stones in the neighbourhood of Inverness. With an appendix on cup-marked stones in the Western Islands. *Proceedings of the Society of Antiquaries of Scotland*, 16 (1881-2), 300-401.

McCartney, P., 1977 *Standing Stone*. Booklet accompanying EMI Classics CD. London: EMI.

Martlew, R.D. & Ruggles, C.L.N., 1996 Ritual and landscape on the west coast of Scotland: an investigation of the stone rows of northern Mull. *Proceedings of the Prehistoric Society*, 62, 117-31.

Maxwell, I., Nanda, R. & Urquhart, D., 2001 *Conservation of Historic Graveyards* (Historic Scotland, Guide for Practitioners 2). Edinburgh: Historic Scotland.

Mercer, R.J., 1981 The excavation of a Late Neolithic henge-type enclosure at Balfarg, Markinch, Fife, Scotland, 1977-78. *Proceedings of the Society of Antiquaries of Scotland*, 111, 63-171.

Piggott, S., 1948 The excavations at Cairnpapple Hill, West Lothian, 1947-48. *Proceedings of the Society of Antiquaries of Scotland*, 82 (1947-8), 68-123.

Ponting, G. & Ponting, M., 1984 *New Light on the Stones of Callanish*. Stornoway: G & M Ponting Publications.

RCAHMS, 1924 Royal Commission on the Ancient and Historical Monuments of Scotland, *Inventory of Monuments and Constructions in the County of East Lothian*. Edinburgh: HMSO.

RCAHMS, 1974 Royal Commission on the Ancient and Historical Monuments of Scotland, *Argyll: An Inventory of the Monuments*, Vol. 2, *Lorn*. Edinburgh: HMSO.

RCAHMS, 1988 Royal Commission on the Ancient and Historical Monuments of Scotland, *Argyll: An Inventory of the Monuments*, Vol. 6, *Mid Argyll and Cowal: Prehistoric and Early Historic Monuments*. Edinburgh: HMSO.

RCAHMS, 1994 Royal Commission on the Ancient and Historical Monuments of Scotland, *South-East Perth: an Archaeological Landscape*. Edinburgh: HMSO.

RCAHMS, 1999 Royal Commission on the Ancient and Historical Monuments of Scotland, *Kilmartin: An Inventory of the Monuments Extracted from Argyll* Vol. 6. Edinburgh: Kilmartin House.

Renfrew, C., 1979 *Investigations in Orkney*. Society of Antiquaries of London Research Report 38. London: Society of Antiquaries of London.

Richards, C., 1992 *Survey & Excavation of Barnhouse, Stenness, Orkney 1991, an Interim Report for Orkney Islands Council on the Survey and Excavations at Barnhouse*. Glasgow: Department of Archaeology, University of Glasgow.

Ritchie, J.N.G., 1974 Excavation of the stone circle and cairn at Balbirnie, Fife. *Archaeological Journal*, 131, 1–32.

Ritchie, J.N.G., 1976 The Stones of Stenness, Orkney. *Proceedings of the Society of Antiquaries of Scotland*, 107 (1975-6), 1–60.

Ritchie, J.N.G., 1988 The Ring of Brodgar, Orkney. In Ruggles, C.L.N. (ed.) *Records in Stone: Papers in Memory of Alexander Thom*, 337–50. Cambridge: Cambridge University Press.

Ritchie, J.N.G., 1997 *The Archaeology of Argyll*. Edinburgh: Edinburgh University Press.

Roy, R., 1999 *Stone Circles: A Modern Builder's Guide to the Megalithic Revival*. Vermont & Totnes: Chelsea Green Publishing Company.

Ruggles, C.L.N., 1999 *Astronomy in Prehistoric Britain and Ireland*. New Haven & London: Yale University Press.

Rutherford, A. & Ritchie, G., 1974 The Catstane. *Proceedings of the Society of Antiquaries of Scotland*, 105 (1973-4), 183–8.

Scott, Sir W., 1822 *The Pirate*. Many editions.

Simpson, D.D.A., 1967 Excavations at Kintrav, Argyll. *Proceedings of the Society of Antiquaries of Scotland*, 99 (1966-7), 54–9.

Simpson, D.D.A., 1996 Excavation of a kerbed funerary monument at Stoneyfield, Raigmore, Inverness, Highland, 1972-3. *Proceedings of the Society of Antiquaries of Scotland*, 126, 53–86.

Smith, I.F., 1965 *Windmill Hill and Avebury: Excavations by Alexander Keiller 1925-1939*. Oxford: Oxford University Press.

Smith, R.A., 1885 *Loch Etive and the Sons of Uisnach*. London & Paisley: Alexander Gardner.

Stewart, M.E.C., 1985 The excavation of a henge, stone circles and metal working area at Moncreiffe, Perthshire. *Proceedings of the Society of Antiquaries of Scotland*, 115, 125–50.

Thom, A., 1967 *Megalithic Sites in Britain*. Oxford: Oxford University Press.

Thom, A., 1971 *Megalithic Lunar Observatories*. Oxford: Oxford University Press.

Thom, A. & Thom, A.S., 1978 *Megalithic Remains in Britain and Brittany*. Oxford: Oxford University Press.

Thomson, W., 1927 Some antiquities in Benderloch and Lorn. *Proceedings of the Society of Antiquaries of Scotland*, 61 (1926-7), 224–33.

West, J.F., (ed.) 1975 *The Journals of the Stanley Expedition to the Faroe Islands in 1789*, Vol 2: Diary of Isaac S Benners. Tórshavn: Føroya Fróðskaperfelag.

4

Time, Space and the Standing Stones Round Calanais

PATRICK ASHMORE

'Archaeologists have been taciturn about Callanish, seeing it as an enigma not easily solved by traditional methods.' (Burl 2000, 204)

'since about 1970... [it had become] increasingly clear that the design of chambered cairns everywhere was largely due to local development and short range influences.' (Henshall & J.N.G. Ritchie 1995, 11)

'... technical and design elements indicating 'foreign' relations are all located in the main ritual focal areas of each archipelago...' (Müller 1988, 35)

INTRODUCTION

To most of the largely urban population of Britain, the Western Isles seem remote. Calanais, on the west coast of the peat-covered mass of Lewis, the northernmost of the Western Isles, seems to be on the far edge of remoteness. Yet excavation of the great stone setting there, along with other sites and stray finds, has shown that it was built by people with connections to nearby islands, to Ireland, Caithness, Orkney and possibly even to eastern Scotland. In the countryside around it are several other stone rings and settings, some buried beneath peat and others standing up through it. Building of the stone setting started long after the first monuments in the great funerary and ceremonial complex at the Bend of the Boyne in Ireland, slightly later than the ring of similarly tall stones at Stenness, Orkney, and significantly earlier than the first sarsen stone circle at Stonehenge (Richards 1990, 269, 273; Ashmore 1999; J.N.G. Ritchie 2000; 2001). A question arises: why were it and the several smaller sites built in this area, and what was special about the period around 2900 to 2600 BC during which the ring of tall stones and small chambered cairn were built?

PHYSICAL BACKGROUND

Lewis is formed largely of gneiss, an acid metamorphic rock, with some Torridonian sandstone. During the last glaciation it was covered by a local icecap (Gilbertson *et al.* 1996, 6). Parts of the island, including the ridge on which Calanais stands, are covered in till. The calcareous sand fringe of parts of the island possibly began to form about 6750 BC, adding to quartzose sand of the periglacial period (Gilbertson *et al.* 1999, 439).

Calanais is near the head of Loch Roag, a sheltered and much indented sea loch. Pollen analyses and birch wood radiocarbon dates from the nearby Tob nan Leobag, a low-lying peninsula, suggest that the birch woodland there declined substantially around the time that Calanais 1 was first built (Bohncke 1988). Field walls of the second millennium BC now run below high water mark at Tob nan Leobag and sea level 5,000 years ago was several metres below the present level; what is now inter-tidal flats was partly dry land (Bohncke 1988). During the Holocene up to some time between 2000 and 500 BC exposed areas supported grass and scrublands, with some pockets of peat in low-lying areas and stands of birch, pine and other trees in sheltered spots. Subsequently blanket peat spread over many areas. Peat did not spread over agricultural ridging immediately east of the stone setting until the early to mid-first millennium BC (Ashmore forthcoming). Excavations to the south-west of the stone setting revealed agricultural ridging covered by peat with basal dates in the mid- to late first millennium BC (Johnston *et al.* forthcoming). Disturbed remains under layers representing use of the stone setting suggest that a similar agricultural system had been created in the area more than 5,000 years ago (Ashmore forthcoming).

PREDECESSORS

The earliest direct evidence of human activity in the Western Isles is provided by early to mid-seventh millennium dates from charred hazelnut shells in basal layers at Northton, on the west coast of Harris (Gregory forthcoming; Simpson *et al.* forthcoming). Pollen analysis suggests that people may have been clearing woodland near Loch an t-Sil in South Uist in the early seventh millennium (Edwards & Whittington 1997, 70-1). It seems most sensible to suppose that people had lived in the Western Isles for at least 3,000 years before farming started there.

Farming was introduced, by immigration or by more complex processes involving an indigenous population, or both, some time in the first half of the fourth millennium BC. The pottery associated with its introduction at Eilean Domhnuill included two vessels tentatively attributed to the Carinated Bowl tradition, which is found in many parts of Scotland (Sheridan 2002; Armit 2003). The handle of an axe head made from Antrim porcellanite, found in deep peat at Shulishader, has been dated to the second half of the fourth millennium, or possibly the first century of the third millennium (Sheridan 1992; Sheridan & Saville 1993). It is reasonable to suppose that the people farming in the Western Isles during the fourth millennium had cultural connections with other farming communities in Scotland and Ireland (Henley in press). However, the nature of these connections requires some thought; they could have taken one (or, over the centuries, more than one) of several forms.

REGIONALISM AND SMALL WORLDS

Direct connections between the Calanais area, Lewis, other parts of the Western Isles, Scotland and Ireland may, on the one hand, have been predominantly short-range, with ideas and techniques being passed along a chain from one community to its neighbours; or there may have been many short-, medium- and long-range connections. Another possibility, however, is that some networks consisted of many small clusters with a few long-range connections. Network theory shows that if the cost of maintaining a long-range two-way connection with a distant community was the same as that of maintaining shorter connections, then the overall connectivity of the system as a whole could be as great as if there was a multitude of short-, medium- and long-range connections. Two variants of this 'Small World' model have been characterised. In one, the egalitarian network, all clusters have roughly the same number of connections with other clusters, mostly short-range but a few long-range (Watts 1999). In the second, the aristocratic network, a few clusters have many more connections than the others (Buchanan 2002, 118-20). There appears to be a feedback mechanism in aristocratic networks. Once dominant clusters have been established they attract more and more connections. The two different kinds of network are both vulnerable to the cutting of a few long distance links, and beyond a certain point failure is catastrophic. The system reverts to sets of local connections.

These Small World model networks become relevant when archaeology suggests that there were persistent links between both local and distant areas, but similar links with intervening areas are not obvious. It implies that there were long-distance two-way connections and that those who maintained them made little of the cost of travelling along them. One question is which models apply best to the Calanais area at what times, and if so, why? I shall return to this.

THE STANDING STONES ROUND CALANAIS

Calanais 1 stretches along a ridge south from the crofting township. It includes a tall monolith central to a ring of standing stones, and five rows of generally shorter stones which radiate from the circle: one due south, one each approximately east and west, and two, forming an avenue, running somewhat east of north. Two more stones lie just outside the circle, to the south west and south east. Between the perimeter of the circle and the central monolith is a small chambered tomb. Outside the north-east quadrant of the circle a stony bank forms in plan part of an oval or ellipse tucked against the side of the stone ring. Accurate plans of it and other settings in the area were made by Tait (1978) and others. A full description of Calanais 1 written prior to the excavations of 1980 and 1981 can be found in Ashmore 1984. Ponting & Ponting (1979; 1981) provide a comprehensive source-book for earlier accounts together with the results of their own work, and an analysis of these and other sources is summarised in their booklet of 1984. A tentative sequence of activities is proposed in Ashmore 1995, in which it is suggested that the avenue, and perhaps some of the other radiating stone alignments, post-date the erection of the stone ring.

Nearby are at least five stone rings. About 2km to the ENE on the high ground at Na Dromannan is a ring of about 11 fallen stones. Nearby is a rock face from which stones could have been extracted for this and other settings (Ballin pers. comm.). About a kilometre to the ESE of Calanais 1, on low-lying land, is Cnoc Ceann a Gharraidh, a ring of eight stones, and Cnoc Fillibhir Beag, a ring surrounding what may be a smaller ring. Ceann Thulabhaig with its tall stones and tiny central monolith stands 3km to the SSE on a gently sloping hill-side. All of these sites lie less than 0.5km from the present shore. Another ring, Cnoc Gearraidh Nighean Choinnich, buried in peat near Breasclete some 2.5km from Calanais 1, has recently been reported by Curtis & Curtis (2003). This is a remarkable cluster of apparently non-domestic stone rings. Some monoliths, pairs and triplets of stones appearing through the peat may be parts of more rings, including Airidh nam Bidearan, Cul a'Chleit, Airigh na Beinne Bige and others (Ponting & Ponting 1981; 1984; Ashmore 1995, 12-13).

It is easy to suppose that these rings (and some of the other sites) are parts of a single ritual landscape, clustered in both time and space. Yet, lacking modern excavation, their chronological relationships are obscure; they are in general earlier than the spread of blanket peat; and it may be supposed (though it cannot be demonstrated for any of them except Calanais 1 and Cnoc Ceann a Gharraidh (Ellice 1860; Stuart 1860, pl. xxv; Ponting & Ponting 1981) that they date after the introduction of farming in the Western Isles, so individual sites could belong anywhere between around 3750 and 500 BC. Strictly speaking, the distance in time between the construction of the earliest and the latest could be measured in millennia. The current orthodoxy, however, is that they are a phenomenon of the early third to mid-second millennia BC, and that they were in use at the same time as each other.

Nor is it entirely clear whether the geographical clustering reflects original distributions of stone rings or survival, or both. There are apparently unfinished or demolished rings in peat-covered areas elsewhere in Lewis, including Achmore and Druim Dubh (Ponting & Ponting 1981; Burl 2000, 427). More broadly, Burl's impressive synthesis of the stone circles of Britain, Ireland and Brittany demonstrates that there are several large areas with abundant stone rings: in Caithness, round Inverness, in Aberdeenshire, Perthshire, Arran, and Wigtownshire, in Fermanagh, Londonderry and Tyrone in Northern Ireland and Cork in Southern Ireland, and in Cumbria, the Peak District and on Dartmoor in England (Burl 2000, 2). Their common feature is that they are mostly on land which has not seen intensive medieval and earlier ploughing. It is entirely clear that there were timber equivalents both on the plough-lands, for instance Carsie Mains near Blairgowrie (Barclay & Brophy 2002, 91) and Dunragit in Wigtownshire (Thomas pers. comm.) and on land which is now marginal, for instance at Machrie Moor in Arran (Haggarty 1991). Thus the visible clusters may be the remains of a once more widespread type of landscape containing both domestic and ritual sites (Gibson 1998; Barclay in press).

There must remain doubts about the meaning of the presently understood distributions of stone rings round Loch Roag. Nevertheless, provisionally accepting firstly that their concentration reflects more than a relatively high local population and the use of large stones in construction, secondly that they (and perhaps some of the other sites) all had a similar purpose, and thirdly that they were all in use at the same time in the third millennium BC, why are they there?

Links Between Calanais 1 and Other Sites

Understanding of the possible links between Calanais and other areas has increased markedly since the early 1950s when Piggott compared the Calanais chamber's projecting side stones with those in the Camster type of tomb (1954, 225). Henshall saw the chambered cairn as unique within the Western Isles, reminiscent of the tombs of Caithness and Orkney (Henshall 1972, 125, 138-9). Megaw and Simpson, in their magisterial survey of British prehistory, simply assigned Callanish to a broad group of passage graves of the period 3000–2000 cal BC (1979, 78,135) within a broad model of regional development of insular forms and styles.

Müller linked the cruciform stone setting at Calanais, as well as what he claimed to be the cruciform chamber, to the cruciform chambers of the Boyne Valley monuments (1988, 24). This point has been adopted and extended by Henley (in press), who sees the stone setting as arising from the same design demands as Maes Howe and the Boyne tombs. In other words, he sees the avenue corresponding to a tomb passage, and the south, east and west alignments to end and side chambers. This attractive insight is weakened by the open nature of the avenue and alignments, and the fact that the axis of symmetry of the ring and the small tomb is east–west, almost at right-angles to the avenue. However at a symbolic level it may be valid and it is thus legitimate to seek analogies amongst the chambered tombs of Scotland and Ireland.

Using Henshall's data for Shetland, Orkney and the Western Isles, and cluster analysis, Müller (1988) classified the small tomb at Calanais as closer to Craonaval and Sig More in the Uists (Henshall 1972, 512, 527) than to other chambered tombs within the Western Isles (Müller 1988, 20); but his broader comparison with tombs in the Western Isles, Orkney and Shetland related it still more closely to the truly cruciform chamber and small cairn at Pettigrath's Field and the heel-shaped cairn with obscured chamber details at Gillaborn in Shetland (Henshall 1963, 171, 160), the small tripartite chambered cairns at Sandyhill Smithy and Kierfea Hill in Orkney (Davidson & Henshall 1989, 158, 130), and the cruciform upper tomb at Taversoe Tuick in Orkney (*ibid.*, 161-3); Müller 1988, 30). Had he extended his analysis he would no doubt also have related Calanais to Dorrery and Earl's Cairn in Caithness (Davidson & Henshall 1991, 111). He argued that there were some long-distance links, direct connections between the Western Isles and Shetland which missed out Orkney and Caithness. He based this on cruciform chambers and façades being stronger elements in both than in Orkney. However, he also suggested that cruciform chambers provided evidence for a direct connection between the Western Isles, Orkney and the Boyne noting that they were in the main ritual focal areas at the Boyne, Callanish, Brodgar (Maes Howe) and Gruting Voe (Gallow Hill) (Müller 1988, 34-6). Again, had he broadened his analysis he might have seen the chamber at Camster Round and the southern chamber at Camster Long as cruciform (Henshall 1963, 96, 103); they are no less so than the tomb at Callanish. They (and I would argue also the Gruting Voe area in Shetland) are not in obvious ritual foci.

Although Müller's analysis was technically flawed by his exclusion of the mainland of Scotland, and some of his connections with Orkney seem to be based on cairn size rather than chamber form, this does not invalidate his central thesis. In Caithness and Sutherland the pattern of chambered cairns seems to be composed of two elements. In addition to many single and paired tombs, such as the two Camster tombs, which may each go with a local settlement, there are several clusters, round Sordale, Yarrows-Warehouse and Ben Freiceadain in Caithness, and Inchnadamph-Loch Ailsh, Upper Kildonan Strath and Helmsdale and mid-Strathnaver in Sutherland (Davidson & Henshall 1991, figs 5 & 6; Henshall & J.N.G. Ritchie 1995, fig. 4). The Yarrows-Warehouse and Sordale Hill complexes at least seem more likely to form ritual landscapes than a collection of territories.

The isolation of the Calanais tomb from other tombs, apart from Breasclete, is typical of much of the Western Isles. Müller showed that the chambered cairns there are dispersed, with each cairn or pair of cairns in an area defined by natural boundaries. The cairns with the largest chambers were equally widely dispersed (1988, 26). That said, the concentration of chambered tombs in North Uist is extraordinary (Henshall 1972, map 4).

Burl noted that the five large oval stone rings in North Uist were juxtaposed with passage graves, and despite the dissimilarity of these tombs to the Clyde and Bargrennan types he saw the connections of the rings there as unequivocal with the ellipses of SW Scotland (2000, 201). On the ground the relationship of the tombs and circles does seem to reflect more than coincidence (Henley in press). This, then, may be a classic example of small territories – polities – each with considerable time-depth. The recent discovery of the peat-buried stone ring measuring 48m by 41m at Breasclete in the Calanais complex (Curtis & Curtis 2003) near to remains of a possible chambered cairn (Henshall 1972, 460) provides a medium-length link between the two main clusters in the Western Isles. It suggests that the model which should be applied at the time that this stone ring at Breasclete was in use is not the Small World model but one in which there were many short-, medium- and long-length connections.

There are two known clusters of tall-stone rings of the late fourth and early third millennia in the north and west of Scotland, one in the area around the Lochs of Stenness and Harray in Orkney, and the other on Machrie Moor in Arran. The Orkney concentration consists of two rings, both larger in diameter than that at Callanish. There may have been a third where Maes Howe now stands (Richards pers. comm.). The Machrie Moor concentration is different again with two tall stone rings and several made of lower stones (Haggarty 1991). The major cluster of chambered tombs and stone circles at the bend of the Boyne is larger and earlier in origin than Calanais 1, and probably earlier than the other stone settings around Loch Roag.

Nevertheless, the implication of most of the evidence is that at the time Calanais 1 was built the long-range connections discussed by Müller were real in the sense that both the grouping of stone rings at Calanais and the small chambered cairn have better analogies far away than they do locally. The Calanais group seems different both in form and connections from those of the southern parts of the Western Isles, and although there are no direct comparanda for the Calanais tomb in Sutherland, there are similar tombs in Caithness and Orkney. Thus the clustering of sites at Calanais is more like an element of the pattern of chambered tombs in Northern Scotland than it is like the rest of the Western Isles apart from North Uist.

More generally, some of the many greater and lesser clusters of ritual sites on the plough-lands may reflect long-distance connections. Broomend of Crichie, Aberdeenshire, is one of the few other known sites in Scotland with a long avenue (J. Ritchie 1920, 158-60; Burl 1993, 42); the pottery from it and Calanais is discussed below together with that from the Avebury avenues.

POTTERY AND SHORT-, MEDIUM- AND LONG-RANGE CONNECTIONS AT CALANAIS

The wide variety of potsherds from Calanais supports the deductions drawn from the structures. The following discussion depends very largely on a draft report on the pottery (Henshall & Johnson forthcoming).

The earliest pottery from the site was made in a fine corky ware; it included carinated bowls. Although appearing in later contexts, they probably all derive from the plough soils underlying the stone setting. The only western Scottish radiocarbon-dated parallels are with Newton, Islay, where similar pottery was found in a pit with a date (GU-1952) in the 2-sigma range 3940-3640 cal BC, from a mixed sample of alder hazel and oak, so perhaps including material old at the time it entered the same pit as the pottery (McCullagh 1989). That said, the potsherds from Calanais are typologically reminiscent of early fine wares, so despite the weakness of the Newton radiocarbon date they do suggest activity at Calanais in the middle half of the fourth millennium, or importation of potsherds of that date in ancestral material. None of the sherds from Calanais seem to be in the Unstan style. These corky plain sherds are similar to others from North Uist, Barra and Skye and there is no specific reason to suppose that they were exotic, even though broadly similar pots in similar fabrics have been found in Orkney and elsewhere.

Numerous sherds decorated in Hebridean styles could, judging by the contexts in which they were found, also belong with pre-ring activity or represent importation of ancestral material. They are in styles well documented at many sites in the Western Isles, with good parallels at the non-funerary sites on Eilean and Tighe, Northton and Eilean Domhnuill.

Several Grooved Ware pots were represented in contexts relating to use of the area defined by the stone ring and central monolith. They go with what seem to be small structures, defined where seen by shallow slots full of darker material than the surrounding layers. Of the fairly numerous other sites excavated in the Western Isles only Unival, an almost square tomb with a façade of tall stones and a nearby conspicuous standing stone, has produced a Grooved Ware vessel, from a secondary level in the chamber (Scott 1948, 21; Henshall 1972, 531; fig. 11). The best preserved pot at Calanais *(25)* was a tub with most of its decoration consisting of loosely horizontal grooved lines but

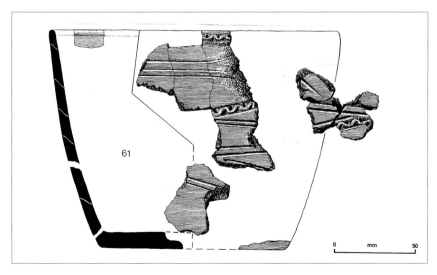

25 Grooved Ware pot from Calanais. *Illustration by Tom Borthwick*

at least one wave-and-dot line. It is broadly similar to pots from Knowth, County Meath (Brindley 1999, illus. 3.2.1), Balfarg, Fife (Mercer 1981, fig. 43.7) and Stenness, Orkney (J.N.G. Ritchie 1976, fig. 6.16). However, use of both line and wave-and-dot line decoration on a single tub is best parallelled at Balfarg Riding School in Fife (Barclay & Russell-White 1993, 97, 106, fig. 28:53a). Charcoal in a ditch layer and a pit at Balfarg Riding School, containing similar Grooved Ware, was dated to between 3340-2910 cal BC (GU-1670), 3330-2880 cal BC (GU-1904) and 3020-2620 cal BC (GU-1902; 2 sigma values cited throughout). The plateau in the calibration curve in the centuries before 3100 BC may explain the earlier parts of the probability distributions for these dates. These Balfarg Riding School dates and Calanais dates related to activities around the time of construction of the ring of stones and cairn are, statistically, unlikely to be exactly contemporary with each other. However, if the tubs are in fact of the same date as the charcoal at both sites, and the charcoal is in fact all of one date, that would constrain that date to between 2910-2880 cal BC (with a 1 in 20 chance of error). Some of the Balfarg charcoal may be more residual than that at Calanais so the attractive possibility that the dates of use of Grooved Ware at both sites can be assigned to a single generation, because of the narrow overlap, is not acceptable; because there are too many 'ifs' in the chain of argument. It does however strengthen the impression that the Grooved Ware at both sites dates to the centuries around 2900 BC. The Grooved Ware found at the timber circle at Machrie Moor Site 1 is associated with a date of 2950-1950 cal BC (GU-2325) and should also relate to dates of 3350-2920 (GU-2316) and 2900-2350 cal BC (GU-2324). The overlap of these dates is again at around 2900 BC.

All that said, in contrast to the corky and Hebridean pots, the Grooved Ware pots currently imply long-range connections in the centuries around 2900 BC, without many short- or medium-range links.

One distinctive set of sherds appears to be from an Impressed Ware pot *(26)*. Much of it came from the upper body of the cairn where it was in earthy material which probably represents modern building up of the surface. Pieces of it were found in several other areas. It is conceivable that it arrived on the cairn from some other part of the site in turf at a recent date. There are no good parallels for it in the Western Isles. One of pots found in pits at Meldon Bridge, Peebles in southern Scotland is similar to the Calanais pot (Speak & Burgess 1999, illus. 35.10). The least unacceptable dates from contexts at Meldon Bridge with abundant broadly similar pottery probably date to the first half of the third millennium BC (SRR-645, SRR-646; SRR-647): *ibid.*, 79). More generally the pottery is found in the south and east of Scotland and in the north of England. Therefore, it is possible that there were long-distance connections between at least one of these areas and Calanais.

Broadly, the dating of the contexts related to the several well-made Beakers implies their use at or before about 2000-1800 cal BC (Ashmore 1999, 129).

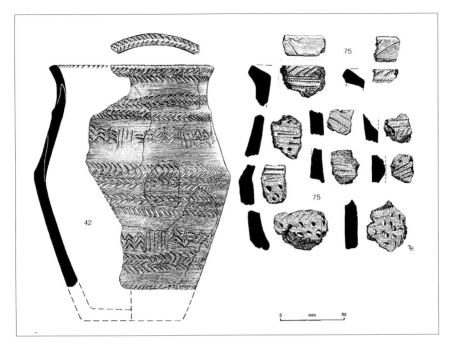

26 Late Northern Insular Beaker (left) and Impressed Ware (right) from Calanais.
Numbers as in the excavation report

It must be noted however that the sherds and the dated charcoal were all found in secondary contexts also containing residual material, and there is no direct evidence that the pieces of charcoal were of the same date as the pot-sherds. The assemblage included fine quality AOC and Bell Beakers broadly similar to examples from Coll, Tiree and Poltalloch. An AOC Beaker from Geirisclett is of lesser quality. A cardium-impressed Beaker with a good quality dark fabric and surface is difficult to parallel, although the deep grooving on some of the sherds is found in other parts of the Western Isles. The best-preserved Beaker is in a late northern British style. Generally comparable pots are found in the upper levels of several chambered cairns in N. Uist, notably at Clettraval (Henshall 1972, 147-8), Skye and Islay, but they have a predominantly eastern and northern British distribution.

The Calanais Beaker assemblage as a whole seems quite unusual in its variety of fine pots. However, some of the northern insular Beaker pottery from cists at Broomend of Crichie (Clarke 1970, 346 figs 542, 544, 360 figs 659-60, 510) is broadly comparable in decoration, and the avenue there strengthens the impression of some connection between the two places. Burl has argued that the northern insular style Beaker pottery at the Avebury Avenues is related to their construction (Burl 1993, 68-9). It may be that at Calanais, Avebury and Broomend the construction of the avenue is related to the occurrence of northern insular Beaker pottery there.

GENERAL DISCUSSION

The evidence from structures and artefacts at Calanais 1 suggests that the site was used for agriculture and subsequently ceremonial activities for at least a millennium and a half from some time in the fourth millennium. Radiocarbon dates suggest that the ring and chambered cairn were built in the first half of the third millennium and probably in the centuries around 2900 BC. The Grooved Ware and structural analogies suggest that this was a time of local clusters of sites with some active long distance connections to major ceremonial and funerary sites elsewhere in Scotland and Ireland, suggesting that a Small World model can be applied. By way of contrast, in the early second millennium BC the Beaker pottery may fit either a Small World model or one in which there were many short-, medium- and long-range connections; for northern insular pottery has been found in many places in Britain (e.g. Clarke 1970, maps 5, 6). The sparser distribution of avenues (Burl 1993, fig. 7), which may be of broadly the same date as the Beakers (*ibid.*, 68-9) would, however, fit a Small Worlds model quite well.

The Calanais cluster of sites may be where it is because in the early third millennium its local environment was favourable for permanent settlement. It seems likely that agriculture was practised locally before its construction. Marine fish may also have provided a rich resource at least seasonally; the sheltered waters of Loch Roag contained abundant cod and ling in the early eighteenth century AD (Macdonald 1978, 95) and may have done so at much earlier dates.

Although I do not wish here to enter into discussion about the precise siting of the main setting, it may have been put here because it allows the viewing of a dramatic interaction between the landscape and movements of the moon, particularly at 18.61 year intervals when the moon's apparent movements are at their most southerly.

That human activity had its own unique trajectory in time in the area around Calanais is incontrovertible. Over the whole period of its existence local and medium-length connections may have predominated for long periods. The patterns explored here have been based largely on analogies with highly visible sites in Ireland and in the agriculturally more marginal areas of Scotland. There are many lowland clusters of ritual and burial sites including earth and timber monuments, and of lowland sites more generally only Avebury, Balfarg Riding School and Broomend of Crichie have been mentioned even in summary detail here, introducing an acknowledged incompleteness in my argument (cf. Barclay in press). The earth and timber sites in particular may prove to be so well connected to one another at a variety of distances as to show that the Small Worlds model is not generally applicable even in the early and the later third millennium BC. However the analogies between aspects of the structures and pottery assemblage at Calanais and other distant ritual and ceremonial centres around 3000 BC, and again in the later third millennium BC, seem to fit a Small World model and may, together with a locally favourable environment, provide the best general explanation for the initiation of the cluster of stone rings and other stone settings at Calanais.

The significance of this is that there must have been compelling reasons to establish and maintain fairly frequent long-distance contacts around 3000 BC. They must have had a value which balanced cost of travel over long distances. The readiest analogy is with trade or with religious or cult practices. There are no obvious signs of widespread trade, unless it is trade in the pots which provide some of the evidence for links. The likelihood seems to be, then, that around 3000 BC and perhaps again towards the end of the third millennium new ideas took hold somewhere in Britain or Ireland which were sufficiently attractive to their adherents to outweigh the costs associated with maintaining connections with people in other places.

BIBLIOGRAPHY

Armit, I., 2003 The Drowners: permanence and transience in the Hebridean Neolithic. In Armit, I., Murphy, E., Nelis E. & Simpson, D.D.A. (eds), *Neolithic Settlement in Ireland and Western Britain*, 93-111. Oxford: Oxbow.

Ashmore, P.J., 1984 Callanish. In Breeze, D.J. (ed.) *Studies in Scottish Antiquity*, 1-31. Edinburgh: John Donald.

Ashmore, P.J., 1995 *Calanais: The Standing Stones*. Stornoway: Urras and Tursachan.

Ashmore, P.J., 1999 Dating the ring of stones and chambered cairn at Calanais. *Antiquity*, 73, 128-30.

Ashmore, P.J., forthcoming The Moon and the Stones: excavations at Calanais 1980-82. *Scottish Archaeological Internet Reports*.

Barclay, G.J., in press. 'Four Nations Prehistory': cores and archetypes in the writing of prehistory. In Philips, R. & Brocklehurst, H. (eds), *History, Nationhood and the Question of Britain*.

Barclay, G.J. & Brophy, K., 2002 Carsie Mains, Perth and Kinross (Blairgowrie parish), rectilinear timber structure; timber ring. *Discovery and Excavation in Scotland*, 3, 91.

Barclay, G.J. & Russell-White, C.J., 1993 Excavations in the ceremonial complex of the fourth to second millennium BC at Balfarg/Balbirnie. *Proceedings of the Society of Antiquaries of Scotland*, 123, 43-210.

Bohncke, S.J.P., 1988 Vegetation and habitation history of the Callanish area, Isle of Lewis, Scotland. In Birks, H.H., Birks, H.J., Kaland, P.E. & Moe, D. (eds), *The Cultural Landscape – Past Present and Future*, 445-61. Cambridge: Cambridge University Press.

Brindley, A.L., 1999 Irish Grooved Ware. In Cleal, R. & MacSween, A. (eds), *Grooved Ware in Britain and Ireland*, 23-35. Neolithic Studies Group Seminar Papers 3. Oxford: Oxbow.

Buchanan, M., 2002 *Small World: Uncovering Nature's Hidden Networks*. London: Weidenfeld & Nicolson.

Burl, A., 1993 *From Carnac to Callanish: the Prehistoric Stone Rows and Avenues of Britain, Ireland and Brittany*. New Haven & London: Yale University Press.

Burl, A., 2000 *The Stone Circles of Britain, Ireland and Brittany*. New Haven & London: Yale University Press.

Clarke, D.L., 1970 *Beaker Pottery of Great Britain and Ireland*. Cambridge: Cambridge University Press.

Curtis, M.R. & G.R., 2003. Cnoc Gearraidh Nighean Choinnich, Breasclete. *Discovery and Excavation in Scotland*, 4, 138.

Davidson, J.L. & Henshall, A.S., 1989 *The Chambered Cairns of Orkney*. Edinburgh: Edinburgh University Press.

Davidson, J.L. & Henshall, A.S., 1991 *The Chambered Cairns of Caithness*. Edinburgh: Edinburgh University Press.

Edwards, K.J. & Whittington, G., 1997 A 12,000-year record of environmental change in the Lomond Hills, Fife, Scotland: vegetational and climatic variability. *Vegetation History & Archaeobotany*, 6, 133-52.

Ellice, H., 1860 [In] Donations: some pieces of charcoal dug up in a Stone Circle near Callernish in the Lewis. *Proceedings of the Society of Antiquaries of Scotland*, 3 (1857-60), 202.

Gibson, A., 1998 *Stonehenge and Timber Circles*. Stroud: Tempus.

Gilbertson, D.D., Kent, M. & Grattan, J., 1996 *The Outer Hebrides: The Last 14,000 Years*. Sheffield: Sheffield University Press.

Gilbertson, D.D., Schwenninger, J-L., Kemp, R.A. & Rhodes, E.J., 1999 Sand-drift and soil formation along an exposed North Atlantic coastline: 14,000 years of diverse geomorphological, climatic and human impacts. *Journal of Archaeological Science*, 26, 439-69.

Gregory, R., forthcoming. Northton, Harris. *Discovery and Excavation in Scotland*, 5.

Haggarty, A., 1991 Machrie Moor, Arran: recent excavations at two stone circles. *Proceedings of the Society of Antiquaries of Scotland*, 121, 51-94.

Henley, C., in press Falling off the edge of the Irish Sea: Clettraval and the two-faced Neolithic of the Outer Hebrides. In Cummings, V. & Fowler, C. (eds), *The Neolithic of the Irish Sea: Materiality and Traditions of Practice*. Oxford: Oxbow.

Henshall, A.S., 1963 and 1972 *The Chambered Tombs of Scotland*. (2 vols). Edinburgh: Edinburgh University Press.

Henshall, A.S. & Johnson, M., forthcoming. The pottery. In Ashmore, forthcoming.

Henshall, A.S. & Ritchie, J.N.G., 1995 *The Chambered Cairns of Sutherland*. Edinburgh: Edinburgh University Press.

Johnston, M., Flitcroft, C. & Verrill, L., forthcoming. *Calanais Fields Project: Excavation of a Prehistoric Sub-peat Field System at Calanais, Isle of Lewis, 1999-2000*.

McCullagh, R.P.J., 1989 Excavation at Newton, Islay. *Glasgow Archaeological Journal*, 15 (1988-9), 23-52.

Macdonald, D., 1978 *Lewis: A History of the Island*. Edinburgh: Gordon Wright.

Megaw, J.V.S. & Simpson, D.D.A., 1979 *Introduction to British Prehistory*. Leicester: Leicester University Press.

Mercer, R.J., 1981 The excavation of a Late Neolithic henge-type enclosure at Balfarg, Markinch, Fife, Scotland. *Proceedings of the Society of Antiquaries of Scotland*, 111, 63-171.

Müller, J., 1988 *The Chambered Cairns of the Northern and Western Isles: Architectural Structure, Information Transfer and Locational Processes*. Edinburgh: University of Edinburgh Department of Archaeology, Occasional Paper 16.

Piggott, S., 1954 *Neolithic Cultures of the British Isles*. Cambridge: Cambridge University Press.

Ponting, G. & M.R., 1979 *Callanish: the Documentary Record*. Callanish: privately published.

Ponting, G. & M.R., 1981 *Callanish: the Documentary Record: Part II: The Minor Sites*. Callanish: privately published.

Ponting, G. & M.R., 1984 *New Light on the Stones of Callanish*. Callanish: privately published.

Richards, J., 1990 *The Stonehenge Environs Project*. London: English Heritage.

Ritchie, J.N.G., 1976 The Stones of Stenness, Orkney. *Proceedings of the Society of Antiquaries of Scotland*, 107 (1975-6), 1-60.

Ritchie, J.N.G., 2000 Stones of Stenness. In Ashmore, P.J., A list of archaeological radiocarbon dates, *Discovery & Excavation in Scotland*, 1, 125.

Ritchie, J.N.G., 2001 Stones of Stenness. In Ashmore, P.J. A list of archaeological radiocarbon dates, *Discovery & Excavation in Scotland*, 2, 125.

Scott, L., 1948 The chamber tomb of Unival, North Uist. *Proceedings of the Society of Antiquaries of Scotland*, 82 (1947-8), 1-39.

Sheridan, J.A., 1992 Scottish stone axe heads: some new work and recent discoveries. In Sharples, N.M. & Sheridan, J.A. (eds), *Vessels for the Ancestors: Essays on the Neolithic of Britain and Ireland in Honour of Audrey Henshall*, 194-212. Edinburgh: Edinburgh University Press.

Sheridan, J.A., 2002 Pottery and other ceramic finds. In Barclay, G.J., Brophy, K. & MacGregor, G. Claish, Stirling: an Early Neolithic structure in its context. *Proceedings of the Society of Antiquaries of Scotland*, 132, 79-88.

Sheridan, J.A. & Saville, A., 1993 Organic artefacts from the National Museums of Scotland collections. In Hedges, R.E.M., Housley, R.A., Bronk Ramsey, C. & van Klinken, G.J. radiocarbon dates from the Oxford AMS system: *Archaeometry* datelist 16. *Archaeometry* 35(1), 155-7.

Simpson, D.D.A. *et al.*, forthcoming. *Excavations at Northton, Harris*. Oxford: British Archaeological Reports.

Speak, S. & Burgess, C.B., 1999 Meldon Bridge: a centre of the third millennium BC in Peeblesshire. *Proceedings of the Society of Antiquaries of Scotland*, 129, 1-118.

Stuart, J., 1860 Note of Incised Marks on one of a Circle of Standing Stones in the Island of Lewis. *Proceedings of the Society of Antiquaries of Scotland*, 3 (1857-60), 212-4.

Tait, D., 1978 *Callanish: A Map of the Standing Stones and Circles at Callanish, Isle of Lewis, with a Detailed Plan of Each Site*. Glasgow: Glasgow University Department of Geography.

Watts, D.J., 1999 *Small Worlds: the Dynamics of Networks between Order and Randomness*. Princeton: Princeton University Press.

5

SCOTTISH PASSAGE-GRAVES: SOME CONFUSIONS AND CONCLUSIONS

AUDREY S. HENSHALL

INTRODUCTION

There are about 270 identified passage-graves in the north mainland of Scotland, the Western Isles and Orkney, and possibly 350 if the little-studied Shetland cairns are included (for present purposes the relatively few passage-graves of Maes Howe type and Clava type have been left aside). Two aspects of the monuments are considered briefly in what follows: their architecture and their funerary use.

ARCHITECTURE

The surviving cairns have been recorded in a reasonably thorough and consistent way[1] and drawing on this material it is now possible to present a balanced account of their design and development. It has to be acknowledged, though, that there has been only partial though informative investigation of the cairn structure at a small number of excavations apart from that of Point of Cott, Westray, Orkney (Barber 1997), which was studied during total demolition. Surface examination of sites generally reveals little except parts of the chambers.

Definition of the basic design and building techniques employed throughout the province has been hampered by two factors. Since the 1930s attention has been focused on the largest and best preserved (and also the most extreme) passage-graves in Orkney, and everywhere primary passage-graves have frequently been hidden within subsequent enlargements. Study of the smaller cairns reveals that the standard passage-grave throughout northern Scotland consisted of a chamber and narrow cairn core built together as a single hollow structure capable of standing unsupported, and this was covered

27 *Opposite* Single-period passage-graves with well-defined round cairns. Key: 1 Diagrammatic reconstruction based on Lower Lechanich, Ross and Cromarty; a cairn core, b cairn casing, c blocking or displaced cairn material. 2 Strathseasgaich, W. Sutherland. 3 Kinloch, N. Sutherland. 4 Kierfea Hill, Orkney. 5 Warehouse Hill, Caithness. 6 Loch Glen na Feannag, North Uist

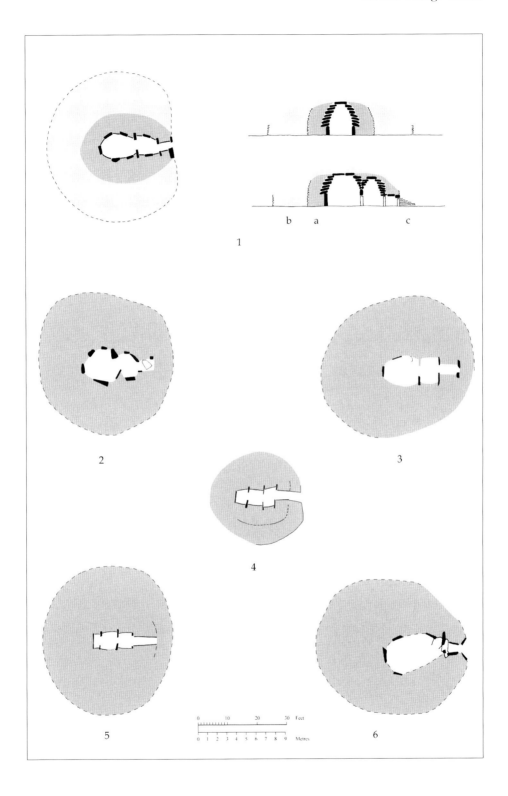

b   a   c

1

2

3

4

5

6

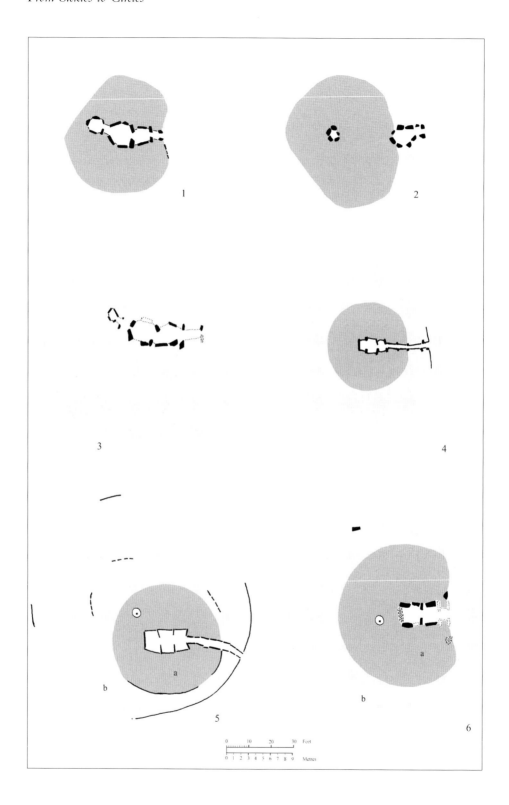

and protected by a casing which formed the outer part of the cairn.[2] The cairn was normally round with the chamber central within it *(27.1)*. Three points need to be stressed: the chambers were generally high (2.5-3.5m), the passages were always very short (1-2m, seldom 3m long), and the cairns were small, indeed sometimes minimal (with diameters of 9-18m when built), even when enclosing large chambers. Cairns with such features can be cited from all parts of the province *(27.2-6)*.

Ground plans dominate our thinking, and too little attention has been paid to the vertical design. To build a structure to these proportions it is necessary to postulate an outer wall-face at least 1.5-2m high, giving the cairns a somewhat drum-shaped profile. The rectangular cairns found in Orkney are adaptations of this minimal cairn design applied to exceptionally long chambers. At round cairns, in order to align the cairn wall-face with the entrance it may have been not uncommon to flatten the ground plan slightly at the front, as revealed by excavation at Kilcoy South in the Central Highlands *(28.1)* and Knowe of Craie in Orkney, or revealed in secondary enlargements (presumably echoing the first phase plan) at The Ord North in Sutherland and Camster Round in Caithness *(28.4)*. Truly round plans apparent on surface examination may be due to external blocking or fallen cairn material, or may have been an assumption until careful planning. It follows that the (seemingly rare) heel-shaped plan peculiar to the north of Scotland may have a genetic origin. The realisation that throughout northern Scotland the ubiquitous design was small-diameter cairns enclosing centrally placed chambers-and-cores enables the essential unity, and the development, of the initial phase of passage-grave building to be better understood.

The variable was the design of the chambers, largely in response to the building material and the desire for greater space: it is difficult not to suppose that in general there was development from small and simple to large and impressive in all parts of the province. In Caithness and Orkney a northern style developed using orthostats for portals, divisions and back-slabs, with fine walling along the sides over sailing towards the roof, and favouring a rectangular plan. Elsewhere a southern style developed using orthostats throughout with limited walling linking them and heavy corbelling above, and favouring a more rounded plan *(29)*. For all the seeming crudity of the latter, the floor area and cubic capacity of the very largest southern style chambers, such as Skelpick Long, Sutherland, were only exceeded by the seven largest stalled chambers in Orkney and perhaps one in Caithness. Occasionally a pre-

28 *Opposite* Multi-period and possibly multi-period cairns. Primary cairns are shown by dark tone. 5-6: the probable structural sequence is indicated; a primary cairn, b enlargement with a white dot at the centre of the enlarged cairn. Key: 1 Kilcoy South, Ross and Cromarty (the possible first phase is not indicated). 2 Achnacreebeag, Argyll. 3 King's Head Cairn, Ross and Cromarty. 4 Camster Round, Caithness. 5 Tulloch of Assery B, Caithness. 6 Balnaguie, Ross and Cromarty

passage-grave phase is apparent, such as the tiny closed chamber at Achnacreebeag, Argyll, or the tiny accessible cist-like or round structures attached to and pre-dating chambers elsewhere *(28.1-3)* (J.N.G. Ritchie 1970; Henshall & Ritchie 2001, 48-50; A. Ritchie, this volume).

It has long been recognised that the Scottish passage-graves may be multi-period structures (rather than multi-phased when additional building was part of the original design). The proposition that the passage-graves were built with minimal cairns itself implies that large round cairns are the result of enlargement. On surface examination the telling indications, besides size, are passage entrances well inside the cairn edge and chambers not central in a round cairn *(28.5-6)*. The most persuasive evidence of a multi-period history comes from the partial excavations of The Ord North, Sutherland, Camster Round and Tulloch of Assery B, Caithness *(28.4-5)*, and Isbister, South Ronaldsay, Orkney (Henshall & Ritchie 2001, 101-2). About 11% of passage-graves are covered by long cairns, some with deep horned forecourts. Two long cairns, Tulach an t'Sionnaich and Camster Long, both in Caithness, have

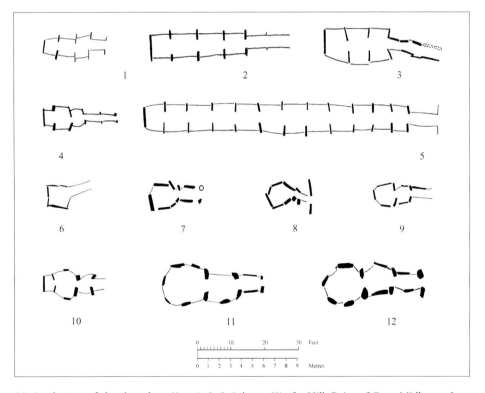

29 A selection of chamber plans. Key: 1, 2, 5 Orkney: Kierfea Hill, Point of Cott, Midhowe. 3, 4, 6 Caithness: Tulloch of Assery B, Camster Round, Tulach an t'Sionnaich. 7 West Inverness-shire: Balvraid. 8 Western Isles: Unival. 9-12 Sutherland: Torboll, Kinbrace Burn, Skelpick Long, The Ord North

been shown by excavation to be complex multi-period structures (Corcoran 1966, 5-22; Masters 1997) *(30.1-2)*. From surface examination it is clear that others comprise an inscrutable and individual series of additions, presumably to a primary passage-grave; in itself a chamber not aligned on the axis almost certainly indicates that the long cairn is a later addition (Henshall & Ritchie 1995, 43-7; 2001, 62-5, 105-6) *(30.2-3)*. A minority of cairns have heel-shaped, short horned or square cairns *(30.1 in second phase, 30.5-7)*, rare forms peculiar to northern Scotland, almost unknown in Orkney, though the dominant forms in Shetland. As mentioned above, the first is likely to be a local development, and the others to be further developments presumably influenced by the appearance of long cairns. Heel-shaped and square cairns have been shown to be secondary to small passage-graves at Tulach an t'Sionnaich, and at Balvraid in west Inverness-shire *(30.1 & 30.7)* (Corcoran 1966, 5-12; Corcoran in Henshall & Ritchie 2001, 62, 68-9, 104, 230-2). However, the excavations of the long cairn at Point of Cott, Orkney, and of the short horned cairn Tulloch of Assery A, Caithness, have shown these to be single-period monuments *(30.4 & 30.6)*, the implication of which is considered below. It can be estimated that roughly 40% of the mainland passage-graves have been encased in later building, and it follows that the size and shape of the covering cairns give no indication of the chronological relationships of the passage-graves within them.

It seems evident that additions to passage-graves, particularly when a concave façade was built, were intended to emphasise the importance of the monument and to provide a setting for ceremonies outside the tomb. Some cairns were enlarged or enhanced whilst the chambers were still in use, and the provision of forecourts in particular seems to reflect a shift away from a purely internal focus. Other cairns were similarly enhanced when access to the chamber was no longer required, implying that the cairns' usage was by then entirely external, the chamber perhaps having been replaced by another passage-grave. At a few long cairns it is clear that the building was cumulative and included differing elements resulting in monuments of astonishing size and complexity; one of the most impressive is Essich Moor in north-east Inverness-shire, 126m long, where four components can be detected. The perceptions and purposes that lie behind the long cairn phenomenon remain an enigma.

It is not surprising that there is no correlation between chamber designs and observed cairn forms. Corcoran's seminal work at Tulach an t'Sionnaich is significant in showing that a stylistically early chamber was primary to two or three additions, the last a long cairn. Barber's work at Point of Cott is equally significant in demonstrating that a chamber which is likely to be relatively late was built as a unitary structure with its horned long cairn (Barber 1997). Corcoran's excavation of the short horned cairn, Tulloch of Assery A, showed that this also was a unitary structure (Corcoran 1966, 22-34).

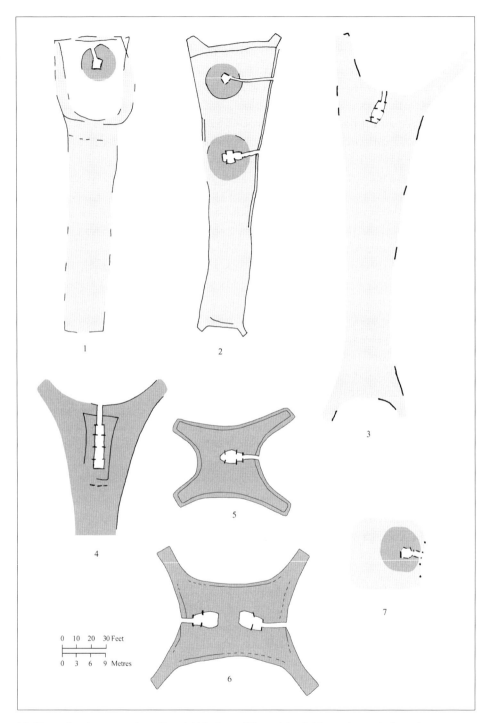

30 Horned and square cairns. Key: 1 Tulach an t'Sionnaich, Caithness (second phase shown white).2 Camster Long, Caithness. 3 South Yarrows South, Caithness. 4 Point of Cott, Orkney (the east side and north end lost to erosion, the original length unknown). 5 Garrywhin, Caithness. 6 Tulloch of Assery A, Caithness. 7 Balvraid, Inverness-shire

Throughout the province the earliest chambers are likely to have been built near the beginning of the earlier Neolithic, soon after 4000 BC. Building skills would have to be developed and maintained, at a time of short life expectancy, implying continuous activity and thus that most of the passage-graves were built during a fairly short period; a span of not more than three centuries seems a reasonable conjecture. The integration of chambers (with varied plans) and horned cairns (perhaps a rare occurrence) brings all the cairn forms within this time frame, a conclusion compatible with the radiocarbon dates from the long cairn at Camster (Masters 1997, 133, 177). It seems likely that most of the passage-graves and their enlargements had been built before the middle of the fourth millennium, the main building period being much shorter than is generally supposed. However, it is clear that some passage-grave building did continue into the second half of the millennium, in Orkney where it contributed to the designs of Maes Howe-type tombs, in Shetland, and at Calanais in the Western Isles (Ashmore 1996, 73). In these cases the chambers are exceptional, either excessively long, or with multiple cells, or extremely small, and at none have the cairns received enlargements perhaps suggesting that the long cairn/horned cairn phase had passed. The length of time individual chambers continued in use for burials in the original tradition is another question. Sealing by additional building in the Neolithic tradition indicates early closure (for instance, the early chamber at Tulach an t'Sionnaich clearly had a short life), but dates from four mainland cairns show that burials continued into the second half of the fourth millennium, and at Point of Cott to the mid-third millennium (summarised in Henshall & Ritchie 2001, 124-5).

FUNERARY USE

It is hard to avoid the assumption that the main purpose of passage-graves was to receive burials, whatever social and mystical imperatives are implied by these powerful structures and the monumental embellishments of some. Excavation of chambers has been concentrated in Orkney but, apart from two modern excavations at Point of Cott and Holm of Papa Westray, it has been variable in quality and in the amount of material recovered. The burial rite seems quite clear and has often been stated; intact cadavers were brought to the chambers, laid crouched, sometimes on benches, and subsequently the bones were gathered and sorted and stored with particular care for the skulls. These processes have been seen most clearly at Midhowe, Orkney (Callander & Grant 1934) *(31)*, and less clearly at four other Orcadian chambers; sorting and storing have been observed in three chambers. Sparse information from the rest of the province gives glimpses of similar procedures. In Caithness two chambers contained crouched burials, and at three there were heaped bones. Stone benches are quite common in Orcadian chambers, and among the few well-reported investigations elsewhere benches are known at one each in Caithness and Sutherland, and in the Western Isles a crouched skeleton lay on a collapsed bench.[3] Evidence of a wooden bench was found at Point of Cott, and may well have been missed elsewhere. At this site the excavator had reason tentatively to suggest that there may have been wooden or stone shelving along the walls for bone storage at a higher level (Barber 1988, 59), an intriguing speculation.

The exceptionally large quantity of bone recovered from the chamber at Isbister (under less than ideal conditions) included no articulated skeletons though much of this bone and whole skulls had been stored or gathered into heaps, and the rest lay in confusion. Detailed study of this material led to the conclusion that the burial rite involved excarnation; that already de-fleshed bones which represented only randomly selected parts of skeletons were brought into the chamber (Hedges 1983, 124-8; 1984, 133-43). A similar conclusion had already been drawn from the bone deposits from the Maes Howe-type chamber at Quanterness (where the circumstances of the actual burial deposits were rather different, Renfrew 1979, 106-7, 166-8). A general perception has followed that excarnation was the normal burial rite in the passage-graves. However, Barber has given cogent reasons for rejecting this interpretation (1997, 68), supported by the results of his investigations at Point of Cott. A few excavations in Orkney and Caithness in the mid-nineteenth century produced large amounts of bone, but there are no details and the material is lost. More generally, throughout the province, the chambers have contained only small amounts of scattered fragmentary bone, or no bone at all. The contrast between the organised inhumation rites and the confused conditions observed in many chambers can be explained to a large extent by two natural phenomena: bone decay and animal activity.

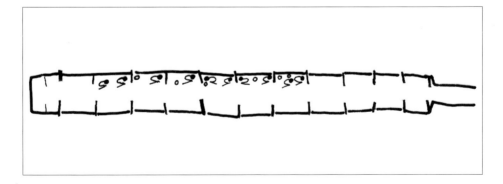

31 Burials in the chamber at Midhowe. Shown are the crouched skeletons and heaped bones on the benches; not shown are two deposits of bone below the benches, one deposit on the floor on the opposite side of the chamber, and two skulls on the floor of the innermost compartment. Total: 17 adults, six adolescents, two children

The effects of both these phenomena become more realistic when the factors that are likely to have affected the chamber deposits, at whatever stage, early or late or intermittently, during the five millennia of the chambers' existence are considered. Most obviously, working in the dark, preparing for new burials and handling bones for storage, would cause skeletal confusion and breakages. The chambers were carefully designed to be dry, and any disturbance of the structure would allow water penetration, perhaps only local dripping, perhaps increasing to extensive dampness. This, together with possible acid soil conditions, would induce variable and changing circumstances for decay, or, conversely, there might be chance local protection; in either case the effect would be random. At Point of Cott there were the partial remains of at least 13 bodies spanning about a thousand years. The earthy layer covering most of the chamber floor had a very high phosphate content only explicable as deriving from a mass of bone, but the quantity, and the proportion coming from animal bone (whether deliberately introduced or intrusive) are, of course, unknown. Study of the bones, most of which were in good condition, suggested that once decay had started it was likely to progress rapidly, though, surprisingly, delicate bones could survive unaffected (see Barber's uniquely detailed examination of the deposits in this chamber and his conclusions in Barber 1988, 60-2; 1997, 23-4, 68-9). Bone loss through decay has long been acknowledged but has mainly been ignored. There can be little doubt that it has been hugely underestimated, and perhaps the several hundred individuals represented at Isbister were not exceptional.

At some stage the chamber structure may have been disturbed sufficiently to allow larger mammals and birds to use the interior as dens or roosts, whether as a cave-like void or by penetrating the chamber filling. The presence of predators, such as otters, foxes, dogs and large birds, is attested at a number of sites by remains of their bodies and parts of other animals that can be interpreted as their prey and their droppings. In many chambers the extent of this activity is hidden by the decay of the organic evidence, but at Point of Cott it was deemed to be very considerable over a very long period (Barber 1988, 60-1; 1997, 24, 69). As far as the burials were concerned, animal activity is likely to have caused disturbance of skeletons as they lay in a void, and, by burrowing, disturbance of bones incorporated in the lowest layers of the chamber filling. At Point of Cott the lowest dark earthy layer (with high phosphate content) contained fragmented and chaotically dispersed human and animal bones, some of which penetrated the whole depth. The excavator concluded that the dark soil matrix was a natural formation and that the whole layer had been totally reworked by animals living in the cairn.

A distinct compact dark floor layer has been reported reliably from only one other Orcadian chamber, Unstan, but it was a recurrent feature of eight chambers in Caithness clustered in the south-east of the county, all excavated in the mid-nineteenth century. The human and animal bone they contained varied greatly in quantity, and was in total confusion, generally in small fragments (and, alone among Scottish passage-graves, included scorched and burnt bone, Davidson & Henshall 1991, 60-2). The writer found a dark earth layer with a little poorly preserved bone at Embo, Sutherland. At the time the layer was thought to have been deliberately laid, but in retrospect it seems likely that the matrix was a natural formation which extended into the base of the surrounding cairn (soil analysis by A.H. Johnson in Henshall & Wallace 1963, 26-9 showed the similarity of dark earth from inside and outside the chamber). Yet it is puzzling that the dark layers formed sufficiently rapidly, and then ceased, for burials to continue above them at Embo, in seven of the Caithness chambers, and at Unstan including several crouched bodies. Investigation of the nature of the floor deposits, whether there is a distinct matrix or not, is obviously a priority in the future now that Barber has brought the implications of animal activity to the fore.

Animal remains found with burials have generally been interpreted as part of funeral ritual, as either food offerings or residual of feasting. At Holm of Papa Westray North some animal remains were deliberately deposited (see A. Ritchie, this volume), but it was argued that most of the animal remains at Point of Cott, including the bones of food animals, could have been introduced by predators. Thus the status and significance of animal remains, particularly of young domesticates, is generally uncertain, and distinguishing the two categories will be a continuing difficulty. The presence of artefacts, principally sherds found either in heaps or scattered, in varying quantity and generally very fragmentary, indicates other ritual activity. Their condition in the chambers, where they were presumably brought as containers, appears similar to that of the human remains, and the possibility that the sherds too have been subject to extensive erosion as well as disturbance should be considered.

CONCLUSION

Thus it is necessary to be aware of the limitations and deceptiveness of our data. No conclusions are possible based on the recorded numbers of individuals identified in each chamber, and any supposed patterning of the disarticulated human remains is probably an illusion. It follows that many conclusions based on this deeply unsatisfactory material should be abandoned, or at very least re-examined. The human remains cannot be used for any demographic studies; there is no evidence for or against occasional clearing out of chambers, nor the addition or removal of specific bones for cult purposes. Animal disturbance on the scale envisaged at Point of Cott may confuse stratigraphy, and possibly could also confuse dating if misplaced or animal-introduced bone were used for radiocarbon assay, as pointed out by Barber (1997, 60). The plausible suggestion that some of the floor deposits were deliberately laid midden material (thus accounting for miscellaneous and jumbled inclusions of animal bone and artefacts) can now be countered by other and perhaps more likely explanations.

As far as the evidence of actual burial procedures goes, based on observation of the last burials which have been least disturbed, it seems a reasonable inference that the placement of crouched bodies and subsequent treatment of the larger bones of the skeletons was consistent throughout the province. Later activities in the chambers seem to have varied. After the passages were closed for the last time some chambers were left empty (as at The Ord North, Sutherland, Boath Short and Allt Eileag, Ross and Cromarty), but others received a deliberate filling layer (as at Holm of Papa Westray North). The complexities that chamber fillings, whether ritual, collapsed masonry, rubbish, or a mixture, present to excavators and readers of old reports lie outside this essay.

With hindsight, interpretations of the results from past excavations have been both surprisingly naive and over-elaborate. Unfortunately the perceived data have sometimes been applied to wider studies of contemporary communities, their economic basis, other ritual activities and cosmographic beliefs, occasionally ending in truly fanciful speculation. Over 30 years ago Stuart Piggott considered these problems, taking a very wide view of chambered tomb studies (1973). He drew attention to the differing functions of the tombs in space and time, the dangers of extrapolating data from them, and the unknowable affects of religious beliefs. It is now time to review the data from the north Scottish chambers, to identify and discard the mis-understood and to re-examine the uncertain (and the writer acknowledges that many of her assumptions and conclusions in the past have to be revised). The immediate result seems negative and sombre. As has been indicated, progress can only come from modern excavations of the highest quality such as those at Point of Cott and Holm of Papa Westray North.

On the other hand, the overview of the structural remains in the whole province, which has allowed recognition of the status of simple passage-graves, is more positive. Small passage-graves in round cairns are found intermittently but widespread through the western seaboard of Europe, and the Scottish passage-graves are presumably part of this wider picture. The phenomenon of long cairns enclosing passage-graves, or other types of chamber tombs, is not unique to northern Scotland of course, but occurs elsewhere in western Britain and western France. The recent excavations of the multi-period long mound with passage-graves at Prissé-la-Charrière, east of La Rochelle, provide insight for consideration of the north Scottish monuments (Scarre *et al.* 2003). The development and later structural history of the Scottish cairns can be viewed from a slightly different perspective if the conclusions offered here are accepted.

Acknowledgements

This paper has benefited from the assistance of Graham Ritchie in word processing and of K.H.J. Macleod in creating the digitised illustrations figures 27-30. Figure 31 is by ASH after Callander & Grant 1934. Anna Ritchie also kindly read the text.

Footnotes

[1] The cairns are listed, described with plans and with references in Davidson & Henshall 1989 (Orkney); Davidson & Henshall 1991 (Caithness); Henshall & Ritchie 1995 (Sutherland); Henshall & Ritchie 2001 (Ross and Cromarty, Inverness-shire); Henshall 1963, 156-82 (Shetland); Henshall 1972, 355-60 (Argyll); 429-30, 460-5, 481-91, 495-534 (Western Isles); 587-92 (Shetland). References to fuller or more recent accounts of cairns and excavations are given in the text. For consistency, the pre-1974 county names are retained in this paper.

[2] As described in Henshall & Ritchie 2001, 36-8, 56-8, 98-101. For Barber's detailed investigation of the techniques for building a chamber and core where sandstone slabs were available see Barber 1992: 1997, 9-13, 60-3. Elsewhere less tractable stone, mainly heavy less regular slabs and boulders, had to be used.

[3] Orcadian burials are discussed in A. Ritchie 1995, 50-5. Besides Midhowe, crouched skeletons were found at Holm of Papa Westray North, Korkquoy, Taversoe Tuick and Unstan in Orkney, M'Cole's Castle and Lower Dounreay in Caithness, and Unival in North Uist. Bones appear to have been gathered and stored at Holm of Papa Westray North, Isbister and Knowe of Yarso in Orkney, Lower Dounreay, Tulloch of Assery A and B in Caithness. Outside Orkney, benches have been found at Tulloch of Assery A in Caithness, The Ord North in Sutherland (the 'slab structure'), and Unival in North Uist (interpreted as a cist by the excavator, Scott 1948).

Bibliography

Ashmore, P.J., 1996 *Neolithic and Bronze Age Scotland*. London: Batsford/Historic Scotland.

Barber J., 1988 Isbister, Quanterness and the Point of Cott: the formulation and testing of some middle range theories. In Barrett, J.C. & Kinnes, I.A. (eds), *The Archaeology of Context in the Neolithic and Bronze Age: Recent Trends*. 57-62. Sheffield: Department of Archaeology and Prehistory, University of Sheffield.

Barber, J., 1992 Megalithic architecture. In Sharples, N. & Sheridan, J.A. (eds), *Vessels for the Ancestors*, 13-31. Edinburgh: Edinburgh University Press.

Barber, J., 1997 *The Excavation of a Stalled Cairn at the Point of Cott, Westray, Orkney*. Monograph No. 1. Edinburgh: Scottish Trust for Archaeological Research.

Callander, J.G. & Grant, W.G., 1934 A long stalled chambered cairn or mausoleum (Rousay type) near Midhowe, Rousay, Orkney. *Proceedings of the Society of Antiquaries of Scotland* 68 (1933-4), 320-50.

Corcoran, J.X.W.P., 1966 Excavation of three chambered cairns at Loch Calder, Caithness. *Proceedings of the Society of Antiquaries of Scotland*, 98 (1964-6), 1-75.

Davidson, J.L. & Henshall, A.S., 1989 *The Chambered Cairns of Orkney*. Edinburgh: Edinburgh University Press.

Davidson, J.L. & Henshall, A.S., 1991 *The Chambered Cairns of Caithness*. Edinburgh: Edinburgh University Press.

Hedges, J.W. 1983 *Isbister: A Chambered Tomb in Orkney*. BAR British Series 115. Oxford: British Archaeological Reports.

Hedges, J.W., 1984 *Tomb of the Eagles: A Window on Stone Age Tribal Britain*. London: John Murray.

Henshall, A.S., 1963 & 1972 (2 vols). *The Chambered Tombs of Scotland*. Edinburgh: Edinburgh University Press.

Henshall, A.S. & Ritchie, J.N.G., 1995 *The Chambered Cairns of Sutherland*. Edinburgh: Edinburgh University Press.

Henshall, A.S. & Ritchie, J.N.G., 2001 *The Chambered Cairns of the Central Highlands*. Edinburgh: Edinburgh University Press.

Henshall, A.S. & Wallace, J.C., 1963 The excavation of a chambered cairn at Embo, Sutherland. *Proceedings of the Society of Antiquaries of Scotland*, 96 (1962-3), 9-36.

Masters, L.J., 1997 The excavation and restoration of the Camster Long chambered cairn, Caithness, 1967-80. *Proceedings of the Society of Antiquaries of Scotland* 127, 123-83.

Piggott, S., 1973 Problems in the interpretation of chambered tombs. In Daniel, G. & Kjaerum, P. (eds), *Megalithic Graves and Ritual*, 9-15. Papers presented at the III colloquium, Mosegård 1969. København: Jutland Archaeological Society.

Renfrew, C., 1979 *Investigations in Orkney*. Report of the Research Committee No. 38. London: The Society of Antiquaries of London.

Ritchie, A., 1995 *Prehistoric Orkney*. London: Batsford/Historic Scotland.

Ritchie, J.N.G., 1970 Excavation of the chambered cairn at Achnacreebeag. *Proceedings of the Society of Antiquaries of Scotland*, 102, (1969-70), 31-55.

Scarre, C., Laporte, L. & Joussaume, R., 2003 Long mounds and megalithic origins in western France: recent excavations at Prissé-la-Charrière. *Proceedings of the Prehistoric Society*, 69, 235-51.

Scott, W.L., 1948 The chambered tomb of Unival, North Uist. *Proceedings of the Society of Antiquaries of Scotland*, 82 (1947-8), 1-49.

6

The Use of Human and Faunal Material in Chambered Cairns in Orkney

Anna Ritchie

Introduction

Excavation of a small chambered tomb on the Holm of Papa Westray in Orkney in 1984-5 revealed new information about the use of human and faunal material (Davidson & Henshall 1989, ORK 21; Ritchie 1995, 41-4), and the purpose of this paper is to set that information, and its interpretation, within the context of other Scottish chambered cairns. The fact that one can do so readily is attributable to Audrey Henshall and her co-workers on the several volumes of her original and revised corpus *The Chambered Cairns of Scotland* (Henshall 1963; 1972; Davidson & Henshall 1989; 1991; Henshall & Ritchie 1995; 2001). Most comparable evidence comes from Orcadian sites, simply because many tombs in the islands are well preserved and soil conditions are conducive to the survival of bone.

Holm of Papa Westray is a small island off the east coast of Papa Westray, one of the most northerly islands of the Orkney group. Changes in sea level over the last five millennia suggest that in Neolithic times the Holm was a promontory on the coast of Papa Westray rather than a separate island (and indeed that Papa Westray was joined to the larger island of Westray to the west). At least two, possibly three, chambered cairns were built on the Holm, including a very large Maes Howe type of tomb (Holm of Papa Westray South, Davidson & Henshall 1989, ORK 22) and a small and ruinous Orkney-Cromarty stalled tomb, Holm of Papa Westray North (ORK 21), the basis of this paper. Following the excavation of the Neolithic settlement at Knap of Howar on the west coast of Papa Westray (Ritchie 1983), Holm of Papa Westray North presented itself as the most likely candidate for the burial place of the family living at Knap of Howar. Aside from its location in relation to Knap of Howar, stalled cairns are associated with Unstan Ware, the type of pottery used at the settlement (Davidson & Henshall 1989, 64-78).

Holm of Papa Westray North

The chamber was partially excavated in three days in September 1854 by George Petrie, but the entrance passage and fourth compartment of the stalled cairn were left intact. Work in 1982-3 directed by the author completed the excavation of the chamber and entrance passage, and revealed the exterior of the cairn at both ends. The building sequence began with the construction of a small corbelled chamber within a round cairn, to which was added a stalled chamber in such a way that the original small chamber became the end-cell of the stalled chamber *(32)*. The stalled chamber was divided by pairs of upright slabs into four compartments, and entry, from the north-west, was by way of a short passage through a rectilinear cairn that incorporated the earlier round cairn. After a period of unknown duration but long enough to allow burials to have taken place in the main chamber, the end-cell was sealed off by horizontal walling and layers of infilling, inserted from within the main chamber. The cairn with its somewhat crescentic façade was later enlarged with a straight façade, and finally an outer skin of cairn was added to make a rectilinear cairn some 11.8m by 6.3m *(33)*. At some stage after the tomb had gone out of use, the roof was removed and the chamber and entrance passage were filled with earth and stones and organic material. The topmost layer of filling in the end-cell also belonged to this act of closure.

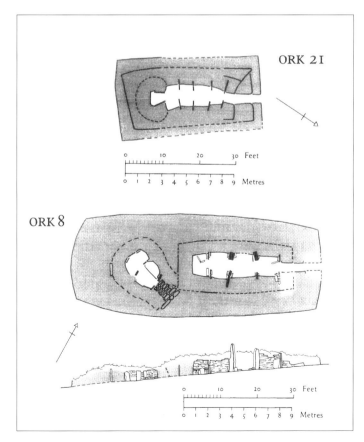

32 Plans of the cairns at Holm of Papa Westray North (ORK 21) and Calf of Eday Long (ORK 8). *After Davidson & Henshall 1989, 121, 108*

John Barber suggested that chambered cairns may have been built initially as temples and used only latterly as ossuaries (2000, 187). This model could fit the structural sequence at Holm of Papa Westray North, for the primary round cairn with its cell might be seen as a small shrine, to which an ossuary was added. The same scenario could explain the juxtaposition of the two chambers at Calf of Eday Long (ORK 8). Here the primary two-compartment chamber within its own small oval cairn may have remained in use after the construction of the adjacent stalled chamber within a rectangular cairn. The entrance into the smaller chamber or temple was subsequently blocked with horizontal walling (Calder 1937, fig. 3), and both cairns were enclosed within a larger rectangular cairn, through which access was provided to the stalled chamber but not to the smaller chamber *(32)*.

A range of human and faunal remains was recovered from the interior of the Holm tomb, from the forecourt and from outside the cairn. Some of this material was found in contexts that suggest deliberate deposition and others in contexts that indicate natural processes of deposition, and each category of material will be discussed separately before considering the broader implications.

FISH

Fish bones are a common component of floor deposits in chambered tombs, and their presence can usually be attributed to the activity of intrusive animals such as otters (Barber 1997, 51). In two instances, however, there are reasons to suggest that human intervention was involved. At Holm of Papa Westray North, a box-like setting of slabs had been constructed in the innermost compartment, after the end-cell had been sealed off, and within the box were 9kg of fish bones, tiny stones and crushed 'fishmeal' *(34)*. The bones all belonged to young fish and represent fishing in shallow waters from the shore, which applies as well to otters as to humans. Otters are known to have frequented chambered tombs, most notably from the evidence at Point of Cott (Barber 1997) but, although an otter might return to the same place over a long period of time, there were no discernable spraints and nothing other than fish bone and stone in the Holm deposit. Davidson and Henshall likened the Holm deposit to dense deposits of frog/small rodent bones in two Caithness tombs (1991, 65). The second example concerns a stalled cairn in the Orcadian island of Burray (ORK 7), which was explored by George Petrie in 1863. An original sketch of the tomb annotated by Petrie and published by Davidson and Henshall (1989, fig. 13) refers to a 'great quantity of bones of sillocks and cuiths with the skeletons literally cartloads of them'. In Orkney and Shetland dialect, sillock means a young saithe at a certain stage in its first year of life, and cuithe refers to the fish in its first to third year. The huge quantity of fish bones involved here seems too great to represent otter activity.

33 Holm of Papa Westray North: looking along the entrance passage, through the stalled chamber to the emptied end-cell. Holm of Papa Westray South is the submarine-shaped outline on the left-hand horizon

34 Holm of Papa Westray North: a mass of tiny fish bones is contained within a setting of stones in the east side of the fourth compartment. *Copyright Jean Comrie*

OTTER

At Point of Cott there was evidence that otters had been using the cairn as a den soon after its construction (Halpin 1997, 47), and the skeletal remains of otters are a common component in the faunal remains from modern excavations of Orcadian chambered cairns (with the notable exception of cairns in Rousay). Their presence may explain the large quantities of fish bones, mostly from small fish, found in the floor deposits at several sites, even where the remains are no longer in the form of recognisable otter spraints. Wet sieving on modern excavations can, as at Isbister and Holm of Papa Westray North, yield quite extraordinary numbers of fish bones where soil conditions are conducive to their survival, and it may be questioned whether all can be attributed to the output from otters' dens. The otters at Isbister and Quanterness were immature, whereas those from Point of Cott and Holm of Papa Westray North were of all ages from immature to adult.

MARINE MOLLUSCA

Despite the fact that shellfish appear to have played a minor role in the human diet in Neolithic times (Evans & Vaughan 1983), their shells have occasionally been found in specific and deliberate contexts within or outside chambered cairns. At Holm of Papa Westray North, 162 periwinkle shells were associated with the remains of a human burial on the floor of the innermost compartment of the main chamber. Within the filling of the entrance passage was a large and virtually soil-free deposit of 10,980 limpet shells, many stacked one inside the other, which indicates that the molluscs had been removed prior to the deposition of their shells, and intermixed with fish bones. Associated with an oval stone structure outside the cairn were 3,586 limpet shells. At the large stalled cairn of Midhowe (ORK 37) in Rousay, 'about three gallons' of limpet shells were found in a pile in one corner of the first compartment (Callander & Grant 1934, 339), while at Isbister (ORK 25) in South Ronaldsay 21 limpet shells lacking their apices were found below a stone shelf in one of the end compartments (Hedges 1983, 21). A significant number of limpet shells were found in the floor deposit in the entrance passage at the stalled cairn of Knowe of Ramsay (ORK 30) in Rousay (Platt 1935, 341). Beyond Orkney, the Clyde cairn of Crarae (ARG 11) in Argyll was associated with two deposits of marine shells: 2,453 mixed shells including pullet carpet, oyster, common periwinkle and cockle were found in a hollow in the forecourt, and more than 2,000 shells, mostly periwinkles and pullet carpet, came from a corner of the innermost compartment of the burial chamber (Scott 1961, 7, 8, 14, 25). Excavation of another Clyde cairn, at Cairnholy 1 in Kirkcudbright (KRK 2), revealed 'two or three handfuls' of densely packed periwinkles and a few limpets, mussels and whelks near the edge of the forecourt blocking (Piggott 1949, 114).

These deposits appear to indicate that there were circumstances in which the use of marine shells was considered appropriate. Periwinkles in particular have attractive shells as well as tasty meat. Discrete piles of limpet shells occur in domestic middens (e.g. Knap of Howar and Skara Brae), but the huge number of shells from the filling of the entrance passage at Holm of Papa Westray North, together with the presence of fish bones, suggests an origin in a specialised seafood midden.

Red Deer

Red deer bones and tines are surprisingly rare in domestic middens on Neolithic settlements in Orkney, but they figure relatively commonly in tombs and in what appear to be 'special' contexts. The most dramatic example was discovered at the settlement on the Links of Noltland in Westray, where the skeletons of 15 deer were found in a pile and lying on their left side on the periphery of the settlement (Sharples 2000, 111-13). Sharples suggested that 'the slaughter of these animals was a special event' for it was clearly not a simple butchery deposit (*ibid.*, 112). That special event would have been long remembered by the stench as the carcasses rotted. Sharples interpreted this and other Orcadian evidence from the Point of Buckquoy and the Bay of Skaill to suggest that there were prohibitions on the consumption of deer, and he argued that deer, recognised as an important symbolic resource in Mesolithic times, remained so and were even enhanced after the introduction of domestic species (*ibid.* 113-14, 109). The special deposits considered by Sharples have radiocarbon dates assigning them to the end of the Late Neolithic and perhaps continuing into Early Bronze Age times.

Two remarkable discoveries of deer remains in chambered cairns were studied in the 1930s by Margery I. Platt of the Royal Scottish Museum (now the Royal Museum of Scotland) in Edinburgh. The stalled chamber at Knowe of Yarso in Rousay (ORK 32) yielded bones and a few antler tines from 36 deer (Platt 1935), and the Knowe of Ramsay contained bones from at least 14 deer in nine of the 14 compartments (Platt 1936, 418). Both immature and mature animals were represented by the bones, but there were no intact skeletons and very little antler. Unfortunately the precise contexts in which the bones were found were not recorded, and both tombs had been severely robbed for stone prior to excavation, with the result that the 'relic bed on the floor' had been much disturbed. In both cases it seems unlikely that these deer had sought refuge in the tomb, especially as one of the Knowe of Ramsay animals was 'of enormous size' (Platt 1936, 417), and more especially because this would not be natural behaviour for the species. Red deer were normally larger in Neolithic times than today (Clutton-Brock 1979, 120) and, unlike sheep, would have found entry through the low passages of chambered tombs very difficult and uninviting. The newborn fawn found in the Maes Howe type tomb of Quanterness was presumably taken into the chamber by some carnivore (Clutton-Brock 1979, 119).

At Holm of Papa Westray North, deer antler was far more common than deer bones (Harman forthcoming). Much antler was found in the 1853 excavation: Petrie recorded 'the crowns and other portions of at least ten pairs of deer's horns' in compartment two alone (1857, 62). Most of the antler appears to have been found in the filling of the tomb, but some came from floor deposits. Some of Petrie's finds were probably left on site and subsequently recovered from disturbed deposits in 1982. From undisturbed areas of the tomb in the modern excavation came 16 tine ends in a total of 62 antler fragments from compartment four, mostly from the filling, and 31 tine ends in a total of 88 fragments from the filling of the end-cell. All of the antler bases are cast and therefore suggest collection of shed antlers rather than slaughter of the animals. At least 17 or 18 sets of antlers are represented in the assemblage, but they could have been shed over the years by fewer than that number of stags. Some of the antlers came from stags of four or five years or more, whereas the few bone fragments were mostly from young animals under three years of age. Antler and deer bone were also a significant component of the faunal assemblages from the forecourt to the tomb and from midden deposits outside the cairn.

The deer antler remains from Holm of Papa Westray North indicate a strong human interest in an animal whose presence within the tomb cannot be attributed to natural processes. The antlers are likely to have been shed within the conjoined area of Papa Westray/Westray by herds of deer that had an important symbolic meaning for their human managers.

The presence of bones from incomplete deer skeletons may be treated rather differently from the evidence of antlers. Comparable to the few immature deer at Holm is the evidence from Point of Cott, where the deer bones from the passage and compartment two were all apparently from one juvenile (Halpin 1997, 47). In both cases the presence of parts of young deer may indicate the activity of animal predators. Yet the relatively large numbers of deer represented by incomplete body parts at the Knowes of Yarso and Ramsay, both mature and immature animals, are more difficult to explain in terms of natural animal processes.

USE OF SKULLS

Processes of sorting human bones within tombs have been recognised since the excavation in 1932-3 of the stalled cairn of Midhowe in Rousay (ORK 37; Callander & Grant 1934, 334-5). In 1934, excavation at the Knowe of Yarso (ORK 32) revealed that the innermost compartment was lined with 23 skulls lacking their mandibles, which appeared to have been set upright and facing into the chamber (Callander & Grant 1935, 333-4, 339). Another clear example of special treatment of human skulls is Isbister, where one of the side-cells contained 23 skulls of adults of both sexes and of children and relatively few other bones (Hedges 1983, 21, 87). Colin Richards interpreted the Knowe of Yarso evidence in terms of the overall discrepancy in human skeletal remains in Orcadian stalled cairns, and he suggested that the Yarso skulls originated in different mortuary contexts elsewhere (1988, 47-9), whereas the excavators and John Barber interpreted them explicitly as ossuary deposits (Barber 1988, 61).

These practices appear to have been connected with the use of the tombs as burial places, whereas at Holm of Papa Westray North skulls, both human and animal, were selected as components of the filling that sealed off the end-cell. Three distinct horizontal layers of filling together yielded just over 7kg of human, animal, bird, rodent and fish bones and deer tines. There were no complete skeletons, only selected bones, and two layers were notable for the presence of skulls: layer 2 contained one human skull, two sheep skulls and one otter skull, while layer 3 contained two human skulls, three sheep skulls and one otter skull. The bone material in layer 3 was concentrated in two discrete deposits against the back wall of the cell *(35)*. All of these human and animal

35 Holm of Papa Westray North: human and animal bones in layer 3 of the filling of the end-cell. Part of the horizontal walling across the entrance has been removed, and the crudely-built face of the round cairn can be seen on either side of the sloping portal slabs. The well-coursed masonry of the main chamber abuts the cairn bottom right

bones could have been derived from deposits in the main chamber, or indeed from the original contents of the end-cell itself. Some physical support for derivation of the remains from the main chamber comes from two sources: Frances Lee identified bones in the end-cell filling as parts of the same human skeletons as found in the main chamber (1985, 44), and Mary Harman found pairs between otter bones in the end-cell and in compartment four (forthcoming). Three radiocarbon dates from human, sheep and otter bone in the filling of the end-cell and one from human bone in compartment four are broadly contemporary and span the period from *c*.3500-2900 cal BC, again suggesting that some at least of the contents of the end-cell were derived from deposits in the main chamber. What remains unfathomable is the extent to which the organic material was truly selected for the purpose rather than simply gathered up in the semi-darkness of the tomb.

Solitary human skulls have been found outside the cairns at Isbister (Hedges 1983, 24) and Holm of Papa Westray North, in the latter case in the forecourt floor deposit close to the entrance to the tomb, but in neither case was there any physical evidence to suggest formal deposition.

36 Holm of Papa Westray North: the portal slabs at the inner end of the entrance passage at an early stage in the excavation of the passage filling

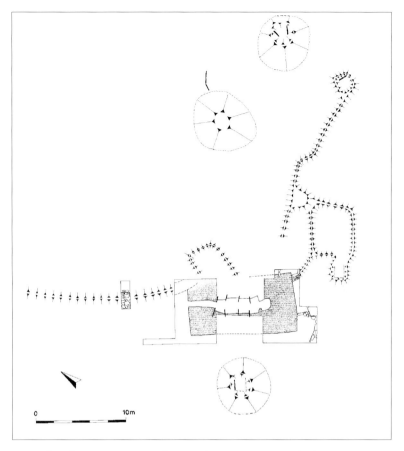

37 Holm of Papa Westray North: secondary structures outside the cairn were associated with Grooved Ware and Beaker sherds. *Illustration by Alan Braby*

DISCUSSION

In the early flush of enthusiasm after the discovery of substantial remains of sea-eagles at Isbister (Hedges 1983; 1984), the notion of animal totemism became very attractive. It explained the concentrations of dog remains at Cuween and Burray and of deer antlers at Holm of Papa Westray North (Hedges 1984, 155; Davidson & Henshall 1989, 84; Ritchie 1995, 63-4). An early note of caution about the interpretation of nineteenth-century excavations had been sounded by the Royal Commission over the Cuween dogs, for the bones had not been examined by experts, and it was thought possible that the skulls were those of foxes rather than dogs (RCAMS 1946, 98). If they were foxes, their presence in the tomb could be the results of natural causes rather than deliberate selection, but the bones have now been examined by a faunal osteologist and their identification as dog confirmed (Dr Anne Tresset pers. comm.). Totemism and deliberate selection of animal remains was ruled out entirely, however, for the assemblage from

Point of Cott: 'there is no secure evidence from the Cott assemblage for the placement of animal bones in the tomb as part of the funerary rite' (Halpin 1997, 48). At Holm of Papa Westray North, it seems inescapable that the fish bone deposit was man-made, and totemism is a possible explanation, alongside appeasement of the natural world and its spirits. It is difficult to interpret the presence of remains of cattle and deer in chambered tombs as anything other than deliberate deposition, simply because the live animals were too big to enter on the hoof.

The animal bone assemblage at Point of Cott was dominated by sheep (over 50%), mostly immature sheep, and it was considered by the excavator that they had been using the tomb as a refuge (Barber 1997, 67). The assemblage from Holm of Papa Westray North was similarly dominated by sheep, and Anne Tresset has come to the same conclusion that their presence was entirely natural (pers. comm.). In both cases, as we know from radiocarbon dating that at least some of the sheep bones are of Neolithic date, such use of the chambers as refuges involves an acceptance that the entrances were not sealed during the life of the tombs as burial places. It may well be that our expectation that tombs would have been sealed between episodes of use relates to our own attitude towards death and the treatment of the dead, rather than to the reality of the past. In most cases, evidence for methods of closure relate only to the final sealing of the tomb, but at Maes Howe the great block of stone that could be swung across the entrance appears to have been part of the original design (Davidson & Henshall 1989, 59-60). Maes Howe is unique in so many ways, however, that it would be rash to assume that any one aspect of it might support a general theory about tomb usage. The weight of the faunal evidence from excavations over the last few decades suggests that access to chambers was possible not just by small mammals and birds but also by sheep, dogs, foxes and otters (though it is puzzling that there is so little evidence of gnawed bones). The living human communities that used chambered cairns clearly had no objection to sharing them with the natural world.

There is no doubt that the chamber and entrance passage at Holm of Papa Westray North were deliberately infilled in order to close the tomb finally *(36)*. The filling was presumably inserted by means first of removing the roof, as Hedges argued at Isbister (1983, 22). At Holm there were plenty of large slabs of stone lying outside the cairn, which may have been roofing lintels. Davidson and Henshall have discussed the evidence for infilling at other Orcadian sites (1989, 60-1), and Barber has argued that such acts of blocking probably took place in Bronze Age or Iron Age times rather than at the end of their Neolithic usage (1997, 7-8, 65). At Holm, two radiocarbon dates from red deer bone in the blocking of the forecourt and from sheep bone in the infilling of the entrance passage suggest that the closure of the tomb took place from *c.* 2900-2400 cal BC. The two bones may, of course, have been redeposited in later times, but their contemporaneity with the act of closure is made more likely by the fact that the latest artefactual material from the site as a whole consists of Grooved Ware and Beaker sherds. Structural modification to the outside of the cairn took place at the same time *(37)*, and it is tempting to link this activity with the on–going use of the huge and architecturally elaborate cairn of Maes Howe type at the south end of the Holm of Papa Westray (ORK 22).

In conclusion, there is evidence to show that selected organic material was deliberately introduced into some chambered tombs by human communities, who used them as shrines, burial places and ossuaries. Modern excavations have above all emphasised the variety of customs associated with chambered cairns, and the need to distinguish between natural and human processes. We must accept that some if not most chambers were left open during their often long period of use and could be entered by any animal of suitable size, with a degree of chaos resulting amongst the 'legitimate' deposits. Some were never closed, at least not by the communities they served, but others were sealed with care and with selection of suitable material. The closure of the end-cell at Holm of Papa Westray North has provided a useful example of the process that is clearly contemporary with the Neolithic use of the monument.

Acknowledgements

As always I am grateful to Graham Ritchie for discussing the subject with me, and my thanks go to him and to Audrey S. Henshall and Alison Sheridan for reading and commenting on a draft of this paper. I am also grateful to Audrey Henshall for allowing me to use her plans in *(32)* and to Alan Braby for drawing *(37)*.

In connection with his own research, Dr Rick Schulting has obtained a further three radiocarbon dates to add to the ten already existing for Holm of Papa Westray North, and I am grateful to him for allowing me to mention them. The new dates extend the probable chronological range for the overall use of the site to 3640-2190 cal BC and suggest that the end-cell was sealed during the period 3640-3340 cal BC.

Bibliography

Barber, J., 1988 Isbister, Quanterness and the Point of Cott: the formulation and testing of some middle range theories. In Barrett, J. & Kinnes, I. (eds), 57–62.

Barber, J., 1997 *The Excavation of a Stalled Cairn at the Point of Cott, Westray, Orkney.* Monograph 1. Edinburgh: Scottish Trust for Archaeological Research.

Barber, J., 2000 Death in Orkney: a rare event. In Ritchie, A. (ed.), 185-7.

Barrett, J.C. & Kinnes, I.A. (eds), 1988 *The Archaeology of Context in the Neolithic and Bronze Age: Recent Trends.* Sheffield: Department of Prehistory and Archaeology, University of Sheffield.

Calder, C., 1937 A Neolithic double-chambered cairn of the stalled type and later structures on the Calf of Eday, Orkney. *Proceedings of the Society of Antiquaries of Scotland*, 71 (1936-7), 115-54.

Callander, J.G. & Grant, W.G., 1934 A long stalled chambered cairn or mausoleum (Rousay type) near Midhowe, Rousay, Orkney. *Proceedings of the Society of Antiquaries of Scotland*, 48 (1933-4), 320-50.

Callander, J.G. & Grant, W.J., 1935 A long stalled cairn, the Knowe of Yarso, in Rousay, Orkney. *Proceedings of the Society of Antiquaries of Scotland*, 49 (1934-5), 325-51.

Clutton-Brock, J., 1979 Report of the mammalian remains other than rodents from Quanterness. In Renfrew, 112-34.

Davidson, J.L. & Henshall, A.S., 1989 *The Chambered Cairns of Orkney*. Edinburgh: Edinburgh University Press.

Davidson, J.L. & Henshall, A.S., 1991 *The Chambered Cairns of Caithness*. Edinburgh: Edinburgh University Press.

Evans, J.G. & Vaughan, M., 1983 The molluscs from Knap of Howar, Orkney, In Ritchie, 1983, 106-14.

Halpin, E., 1997 Animal bone. In Barber, 1997, 43-50.

Harman, M., forthcoming. The animal bones. In Ritchie, forthcoming.

Hedges, J.W., 1983 *Isbister: A Chambered Tomb in Orkney*. BAR British Series 115. Oxford: British Archaeological Reports.

Hedges, J.W., 1984 *Tomb of the Eagles: a Window on Stone Age Tribal Britain*. London: John Murray.

Henshall, A.S., 1963 & 1972 *The Chambered Tombs of Scotland* (2 vols). Edinburgh: Edinburgh University Press.

Henshall, A.S. & Ritchie, J.N.G., 1995 *The Chambered Cairns of Sutherland*. Edinburgh: Edinburgh University Press.

Henshall, A.S. & Ritchie, J.N.G., 2001 *The Chambered Cairns of the Central Highlands*. Edinburgh: Edinburgh University Press.

Lee, F., 1985 *The Contribution of Human Bone Studies to our Understanding of the Neolithic Population and their Burial Rites in Orkney, with Particular Reference to the Sites of Points of Cott, Westray, and Holm of Papa Westray North*. Unpublished MA dissertation, University of Sheffield, Department of Prehistory and Archaeology.

Petrie, G., 1857 Description of antiquities in Orkney recently examined, with illustrative drawings. *Proceedings of the Society of Antiquaries of Scotland,* 2 (1854-7), 56-62.

Piggott, S., 1949 The excavation of three Neolithic chambered tombs in Galloway, 1949. *Proceedings of the Society of Antiquaries of Scotland*, 83 (1948-9), 103-61.

Platt, M.I., 1935 Report on the animal bones. In Callander, J.G. & Grant, W.G. A long, stalled cairn, the Knowe of Yarso, in Rousay, Orkney, 341-3. *Proceedings of the Society of Antiquaries of Scotland*, 69 (1934-5), 325-51.

Platt, M.I., 1936 Report on the animal bones found in the chambered cairn, Knowe of Ramsay, Rousay, Orkney. In Callander, J.G. & Grant, W.G. A stalled chambered cairn, the Knowe of Ramsay, at Hullion, Rousay, Orkney, 415-19. *Proceedings of the Society of Antiquaries of Scotland*, 70 (1935-6), 407-19.

RCAMS., 1946 Royal Commission on the Ancient Monuments of Scotland. Inventory of the Ancient Monuments of Orkney and Shetland, vol. 2, Orkney. Edinburgh: HMSO.

Renfrew, C., 1979 *Investigations in Orkney*. Research Report 38. London: Society of Antiquaries of London.

Richards, C., 1988 Altered images: a re-examination of Neolithic mortuary practices in Orkney. In Barrett, J. & Kinnes, I. (eds), 42-56.

Ritchie, A., 1983 Excavation of a Neolithic farmstead at Knap of Howar, Papa Westray, Orkney. *Proceedings of the Society of Antiquaries of Scotland*, 113, 40-121.

Ritchie, A., 1995 *Prehistoric Orkney*. London: Batsford/Historic Scotland.

Ritchie, A., (ed.) 2000 *Neolithic Orkney in its European Context*. Cambridge: McDonald Institute Monograph.

Ritchie, A., forthcoming. Excavation of a stalled cairn on the Holm of Papa Westray, Orkney. *Proceedings of the Society of Antiquaries of Scotland*.

Scott, J.G., 1961 The excavation of the chambered cairn at Crarae, Loch Fyneside, Mid Argyll. *Proceedings of the Society of Antiquaries of Scotland*, 94 (1960-1), 1-27.

Sharples, N., 2000 Antlers and Orcadian rituals: an ambiguous role for red deer in the Neolithic. In Ritchie, A. (ed.), 107-16.

7

'A Truth Universally Acknowledged': Some More Thoughts on Neolithic Round Barrows

Ian Kinnes

Introduction

As we shall see, the history of study of this particular aspect of insular Neolithic archaeology is fairly recent for, mainly, the usual reasons. As it turns out, by accident or design given the eclectic factors which allowed excavations at the time, Derek contributed significantly to the non-megalithic (NM) round barrows thesis: Rainham (gravel quarry rescue, just another ring-ditch), Seamer Moor (plough threat on known important barrow cemetery) and Pitnacree (research, but should have dug the rest) – all, as it happens, of critical importance; and, in this burgeoning complexity of Neolithic practice, we might add the structures and sequence at Raigmore.

Non-Megalithic Round Barrows Since 1979

A quarter of a century ago I addressed the matter of the existence of circular mortuary monuments in non-megalithic traditions for Neolithic Britain (Kinnes 1979) with some subsequent thought and amendments (Kinnes *et al.* 1983; Kinnes 1992). The initiative was necessarily proselytising since examples, largely dredged from the wealth of Victorian barrow-digging literature, had been broadly disregarded or seen as some form of 'native' response to the new Beaker mode, the latter easier to accommodate within a short chronology which, in retrospect, seems to have guided interpretation for a surprisingly long time and even now can retain a subconscious influence on aspects of overall structuring.

The original sought not only to authenticate such sites, and enforce consideration of relationships with, for at least the fourth millennium, NM long barrows, but also to create a series of sets by structural format, mortuary practice and/or material associations. The stages thus formed, not phases or periods although with a broad chronological sense, now seem too exact and certainly took little account of regional variation. Although the corpus has increased, notably from salvage excavations on alluvial gravels, it still suffers from the necessary limitations of interpretations of nineteenth-century archives and on an insufficient quantity of radiometric dates. For the former it is quite possible that genuine sites have been rejected on the grounds of insufficient evidence but strict limits must be set. In this regard it is interesting that there are *c.*120 acceptable examples (with others awaiting confirmation by publication) and 59, claimed as Neolithic by various authors (of which eight by myself in 1979), non-acceptable.

This makes for an interesting process: a broad acceptance of the original thesis with the evidence and its possibilities rightly expanded by some, its strictures blithely ignored by others as dubious dots were added to maps. Some examples might be mentioned in five categories. Multiple inhumations of unknown date and fragmentary or disarticulated deposits occur in later periods, as three adults 'hastily deposited' at Winterborne St Martin 5c or 'disturbed' inhumations at Galley Hill 3 (some or all post-prehistoric). There are invalid associations with Neolithic material in mound or ditch but essentially *termini post quos* for burials, as at Alton 13. There are also misidentified associations with material variously identified as Neolithic but assigned a later date by typology or context, as Ganton 21 (leaf arrowhead with Food Vessel) or Hambleton Moor (jet toggle — not belt-slider — with iron spearhead). There are those solely dependent on radiocarbon determinations, usually on charcoal and of no proven mortuary association, as Low Farm (in mound). Finally, some are dependent on typological perceptions: there are misidentified structures, as Cowlam 277 (now long barrow, shown by aerial survey) or Black Beck (probably corn drying kiln, cf. Ewanrigg).

I believe that there are two outstanding problems. The first is that post-war (no, that war) excavations and fieldwork continue to demonstrate not only a massively increased level of Neolithic activity but also a quite astonishing variety of formats and practices which often is hard to reconcile with traditional cate-gories, notably for those of enclosures of whatever scale. Second, there is a great need for re-excavation of some sites, especially those relatively well preserved, as was shown at Callis Wold, Seamer Moor and Ayton East Field; Whiteleaf (rich assemblage, structures), Duggleby Howe (remarkable sequence) and Wold Newton 284 (environmental potential, structures) come easily to mind.

Before moving to my particular theme I should complete this rough update with one last point. In 1979 enclosed cremation cemeteries formed the bulk of my stage F; it now seems clear that this was based on a thorough misconception. It is a matter of venturing into the nebulous area of pit (post) circles, some smallish henges and some ring-ditches (either embanked or erased barrows). The Dorchester sites remain the classic examples and serious reconsideration has been given to questions as to open or mounded, post-framed or not. Whatever, it seems clear that the cremation deposits here and elsewhere are systematically secondary in ditch fill and bank/mound. In other words, just as at Duggleby Howe these 'cemeteries' simply utilise existing monuments, always circular but not otherwise unified. There may, between the original structure and these deposits, be a gap of half a millennium (Stonehenge, Duggleby Howe etc.) or perhaps a couple of generations (Dorchester etc.). Some systematic associations lend coherence to a number of sites: skewer pins, transverse arrowheads, fabricators, and the odd stone mace head; pottery is lacking but by a series of linkages through to occasional pits (as Yeavering) Grooved Ware affiliation, at least south of the Forth, seems likely. On the other hand, caution is expressed by separate cremation deposits from the earlier Neolithic as at Midtown of Pitglassie, crematoria being, in observation at least, a separate phenomenon; by a cremation with skewer-pin and flint flakes secondary to a Food Vessel inhumation at Aldro 52, or dismayingly by a pit-circle with Aldbourne Cup associations at Hungerford (see Gibson 1994). There are times when I think that we, all right then, I, have got some things deeply wrong.

The foregoing simply illustrates the point that the accumulated archive is not easy of assimilation and highly vulnerable to the paired sins of neglect or over-interpretation.

Single Burial

Against this background might be briefly considered the matter of single burials beneath round barrows or within ring-ditches *(38)*. Ever since Thurnam's classic anatomy of long barrows: long heads (dolichocephalic); round barrows: round heads (brachycephalic) – perhaps he and Rolleston were only seekers after trophy bones rather than antiquities – a form of Neolithic-Bronze Age absolutism came into force, reinforced by communal versus single interment. This may hold broadly true but there are many exceptions, unsurprising over four millennia of chronological, cultural and regional variation, plus, of course, the inevitable matter of there being a vast proportion of undated mortuary contexts, monumental or otherwise.

Without going into the refined realms of how far single inhumations accumulated in a defined space (ideally a recognisable structure, quite often the limits of a barrow-digger's 'howk') or fragmentary – the results of on or off-site processing (and taphonomy) – it would be best to stay with the discrete deposition of, observably, an individual, classically in crouched position. Even this is not easy; Gibson (2004) has observed the frequency in this state, where the lamentably few good osteological analyses exist, of odd bones missing (not here taphonomic), misplaced or reversed, such as could not occur in a fully-fleshed individual. If this can be sometimes discerned in modern times (and perhaps not always even now) some dread descends over the perception of the accumulated, still largely antiquarian, archive. The passing thought that a crouched inhumation in its own grave might actually comprise rearranged bones of more than one individual leads inevitably to memories of Kurtz-trauma at the head of some distant river, or should we say, creek.

38 The Antiquarian view. The reconstruction of the burial of a man with Beaker and dagger. *From Bateman 1848*

Enough of that, back to what we can do with the record. Single inhumations, sometimes in cemeteries, seem standard for the earlier Continental Neolithic; thereafter, until the third millennium with such as Corded Ware, they are rare. In Britain this is not so. A number of flat graves, as at Radley, are known and some inhumations are separately placed within causewayed enclosures, as at Windmill Hill; these are largely without associations and dependent on direct bone dating or context for attribution.

For round barrows and ring-ditches, individuals are placed in graves or on the old surface, commonly in crouched position; insofar as reliable identification exists both males and females are represented, rarely children, with no apparent sexual division of associations.

Pottery is infrequent, just as in most long barrows or chambered tombs. At Four Crosses 5, Duggleby Howe (basal shaft-grave), Aldro 94 (this with two adults) and Goldington 2 were plain Bowls, typologically of Early Middle Neolithic date. The curious vessel from Liff's Low *(39)* does have some decorative affinity with Mortlake but its cylindrical neck and simple rim profile is unique. Comparisons with TRB collared flasks can be safely discounted. Mortlake sherds, in sufficient quantity to suggest formal placement in ditch or on old surface, are linked to single inhumations at Handley 26 and Shepperton, the latter in the re-cutting of a ditch with Bowl material.

Thus for the single burials, but it should be remembered that even regionally considerable mortuary variation might exist within the same ceramic tradition: contemporary round and long barrows, graves and chambers, inhumation and cremation, single and multiple, with East Yorkshire providing

39 The Liff's Low grave group. *From Bateman 1861*

perhaps the most dramatic illustrations. I shall confine this treatment to a series which might be defined by the possession of components of a particular artefact set, distinguished by the use of exotic materials and/or fine craftsmanship. How much variation might exist regionally or with a refined chronology is currently unclear but there is a sufficiency of repetitive associations to establish some sort of pattern, although it must be stressed that there are no invariable associations.

The finely-worked edge-polished axes and adzes are often made in selected multi-coloured flint with, for the North at least, a strong likelihood of origin in Yorkshire coastal deposits and known 'workshop' sites in the area. Association with round barrow burials is confined to the Wolds and Peak and, in Scotland, there is a flat grave at Knappers and the probable cist inhumation at Greenbrae. A notable association in a pit central to a later ring-ditch at Eynesford is with a half of a Mortlake bowl, adjacent debitage and a stone rubber, apparently attesting manufacture on the spot (inf. Herne). Axe hoards are known from the Midlands, East Anglia and Wessex with a notable polished discoidal knife association in the formal deposit at Great Baddow (Varndell, this volume).

Edge- or all-over polished knives are recurrent over a wide area, with polished examples of remarkable fineness from Duggleby Howe and Aldro 175. Manufacture can be shown on the same sites in East Yorkshire as for the axes. Lozenge arrowheads and leaf points are, of course, widespread but for single graves confined to a very few sites; those from Liff's Low and Ayton East Fields are rough-outs.

Antler maceheads (Simpson 1996), with one exception, are confined to the North for single burials but a full inventory shows a massive preponderance of finds from riverine and wet sites between the Trent and Thames with a possible 'hoard' of 13 from Brentford; one example is known from a domestic context at Northton. Paired boar tusks (12 at Duggleby Howe) are worked to chisel points as with the beaver incisors (only at Duggleby).

Belt-sliders occur widely but remain rare. As with the antler maces their chances of survival outside protected dry land or wet contexts are slender so distribution is inevitably skewed. Where identifiable, most but not all appear to be of Whitby jet (inf. Sheridan). There are some informative associations: with edge-polished axe and inhumation dated to the late fourth millennium at Whitegrounds and with Mortlake sherds in primary ditch fill and on old surface at Handley 26. Elsewhere the double inhumation in the Radley 'long barrow' (slider, polished knife, leaf point) has dates in the mid-third millennium, although those for antler here point a good 500 years earlier. Two examples from the Gop Cave massive cist are with multiple burials, Mortlake pottery and a polished knife. Those from Beacharra and Giant's Hills 1 are secondary to earlier Neolithic monuments.

Several notable features emerge from this array. None of the objects shows any trace of use, with the possible exception of sliders (found at the hip when *in situ*). There is considerable interest in exceptional raw materials – colourful flint, jet and, if Greenbrae is included, amber. The latter is rare in the Neolithic but it seems, for the western coastline of the North Sea, dependent for availability on occasional breaking-up of offshore reefs so that periods of exceptional use can be isolated as for the earlier Bronze Age or the sixth-seventh centuries AD. Visible craftsmanship is as good as it gets in the insular Neolithic. Putting the pieces together there are recurrent, if somewhat eclectic, associations and contexts sufficient to argue a particular social (cultural, ritual, chronological) phenomenon.

The likelihood is, of course, that these linkages conceal a whole realm of sub-sets, that is that we are reducing a complex of variables to a single circumstance whereas we must allow for factors for which we simply lack evidence at present. What period of time do these represent? If we credit human bone dates for slider associations (Radley, Whitegrounds) then maybe half a millennium; if the edge-ground axes in the Upton Lovell 2a grave show contemporary use or manufacture in the earlier Bronze Age, then as much as 1,000 years (or here did the burial fortuitously wreck and then incorporate the contents of an earlier deposit?). Should we, to anticipate a later point, see sequential associated burials in shaft-graves at Duggleby Howe (Neolithic through and through) *(40)* and not too distant Rudston 62 (with Beakers and then Food Vessel, whilst incorporating many Bowl sherds) as in any way related? Clearly it must be allowed that the mortuary record over space and time can often produce close resemblances which bear little further scrutiny: global *mégalithisme* being a good example. I would nonetheless insist for the sites, perhaps not all, that there is some form of entity; if, to some perceptions, this might seem to weaken an argument then it simply posits the abiding need for the advocate to retain *autocritique* lest others are too easily moved in one direction or another.

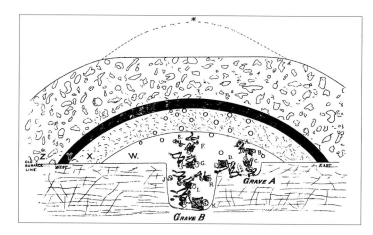

40 Mortimer's (1905) section through Duggleby Howe

DISCUSSION

It is perhaps worthwhile to review the role of the associated material. It seems unsafe to assume that these individuals necessarily had personal ownership of the objects finally deposited with them, with the possible exception of belt-sliders: even here there is little evidence for everyday wear as opposed to being part of a special costume. There did seem a case for these having different roles regionally with (outside the production area) a preponderance of non-mortuary finds, notably in wet contexts. This invokes several qualifications. Firstly, with the dead, four from East Yorkshire, three from distant Wessex (and two with a bone mass in North Wales); sooner or later landscape excavations incorporating barrows such as Irthlingborough/West Cotton or the Nene valley should fill the gaps created by the Victorian archive. Secondly, a matter of survival when unprotected and a record dominated by intensive river-dredging, notably the Thames with attentive collectors such as Lawrence, or peat-digging in North Britain; interestingly, however, three (not recorded in McInnes 1968; inf. Manby) are known from the Whitby area as 'surface' finds, one, it seems, with a prolific flint scatter. The dredged-Thames effect can also be seen for the antler maces and indeed for intact Mortlake vessels which might be suggestive for particular depositional practices were it not for a comparable preponderance in the record for Mesolithic bonework, flint and stone axes or prolific metalwork from the Bronze Age to post-Medieval. Whilst not denying the widespread evidence for deliberate wet-place sacrifice of important possessions, the factors of the changing courses of riverine history or peat formation deserve further consideration.

The axe-head in stone or flint is the famous (notorious) definer of the Neolithic, initially to classify museum collections, later as the agent of forest clearance, more recently a symbol of the means and purpose of production. Aside from the particular edge-ground forms treated here, they are rare in Neolithic mortuary contexts; more often than not in NM or stone chamber retrieval as fragmentary (there is good evidence from sites, such as Runnymede (inf. Needham) or Etton, for deliberate breakage). There are single round barrow inhumations with axes such as Gospel Hillock or Blackpatch which might well be Neolithic but a cautionary note must be entered as to the duration of production and use, perhaps into the currency of metal. Whatever, the occurrence of groups of axes in some of the graves in question echoes that of hoard practice and signals the particular role of the artefact.

Arrowheads are, of course, familiar across the mortuary record. Arguably, in many, perhaps all, occurrences in the Earlier Neolithic, they accompany the body only in the sense of being the embedded cause of death. Hunting apart – and, for, the record, how interesting that, although large game features strongly in utilised fauna, no arrowhead has been attested as means of demise (although surely so: just another quiddity of the record) – archers with the longbow, dominant in warfare as far apart as the insular earlier Neolithic (more correctly flat bows in the Neolithic – eds.) to Agincourt, are well-attested on no mean scale at Crickley and Hambledon Hills. For the single graves the arrowheads are placed with, not within, the body; again, like the axes, a different perception of deposition. Leaf points, presumptively spearheads (or just aggrandised 'display' arrowheads) are known as an occasional component of retrieved flint assemblages and are otherwise without context; their appearance as roughouts at Liff's Low and Ayton East Field forms a curious contrast with the accomplished appearance of other associations.

The antler maces have no obvious function, not even from their surface condition when well-preserved as soft hammers for lithic retouch. The raw material is not rare and employed in some quantity as ubiquitous picks demonstrate, obtained as a by-product of deer hunting or, more commonly, by collection after shedding. The latter is of more than passing note in that detailed woodcraft knowledge is necessary for systematic rather than fortuitous supply. Equally, the notorious Neolithic preoccupation with digging holes, often of no surviving apparent function or rather more elaborate in scale or repetition than seems strictly necessary, might lead further status to an otherwise mundane material, as placed deposits of antler picks – apparently the main excavation tool – amply show. The mace heads may not be the personal symbol that the nomenclature suggests, given their prolific retrieval from a recorded short stretch of the Thames, or even of invariable status but, as selected for certain contexts, must transcend the mundane.

An easy postulate, as I have regrettably perpetrated before, would identify social changes linked to new hierarchies based on resource control. I do not believe that, currently, we have a sufficient information base for this but would settle for the particular referential treatment of selected individuals within a broad and fluid series of circumstances.

Not without interest is the indirect but provable linkage to users of Peterborough, notably Mortlake-style, pottery whose mortuary practice is otherwise thinly in evidence. The freeing of Peterborough from its confined chronological span and, probably, its strict typology by an immediately few but reliable dates (Gibson & Kinnes 1997) assists in this process of loosening over-tight 'cultural' definitions. North British Impressed Wares can be closely linked here.

Interesting also is the more or less contemporary appearance of the Linkardstown single burials in Ireland, here distinguished by elaborately-decorated vessels, but by little on the non-ceramic front. Whether they reflect comparable processes or some parallel insular phenomenon is at best unclear (Brindley *et al.* 1983; Kinnes 1992).

On the latter, their formerly long-standing attribution to an earlier Bronze Age date, even argued from the resemblance of one bone object to the remote Únetiče of Central Europe, finds ready echoes in Britain. Here, the concurrence of single graves beneath round barrows with 'individual' or 'personal' associations and few in number could readily, especially in the all-too-recent days of short chronology, be set aside as occasional native response to intrusive and rapidly-dominant Beaker users, a nice colonial circumstance. To be fair, superficial resemblances of leaf points to flint daggers, the lack of detailed analyses and the consequent looseness of identification and terminology of flint-work, the linkage of sliders to belt-toggles (the interesting separation of nomenclature) and so on were all reasonably plausible and, as Atkinson (1972) said: even if there were Neolithic round barrows they were too few to be of any significance.

I think, on balance, these endowed singles do represent a single phenomenon, probably of short duration and with no obvious antecedents and no particular descendants, given what seems a reasonably secure florescence *c.*3000 BC. There is no visible external mechanism since we can discard chronologically the passing resemblance to Beaker practice. They occur notably in their very own monuments but also as secondary to earlier ones and, occasionally, in flat graves. There are two focal points: single inhumation and recurrent sets of quality artefacts. As once suggested, I think it no longer plausible that such is any real indicator of the emergence of particular social hierarchies; rather, I think it as likely, in various forms of deposition, that the material of the artefacts is the importance and that, for 'graves', the body in this case is the accompaniment.

Another marker in this attempt to account for and widen the reference for this material bears on the ceramic record. Peterborough, despite the magisterial efforts of Isobel Smith, has never achieved a coherent role in our perception. For its defined components, Ebbsfleet, apart largely from the eponymous site whose ceramics are in urgent need of review (as a real tester, is this our sole contender for an Ertebølle/Swifterbant circumstance?), fades off into a nebulous series of vaguely-necked vessels; Fengate is quite distinctive in appearance and manufacture and if, as some think (Gibson & Kinnes 1997), no longer proto-Collared Urn, another contender for the quiddity class as with Grooved Ware outside its Orcadian home. Mortlake, an elaborate form as I trust I have shown, is the ceramic component of the assemblages under assessment and, I suspect, just as special; the ornate Linkardstown vessels provide an intriguing comparison.

So, more excavation or re-excavation, more human bone dating on the lines accomplished by Rick Schulting for the earlier Neolithic, more sifting of the archive. Along with Tennyson one might urge, 'some work of noble note may yet be done' (although sentiments expressed in much of the rest of the poem may jar).

To end with a fine quote from Clint Eastwood: 'some people dig, some watch': Derek has done both admirably.

ACKNOWLEDGEMENTS

Thanks to many, but for immediate purposes D. Clarke, A. Gibson, T. Manby, A. Sheridan and D. Simpson.

BIBLIOGRAPHY

Atkinson R.J.C., 1972 Burial and population in the British Bronze Age. In Lynch, F.M. & Burgess, C. (eds), *Prehistoric Man in Wales and the West*, 107-16, Bath: Adams & Dart.

Bateman, T., 1848 *Vestiges of the Antiquities of Derbyshire*. London: John Russell Smith.

Bateman, T., 1861 *Ten Years Diggings*. London & Derby: J.R. Smith & Bemrose & Sons.

Brindley A., Lanting, J. & Moore, W.G., 1983 Radiocarbon dates from the Neolithic burials at Ballintruer More and Ardcony. *Journal of Irish Archaeology*, 1, 1-9.

Gibson, A.M., 1994 Excavations at the Sarn-y-Bryn Caled complex and the timber circles of Great Britain and Ireland. *Proceedings of the Prehistoric Society*, 60, 143-223.

Gibson, A.M., (2004). Burials and Beakers: seeing beneath the veneer in late Neolithic Britain. In Czebreszuk, J. (ed.), *Similar But Different. Bell Beakers in Europe*, 173-92 Poznan: Adam Mickiewicz University.

Gibson, A.M. & Kinnes, I., 1997 On the Urns of a Dilemma: radiocarbon and the Peterborough problem. *Oxford Journal of Archaeology*, 16 (1), 65-72.

Gibson, A.M. & Simpson, D. (eds), 1998 *Prehistoric Ritual and Religion*. Stroud: Allan Sutton.

Kinnes, I., 1979 *Neolithic Round Barrows and Ring-Ditches in the British Neolithic*. London: British Museum.

Kinnes, I., 1992 Balnagowan and after: the context of non-megalithic mortuary sites in Scotland. In Sharples, N. & Sheridan, J.A. (eds), *Vessels for the Ancestors*, 83-103. Edinburgh: Edinburgh University Press.

Kinnes, I., Schadla-Hall, T., Chadwick, P. & Dean, P., 1983 Duggleby Howe reconsidered. *Archaeological Journal*, 140, 83-108.

McInnes, I., 1968 Jet sliders in prehistoric Britain. In Coles, J. & Simpson, D.D.A. (eds), *Studies in Ancient Europe*, 137-44. Leicester: Leicester University Press.

Mortimer, J.R., 1905 *Forty Years' Researches into British and Saxon Burial Mounds of East Yorkshire*. London: Brown & Sons.

Simpson, D.D.A., 1996 Crown antler maceheads and the Later Neolithic in Britain. *Proceedings of the Prehistoric Society*, 62, 292-310.

8

THE GREAT BADDOW HOARD AND DISCOIDAL KNIVES: MORE QUESTIONS THAN ANSWERS

GILLIAN VARNDELL

INTRODUCTION

In 1949 Mr Herbert Haddock was starting work on a new garden path at his house in Great Baddow, near Chelmsford, Essex (TL 720091). Fourteen inches down in mixed clay and gravel subsoil he found a cache of five flint axes, a stone axe and a flint discoidal knife. Mr Haddock evidently had an eye for detail and some knowledge of archaeology, for his notes and sketches provide an excellent record of the context of this find and its original position in the ground *(41)*. He records also 'traces of what appear to be burnt material in very small pieces, of a dark or blackish brown colour and which snap very easily when twisted.' He took samples but regrettably these do not survive; it may have been merely mineral enrichment. The hoard was acquired by the British Museum.

DESCRIPTION

1. BM 1950 7-5.1 *(42a)* Pale grey-brown mottled flint axe, flaked all over and with the marked flake scars and wavy edges of an unfinished piece. Broad in appearance with broad, rounded blade tapering to rounded butt. Length 193mm; width 83mm; thickness 34mm; weight 540.1g.
2. BM 1950 7-5.2 *(42b)* Mid-brown flint axe, flaked all over, edges wavy. Very similar in shape to axe 1. Length 164mm; width 75mm; thickness 34mm; weight 423.6g.
3. BM 1950 7-5.3 *(43a)* Pale grey-brown mottled flint axe, flaked and partially polished, chiefly at blade end; edges also ground but uneven. Asymmetrical butt, otherwise similar in shape to the above. Fossil cast on one face. Length 159mm; width 74mm; thickness 37mm; weight 446.9g.
4. BM 1950 7-5.4 *(43b)* Pale grey-brown mottled flint axe, flaked and partially polished, chiefly at blade end but extending towards butt; one edge is ground. In outline, tapers rather less towards a proportionately broader butt than the above three. Length 128mm; width 56mm; thickness 30mm; weight 231.8g.

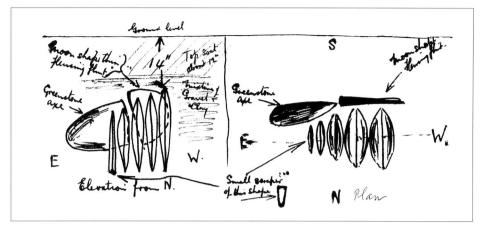

41 Haddock's sketch of the Great Baddow hoard *in situ*

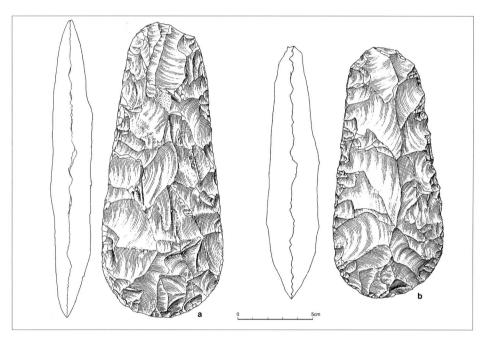

42 Axes from the Great Baddow hoard

5. BM 1950 7-5.5 *(44a)* Dark grey flint axe with paler banding, very finely flaked all over; edges are well finished and straight in profile but unground. Polished at blade edge, more extensively on one face; blade is bevelled to sharp edge. Much more angular in shape than the others, with a near-straight blade, tapering to a narrow rounded butt. Length 127mm; width 61mm; thickness 19mm; weight 133.4g.

6. BM 1950 7-5.6 *(44b)* Axe of coarse-grained igneous rock not sectioned but identified as greenstone (Clough and Cummins 1988, 177, Essex 55).

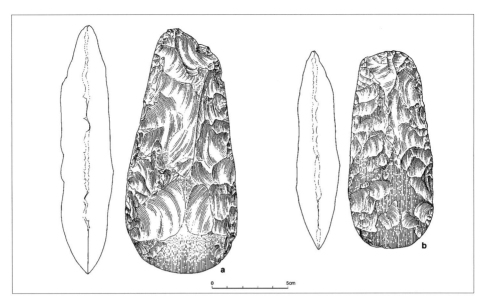

43 Axes from the Great Baddow hoard

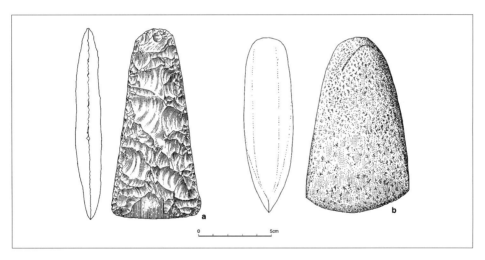

44 Axes from the Great Baddow hoard

Ground all over with particular attention to blade. Length 117mm; width 71mm; thickness 35mm; weight 420.5g.

7. BM 1950 7-5. 7 *(45)* Discoidal knife, subtriangular, of flint similar to axes 1-4 though a shade darker. Flaked all over; two edges and some ridges polished. Third edge tapers in section in the same way as the other two, but bears some fine blunting. Length ('apex' to mid-point of unpolished base of triangle) 80mm; width 95mm; thickness 11mm; weight 90.1g.

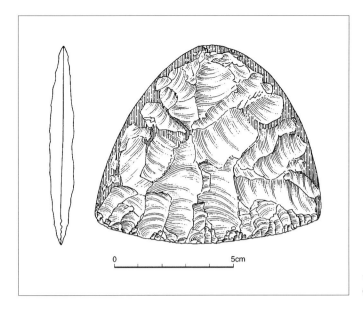

45 Discoidal knife from Great Baddow

DISCUSSION

The hoard is interesting for more than one reason. Firstly it comes with clear evidence of careful deposition – in this case its original position carefully recorded by the finder, the flint axes blade upwards and graduated, placed so close together that some perishable container seems likely – mention of the fugitive samples of blackish material is tantalising. Such finds are inevitably almost always accidental. However, a controlled archaeological excavation ahead of development at Carlton Colville, Suffolk, revealed three flint axes, two unpolished and one with polish (Varndell 2001). Two are of very large size and none appears to have been used. They were packed together, similarly aligned, within a darker area in a large, irregular pit. Rarely some useful information about old finds survives, as with the Clarence Road, Teddington, hoard of five flint axes 'arranged edgeways in a row' (Pitts 1996, 356).

Secondly there is the combination of part-polished/unpolished items, arguably stages in finishing. Pitts has considered such hoards in detail *(ibid.)*. It is generally agreed that grinding/polishing adds strength; it may also add value. The three Baddow axes which are ground at the blade are considered by Pitts to bear evidence of 'light use'. Indeed, at low magnification they appear to have slight damage to the blade edges which does not seem to be recent (so does the stone axe). A pair of part-polished flint axes from Playford, Suffolk, are reported as having traces of hafting and use wear (Martin *et al.* 1995), while another pair from Kessingland, Norfolk, had slight chipping of the blades suggesting use, but neither was polished and neither bore evidence of hafting (John Newman, pers. comm.).

In some hoards, the similarity in shape of the axes tempts one to see the same hand at work, or at least some tightly defined manufacturing tradition.

Of the Baddow flint axes, 1–3 are similar in outline; 5 is very different. Visually the flint used for 1–3 is similar; 5 again differs. Four of the axes were drilled for analysis as part of a programme of trace element analysis (Craddock *et al.* 1983). 1 and 2 were attributed to South Downs B as likeliest source, 3 to Clanfield and 4 to South Downs A, the results from 2 and 3 having very low probabilities. The fifth axe was drilled at the same time but the sample was not run; the analysis has now been carried out and the flint provenanced to Great Massingham, Norfolk; again the probability was not high. This site was recently discredited as a flint mine (Barber *et al.* 1999, 2, 8, 78) but this does not preclude its being a source; surface flint here could well have a similar signature.

Finally, the combination of artefact types poses yet more questions, particularly in the light of a hoard discovered somewhat over ten years ago in Banham, Norfolk, and noted in Norfolk Archaeology (Gurney 1990, 98). Described as a 'disturbed hoard', it comprises two flint axes, both with some polish, a subtriangular discoidal flint knife 'in perfect condition', a weathered greenstone axe (N308) and a partly-perforated mace head of igneous rock (N307). The larger axe (*c.*186mm long) resembles the Great Baddow axes 1–3 in outline; the smaller (*c.*156mm) is narrow, with a straighter blade and narrow, rounded butt. The discoidal knives suggest a deposition date for both hoards in the Late Neolithic, and while the cultural background of this type as a whole remains somewhat murky, the evidence we have relates them to Grooved Ware activity. Roughouts from both early and late twentieth century excavations at Grimes Graves are plentiful, and include the sub-triangular variety (Varndell forthcoming). Cotton (1984, 229 and microfiche) mentions another sub-triangular example from Burrows Cross, Peaslake, Surrey, said to have been found 'in an arable field with a re-chipped polished axe'. (Three fresh-looking flaked axes, one with some polish on ridges, were found at Burrows Wood, Peaslake: Bruce-Mitford, 1938).

Banham and Great Baddow add to the rather small number of secure discoidal knife associations other than flint scatters. Polished discoidal knives may be presumed to belong to a range of prestige artefacts by reason of the care invested in their manufacture and appearance. If they are high-status and 'special', contexts other than these two deposits do not provide corroboration. Discoidal knives do not feature at the great henge sites, or indeed at others, in any useful way – either henges were not a context for their use, or they were disposed of elsewhere. One from Lawford mentioned in the Durrington Walls report (Wainwright & Longworth 1971, 260) is unstratified (Healy 1985). They are not found in burials (neither is Grooved Ware as far as England and Wales are concerned); other types of fine polished flake knives are (e.g. Kinnes 1979). Shetland knives of felsite (which also have the look of 'special' artefacts and have features in common with discoidal knives) are found singly and in hoards and have been associated with stone axes (e.g. Munro 1906). A hoard of 19 was found near Walls some 20 years ago, carefully stacked edgewise.

Perhaps, despite their fine workmanship, the natural habitat of discoidal knives is the domestic sphere, like the Skaill knives at Skara Brae and other island settlements. At Skara Brae, a site exceptional perhaps chiefly in the degree of preservation, one may observe all manner of enigmatic things rubbing shoulders with each other: stone balls, passage-grave art, Grooved Ware. Saville (1994) published a newly recognised, decorated Skaill knife from Skara Brae. The incised geometric decoration is compared with designs on the Grooved Ware pottery of Orkney. In the same paper he published a new drawing of an old find, the decorated ground-edge stone knife from the same site (109,3), and suggested that this must be related to the other Late Neolithic discoidal knives. A wholly practical scenario is presented, with Skaill knives as short-lived and expedient, and discoidal knives as carefully made and curated. Skaill knives were frequently discarded on middens. Clarke's work on the type (1992, 244-58) demonstrates their functionality; experimentation has found them to be efficient butchering tools. What of discoidal knives? Clark (1929, 44) suggested that these 'would be sharp enough to cut thin materials such as hides, and would be useful in their preparation.'

Perhaps they were particular tools for a particular job such as the careful processing of skins. There is little enough hard evidence for clothing or 'soft furnishings' at this period; the paucity of settlement evidence also skews our understanding of subsistence patterns and ways in which domesticated and wild faunal resources might have been used. Add in the possible manipulation of material carrying 'wild' and 'tame' significance, and meanings become even more elusive. With fur animals, carcasses might have been left in the wild – understandable if they were not valued (or allowed) as meat. Patchy settlement evidence, the separation of activity areas (some of these off site), the social and ideological rules governing burial or other means of disposal of human remains and material goods – all serve to make interpretation more difficult and reduce our ability to compare like with like.

The combination in two hoards of flint axes, a stone axe and a polished discoidal knife is surely significant. The Banham find has not been published in detail, but the drawings of the two flint axes suggest different stages of finishing. The stone axe appears to be considerably weathered; the discoidal knife, which is the same sub-triangular shape as the Baddow example, appears to be similar in other respects as well – finely flaked, and edge polished on two edges, apparently a finished tool. The Banham knife is described as 'in perfect condition'; the Baddow one has very slight edge damage but extensive areas of the blade edges look in mint condition. These do not look like toolkits. It seems fair to surmise that the elements combined in these caches may relate to two or more different activities and/or motives; however, the bringing together of these different items may have some particular meaning. Two instances do not constitute a habit, they merely hint at one: only future discoveries will tell.

Acknowledgements

I am grateful to Stuart Needham for his comments on the draft, and to Mike Cowell for analysis of the fifth sample, to Karen Hughes for the drawings and to Steve Crummy for technical help with the illustrations. Photograph reproduced by permission of the Trustees of the British Museum.

Bibliography

Barber, M., Field, D. & Topping, P., 1999 *The Neolithic Flint Mines of England*. Swindon: English Heritage.

Bruce-Mitford, R.L.S., 1938 A hoard of Neolithic axes from Peaslake, Surrey. *Antiquaries Journal*, 18, 279-84.

Clark, J.D.G., 1929 Discoidal polished flint knives – their typology and distribution. *Proceedings of the Prehistoric Society of East Anglia*, 6 (5), 41-54.

Clarke, A., 1992 Artefacts of coarse stone from Neolithic Orkney. In Sharples, N.M. & Sheridan, J.A. (eds), *Vessels for the Ancestors: Essays on the Neolithic of Britain and Ireland in Honour of Audrey Henshall*, 244-58. Edinburgh: Edinburgh University Press.

Clough, T.H.McK. & Cummins, W.A. (eds), 1988 *Stone Axe Studies* Vol. 2. Research Report 67. London: Council for British Archaeology.

Cotton, J., 1984 Three Later Neolithic discoidal knives from north-east Surrey with a note on similar examples from the county. *Surrey Archaeological Collections*, 75, 225-34.

Craddock, P.T., Cowell, M.R., Leese, M.N. & Hughes, M.J., 1983 The trace element composition of polished flint axes as an indicator of source. *Archaeometry*, 25, 135-63.

Gurney, D., 1990 Archaeological finds in Norfolk 1989. *Norfolk Archaeology*, 41 (1), 96-106.

Healy, F., 1985 In Shennan, S.J., Healy, F. & Smith, I.F., The excavation of a ring-ditch at Tye Field, Lawford, Essex. *Archaeological Journal*, 142, 150-215.

Kinnes, I., 1979 *Round Barrows and Ring-ditches in the British Neolithic*. Occasional Paper no. 7. London: British Museum.

Martin, E.A., Pendleton, C., Plouviez, J., Wreathall, D. & Holden, S., 1995 Archaeology in Suffolk 1994. *Proceedings of the Suffolk Institute of Archaeology and History*, 38 (3), 335-62.

Munro, R., 1905-6 Notes on a hoard of eleven stone knives found in Shetland. *Proceedings of the Society of Antiquaries of Scotland*, 40, 151-64.

Pitts, M., 1996 The stone axe in Neolithic Britain. *Proceedings of the Prehistoric Society*, 61, 311-71.

Saville, A., 1994 A decorated Skaill knife from Skara Brae, Orkney. *Proceedings of the Society of Antiquaries of Scotland*, 124, 103-11.

Varndell, G., 2001 In Gill, D. (ed.) *Carlton Park, Carlton Colville CAC 017 and CAC 020. A Report on the Archaeological Excavations, 1999*. SCCAS Report no. 2001/24.

Varndell, G., forthcoming. In Lech, J., Longworth, I. & Varndell, G. *Excavations at Grimes Graves*, fascicule 6. London: British Museum Company.

Wainwright, G.J. & Longworth, I.H., 1971 *Durrington Walls: Excavations 1966-68*. London: Society of Antiquaries.

9

Spiralling Outwards –
The Problems and Possibilities of a
Later Neolithic *Leitmotiv*

Roy Loveday

Introduction

The spiral has become the *leitmotiv* of Later Neolithic Ireland. Its sculptural splendour on the entrance stone at Newgrange, offset by the theatrically white backdrop of the reconstructed mound, has ensured a place close to the hearts of jewellers, tourist boards, new age mystics and even learned societies. Interestingly the equally splendid Orcadian stone from Pierowall, imprisoned in the Orkney Museum in Kirkwall, has had far less impact – a clear illustration of the fact that the sculptors knew best how to display their work. Behind the artistic splendour of course lies the enigma of meaning – endlessly attractive but ultimately as incapable of resolution as an attempt to establish even the basic rudiments of Christianity from no more than the symbols of the fish and the *chi ro*. Another enigma, however, lies here that should be capable of resolution within the limits imposed by the partial nature of archaeological evidence: that of artistic origins.

George Eogan has stated: 'All the elements of the angular style could be based on Iberian motifs… On the other hand it is the one of the most common of the Irish motifs, the spiral that presents problems. Common on pottery of central European Danubian *(Linearbandkeramik)* culture, but found only sporadically at Gavr'inis and wholly absent from other Breton sites, the spiral's abundance in Ireland is an unexplained surprise, but a native origin has not yet been demonstrated.' (1986, 170-1). Thirty years earlier Piggott had come to the same conclusion: 'Boyne culture art is closely related to that employed upon the anthropomorphic idols of Southern Iberia… the spiral motif, *of uncertain origin*, links the Boyne art with Gavrinnis' (1954, 218: my italics). Spiral motifs on British Grooved Ware could be assumed to derive from Irish megalithic art (Childe 1931b, 133; Wainwright & Longworth 1971, 246), and rock art spirals conceivably from either (Bradley 1997, 64), but how did the spiral originate? A range of natural triggers exist – ammonites, coiled snakes, snail shells, emerging bracken fronds – but the fact that the motif is strongly concentrated in the Boyne–Loughcrew area restricts such possibilities: stones bearing ammonite fossils were not incorporated in the structures (unlike at the tomb at Stoney Littleton in Somerset: Frodsham 1996, 123); bracken is unlikely to have been a feature of the rich soils of the Boyne valley; snakes are not recorded in Ireland and *escargots* seem an unlikely speciality of funerary feasts!

ENTOPTIC PHENOMENA

In 1988 publication of investigations into entoptic phenomena appeared to furnish an answer (Lewis-Williams & Dowson 1988). These are largely geometric visual forms generated within the central nervous system during altered states of consciousness, most notably brought on by psychoactive drugs, and thus possessing cross-cultural commonality. Irish art was central to the case for recognising such images in the passage tombs of Western Europe (Bradley 1989, 73; Lewis-Williams & Dowson 1993) and, as the spiral is central to Irish art, the two were in considerable measure interdependent. The motif has particular relevance since a tunnel/vortex experience appears common to those entering trance states. It is surprising therefore that Lewis-Williams and Dowson's re-grouping of Shee Twohig's megalithic art motifs into entoptic and non-entoptic types (1993, fig. 9) only re-affirms both its regional restrictiveness and that of allied concentric circle forms. Predicted inter-regional commonality is largely restricted to basic zigzag and U figures *(46)*. Criticism that their claimed entoptic shapes were in fact ubiquitous was rigorously addressed by Dronfield (1995a & b; 1996). Through an evaluation of arts known to have derived from subjective visual phenomena in altered states of

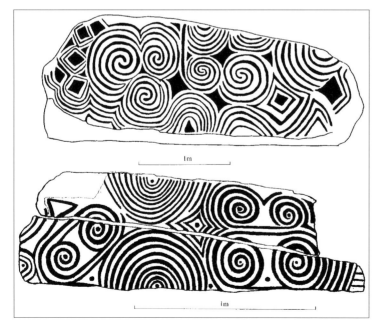

46 Spiral extravagance. Top: the entrance stone (K1) at Newgrange. *After O'Kelly 1982.* Bottom: the Pierowall stone. *Based on Sharples 1984*

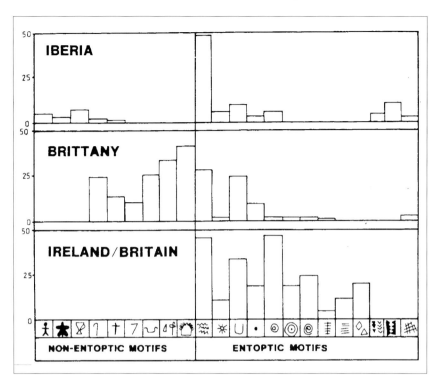

47 The geographical distribution of entoptic and non-entoptic motifs in megalithic art.
From Lewis-Williams & Dowson 1993

consciousness (ASC), and those emphatically not, he was able to demonstrate a clear separation of art types and isolate securely diagnostic entoptic motifs. Amongst these was the double, here termed interlocking, spiral (after Frodsham 1996, 103); the single spiral was considered undiagnostic since it appeared strongly in non-ASC arts such as those of Rome and Benin. The importance of the interlocking spiral motif to Dronfield's analysis is increased by the fact that three of the motifs occurring more frequently than it – the filigree, meander and 'fortification' – appear in Irish megalithic art to be largely interchangeable (1995a, *Table 1* and figs 5, 6 & 8) and distinguishable from his *undiagnostic* zigzag motif only on the most subjective terms: lack of accomplishment or visual 'drift' in execution might easily result in a zigzag motif appearing as a meander or, if repeated, as a 'fortification'. All are also capable of employment in representational or semi-representational contexts (e.g. the hangings depicted on the Göhlitsch tomb and as waves on the Caergurle boat/bowl (Miller 1997; Grimes 1951, 85). His remaining, more numerous motif ('small circular (arc)') is almost exclusive to one cemetery, Loughcrew, and overwhelmingly a feature of just one site within it (tomb F).

Doubts about these motifs leave the interlocking spiral as the principal secure diagnostic motif – others score below 3.0% in Dronfield's sample, and most below 1.5% (Dronfield 1995a, fig. 4). Yet this motif appears almost equally restricted. Except for single examples at Loughcrew, Clear Island and possibly the Calderstones, across the Irish Sea in Liverpool (Forde-Johnston 1957), the motif is restricted to the Brugh na Bóinne (Shee Twohig 1981, 114). Even there it is not numerous: 13 depictions on six stones at Newgrange (O'Kelly 1982); two certain and two possible examples on the kerbstones of site 1, and one on kerb 10 of site 3, at Knowth (Eogan 1984, fig. 6; 1986, pls. 66-76); and one on kerb 17 at Dowth (O'Kelly & O'Kelly 1983). In all perhaps as few as 20 depictions, overwhelmingly concentrated at one site – Newgrange. This is scarcely an acceptable diagnostic base for interpretation of an entire tradition, particularly one of such versatility. Additional problems are that many of these depictions have straightened central elements quite unlike the even reciprocating curvature of the endogenously generated vortex, and that most could have been added to the sites at dates later than the rest of the art. The interlocking spiral is certainly not a feature of the pre-tomb art recognised by Eogan at Knowth (1998) yet dominates the entrance stone and K52 at Newgrange, stones that exemplify O'Sullivan's developed 'plastic style' (1997).

Significantly the motif does not feature at Sess Kilgreen, despite the fact that it is one of only three sites that Dronfield's analysis suggests are likely to display art induced by hallucinogens; the others are Newgrange and Knowth (Dronfield 1995b, fig. 1 & *table 6*). It was considered more likely that Irish art elsewhere originated from migrainous syndromes or light flicker (but based on clinical studies using a light source in the order of 500 watts: *ibid.*, n.1). Equally problematic is the fact that Lewis-Williams and Dawson's own diagnostic elements of polyopia (repeated images) and integration (framing with entoptic elements) are largely restricted to the highly atypical tomb of Gavr'inis and the two famous kerbstones at Newgrange (Lewis-Williams & Dawson 1993). Given these reservations, the charge that the passage tomb builders of Ireland were high on magic mushrooms must, it seems, be declared unproven, at least as an explanation for the genesis of the art, thus saving the reputations not only of jewellers but also of a famous learned society whose proceedings bear triple interlocking spirals!

European Context

If the origin of the spiral appears to lie neither in the commonality of the human central nervous system nor in natural sources peculiar to Ireland, we are forced to look farther afield. Iberian elements are well attested in the Irish repertoire (Piggott 1954, 218; Eogan 1999) but the spiral is missing, whilst the widely splayed, normally single, curls decorating some Western LBK pottery lack temporal or stylistic proximity. Nevertheless the spiral does occur in Northern Europe in a form more immediately reminiscent of Boyne art – the copper spectacle spiral ornament (Ottaway 1973). This is most familiar from the

48 The European context: a) Vinca clay plaque from Vrsac, Serbia. *After Gimbutas 1974, fig. 161;* b) Cucuteni terracotta stamp seals from Frumusica, north-eastern Romania. *After Gimbutas 1976, figs 3 & 4;* c) Cucuteni vase decoration: detail. *After Gimbutas 1974, fig. 58;* d) Copper spectacle spiral. *After Ottaway 1973, fig. 3;* e) Incised spiral decoration from a Grooved Ware sherd, Skara Brae, Orkney. *After Ritchie 1995, fig. 49a.* Various scales

exceptional copper rich late Lengyel graves at Breść Kujawski and Osłonki in Poland, and at Jordanów in Silesia (Jaźdźewski 1938; Grygiel & Bogucki 1997). Jaźdźewski suggested that the spectacle spiral was associated with males, whilst copper arm spirals and beads were confined to female graves. Like spondylus shells these were clearly exotic exchange goods emanating from SE Europe where spiral motifs had been evident from not later than 6000 cal BC in the Starčevo culture, reaching their climax in the Dimini, Vinča, Butmir, Karanovo V and Cucuteni cultures (Lichardus & Lichardus-Itten 1985; Gimbutas 1974; Ellis 1984). In addition to their application to pottery, spirals were used to decorate stamp seals and apparent cult models (e.g. Gimbutas 1976, fig. 13; Whittle 1996, fig. 4.8). In all cases single and interlocking spirals were depicted precisely as in Irish megalithic art *(48a-c)*, as O'Sullivan has noted (1997). This fifth-millennium Balkan background furnishes a context for the copper spectacle spirals of Poland and Silesia – late Lengyel pottery in its southern heartland itself possessing spiral decoration (Lichardus & Lichardus-Itten 1985, fig. 18).

But copper ornaments ceased to be deposited in graves at Osłonki after the 'classic' phase (ending *c.*4000 BC) and spectacle spirals all but disappear from the record for nearly two millennia before returning and proliferating from Únetičeto Hallstatt. Understandably, this hiatus, and the distances involved, have prevented them being advanced as the progenitors of the Irish motif. Nevertheless a number may be linked to the brief Eastern Alpine copper industry flourishing between 3500 and 3000 BC – precisely the target period for the construction of the great Boyne tombs. From Unterach at the eastern end of the Mondsee a spiral with an unwound section was recovered from the same alluvial deposits as several type Altheim copper flat axes, a type Vinca axe, crucible fragments and typical Mondsee pottery (Mayer 1977, 54, taf 115). Posts produced dates of 4910±130 BP (*c.*3730 cal BC *Radiocarbon*, XII, 1970, 314) and 4560±100 BP (*c.*3370 cal BC *Radiocarbon*, XV, 1973, 433). Lack of stratification prevents certain association as do the circumstances of the discovery of the Stollhof hoard. This included two complete spectacle spirals, two gold discs with indentations (identical except in material to those from Breść Kujawski), and axes and spiral cylinders which can be paralleled in the Bygholm hoard in Denmark found in a TRB Vollung phase pot. The spiral cylinders also link the hoard to Cucuteni horizons. Suggested cultural ascriptions range from Bodrogkeresztúr to Baden (Mayer 1977, 47) as they do for a fragment of spectacle spiral from a hoard at Malé Leváre in Slovakia (Novotná 1970, 14, taf. 48b; Mayer 1977, 60). Some female graves of the Bodrogkerseztúr culture and settlements of Cucuteni B are also reported to have produced spectacle spirals (Ottaway 1973, 301). Interestingly Boleráz pottery from Hungary, broadly datable to 3600–3400 BC, exhibits spiral motifs closely comparable to contemporary pottery from Petromagoula in Thessaly on the one hand (Johnson 1999, fig. 5) and to the Unterach copper spiral from Austria on the other. Thus, although dating remains imprecise, it does appear that copper spirals and spiral motifs were current in central and south-eastern Europe in the centuries prior to the construction of the great passage tombs of Newgrange and Knowth.

Bridging the Gap

Problems of the yawning geographical gulf and distinct lack of intervening evidence remain. It may, however, be significant that amongst the items from Unterach and Stollhof were rectangular copper flat axes (Type Vinča), since they can be traced from presumed Eastern Alpine production centres through Eastern Europe as far as Denmark (Vandkilde 1996, 178) and arguably have a strong claim to be the progenitors of the English polished rectangular flint knife series. Trapezoidal flat axes of Altheim type are similarly distributed and may equally be echoed in flint as axes/adzes of 'prestige' Seamer and Duggleby types (Loveday forthcoming). The only explanation for such sophisticated replication would appear to be the extreme rarity value of copper artefacts during an impact phase. And, if we grant the possibility of copper axes appearing to be 'gifts from the gods', how much more enigmatic and potentially awesome might copper spirals have appeared?

It is not without interest that amongst those items conceivably transferred by Baltic and North Sea littoral groups along with copper artefacts were antler hammers/maceheads *(ibid.)*. One such from Garboldisham in Suffolk (Simpson 1996) is decorated with three separate spirals with long arms reminiscent of the unfinished copper spiral from Unterach (Mayer 1977, taf. 115). Its open spirals are echoed at a vastly higher level of craftsmanship on the exquisite flint macehead found at the entrance to the right hand recess of the eastern tomb at Knowth (Eogan 1986, 141). Facetting on the ends of this implement finds immediate parallel in the antler macehead series, particularly examples from the Lower Thames which appear to date to the mid-fourth millennium BC.

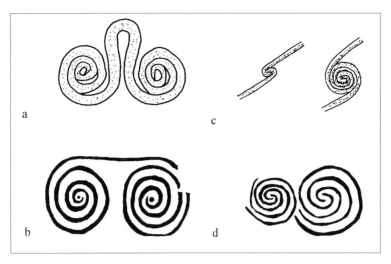

49 Metallurgy and art motifs: a) Copper spectacle spiral. *After Arnal et al, 1978, fig 11;* b) Pierowall stone: detail. *After Sharples 1984;* c) Coiling a double spiral. *Based on Ronne 1989, fig. 10;* d) Newgrange entrance stone: detail. *After O'Kelly 1982*

In seeking parallels for its spiral ornament Derek Simpson has pointed to the Calderstones and to Orkney (Simpson 1988; Simpson & Ransom 1992). In both these locations, and on the top of the macehead, spirals are depicted in spectacle form albeit with straightened, not looped, central bars. The fact that the spectacle motif overwhelmingly dominates the admittedly small corpus of Orcadian art calls for particular comment since it does *not* occur on tombs in Ireland (Shee Twohig 1981, 114; Sharples 1984, 102). If the generally accepted view is adhered to that Orcadian art derived from Ireland, we are at some difficulty to explain this. Had the motif been developed at a late date in Orkney how did it reach the 'Irish' tombs of the Anglesey-Mersey region without apparently impacting on the Irish repertoire? If, on the other hand, we hypothesise that copper spectacle spirals (complete or partial) emanating from Eastern and Northern Europe triggered the motif we might expect it to be depicted in its truest form precisely in those areas *between* the continent and Ireland. Orkney would be well placed for that role.

The Pierowall stone may offer valuable supporting evidence. Since great care was clearly taken in its production details of spiral depiction can be considered significant. Two features stand out: a hole created at the centre of each spiral and the tapered termination of the coil adjacent to it (Sharples 1984, illus. 28). This is quite unlike the rounded amorphous form of the arms on the equally splendid stones at Newgrange. It can be argued that holes have been created at other points on the stone but only in the case of the spirals does there appear to be evidence of consistency and care in placement. The effect of both features is to replicate the tapered end of a hammer-cut copper spiral and the hole left at its centre. This is particularly obvious in the case of the smaller of the back-to-back spectacles *(49a-b)*. Tapered ends also characterise the roughly picked spirals depicted on the other stones from the site *(ibid.,* 103).

Occurrence of spiral decoration on Grooved Ware in Orkney therefore attains considerable significance. It appears to be restricted to Skara Brae (MacSween 1992, tab.19.1) where two sherds with simple incised spiral ornament were recovered from the midden during recent excavations (Clarke 1976: stratigraphic details awaited) and the famous sherd by Childe (1931a, 68): 'just outside the cell of Hut 10 on the level of the hut floor in a deposit indubitably belonging to period II' (Clarke's phase 1). The fact that the latter is recorded as being sealed successively by sand, a greenish deposit from the drain in house 5, and a fragmentary stone pavement extending over the ruined walls of house 10, upon which the platform around house 4 (phase 2) was built, leaves little doubt regarding date. The incised nature of the decoration is consistent with this. Significantly house 10 appears to have been very much the largest of those surviving from phase I.

Childe was certain that the affiliations of the motif lay with Irish megalithic art (1931b, 132), and radiocarbon dating of the early phase of the village has supported that assertion: *c.*3300–2900 BC (Ashmore 1998), in contrast to dates spanning 2600–2100 BC from those contexts producing the only two certain spiral ornamented Grooved Ware sherds from southern Britain – Radley and Durrington Walls (Barclay & Halpin 1999; Wainwright & Longworth 1971). The case for an Irish derivation then rests upon phase I Skara Brae since only there are both motif and ceramic early enough to be contemporary with the construction of the great Boyne tombs. Questions of priority are bedevilled by the calibration plateau, however. Equally Kinnes's wise caution must be heeded that it is not very clear thinking to conclude that because Boyne mural art is durable and visible, it must be, if only numerically, the inspiration for other media in other places (1995, 49). Stylistic features attain a central importance therefore. Here the exceptional nature of the decoration on the Skara Brae pot, and the close parallels that its lozenge motif finds in decoration applied both to stones and a Skaill knife from phase 1 of the site become significant (Shepherd 2000). There is little so close in the Irish tomb art repertoire except K67 at Newgrange, and even here the spiral is of S rather than spectacle form. Perhaps significantly the spectacle spiral motif on C1 at Barclodiad y Gawres appears closer (Shee Twohig 1981, fig. 266). Since, then, there is no evidence of slavish, or even particularly close, copying of Irish megalithic art to decorate Orcadian Grooved Ware (Brindley 1999, 136), or of the long distance movement of such ceramics to explain the extreme northern and southern British occurrence of spiral decoration, an alternative medium must be envisaged to explain the spread (Cleal 1999). The copper spectacle spiral would appear ideally suited for this role and would, if worn upon material possessing novel, angular stitching, furnish a source for these recurrent Later Neolithic 'signifiers' (cf. the Sion decorated stelae: Gallay & Spindler 1972).

Derek Simpson's work (1988, 31–5; Simpson & Ransom 1992) has high-lighted another strand of evidence detailing the relationship between Orkney and Ireland. Pestle maceheads are concentrated in Northern and Eastern Ireland (20 examples as against 1 cushion and 2 ovoid), and in Orkney (nearly 50% of the total within the densest concentration of such implements in the British Isles). That Orcadian concentration, the Irish distributional coincidence with passage tombs and the apparent copying of pestle forms as pendants found within the Irish tombs, he implies, points to movement of either implements or the concept from the north (Simpson 1988, 33–5). Certainly the opposite case would be difficult to make since pendants are unlikely to generate full-scale artefacts. Only the generalised forms of bulb-headed and giant pins suggest any copying of Boyne artefacts in Orkney (Wainwright & Longworth 1971, 263). If evidence for the movement of people and ideas then appears to favour a southern course from Orkney to the Boyne, how are we to explain the sudden appearance of the Maes Howe passage tomb type and the attendant transformation of Orkney? Richards has made a strong case for inverting Renfrew's model of an evolving Grooved Ware society there but this poses the problem of apparently sudden cultural transformation (1998).

The Early Grooved Ware Phenomenon in Orkney

Orkney generates more questions than answers: how does the Grooved Ware complex emerge? Why does it collapse so totally with virtually no Beaker and Earlier Bronze Age successor? Where did the tradition of fine stone working witnessed at Maes Howe and the Howe originate (Davidson & Henshall 1989)? Why did substantial villages develop there when the pattern in comparable geological regions is of no more than slight, double unit settlements (Armit 1996; Barclay 1996)? Why are maceheads mostly found in settlement contexts there and frequently in a fragmentary condition (Simpson & Ransom 1992)? Of course more deeply stratified sequences such as Pool (Hunter & MacSween 1991) may clarify ceramic origins and further disco-veries such as at the Howe may furnish intermediate tombs of the eminently destructible Maes Howe series, but questions relating to the nature of the settlements are less easy to resolve (Russell 2002, 163–5). One has the uneasy feeling that there are external elements in their makeup. Obsessive rebuilding (not determined by the decay of organic materials), drains, burials within or under houses (Brae and Barnhouse), ovens (Rinyo), a profusion of mortars, furniture and floor boxes appear from current evidence unparalleled in Hebridean, Irish or even Danish settlements but many find echoes in SE Europe. Significantly this is also the region where spiral designs were commonplace and whence the copper spectacle spiral probably originated.
   Yet can we seriously entertain the movement of ideas and people over such distances, and why to Orkney of all places? Contact, albeit indirect, within

continental Europe is indicated by the movement of copper north and amber south (Midgeley 1982, 290-6). Shared coloration and 'magical' properties may have led to a mythological equation being drawn between these materials, hence the production of discs in gold, copper and amber. This indeed seems to explain the complementary distribution patterns of copper and amber articles in Denmark (Randsborg 1979; Whittle 1988, 119). If so when copper supplies began to falter in the Eastern Alps we could speculate that attention might be re-directed to the distant amber zone. The potential for renown in locating new sources is likely to have been high thus attracting members of structurally disadvantaged lineages seeking higher status through access to prestige material. Failure would be inevitable on the Jutland amber coast yet the magical emergence of amber from the sea 'being swept along so easily that it seems to hover in the water' (Pliny, *Natural History* 11.42) may have focused attention beyond the north western horizon, particularly if a sun→amber→copper mythological equation existed. Out there Pytheas was to record 'the barbarians often pointed out the place where the sun lies down for so short a period at midsummer before it straightaway rises up again' (Hawkes 1975), a phenomenon possibly known to Danish littoral groups blown north–west whilst traversing their highly accessible coastline. A sea crossing in such a direction would lead to a landfall somewhere in Scotland where their foreign nature, artefacts (including perhaps copper spiral ornaments) and dress (conceivably chevron/lozenge decorated) could be predicted to result in either local aggression or veneration. That the latter was not uncommon is confirmed by the origin myths of many Mayan and African royal lineages which speak of the lineage founder as a migrant who arrived from a distant country, attracted clients among the local population and established his own ranked polity (Anthony 1997, 23). Accounts of hundreds of Indian people following and worshipping Cabeza de Vaca's ragged group of conquistadors ('This people hysterically crowded upon us... they brought every single inhabitant ... for us to touch and bless. ... When we left next day, all the people of the place went with us, and the next people received us as well as the last': trans. Covey 1983, 102), and of the Miwok of California sacrificing to Drake and his men as gods (James 1998, 13) furnish historically attested examples of the veneration process, whilst the Slavs' invitation to the Varangian Russes to rule over them to prevent internal dispute (*Primary Chronicle*: trans. Cross 1930) furnishes an example of the more hard-headed process of elevating outsiders as non-partisan rulers.

The archaeological correlates of such an adoption of an external elite might include:

1. A limited new artefact range
2. Novel, but in origin mundane, artefacts accorded prestige/ritual significance

3. New decorative schemes accorded prestige/ritual significance and transferred from one medium to another
4. New settlement hierarchies and gradual transformation of peripheries
5. Exceptional burials and/or burial structures
6. Continuity of exploitation patterns whether agricultural or stone/clay procurement.
7. Continuity of local technologies

Most of theses features characterise the advent of the Grooved Ware phenomenon in Orkney (Richards 1998; Ritchie 2000). As with an internally generated elite (e.g. Later Neolithic Eastern Yorkshire: Thorpe & Richards 1984; Loveday forthcoming) position would depend upon control of important ceremonies and exotic artefacts. And here there appears a problem since the quest for copper, that it is speculated could have fuelled the process, would be doomed to failure in Orkney. Or was it?

COPPER WORKING IN ORKNEY?

In 1774 it was reported that on Burray: 'In breaking through a crumbling sort of rock they found pure virgin copper in the form of leaves and sprigs of trees' (quoted in Richardson 1974, 78). More significantly exposures of secondary ores are known on Rousay and can still be seen by the cliffs at Yesnaby some 3.5km from Skara Brae (Mykura 1976, 119). Earliest recognition and working may well have been at coastal exposures (cf. O'Brien *et al.* 1990, 35). In itself, of course, this only adds opportunity to motive; hard evidence is needed to confirm working and cliff exposures are highly vulnerable to erosion. However, given the secrecy and magic assumed to surround production (Budd & Taylor 1995), which in this instance could have been the key factor in elevating revered outsiders to the role of agents of the gods, it may be more profitable to seek evidence on or near settlements.

At Skara Brae a hammerstone with a groove worked around the waist, and another groove around the butt end, came from House 9, a first phase building adjacent to the large house from which the spiral-decorated sherd was recovered. Childe (1931a, 61-2 & fig. 18) immediately recognised it as a type 'associated with the earliest metal using cultures of Europe and now intimately linked to copper mining' (Pickin's class 6a: 1990). It appears to be the sole example from the site but that is not perhaps surprising at a location where processing installations and tools might be better predicted than extractive ones.

House 8 at Skara Brae was unique both in being placed outside the midden and in having no domestic furniture. A narrow, 370mm wide gap in the wall opposite the door is too small to have been another entrance, nor can it have been the remains of a collapsed cell since upright slabs lined its sides. Its role as a flue for the adjacent $2m^2$ paved hearth arrangement packed with heat-fractured volcanic stones seems certain. This was clearly the *raison d'être* of the house and has been interpreted as an instillation for heating chert to improve its flaking qualities; '... the heated volcanic stones being a prime means of attaining the required temperature' (Clarke & Sharples 1985, 67-8). It seems inordinately large for that purpose yet compares well with roasting hearths used to prepare ore for smelting. These have been postulated at Mount Gabriel (O'Brien *et al.* 1990, 34) and are recorded at the Mitterberg smelting sites as rectangular paved areas 2m x 1m in size (Tylecote 1987, 111-2 & 130). Clay banked around the edges of the Skara Brae installation accords with the evidence of stall roasters (*ibid.*, fig. 4.5) and would assist in containing air from the flue. Induced draft rather than high temperature was the prerequisite, heated stones perhaps being the best means of maintaining the latter in a fuel-scarce environment. Smelting could have been achieved in such an installation but a role in ore preparation seems more likely (*ibid.*, 129-30, fig. 4.16). Given the precocious (and presumably secretive and ritualised) nature of smelting it seems more likely that this would have been tightly controlled at the elite centre. Here the industrial/transformation' area at Barnhouse becomes significant. Although slag has not been recognised amongst the extensive evidence of burning this is not unusual at early smelting sites (Craddock 1995, 136-46); its central location within the settlement certainly appears to indicate something beyond a simple pottery firing site (Jones 2000,130 & fig. 11.3).

With the possibility of such activities in mind it is worth recalling Piggott's comment on the concentration of maceheads in Orkney: '... almost invariably broken and particularly found in the Maes Howe-Stenness region' (1954, 331). As Derek Simpson has pointed out this condition is highly unusual (1988, 31). A workaday origin for Orkney pestle maceheads as just that, pestles used in fine crushing and grinding, is not inconceivable given their unique occurrence on settlement sites. The surviving end of an example from house K at Rinyo was described as '... abraded as if through use as a hammer stone'. (Childe & Callander 1947, 41). The accompanying elements – mortars – are found in abundance at Skara Brae. Many, such as that illustrated by Childe and Grant from Rinyo (1939, pl. xxiii) seem inappropriate to cereal preparation and 'over built' for fish bone or shell pounding, their other assumed use. At the comparably preserved sites of Knap of Howar and Eilean Domhnuill, single querns appear to have been the norm and small bowls or mortars are absent. Potentially more significant are a series of distinctive stones found at Barnhouse with deep hollows formed on the faces and sides (Clarke 1992, 252, fig. 18.2). They closely resemble mortar stones, often with hollows on more than one face, that were used for the fine grinding of copper ore. Their associated pounders appear to have predominantly taken the form of rounded balls of stone (Dutton 1990, 13; Thorburn 1990, 45-6; Tylecote 1986, 58). Stone balls also occur on Orcadian settlement sites and form an enigmatic feature of the

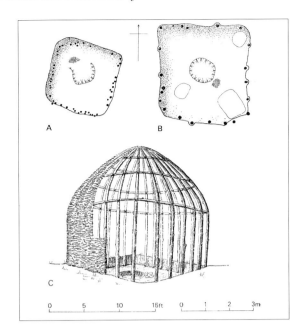

50 Houses from phase III at the
Goldberg. *From Simpson 1971*

repertoire. They are not dissimilar in size to the preferred range of 80-100mm for pounders from the Great Orme mine (e.g. 126mm, Rinyo; 62mm, Skara Brae). Finely carved specimens point to a ritual as well as a functional aspect which links them to the tradition centred in Aberdeenshire (97% of which are some 70mm in diameter, several displaying spiral ornamentation: Marshall 1977). Equally uncarved specimens suggest a link to those from Irish passage tombs (e.g. Loughcrew cairns L & F: 67mm & 78mm in diameter), that have been demonstrated to fit neatly into cup marks on orthostats (McMann 1994, 540). Miniature balls found in the same tombs, like miniature pestle maceheads, suggest a talismanic quality. The disparate symbolic messages presented by these artefacts are rendered coherent if related to the precocious processing of copper. This is equally true of the obsessive use of haematite at Skara Brae, both as a pigment and possibly to inscribe the walls (Isbister 2000, 191) – its translucent copper orange colour suggesting a symbolic, sympathetic dimension.

There is much at Skara Brae and Barnhouse then that recalls Herdits' description of the Muhlbach processing site at the Mitterberg: 'The ore… (was)…crushed with round, usually apple-sized stone ore pounders, anvil stones with hollows worked into them over time…and querns not dissimilar to prehistoric corn grinding querns' (2003, 70). When coupled with the novel size and shape of the houses, their village agglomeration and the sudden appearance of flat-based pottery, all of which can be paralleled amongst Altheim copper working groups *(50)* (Bersu 1937; Last 1996, 37; Driehaus 1960, taf. 3), a case, albeit circumstantial, emerges for the presence of an adopted external elite with knowledge of the working of copper. If driven by mythological correlations, they and their monuments, rather than any natural phenomenon, might explain Orkney's suggested emergence as an inter-regional centre – pilgrimage being the consequence rather than the agency in the process (Renfrew 2000). Thus instead of the current, strangely diffusionist driven image of native Orcadian developments dependent on the movement of ideas along the Atlantic seaboard through Ireland, with all the attendant problems of differing tomb design, agglomeration and burial rite (Sharples 1984, 117), the opposite might in some measure hold true. The exceptional Boyne pheno-menon could then be ascribed to a dynamic mixing of native, Iberian (Eogan 1999), Breton (O'Sullivan 1997) and Orcadian influences. Looking beyond the art, it is not without interest that the site chosen for the Brugh na Bóinne cemetery lies in the heart of an area of copper deposits (Stout 1991, fig. 5).

CHANGED PERSPECTIVES

Re-positioning of Orcadian Grooved Ware groups as possible agents rather than receptors in the development of the key spiral element in the Irish artistic (and presumably religious) repertoire forces us to confront the question of the source of the angular-spiral art that characterises the early, re-used stones at Knowth, one of which (corbel 5D/6E at Site I East) appears to furnish a close parallel for the Skara Brae sherd design (Eogan 1998, fig. 10). It also forces us to question the origin of O'Sullivan's step 2 'plastic' art (1997, 84). Could it have developed in response to that recorded at Pierowall rather than *vice versa*? It is principally a feature of kerbstones, and can be demonstrated to have been accomplished *in situ* at Newgrange where interlocking spirals have very distinctive straight central elements closely resembling the pattern produced in winding double copper spirals *(49c-d)*. Equally O'Sullivan's step 4 art (amorphous areas of dense picking) might be referable to uncertain application of a technique used architecturally at Maes Howe. This again appears to have been applied when the structures were already in place (*ibid.*, 87).

CONCLUSION

The central case made here – that spiral tomb decoration may have ultimately derived from Altheim-Mondsee copper spectacle spirals – can of course be dismissed as unsupported speculation in the absence of the key artefacts. Nevertheless it has forced a re-examination of the Orcadian evidence, where release from the Irish umbilical cord has opened up the possibility of a very different European perspective. From this changed standpoint the unique monument of Maes Howe appears less like a highly refined megalithic cruciform chamber and more like a copy of a wooden one with corner buttresses, significantly akin to the internal quartet of posts that characterise later southern Grooved Ware structures from Wessex to the Boyne (Wainwright & Longworth

1971, 42; Eogan & Roche 1999). Although highly improbable as a native Orcadian development in a timber-scarce environment this has distinct European resonances. Mortuary houses in Jutland (Herrup 43 & 46) are of comparable size to the chamber (Becker 1993), while beneath the almost identically sized mound of Spitz Hoch, at Latdorf in Bernburg, oak timbers wrapped in decorated textiles divided a 'stone rotunda' into upper and lower chambers (Schlabow, 1959), or equally plausibly given the uncertainties of the 1880 excavation, defined a wooden chamber capped by stone. This use of cloth (later carbonised by fire) in a tomb datable to at least the opening of the third millennium BC by the inclusion of Bernburg pottery, recalls the placing of geometric art on corbels and lintels in Irish tombs (Eogan 1986, fig. 73) and suggests that its role may primarily have been decorative – to be seen by the deceased who occupied the chambers rather than initiates in a state of narcosis. From the same Central European region come the only external parallels for that other early Orcadian feature – the henge (Harding with Lee 1987, 57). Thus the spiral has returned us, unexpectedly and by a different route, to Childe's comment on the Orcadian evidence: '... such a cluster of one roomed dwellings as is planned on the Goldberg bears a striking similarity to the clusters of stone huts we know at Skara Brae and Rinyo. Moreover the house plans with their rounded corners are similar, while the relics from the Orcadian hamlets notoriously include some types suggestive of Horgen connections. Curiously enough we have from Rinyo the first ovens found in Britain' (1949, 86). Research over the intervening half century has only deepened this enigma.

ACKNOWLEDGEMENTS

I owe a deep debt of gratitude to the late Ted and Jean Holmes – enthusiasts for the past – whose curiosity was always a stimulus and whose books on Orkney and Ireland have been of enormous value. I am also very grateful to Derek Barker for his discussion and assistance with the historical aspects of the case set out here.

BIBLIOGRAPHY

Anthony, D., 1997 Prehistoric migration as social process. In Chapman, C. & Hamerow, H. (eds), *Migrations and Invasions in Archaeological Explanation*, 21-32. BAR International Series 664. Oxford: British Archaeological Reports.

Armit, I., 1996 *The Archaeology of Skye and the Western Isles*. Edinburgh: Edinburgh University Press.

Arnal. J., Bocquet, A., Robert, A. & Verras, G., 1978 La Naissance de la metallurgie dans le sud-est de la France. In Ryan, M. (ed.) *The Origins of Metallurgy in Atlantic Europe 35-63*. Dublin: Stationery Office.

Ashmore, P., 1998 Radiocarbon dates for settlements, tombs and ceremonial sites with Grooved Ware in Scotland. In Gibson, A. & Simpson, D. (eds), *Prehistoric Ritual and Religion. Essays in Honour of Aubrey Burl*, 139-47. Stroud: Allan Sutton.

Barclay, A. & Halpin, C., 1999 *Excavations at Barrow Hills, Radley, Oxfordshire: Vol. 1. The Neolithic and Bronze Age Complex*. Oxford: Oxford Archaeological Unit.

Barclay, G., 1996 Neolithic buildings in Scotland. In Darvill, T. & Thomas, J. (eds), *Neolithic Houses in Northwest Europe and Beyond*. Neolithic Studies Group Seminar Papers 1, 61-76. Oxford: Oxbow.

Becker, C.J., 1993 Cult houses of the Funnel Beaker Culture. In Hvass, S. & Storgaard, B. (eds), *Digging into the Past: 25 Years of Archaeology*, 110-11. Aarhus: Jutland Archaeological Society.

Bersu, G., 1937 Altheimer Wohnhäuser vom Goldberg, O.A. Neresheim Württemberg. *Germania*, 21, 149-58.

Bradley, R., 1989 Deaths and entrances: a contextual analysis of megalithic art. *Current Anthropology*, 30, 68-75.

Bradley, R., 1997 *Rock Art and the Prehistory of Atlantic Europe: Signing the Land*. London: Routledge.

Brindley, A., 1999 Sequence and dating in the Grooved Ware tradition. In Cleal, R. & MacSween, A. (eds), *Grooved Ware in Britain and Ireland*, 133-44. Oxford: Oxbow.

Budd, P. & Taylor, T., 1995 The fairie smith meets the bronze industry: magic versus science in the interpretation of prehistoric metal making. *World Archaeology*, 27, 133-43.

Childe, V.G., 1931a Final report on the operations at Skara Brae. *Proceedings of the Society of Antiquaries of Scotland*, 65 (1930-1), 27-77.

Childe, V.G., 1931b *Skara Brae. A Pictish Village in Orkney*. London: Keegan Paul, Trench & Trubner.

Childe, V.G., 1949 Neolithic houses-types in temperate Europe. *Proceedings of the Prehistoric Society*, 15, 77-86.

Childe, V.G. & Grant, W.G., 1939 A Stone Age settlement at the Braes of Rinyo, Rousay, Orkney. *Proceedings of the Society of Antiquaries of Scotland*, 73,(1938-9) 6-31.

Childe, V.G. & Grant, W.G., 1948 A Stone Age settlement at the Braes of Rinyo, Rousay, Orkney (second report). *Proceedings of the Society of Antiquaries of Scotland*, 81 (1946-7), 16-42.

Clarke, A., 1992 Artefacts of coarse stone from Neolithic Orkney. In Sharples & Sheridan (eds), 44-58.

Clarke, D.V., 1976 The Neolithic village at Skara Brae, Orkney. Excavations 1972-73: an interim report. Edinburgh: National Museum of Antiquities of Scotland.

Clarke, D.V. & Sharples, N., 1985 Settlements and subsistence in the 3rd Millennium BC. In Renfrew, C. (ed.) *The Prehistory of Orkney*, 54-82. Edinburgh: Edinburgh University Press.

Cleal, R., 1999 Introduction. The what, where and why of Grooved Ware. In Cleal, R. & MacSween, A. (eds), *Grooved Ware in Britain and Ireland*, 1-8. Oxford: Oxbow.

Covey, C. (trans.), 1983 *Cabeza de Vaca's Adventures in the Unknown Interior of America*. Albuquerque, N.M: University of New Mexico Press.

Craddock, P., 1995 *Early Metal Mining and Production*. Edinburgh; Edinburgh University Press.

Cross, S.H. (trans.), 1930 *The Russian Primary Chronicle*. Cambridge, Mass.: Medieval Academy.

Davidson, J.L. & Henshall, A.S., 1989 *The Chambered Tombs of Orkney*. Edinburgh: Edinburgh University Press.

Driehaus, J., 1960 *Die Altheimer Gruppe und das Jungneolithikum in Mitteleuropa*. Mainz: Römisch-Germanisches Zentralmuseum zu Mainz.

Dronfield, J., 1995a Subjective vision and the source of Irish megalithic art. *Antiquity*, 69, 539-49.

Dronfield, J., 1995b Migraine, light and hallucinogens: the neurocognitive basis of Irish megalithic art. *Oxford Journal of Archaeology*, 14, 261-75.

Dronfield, J., 1996 The vision thing: diagnosis of endogenous derivation in 'abstract' arts. *Current Anthropology*, 37, 373–90.

Dutton, L.A., 1990 Surface remains of early mining on the Great Orme. In Crew, P. & S. (eds), *Early Mining in the British Isles*, 11–14. Plas Tan y Bwlch: Snowdonia National Park.

Ellis, L., 1984 *The Cucuteni-Tripolye Culture*. BAR International Series 217. Oxford: British Archaeological Reports.

Eogan, G., 1984 *Excavations at Knowth, vol. 1: Smaller Passage Tombs, Neolithic Occupation and Beaker Activity*. Dublin: Royal Irish Academy.

Eogan, G., 1986 *Knowth and the Passage Tombs of Ireland*. London: Thames and Hudson.

Eogan, G., 1998 Knowth before Knowth. *Antiquity*, 72, 162–72.

Eogan, G., 1999 Megalithic art and society. *Proceedings of the Prehistoric Society*, 65, 415–46.

Eogan, G. & Roche, H., 1999 Grooved Ware from Brugh na Bóinne and its wider context. In Cleal, R. & MacSween, A. (eds), *Grooved Ware in Britain and Ireland*, 98–111. Oxford: Oxbow.

Forde-Johnson, J.L., 1957 Megalithic art in the north-west of Britain: the Calderstones, Liverpool. *Proceedings of the Prehistoric Society*, 23, 20–39.

Frodsham, P., 1996 Spirals in Time: Morwick Hill and the Spiral Motif in the British Isles. In Frodsham, P. (ed.) *Neolithic Studies in No-Man's Land. Papers on the Neolithic of Northern England from the Trent to the Tweed. Northern Archaeology* 13/14, 101–38. Newcastle: Northern Archaeology Group.

Gallay, G. & Spindler, K., 1972, Le Petit-Chasseur. Problèmes Chronologique et culturels. *Helvetica Antigua*, 10-11, 62–88.

Gimbutas, M. 1974. *The Gods and Goddesses of Old Europe, 6500-3500BC. Myths and Cult Images*. London: Thames & Hudson.

Gimbutas, M., 1976 Ideograms and symbolic design on ritual objects of Old Europe (Neolithic and Chalcolithic South-east Europe). In Megaw, J.V.S. (ed.) *To Illustrate the Monuments. Essays on Archaeology presented to Stuart Piggott on the Occasion of his Sixty-fifth Birthday*, 77-98. London: Thames & Hudson.

Grimes, W.F., 1951 *The Prehistory of Wales*. Cardiff: National Museum of Wales.

Grygiel, R. & Bogucki, P., 1997 Early Farmers in North-Central Europe: 1989-1994 Excavations at Osłonki, Poland. *Journal of Field Archaeology*, 24, 161–78.

Harding, A.F. with Lee, G.E., 1987 *Henge Monuments and Related Sites of Great Britain. Air Photographic Evidence and Catalogue*. BAR British Series 175. Oxford: British Archaeological Reports.

Hawkes, C.F.C., 1975 *Pytheas: Europe and the Greek Explorers*. Oxford: Blackwell.

Herdits, H., 2003 Bronze Age smelting site in the Mitterberg mining area in Austria. In Craddock, P. & Lang, J. (eds), *Mining and Metal Production Through The Ages*, 69-75. London: British Museum Press.

Hunter, J.R. & MacSween, A., 1991 A Sequence for the Orcadian Neolithic? *Antiquity*, 65, 911–14.

Isbister, A., 2000 The Neolithic Fair, Skaill House, Sandwick: burnished haematite and pigment production. In Ritchie, A. (ed.) 191-5.

James, L., 1998 *The Rise and Fall of the British Empire*. London: Abacus.

Jaźdźewski, K., 1938 Die Gräberfelder der Bandkeramischen Kultur und die mit ihnen verbundenen Siedlingsgruppen in Breść Kujawski Kr. Włoclawek. *Wiadomości Archaeologi*, 15, 1–105.

Johnson, M., 1999 Chronology of Greece and South-east Europe in the Final Neolithic and Early Bronze Age. *Proceedings of the Prehistoric Society*, 65, 319–36.

Jones, A., 2000 Life after death: monuments, material culture and social change in Neolithic Orkney. In Ritchie, A. (ed.), 127–38.

Kinnes, I.A., 1995 An Innovation Backed by Great Prestige: the Instance of the Spiral and Twenty Centuries of Stony Sleep. In Kinnes, I. & Varndell, G. (eds), *Unbaked Urns of Rudely Shape. Essays on British and Irish Pottery for Ian Longworth*, 49-54. Oxford: Oxbow.

Last, J., 1996 Neolithic houses – A central European perspective. In Darvill, T. & Thomas, J. (eds), *Neolithic Houses in Northwest Europe and Beyond. Neolithic Studies Group Seminar Papers 1*, 27-40. Oxford: Oxbow.

Lewis-Williams, J.D. & Dowson, T.A., 1988 The signs of all times: entoptic phenomena in Upper Palaeolithic art. *Current Anthropology*, 29, 201-46.

Lewis-Williams, J.D. & Dowson, T.A., 1993 On vision and power in the Neolithic: evidence from the decorated monuments. *Current Anthropology*, 34, 55-65.

Lichardus, J. & Lichardus-Itten, M., 1985 *La Protohistoire de l'Europe*. Paris.

Loveday, R., forthcoming. From ritual to riches – the route to individual power in later Neolithic eastern Yorkshire? In Barclay, G. & Brophy, K. (eds), *Regional Neolithics of the British Isles*.

MacSween, A., 1992 Orcadian Grooved Ware. In Sharples & Sheridan (eds), 259-71.

MacSween, A., 1995 Grooved Ware from Scotland: aspects of decoration. In Kinnes, I. & Varndell, G. (eds), *'Unbaked Urns of Rudely Shape', Essays on British and Irish Pottery for Ian Longworth*, 41-8. Oxford: Oxbow.

Marshall, D.N., 1977 Carved stone balls. *Proceedings of the Society of Antiquaries of Scotland*, 108 (1976-7), 40-72.

Mayer, E.F., 1977 *Die Äxte und Beile in Österreich*. Prähistorische Bronzefunde Abteilung IX, 9. München: Beck'sche.

McMann, J., 1994 Forms of power: dimensions of an Irish megalithic landscape. *Antiquity*, 68, 525-44.

Midgeley, M.S., 1982 *TRB Culture. The First Farmers of the North European Plain*. Edinburgh: Edinburgh University Press.

Müller, D., 1997 Ornamente, Symbole, Bilder – zum megalithischen Totenbrauchten in Mitteldeutschland. In L'Helgouac'h, J., Le Roux, C-T. & Lecornec, J. (eds), *Art et Symboles du Mégalithisme Européen. Revue Archéologique de l' Ouest Supplément 8*, 163-76.

Mykura, W., 1976 *British Regional Geology. Orkney and Shetland*. Edinburgh: HMSO.

Novotná, M., 1970 *Die Äxte und Beile in Slowakei* Prähistorische Bronzefunde Abteilung IX, 3. München: Beck'sche.

O'Brien, W., Ixer, R. & O'Sullivan, M., 1990 Copper resources in Prehistory: an Irish perspective. In Crew, P. & S. (eds), *Early Mining in the British Isles*, 30-5. Plas Tan y Bwlch: Snowdonia National Park.

O'Kelly, M.J., 1982 *Archaeology, Art and Legend*. London: Thames and Hudson.

O'Kelly, M.J. & O'Kelly, C., 1983 The tumulus of Dowth. *Proceedings of the Royal Irish Academy*, 83C, 135-90.

O'Sullivan, M., 1997 Megalithic art in Ireland and Brittany. Divergence or convergence? In L'Helgouac'h, J., Le Roux, C-T. & Lecornec, J. *Art et Symboles du Mégalithisme Européen. Revue Archéologique de l' Ouest Supplément 8*, 81-96.

Ottaway, B., 1973 The earliest copper ornaments in Northern Europe. *Proceedings of the Prehistoric Society*, 39, 294-323.

Pickin, J., 1990 Stone tools and early metal mining in England and Wales. In Crew, P. & S. (eds), *Early Mining in the British Isles*, 39-42. Plas Tan y Bwlch: Snowdonia National Park.

Piggott, S., 1954 *Neolithic Cultures of the British Isles*. Cambridge: Cambridge University Press.

Randsborg, K., 1979 Resources, distribution and the function of copper in Early Neolithic Denmark. In Ryan, M. (ed.) *The Origins of Metallurgy in Atlantic Europe. Proceedings of the 5th Atlantic Colloquium*, 303-18.

Renfrew, C., 2000 The Auld Hoose speaks: society and life in stone age Orkney. In A. Ritchie (ed.) *Neolithic Orkney in its European Context*, 1-22. Cambridge: McDonald Institute for Archaeological Research.

Richards, C., 1998 Centralising tendencies? A re-examination of social evolution in Late Neolithic Orkney. In Edmonds, M. & Richards, C. (eds), *Understanding the Neolithic of North Western Europe*, 516-32, Glasgow: Cruithne Press.

Richardson, J.B., 1974 *Metal Mining: Industrial Archaeology, 12.* London: Allen Lane.

Ritchie, A., 1995 *Prehistoric Orkney.* London: Batsford/Historic Scotland.

Ritchie, A., (ed.) 2000 *Neolithic Orkney in its European Context.* Cambridge: McDonald Institute for Archaeological Research.

Ronne, P., 1989 Early Bronze Age spiral ornament – the technical background. *Journal of Danish Archaeology*, 8, 126-43.

Russell, M., 2002 *Monuments of the British Neolithic. The Roots of Architecture.* Stroud: Tempus.

Schlabow, K., 1959 Beiträge zur Erforschung der jungsteinzeitlichen und bronzezeitlichen Gewebetechnik Mitteldeutschlands. *Jahresschrift für Mitteldeutsche Vorgeschichte*, 43, 101-20.

Sharples, N.M., 1984 Excavations at Pierowall Quarry, Westray, Orkney. *Proceedings of the Society of Antiquaries of Scotland*, 114, 75-125.

Sharples, N.M. & Sheridan, J.A. (eds), 1992 *Vessels for the Ancestors. Essays in Honour of Audrey Henshall.* Edinburgh: Edinburgh University Press.

Shee Twohig, E., 1981 *The Megalithic Art of Western Europe.* Oxford: Oxford University Press.

Shepherd, A., 2000 Skara Brae: expressing identity in a Neolithic community. In Ritchie, A. (ed.) 139-58.

Simpson, D.D.A., 1971 Beaker houses and settlements in Britain. In Simpson, D.D.A. (ed.) *Economy and Settlement in Neolithic and Early Bronze Age Britain and Europe*, 131-52. Leicester: Leicester University Press.

Simpson, D.D.A., 1988 The stone maceheads of Ireland. *Journal of the Royal Society of Antiquaries of Ireland*, 118, 27-52.

Simpson, D.D.A., 1996 'Crown' antler maceheads and the Later Neolithic in Britain. *Proceedings of the Prehistoric Society*, 62, 293-310.

Simpson, D.D.A. & Ransom, R., 1992 Maceheads and the Orcadian Neolithic. In Sharples, N. & Sheridan, A. (eds), 221-4.

Stout, G., 1991 Embanked enclosures of the Boyne region. *Proceedings of the Royal Irish Academy*, 91, 245-84.

Thorburn, J., 1990 Stone tools and early mining in England and Wales. In Crew, P. &. S. (eds), *Early Mining in the British Isles*, 43-5. Plas Tan y Bwlch: Snowdonia National Park.

Thorpe, I.J. & Richards C., 1984 The decline of ritual authority and the introduction of Beakers into Britain. In Bradley, R. & Gardiner, J. (eds), *Neolithic Studies. A Review of some Recent Research*, 67-84. BAR British Series 133. Oxford: British Archaeological Reports.

Tylecote, R.F., 1987 *The Early History of Metallurgy in Europe.* London: Longmans.

Vandekilde, H., 1996 *From Stone to Bronze: The Metalwork of the Late Neolithic and Early Bronze Age in Denmark.* Aarhus: Jutland Archaeological Society Publications xxxii.

Wainwright, G.J. & Longworth, I.H., 1971 *Durrington Walls: Excavations 1966-1968.* London: Society of Antiquaries.

Whittle, A., 1988 *Problems in Neolithic Archaeology.* Cambridge: Cambridge University Press.

Whittle, A., 1996 *Europe in the Neolithic. The Creation of New Worlds.* Cambridge: Cambridge University Press.

10

Hostilities in Early Neolithic Ireland:

Trouble with the New Neighbours – The Evidence from Ballyharry, County Antrim

Dermot G. Moore

Introduction

This paper on a rather overlooked aspect of Irish Neolithic archaeology is my small tribute to Derek Simpson, whom I have known for almost 20 years, first as a student and then as a colleague and friend. Derek's encyclopaedic knowledge and understanding of all aspects of Irish and British prehistory has constantly been a source of inspiration for me and in many ways, I am still his student. Unfortunately, Derek, we do not know who exactly the cowboys and indians were but we do have the bow and arrow.

The excavation of the substantial Early Neolithic rectangular house structure in Ballyharry townland on Islandmagee in County Antrim and the excavation of an enclosed Neolithic settlement at Thornhill, County Derry (*51*) has provided a significant degree of evidence for conflict during the Neolithic in Ireland. Prior to this, with the exception of some human skeletal remains, one with a blunt trauma to the head and one with a chert arrowhead tip embedded in the pelvis at Poulnabrone (Lynch & O'Donnabháin 1994) and another blunt trauma to an adult male skull from a Linkardstown burial in Carlow (Raftery 1944), there is little direct evidence for human aggression in the Irish Neolithic. It would appear from the analysis of human remains that in comparison to the rest of Britain and Europe, Ireland during the Neolithic was a relatively peaceful place.

Several theories regarding the nature of the settlement and general domestic activities of the first agriculturists in the Early Neolithic have now been put forward (Cooney & Grogan 1994; Cooney 2000). What we have at present is a series of dispersed settlements, some as single structures as at Ballynagilly, County Tyrone (ApSimon 1976) and Newtown, County Meath (Halpin 1995) and grouped structures such as Ballygalley, County Antrim (Moore & Simpson forthcoming), Thornhill, County Derry (Logue 2003) and Corbally, County Kildare (Purcell 2002; Tobin 2003). The initial impression one gets from the description of these excavated rectangular houses and their associated artefactual remains is of a settlement where conflict had no impact. That was the general assumption prior to the excavation of Ballyharry House 1.

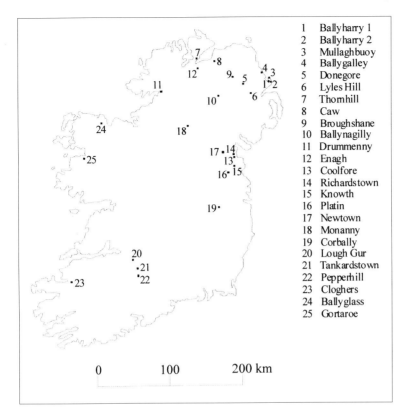

1	Ballyharry 1
2	Ballyharry 2
3	Mullaghbuoy
4	Ballygalley
5	Donegore
6	Lyles Hill
7	Thornhill
8	Caw
9	Broughshane
10	Ballynagilly
11	Drummenny
12	Enagh
13	Coolfore
14	Richardstown
15	Knowth
16	Platin
17	Newtown
18	Monanny
19	Corbally
20	Lough Gur
21	Tankardstown
22	Pepperhill
23	Cloghers
24	Ballyglass
25	Gortaroe

0   100   200 km

51 Location map of sites mentioned in Chapter 10

THE EVIDENCE FROM BALLYHARRY

Although all the Early Neolithic houses were eventually abandoned, House 1 at Ballyharry underwent a series of distinct periods of activity prior to final abandonment. It is one of the periods of activity prior to abandonment that primarily concerns us here.

The site under discussion (Ballyharry House 1) was excavated in the townland of Ballyharry on Islandmagee in 1996 (Moore 1999; 2003) as part of a series of rescue excavations on the gas pipeline route from Ballylumford on Islandmagee to Trooperslane, near Carrickfergus, County Antrim. The site, which was located at *c*.120m OD, consisted of a succession of different structural phases and associated occupation deposits. The first phase was a sub-rectangular post-built structure with only a small quantity of artefactual material. The second phase was the rectangular plank-built structure with a later annex on its northern gable enclosing a hearth pit and an associated ancillary structure further to the north. A large quantity of lithic material was recovered such as scrapers, axes and knives.

During or immediately following this phase, the site seems to have been attacked as indicated by a substantial portion of the main rectangular structure (enclosing the living space) having been subjected to intense burning and a profusion of projectile points several of which were broken and some burnt

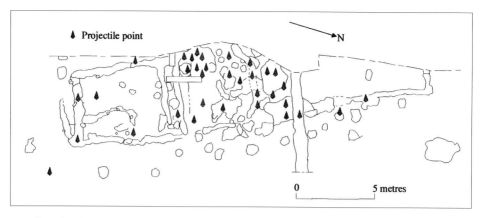

52 Plan of Ballyharry House 1 showing *in situ* burnt planks and posts and projectile distribution

(52). The next phase was one of reconstruction with a ritual element – the deposition of a perfect laurel leaf arrowhead in the central post-hole of the western foundation trench and the deposition of a perfect basaltic axe in the corresponding central post-hole in the eastern foundation trench. Both these artefacts had been placed upright in each of the post-holes with the point of the projectile and axe blade edge pointing downwards.

The last phase of activity was defined by a series of large shallow pits which contained a wide range of flint and stone tools and a large amount of pottery. These features also contained exotic stone such as polished flakes of Group VI axes. The construction and occupation activity appears to have ceased around 3700–3600 BC.

A notable aspect of the material remains from the house was the presence of a large amount of pottery (1,201 sherds). Preliminary analysis by Helen Roche (pers. comm.) suggests that two types are represented: undecorated, round-based shouldered bowls of the Dunmurry-Ballymarlagh style and plain unshouldered bowls. In addition to the pottery and lithic remains, a large amount of charred cereal remains (predominantly wheat with some barley) and wild plant seeds were recovered from all phases along with quernstones, rubbers and a broken ard point. The presence of burnt animal bone shows that a mixed agricultural economy was being undertaken on Islandmagee during the Early Neolithic.

So what is the nature of the evidence from Ballyharry House 1? Firstly, the primary evidence of a period of aggression was the uncovering of the *in situ* remains of completely charred wooden planks and posts and scorched packing stones within the main foundation trenches of the house. Re-fired pottery and burnt flint also attest to a severe conflagration. Analysis of the cereal and seed remains by Brenda Collins show that many were severely heat blistered and deformed, indicating severe heat stress (Collins pers. comm.).

Secondly, the large number of projectile points – 34 in total, making up over 13% of the secondary worked assemblage *(Table 3)* – found in close

	total	percentage
Ret. Flake	82	32.03
Ret. Blade	24	9.38
G.P. Scraper	26	10.16
End Scraper	22	8.6
End + 1	8	3.13
End + 2	6	2.34
Double End	1	0.39
End of Blade	3	1.17
Sidescraper	21	8.2
Knife	22	8.59
Projectile	34	13.28
Axe	4	1.56
Notched Sc.	1	0.39
Hollow Sc.	1	0.39
Borer	1	0.39
TOTAL	256	100

Table 3 Secondary worked flint from Ballyharry House 1

proximity to the main area of burning also confirms that the house was the subject of an attack. The large number of projectiles associated with the areas of burning and charring shown on *(52)* are quite conclusive evidence for a period of instability and hostility in this area of Antrim. The projectiles centre on the area of the northern wall-slot and the annex and apparently show that the northern side of the house was the particular focus of the attack.

The projectiles recovered from the site were of varying condition and manufacture. With the exception of the laurel leaf in a votive deposit, only six projectiles were complete and of these only two could be classed as fine quality. The type of projectiles recovered from the excavation was predominantly leaf-shaped arrowheads with a number of larger laurel leaf points *(Table 4)*. Six of the projectiles were partially or totally burnt/calcined. One example was completely porcellanised (burnt white) indicating it had been exposed to temperatures between 800°C and 1,000°C. Over 2kg of burnt flint were recovered from the excavated area especially in the main area of burning.

Arrowhead manufacture and reworking was also evidenced on the site by the presence of fine pressure flaking micro-debitage associated with the tip of a leaf arrowhead and laurel leaf trimming flakes. The occurrence of leaf, lozenge and the laurel leaf forms on the same site also shows that these forms were contemporaneous with each other.

EVIDENCE FROM OTHER IRISH NEOLITHIC RECTANGULAR HOUSES

There are now (in late 2003) some 36 Early Neolithic rectangular house structures in Ireland *(51, Table 5)*. The number has been growing almost every month since the publication of Grogan's (1996) list of houses. In many cases, the

Phase	Projectile	Description
1	2	1 tip of kite and 1 portion of laurel leaf
2	4	1 tip of leaf, 3 butt-ends of laurel leaves (1 burnt)
3	3	1 perfect leaf, 1 tip and 1 laurel with tip missing
4	13	5 leaf tips, 2 laurel tips, 2 laurel butts, 1 leaf (burnt), 1 laurel leaf, 2 laurel roughouts
Context 2	10	2 leaf mid sections, 1 burnt lozenge mid section, 1 leaf roughout, 6 laurel roughouts
Topsoil	2	1 leaf (burnt) and 1 javelin tip

Table 4 Projectile numbers from Ballyharry 1 structural phases

evidence (burnt posts, planks and wattle) would suggest that destruction or partial destruction by fire was an everyday hazard with wooden structures and hearths in close proximity to each other. Unfortunately it cannot be shown whether the burning was by accident or by design. From *Table 5* it can be seen that the only definite evidence for hostile acts (in the form of large quantities of projectile points and burnt structural remains) is that from Ballyharry 1 and Thornhill.

The site of Thornhill, excavated by Paul Logue (Logue 2003), has produced probably the best evidence from Ireland of a site that had been attacked. Here there is evidence of the enclosing palisade having been under threat from a group of archers who burnt down part of it and one of the rectangular houses inside. A range of projectiles, predominantly in the form of leaf arrowheads, were recovered in and around the outer palisade. The initial interpretation was that there was a hail of arrows fired at and over the palisade and that the attackers used poor quality projectiles possibly because they were being used as fire arrows (Logue pers. comm.). What is of note is that the palisade appears to have been rebuilt suggesting that the defenders won the battle. On Islandmagee, located approximately 200m to the south-west of Ballyharry House 1 was Ballyharry House 2, situated at a height of *c*.110m OD. Only a small portion of the site was excavated and this uncovered the gable end of a rectangular structure with deep foundation trenches and the preserved remains of charcoal-filled post-pipes. A small number of finds were recovered from the site with the majority of the pottery and lithic material being recovered from an area of occupation just east of the structure. Further north on Islandmagee, the site of Mullaghbuoy, excavated by Ciara MacManus, produced the remains of a substantial rectangular Neolithic house measuring 23m in length with two phases of occupation which also exhibited areas of intense burning. These were defined by *in situ* posts and planks (MacManus pers. comm.). A single laurel leaf point and a crude leaf projectile roughout were recovered in association with a large amount of knapping debris.

At Croft Manor, Ballygalley (Simpson 1996; Moore & Simpson forthcoming), three rectangular houses were excavated. The material remains from the houses were rather paltry with only a small amount of pottery and lithic material directly associated with slots and post-holes. The evidence from the three houses indicates that they were dismantled and the slots either deliberately filled in, as was the case for Houses 1 and 3, or allowed to silt up as in House 2. A total of 82 projectile points were recovered from the whole excavation comprising leaf, lozenge and kite-shaped varieties as well as javelins of Collins' classes A-C (Collins 1981). Of the leaf arrowheads, one was recovered from the annex slot of House 1 and one was recovered from House 2, in the fill of one of the central supporting post-holes. Eighty of the projectiles were associated with occupation deposits overlying the houses. After the dismantling of the houses the site continued to be occupied. This continued

Site	County	Abandonment condition	Projectiles in association with structure	Pottery	Ritual deposition
Ballygalley 1	Antrim	dismantled	1 perfect leaf (flint) from annex slot	W. Neo	projectile
Ballygalley 2	Antrim	dismantled	1 leaf (flint) from internal posthole	W. Neo	projectile
Ballygalley 3	Antrim	dismantled	n/a	W. Neo	
Ballyglass	Mayo	dismantled	leaf arrowheads	W. Neo	
Ballyharry 1	Antrim	burnt or attacked	34 leaf, lozenge and laurel leaf (flint) from various locations	W. Neo	axe, projectile
Ballyharry 2	Antrim	burnt	2 leaf (flint)	W. Neo	
Ballynagilly	Tyrone	burnt	9 (flint) (3 within house; 3 just outside; and 3 others	W. Neo	
Broughshane	Antrim	partially burnt	n/a	W. Neo	
Caw	Derry	dismantled	n/a	W. Neo	
Cloghers	Kerry	burnt	1 leaf (flint)	W. Neo	
Coolfore 1	Louth	unfinished	none	W. Neo	
Coolfore 2	Louth	burnt	1 lozenge (chert)	W. Neo	
Corbally 1	Kildare	dismantled	3 leaf-shaped (flint)	W. Neo	
Corbally 2	Kildare	burnt or demolished	1 leaf-shaped (flint)	W. Neo	
Corbally 3	Kildare	dismantled	1 leaf-shaped (flint)	W. Neo	
Corbally 4	Kildare	partially burnt	n/a	W. Neo	axe
Corbally 5	Kildare	partially burnt	n/a	W. Neo	
Corbally 6	Kildare	partially burnt	n/a	W. Neo	
Corbally 7	Kildare	partially burnt	n/a	W. Neo	
Drummenny	Donegal	partially burnt	1 leaf-shaped (flint)	W. Neo	
Enagh	Derry	burnt	none	W. Neo	
Gortaroe	Mayo	burnt	1 javelin (flint)	W. Neo	
Knowth 2	Meath	dismantled	none	W. Neo	
Lough Gur Site A	Limerick	partially burnt	1 leaf (chert)	W. Neo	
Monanny 1	Monaghan	partially burnt	none	W. Neo	
Monanny 2	Monaghan	dismantled	none	W. Neo	
Monanny 3	Monaghan	burnt	none	W. Neo	
Mullaghbuoy	Antrim	burnt	2 leaf, and javelin (flint)	W. Neo	
Newtown	Meath	partially burnt or dismantled	1 leaf-shaped (chert) from slot posthole	W. Neo	
Pepperhill	Cork	partially burnt	none	W. Neo	
Platin	Meath	partially burnt?	n/a	W. Neo	
Richardstown	Louth	partially burnt	n/a	W. Neo	
Tankardstown 1	Limerick	burnt	1 leaf-shaped (flint)	W. Neo	
Tankardstown 2	Limerick	burnt	none	W. Neo	
Thornhill A	Derry	burnt or attacked	1 lozenge (flint)	W. Neo	
Thornhill B	Derry	burnt or attacked	1 lozenge (flint) and 1 burnt tip	W. Neo	
Thornhill D	Derry	burnt or attacked	none	W. Neo	
Thornhill E	Derry	burnt	1 leaf (flint)	W. Neo	

Table 5 List of Irish rectangular Neolithic house structures

use was attested by an increase in occupation activity but with no structures. The occupation activity included an increase in animal husbandry shown by the large quantity of cattle, pig and some ovacaprid teeth (the only animal remains that survived in the soil). Cereal cultivation also continued but appears to have been of lesser importance *(Table 5)*.

At Corbally, County Kildare (Purcell 2002; Tobin 2003), where there are now seven structures, there was a mixture of activities during the final stages of the settlement. Some houses were burnt, others partially burnt and some were dismantled. Of note was the excavation of House 4 which had a mudstone axe set into the foundation trench with its blade edge pointing upwards (Tobin 2003, 33).

The three rectangular houses excavated by Fintan Walsh on the edge of a small river in Monanny townland in County Monaghan in 2003 also show the disparity of grouped Neolithic settlement. Here, the smallest of the three structures was only partially burnt; the second was abandoned with no evidence of burning; and the third was totally destroyed by burning (Walsh pers. comm.). The lithic assemblage was paltry with no projectiles and only one polished stone axe being recovered from any of the structures or surrounding area. At Coolfore, County Louth, one of the houses was burnt and the other left unfinished (O'Drisceoil 2003).

The evidence from single rectangular structures such as Drummenny Lower, County Donegal (Dunne 2003), Broughshane, County Antrim (McConway pers. comm.), Cloghers, County Kerry (Dunne & Kiely 2003), and Ballynagilly, County Tyrone (ApSimon 1976) also provide evidence of destruction or partial destruction by fire. However, these all appear to have been abandoned after the conflagration. Some structures appear to have had only a temporary occupation such as Platin, County Meath (Moore 2001), Enagh, County Derry (McSparran 2003), Gortaroe, County Mayo (Gillespie 2002, 7) and Richardstown, County Louth (Byrnes 1999, 33).

Although no rectangular structures were uncovered, the evidence from Donegore Hill (Mallory & Hartwell 1984) and Lyles Hill (Evans 1953; Simpson & Gibson 1989) shows that large-scale defences (banks, ditches and palisades) were being constructed in south Antrim during this period. Unfortunately we cannot determine the precise relationship between these two hilltop enclosures but Donegore may also have been attacked as shown by the small concentration of leaf arrowheads near the possible western entrance.

From the available excavated material, we have much contradictory evidence regarding the activity during the final days of occupation of these settlements. Sites which have more than one structure have also produced evidence of burning in one and dismantlement in others. Could this contradictory evidence be a result of conflict? In the absence of human remains with trauma injuries on these domestic sites we have to look at the material remains for evidence of violent activity.

WEAPONS OF CHOICE

The Neolithic is dominated by a range of projectile points, most notably the leaf-shaped arrowhead. Unfortunately, there is very little evidence in Ireland of the bows used to shoot the arrows; a bow fragment from Drumwhinny in County Fermanagh was found to be of Bronze Age date (Glover 1979). The leaf arrowheads are by far the most distinctive and homogenous implement type of the whole of the Neolithic not just by their shape but by their method of manufacture (Green 1980, 149). The large number of a range of projectiles, in particular leaf arrowheads, at Ballyharry can be compared with other settlement sites such as Thornhill (Logue 2003).

Positive evidence for conflict can be found at a number of English sites such as Carn Brea, Cornwall (Mercer 1981), Hambledon Hill, Dorset (Mercer 1980) and Crickley Hill, Gloucestershire (Dixon 1989). All have the defensive architecture (ditches etc), large numbers of projectiles, areas and episodes of intense burning and destruction, and in some cases human remains showing combat wounds. From this it would seem that in the Early Neolithic, the bow and arrow appears to be the weapon of choice for any offensive undertaking. This is comparable to the evidence from sites on the continent (Clark 1963). However, there are problems with the archaeological visibility of the weapons of early prehistoric warfare. The bow and arrow have been perceived as a non-specialised weapon in that 'their use can only be detected by their effects on human skeletal remains' (Vencl 1999, 65). Polished stone axes and knives fall into this category of non-specialised weapons or 'tool-weapons' (Vencl 1984). However, Chapman (1999, 108) in the same volume mentions that although a single tool-weapon cannot support the idea of warfare a large number in a localised area could. One thing is certain: the bow and arrow, like the gun, is designed for one thing only and that is to kill humans and animals.

The evidence for other offensive weapons is scant or non-existent. The use of axes and knives as offensive weapons has yet to be proved. The evidence of blunt trauma on a number of skeletal remains such as that from Poulnabrone is more than circumstantial but this could have been caused by a club or even a suitably sized rock. At Ballyharry, a number of flint axes and porcellanite axes were recovered. The two polished flint axes had damage to their blade edges and were broken at their haft points suggesting breakage through use. However, these breakages may have resulted from tree felling or for that matter any number of uses. Their occurrence on sites in association with projectiles does lend weight to the possibility of them being used as weapons. A number of flint knives were also recovered from Ballyharry but their use as weapons would be very difficult to prove.

One rather overlooked tool of aggression is that of fire. It is the one common element in the destruction of Early Neolithic rectangular houses.

Fire would have been a very powerful weapon with attackers using brushwood torches to set houses alight. However, to deliver fire safely to an opponent's position, distance would be needed, and for that, the bow and arrow would have been ideal.

THE METHOD OF AGGRESSION

From the evidence of the sites mentioned above, we can say that at least two sites in Ireland were attacked with people shooting arrows from bows. What we cannot say with any certainty is how long the attacks lasted or the methods by which these were orchestrated. At Ballyharry House 1 (as at Thornhill), the act of aggression may have lasted only a few minutes but there also may have been several acts possibly over a very short period of time. It is likely that when an attack occurred, and there is no reason to suspect otherwise, it was probably by a group of archers from a distance of less than 50m. Arrow fusillades have certainly more impact than one single archer even with a grudge. Having experimented using replica Neolithic bows with leaf arrowheads, I (and other modern archers) have found that for consistent accurate shooting one has to be as close as 25m to the target (Moore in prep.). However, if the target is large enough (and a barn door comes to mind), this distance can be doubled or trebled.

If a group of archers attacked Ballyharry then it is possible that there was a plan of attack. There is evidence for what appear to be plans of attack by archers (during the Neolithic) from cave paintings in southern Spain such as Les Dogues (Guilaine & Zammit 1998, 170, fig. 36). Such episodes may have been very short-lived. Analysing the material remains alone cannot give an accurate view of what really happened. The location of the projectiles (both of defenders and attackers) and the subsequent rebuilding phase makes the suggestion of who won a matter of conjecture but the presence of votive objects and continued manufacture of projectiles do suggest that the defenders won the day. The rebuilding phase at Thornhill would also suggest that the defenders prevailed over their attackers.

CAUSES OF INTERNECINE STRIFE

Defining the causes of conflict in early prehistoric society is difficult with the limited evidence we have available. It is even more difficult to define the causes of conflict at Ballyharry and Thornhill when these are presently the only two sites in Ireland which do exhibit material evidence of attack.

Chapman (1999, 140) defines three principal contexts for the probability of conflict. In the Early to Middle Neolithic these could be frontier contexts with new people entering already established settled zones (new settlers infilling niches in a settled landscape); differential distribution of resources where such resources (arable or pastoral or hard resources such as flint and porcellanite) could provoke raiding to acquire such wealth from already settled and richer communities; and cultural factors such as the emergence of a more hierarchical society where it was found necessary to subjugate others and accumulate wealth. At Ballyharry and Thornhill, the attackers could have been either new settlers or raiders who were looking to expand their influence that did the attacking or some other group of original settlers who due to pressure on resources were forced to attack other settlements for booty. There is no evidence that it was the indigenous hunter-gatherers of the Later Mesolithic who attacked these sites. The booty may have been food, raw material resources or people. It also may have simply been to show their hegemony in a particular area and over a particular group of people. If it was a simple act of raiding, why were the other Early Neolithic houses burnt or dismantled during this period? The evidence from Ballyharry may indicate raiding, but in conjunction with the evidence from other houses this hypothesis does not hold up. Raiding would have to have been a widespread and organised phenomenon and this cannot be seen from the excavated evidence.

Change did occur, but unfortunately from the evidence it cannot be said whether this was from within or without. There is no evidence in Ireland that there was any significant environmental change to cause a breakdown in the old order with the possible resultant consequence of conflict. We are therefore left with the possibility of new peoples entering already settled areas of Ireland and that these brought with them a reliance on a pastoral economy. At Croft Manor, Ballygalley where there was no evidence of conflict, there is a dramatic increase in the evidence for animal husbandry in association with an increase of new pottery styles and the appearance of exotic goods. The move to – or the importation of – a pastoral economy may also suggest a possible reason for the appearance of the large leaf points and javelins (Woodman 1994; Moore 1999). If the economy was based around domesticated livestock then the use of the small leaf arrowhead would become redundant as hunting would have played a lesser role.

At this time we also see the introduction of additions to the ceramic and lithic repertoire. In particular hollow scrapers and javelins appear in association with modified forms of the earlier undecorated pottery and new highly decorated pottery. The new settlers may have created pressure on the available land and this may have resulted in conflict. Court tombs cease to be constructed (although they were still being used) at this time suggesting that the colonists had new ideas about territoriality. The widespread acts of burning, dismantlement and abandonment of the rectangular houses may have been an aspect of low-level skirmishing during this new colonising phase.

So the question is: why do we only have definitive evidence for actual conflict at two sites? Could it be that the locations of both these sites were important focal points? Both overlook major river estuaries/loughs and both are situated on the coast. Although these locations have commanding views over the surrounding areas they cannot have been the only reason for them to be attacked. It is possible that these sites symbolised some form of power and control of resources. Ultimately, it is only with the excavation of more sites like Thornhill that we may get a more coherent picture of the transition from the Early to Later Neolithic.

CONCLUSION

Conflict at the end of the Early Neolithic in Ireland was more than an occasional occurrence than the human remains would have us believe. From the excavated sites, Thornhill and Ballyharry are our best evidence for the sites having been attacked and burnt. Whether this conflict was simply a local aspect in the north of Ireland or part of a widespread phenomenon cannot be stated with certainty. The evidence from the other sites with rectangular houses does suggest a period of upheaval and change around 3700–3600 BC.

The causes of such conflict may have been pressure on land availability and control of resources. In the absence of an environmental event to put pressure on the early farmers it would seem likely that, in some cases, such pressure and change came about by the arrival of new peoples. This possibly occurred first in the north of Ireland where the new arrivals defined their presence at Thornhill and Ballyharry. These new arrivals brought with them a reliance on a pastoral economy with new additions to the ceramic and lithic repertoire and the mental attitude to define and keep what was theirs and to acquire more. They may have started a pattern of clearance resulting in the destruction of the rectangular house form. The period of upheaval appears to have been short-lived and physical attack may have not been necessary in all cases. One does not need to destroy a site or its inhabitants totally to show power or enforce will. The simple act of attacking (and then withdrawing) may have given the preferred outcome such as subservience, obedience and or tribute. This could be seen as the prehistoric version of 'gunboat diplomacy' or in this case arrowhead diplomacy.

The period of stress and conflict may have ended peacefully. The recovery of the votive deposits of a perfect laurel leaf arrowhead and a basalt axe may have signified a symbolic act – that of the burying of weapons, showing that hostilities were at an end and a period of reconstruction could begin. The primary weapon of the attackers was the bow and arrow and this period in the Neolithic represents its zenith as a tool of aggression. The later arrowheads appear not to have been used to kill humans. As Edmonds has noted (Edmonds 1995, 101), the decline of the leaf arrowhead in favour of forms such as the large laurel leaf and javelin may suggest that conflict was not a regular occurrence during the later stages of the Neolithic.

Therefore, the rural idyll previously envisaged for the Early Neolithic in Ireland and in Britain ended in a period of upheaval and in places by violent activity. It is a pity that we do not have better evidence of arrow shafts and feathers which might differentiate between the warring communities. If we did, we could, like John Wayne in the movies, pick up an arrow and say 'Apache'.

ACKNOWLEDGEMENTS

Many thanks are due to all those who freely gave me permission to use unpublished information and gave access to the lithic assemblages from their sites.

BIBLIOGRAPHY

ApSimon, A., 1976 Ballynagilly and the beginning and end of the Irish Neolithic. In de Laet, S.J. (ed.) *Acculturation and Continuity in Atlantic Europe*, 15-38. Bruges: Dissertationes Archaeologicae Gandenses.

Armit, I., Murphy, E., Nelis, E. & Simpson, D. (eds), 2003 *Neolithic Settlement in Ireland and Western Britain*. Oxford: Oxbow.

Byrnes, E., 1999 Recent excavations at Richardstown, County Louth. *Archaeology Ireland*, 13 (4), 33.

Carman, J. & Harding, A. (eds), 1999 *Ancient Warfare*. Stroud: Sutton Publishing Ltd.

Chapman, J., 1999 The origins of warfare in the prehistory of Central and Eastern Europe. In Carman, J. & Harding, A. (eds), 101–42.

Clark, J.G.D., 1963 Neolithic bows from Somerset, England, and the prehistory of archery in north-western Europe. *Proceedings of the Prehistoric Society,* 29, 50-98.

Collins, A.E.P., 1981 The flint javelin heads of Ireland. In Ó Corráin, D. (ed.) *Irish Antiquity*, 111-33. Cork: Tower Books.

Cooney, G., 2000 *Landscapes of Neolithic Ireland*. London: Routledge.

Cooney, G. & Grogan, E., 1994 *Irish Prehistory: A Social Perspective*. Dublin: Wordwell.

Darvill, T.C. & Thomas, J. (eds), 1996, *Neolithic Houses in Northwest Europe and Beyond*. Neolithic Studies Group Seminar Papers 1. Oxbow Monograph 57. Oxford: Oxbow.

Dixon, P., 1989 Crickley Hill. In Burgess, C., Topping, P., Mordant, C. & Maddison, M. (eds), *Enclosures and Defences in the Neolithic of Western Europe*, 75-87. BAR International Series 403. Oxford: British Archaeological Reports.

Dunne, C.M., 2003 Neolithic structure at Drummenny Lower, Co. Donegal: an environmental perspective. In Armit *et al.* (eds), 2003, 164-71.

Dunne, L. & Kiely, J., 2003 A Neolithic house at Cloghers, County Kerry. In Armit *et al.* (eds), 182-7.

Edmonds, M., 1995 *Stone Tools and Society*. London: Batsford.

Evans, E.E., 1953 *Lyles Hill: A Neolithic Site in County Antrim*. Belfast: HMSO.

Gillespie, R., 2002 Neolithic house at Gortaroe, Westport, County Mayo. *Archaeology Ireland*, 16 (1), 7.

Glover, W., 1979 A prehistoric bow fragment from Drumwhinny Bog, Kesh, County Fermanagh. *Proceedings of the Prehistoric Society*, 45, 323-7.

Green, S., 1980 *The Flint Arrowheads of the British Isles (Parts I and II)*. BAR British Series 75. Oxford: British Archaeological Reports.

Grogan, E., 1996 Neolithic houses in Ireland. In Darvill, T. & Thomas, J. (eds), 41-60.

Grogan, E. & Mount, C. (eds), 1995 *Annus Archaeologiae*. Proceedings of the OIA Winter Conference 1993. Dublin: The Office of Public Works.

Guilaine, J. & Zammit, J., 1998 *Le Sentier de la Guerre: Visages de la Violence Prehistorique.* Paris: Sueil.

Halpin, E., 1995 Excavations at Newtown, County Meath. In Grogan, E. & Mount, C. (eds), 45-54.

Logue, P., 2003 Excavations at Thornhill, Co. Londonderry. In Armit, *et al.* (eds), 2003, 149-55.

Lynch, A. & O'Donnabháin, B., 1994 Poulnabrone portal tomb, *The other Clare,* 18, 5-7.

Mallory, J. P. & Hartwell, B., 1984 Donegore. *Current Archaeology,* 8 (9), 271-5.

McSparran, C., 2003 The excavation of a Neolithic house in Enagh townland, County Derry. In Armit *et al.* (eds), 172-5.

Mercer, R., 1980 *Hambledon Hill: A Neolithic Landscape.* Edinburgh: Edinburgh University Press.

Mercer, R., 1981 Excavation at Carn Brea, Illogan, Cornwall, 1970-73. *Cornish Archaeology,* 20, 1-204.

Mercer, R., 1999 The origins of warfare in the British Isles. In Carman, J. & Harding, A. (eds), *Ancient Warfare,* 143-56. Stroud: Sutton Publishing Ltd.

Moore, D.G., 1999 *Analysis of the Lithic Assemblages from Early Prehistoric Sites along the South Antrim Coast.* Unpublished MPhil thesis, Queen's University, Belfast.

Moore, D.G., 2001 Platin. In Bennett, I. (ed.) *Excavations 2001.* Dublin: Stationery Office.

Moore, D.G., 2003 Neolithic houses in Ballyharry townland, Islandmagee, County Antrim. In Armit *et al.* (eds), 156-63.

Moore, D.G., in prep. Delivering the point: archery in the Neolithic of Britain and Ireland

Moore, D.G. & Simpson, D.D.A., forthcoming *Excavations at Croft Manor, Ballygalley, County Antrim.*

Ó Drisceoil, C., 2003 Archaeological excavations of a Neolithic settlement at Coolfore, C. Louth. In Armit *et al.* (eds), 2003, 176-81.

Purcell, A., 2002 Excavation of Three Neolithic Houses at Corbally, County Kildare. *Journal of Irish Archaeology,* 11, 31-76.

Raftery, J., 1944 A Neolithic burial in Co. Carlow. *Journal of the Royal Society of Antiquaries of Ireland,* 74, 61-2.

Simpson, D.D.A. & Gibson, A., 1989 Lyles Hill. *Current Archaeology,* 10 (7), 214-5.

Simpson, D.D.A., 1996 Ballygalley houses, Co. Antrim, Ireland. In Darvill, T. & Thomas, J. (eds), 123-32.

Tobin, R., 2003 Houses, enclosures and kilns – excavations at Corbally, County Kildare. *Archaeology Ireland,* 17(3), 12-14.

Vencl, S., 1984 War and warfare in archaeology. *Journal of Anthropological Archaeology,* 3, 116-32.

Vencl, S., 1999 Stone Age Warfare. In Carman, J. & Harding, A. (eds), *Ancient Warfare,* 57-72. Stroud: Sutton Publishing Ltd.

Woodman, P.C., 1994 Towards a definition of Irish Early Neolithic lithic assemblages. In Ashton &. David (eds), 1994, *Stories in Stone: Proceedings of the Anniversary Conference at St. Hilda's College, Oxford,* 213-18. Lithic Studies Society Monograph 4. London: Lithic Studies Society.

11

Neolithic Flint-Work from the North of Ireland: Some Thoughts on Prominent Tool Types and Their Production

Eiméar Nelis

Introduction

A recent study of the lithic material from Donegore Hill, a causewayed enclosure in County Antrim, explored one of the more prolific assemblages of flint and other stone artefacts relating to the Irish Neolithic (Nelis 1998; 2003a; in press: Mallory *et al.* in press). In the course of the study, an attempt to view the results comparatively with contemporary sites within the region highlighted something of a lacuna in the field of chipped stone assemblage studies in an Irish Neolithic context, and a synthesis of known Neolithic flint-work in the area was lacking. Consequently, a project was devised to look at this area of study, focusing geographically on the north of the island, and aimed at establishing a clearer view of the flint industry during this period.

The project has recently been completed (Nelis 2003b) and, it is hoped, will offer some insight into developments in the primary and secondary flint technologies of the region *(53)*. This paper attempts to offer a brief overview of some of the results of the study, concentrating in this case on some of the particular tool types that we have come to expect within Neolithic flint assemblages (e.g. Woodman 1994), during the Early (4000–3600 BC), Middle (3600–3100 BC) and Late (3100–2500 BC) phases (Sheridan 1995): namely projectiles, hollow scrapers, scrapers and knives, as well as other less well defined tools.

Two-Faced Ambiguity: Bifaces and Arrowheads

Perhaps the most distinctive element of Early Neolithic assemblages in the study area is the strong component of projectiles in settlement contexts, mainly comprising small pressure flaked arrowheads *(54e-g)*, but often including large percussion flaked bifaces *(54a-c)*. The artefacts which fall into these groups often embody a complex array of finished and unfinished tools, which span a continuum from blanks to finished artefacts; a common difficulty, therefore, with the interpretation of such assemblages lies in the feasibility of

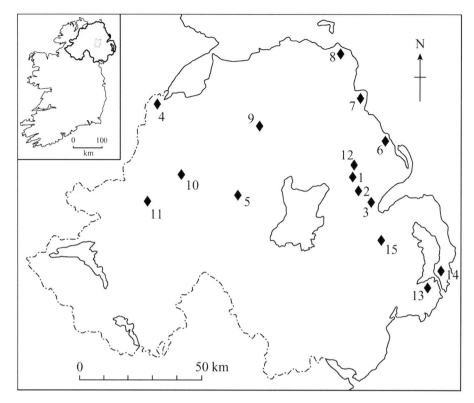

53 Map of north of Ireland, showing nos 1-15: the site location of analysed assemblages mentioned in text. 1 Donegore Hill, County Antrim; 2 Lyles Hill, County Antrim; 3 Squires Hill, County Antrim; 4 Thornhill, County Derry; 5 Ballynagilly, County Tyrone; 6 Ballygalley Hill, County Antrim; 7 Windy Ridge, County Antrim; 8 Goodland, County Antrim; 9 Tamnyrankin West, County Derry; 10 Barnes Lower, County Tyrone; 11 Legland, County Tyrone; 12 Browndod, County Antrim; 13 Ballyalton, County Down; 14 Audleystown, County Down; 15 Ballynahatty, County Down

establishing clear divisions between the different types or stages of production (e.g. Whittaker 1987).

In a north Irish Neolithic context, one end of the spectrum of bifacial tools is populated by flaked flint axes, a tool type not particularly commonly found in the region, with only a few examples being identified (see Woodman 1992 for discussion). Although it is probable that flaked axes and other large leaf-shaped bifaces were both conceptually and functionally distinguishable to those who produced and used them, it is not always clear to analysts where such distinctions may lie. This was particularly apparent during the analysis of the Neolithic assemblage from Squires Hill, County Antrim (Evans 1938; Nelis 2003b), which included many large and apparently unfinished bifaces of questionable type *(54a)*. At its neighbouring hilltop settlements of Donegore Hill and Lyles Hill (Evans 1953;

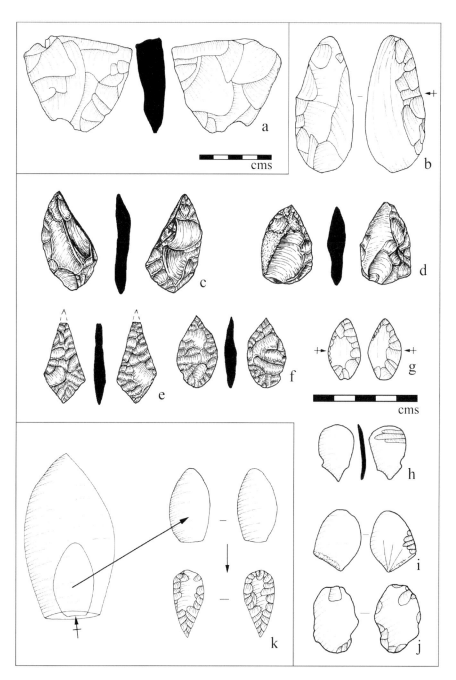

54 Bifaces and arrowheads. a biface fragment, Squires Hill; b side-struck laurel leaf, Lyles Hill; c obliquely fractured laurel leaf, Donegore Hill; d small laurel leaf/arrowhead preform?, Donegore Hill; e lozenge-shaped arrowhead, Donegore Hill; f leaf-shaped arrowhead, Donegore Hill; g side-struck leaf-shaped arrowhead on double ventral flake, Thornhill; h-i double ventral arrowhead blanks, Thornhill; j double ventral arrowhead blank, Lyles Hill; k process of double ventral flake production

Simpson & Gibson 1989; Nelis 2003a; 2003b) and on the nearby coastal promontory at Ballygalley Hill (Collins 1978; Nelis 2003b), smaller leaf-shaped bifaces, more commonly identified as 'laurel leaves', were dominant *(54c-d)*. It can be said that similar techniques were used in the bifacial production of all of these tools, but it is more difficult to ascertain the function of many of these artefacts, or to say whether or not they were perceived to have been completed.

There is, of course, debate as to whether laurel leaves should be considered as preforms of arrowheads, rather than as functional and finished tools. Certainly, some laurel leaves have been edge trimmed, shaped and therefore evidently 'finished', as at Donegore Hill and Lyles Hill, *(54d)*, but even these stand clearly apart from pressure flaked arrowheads, which tend to be significantly smaller and lighter. A critical factor in establishing the purpose of laurel leaves lies in the production methods behind these and arrowheads, and it is clear that arrowheads relating to the north Irish Neolithic were produced using very different methods from those deployed in the production of laurel leaves: not only are they modified by pressure flaking rather than percussion flaking, but many of the unfinished and finished arrowheads studied have clearly been formed on double ventral flake blanks *(54g-j)*; the creation of such a blank involves the removal of one flake from the ventral surface of another flake *(54k)*, so that the resulting blank carries two smooth, unfaceted ventral faces. The component of arrowheads formed on double ventral flakes is often substantial within a given assemblage, but unequivocal recognition of the technique is not always possible, as the method can only be clearly identified when parts of both faces are left unworked (i.e. not fully invasively pressure flaked *(54g)*. It can sometimes be inferred, however, from examples which exhibit remnants of ventral features on one face only.

A number of artefacts were studied which show the very early stages of double ventral arrowhead production (as at Thornhill, County Derry; Logue 2003: Ballynagilly, County Tyrone; ApSimon 1969; 1976: and Lyles Hill, County Antrim, for example *54h-j*; Nelis 2003b) and these suggest that the flakes were themselves created by indirect percussion, thus facilitating a very specifically aimed strike on a fine platform. One of the benefits of the use of double ventral flakes may have been that they allowed for the production of an arrowhead on a flake that could have something close to uniform surface morphology on both faces, thus precluding the potentially risky reduction of dorsal ridges and heavy bulbs and platforms; features which can be more prominent on 'ordinary' flakes. It is also arguable that the production of an arrowhead from a laurel leaf type preform invited many more opportunities to encounter knapping errors, since more extensive early stage preparation and shaping would be required; the early-stage double-ventral blanks which were studied indicate that only minimal shaping and modification would have been required in order to produce fine, functional arrowheads *(54g-h & k)*. The latter method therefore potentially allows for a reasonably minimalist (although highly skilled) commitment of time, and a limited range of retouch techniques *(54g)*.

The desire for a double ventral flake does, however, add a further layer of complexity to the process of producing and selecting blanks. Such flakes may, of course, have been a by-product of bifacial thinning, but this need not necessarily have been the case, and the technique of double ventral flake production may explain the occurrence of irregular flake cores which are occasionally found at sites such as Lyles Hill; indeed, their production may also explain the existence of at least some of the more irregular bifaces recovered from Early Neolithic sites, which may simply have served as curated cores. At Thornhill, for example, where raw material seems to have been scarce and tools were frequently refurbished, a scraper was heavily amended by being secondarily reduced on the ventral face, and it appears that a desire for a double ventral blank compelled the reworking in this case.

The double ventral flakes used in arrowhead production differ significantly from the majority of flakes used in the production of laurel leaves, and it is clear that when double ventral features are evident on an arrowhead, then it follows that the arrowhead cannot have been reduced from a laurel leaf 'preform'; likewise, it is notable that none of the laurel leaves which were analysed were formed on double ventral flakes. Many laurel leaves seem to have been based on quite heavy 'ordinary' flakes which are side-struck (i.e. the longitudinal axis of the laurel leaf is often perpendicular to the axis of percussion of the original flake: see *(54g)*; as such, the use of side-struck flakes allowed for the production of a 'long' blank from a 'short' core. Therefore, the frequent occurrence of laurel leaves on side-struck heavy flakes implies that (as with arrowheads) a specific methodology for their manufacture was in practice, and was collectively understood by the relevant specialists.

There is of course some overlap between the production methods of both artefact types (compare, for example, *54b & g*, both of which are side-struck) and some arrowheads and arrowhead preforms may well have been reduced from laurel leaves, since occasional artefacts which seem to fall between both types occur *(54d)*. While some laurel leaves may have been thought of as arrowhead preforms, this cannot explain the function of all such artefacts (see Saville 2002 for discussion). Many of the Irish laurel leaves may have functioned as javelin heads (see Collins 1981), and it is perhaps significant that their occurrence appears to diminish by the Middle Neolithic, at a time when 'javelin heads' proper begin to emerge (the latter being, in fact, quite rarely found in excavated assemblages). If laurel leaves did function as javelin heads, it is worthy of note that they rarely exhibit tip or lateral burin fractures which are seen as indicators of projectile usage (Ahler 1971; Bergman & Newcomer 1983); however, such damage will depend on the material with which they were in contact. The cause of the more commonly found oblique medial fractures; however, is an issue of debate (e.g. Donegore Hill: *54c*; Hedges & Buckley 1978; Healey & Robertson-Mackay 1987; Brown 1995), but it is clear that not all of these fractures can be explained by knapping error, which was once assumed to be the case. It is also plausible that some laurel leaves had ritual significance, and certainly by the Middle and Later Neolithic the occasional javelin heads which are known are commonly found in ritual contexts (Collins 1981; Nelis 2003b), at court tombs such as Tamnyrankin West, County Derry (Herring 1941; Nelis 2003b), and at Ballynahatty timber circle, County Down, for example (Hartwell 2002; Nelis 2003b). Much more detailed analysis is required to further explore these possibilities, and of course, there is no reason for just one explanation of function and use to emerge.

The study also showed that arrowheads of both leaf and lozenge shape are found in the earliest Neolithic settlement contexts (e.g. Thornhill, Ballynagilly and Donegore Hill; *(54e-f)*, and therefore both types seem to appear concurrently. However, it is apparent that lozenge forms become particularly dominant during the Middle Neolithic, in an almost exclusively funerary context (e.g. at court tombs such as Audleystown, County Down; Collins 1954; 1959a: Ballyalton, County Down; Evans & Davies 1934: Barnes Lower, County Tyrone; Collins 1966).

The production of a lozenge-shaped arrowhead differs from that of a leaf-shaped arrowhead in that it essentially involves a further stage of manufacture: the creation of the lozenge form requires a realignment of the blank during production, whereas the leaf morphology allows for production to follow the existing curvature of the blank; the creation of a lozenge form, therefore, is very much a cognitive and determined act which shows a particular concern for the stylistic value of the piece. The significance of the lozenge morphology in the context of ritual monuments extends beyond the recovery of arrowheads at court tombs: at passage tombs, lozenge motifs are among many replicated inscribed forms which appear on rock art (e.g. the entrance stone at Newgrange: O'Kelly 1982). Such motifs are less commonly found in non-passage tomb contexts, but were found on a cairn stone at Goward court tomb (Davies & Evans 1933), as well as at Lyles Hill cairn (Evans 1953), for example. It is entirely plausible that the trend for lozenge-shaped arrowheads at this time and in these contexts was in some way linked to the same incentives that were behind the form in rock art and other manifestations.

By the Middle Neolithic, fewer arrowheads seem to have been required in settlement contexts (such as at Goodland, County Antrim; Case 1973; Nelis 2003b and Windy Ridge, County Antrim; Woodman *et al.* 1992), and those which occur tend to be reasonably heavy, not particularly well made, and of variable morphology. The apparent change in focus which sees arrowheads being concentrated in settlement sites during the Early Neolithic, to more overtly ritualised contexts towards the Middle Neolithic, would seem to imply something of a shift in the functional status of the tools. This possible change

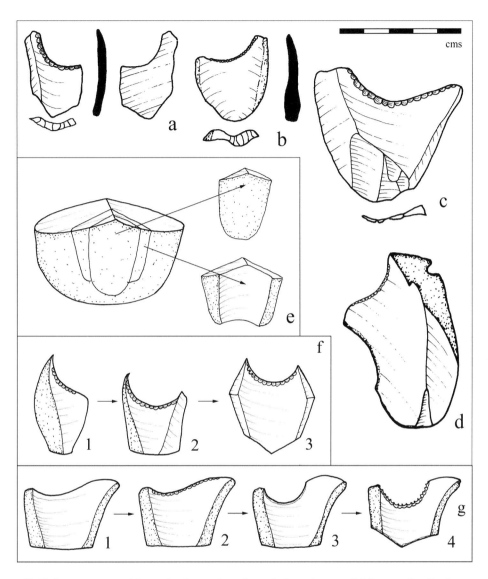

55 Hollow scrapers. a with pseudo-*chapeau de gendarme* platform along medial fracture, Goodland; b–c Goodland; d Ballyalton court tomb; e process of trapezoidal flake production; f developing complexity of hollow scraper forms, beginning on (1) 'regular' flakes, (2) onto simple trapezoidal flake, (3) culminating with elaborate trapezoidal flake with dual faceted lateral edges and *chapeau de gendarme* platform; g theoretical production sequence for hollow scraper, (1) simple trapezoidal flake with subtle naturally occurring concave, (2) utilisation or retouch of existing concave, and/or (3) application of force to produce concave fracture, which is then (4) retouched or utilised, with application of pressure-faceted *chapeau de gendarme* platform, either on existing dihedral platform, or manipulating planar platform *(Nelis 2003b)*

in significance may be echoed by the quality of the projectiles (and therefore the continuation of projectile manufacture as a specialism): highly crafted examples appear to be less available (and perhaps less necessary) in settlement contexts, but seem to continue in ritual contexts.

Towards the Late Neolithic, it would seem that petit tranchet and derivative arrowheads types dominate the projectile assemblage, although the detail of their context is often far from clear since most of the known examples relate to antiquarian collections rather than excavation. The few examples identified during the study rest comfortably with Flanagan's simple classification system, with those recovered from Ballynhatty and from final Neolithic contexts at Ballynagilly being either transverse, short or elongated pointed forms (Flanagan 1966). It is worthy of note, however, that the limited evidence to date suggests that the elongated forms, the particularly Irish type, may well have been used as knives, being commonly worn along their unmodified edge, and it is entirely plausible that they functioned both as projectiles and as knives.

HOLLOW SCRAPERS

Hollow scrapers are generally perceived to be idiosyncratic tools, apparently unique to the Irish Neolithic (e.g. Flanagan 1965, fig. 3). More is now known of their distribution since Flanagan's early studies suggested that they had a predominantly north-eastern concentration in the island *(ibid.)*, and subsequent discoveries have pointed to their recovery in substantial numbers to the north-west (e.g. Bengttson & Bergh 1984); currently, their main area of production and use still appears to be the northern half of the island.

The type of flake selected as the basis for a hollow scraper has long been recognised and presented as a distinctive signature of the tool type (e.g. Woodman 1967a; 1967b). The most commonly recognised examples are formed on thin, often squarish flakes which are trapezoidal in section, and the retouched hollows tend to be formed along a fine distal or lateral edge (e.g. *55b*) Some studies have looked at the location and direction of these elements (e.g. Eogan 1963) or have focused on the nature and extent of the hollow and its modification (e.g. Woodman 1967a; 1967b); the common occurrence of distinct *chapeau de gendarme* platforms has also been highlighted as an important element of the tool *(ibid.)*.

The study offered some evidence to suggest that hollow scrapers were initially developed on non-trapezoidal flakes. Some early contenders include examples from Ballyalton court tomb (within the cache at the base of one of the court façade stones – *55d*, for example), and Ballynagilly. The example within the Ballyalton cache is particularly unusual in that it is formed on a heavy long flake: the hollow is formed on a naturally occurring concave and the tool is generally only minimally modified and contrived, but (bizarrely) the platform has undergone elaborate pressure-faceting; in essence, some of the features of a hollow scraper exist, but they are presented using a very different technical language from that found on 'classic' examples (e.g. *55a-b*).

It may be that the technology behind the production of a trapezoidal flake may have developed in response to an increasing use of concave-edge cutting tools on non-trapezoidal flakes during the Early Neolithic. With time, it seems that trapezoidal flakes were recognised as being well suited for manufacturing such tools. The benefit of the trapezoidal flake is mainly this: in having a double dorsal ridge, two distal points of termination are encouraged, therefore increasing the likelihood that the intervening edge between the two points will be at least slightly concave (e.g. *55c*). The development of this flake production technique was quite an innovation, but it is possible that it may have been borne out of the accidental production of such flakes: occasionally a single strike can simultaneously remove two flakes in a sequence, the second of which would be trapezoidal (Jelinek *et al.* 1971; *55e*). The abundance of such flakes relating to hollow scrapers in the Irish Neolithic clearly indicates that the technique was intentional rather than accidental. Nonetheless, the discovery of the technique may have been the result of knapping accidents, and the suitability of the resulting flakes may have encouraged the development of the method. The intentional production of trapezoidal flakes would involve two individual strikes, rather than attempting to create two flakes at once. To begin with, the flakes may have been struck on flat, planar platforms *(55f:2)*, but as the technique developed, it seems that dihedral ridged platforms (i.e. the basis of *chapeau de gendarme* platforms) became more common *(55f:3)*; the development of ridged platforms would have helped direct the forces downward and along the lines of the dorsal ridges. Examples, therefore, with dihedral ridged platforms (or 'apex tangs') may signal a more developed stage of hollow scraper production, and a further stage of tool development may be indicated by the large and elaborate types with prominent tangs and dual faceted lateral edges (e.g. Audleystown, *55f:3*). This latter form may represent the final phase in the development of hollow scrapers, although more study is needed in order to clarify the context and timing of these changes.

The sequence of developments, of course, need not have been linear, and with the emergence of more elaborate types, the more simple forms probably continued. However, the apex tang certainly seems to become a significant element of hollow scraper production: examples of hollow scrapers exist which have had pseudo-*chapeau de gendarme* platforms created along non-platform edges in order to emulate the typical basal morphology (e.g. *55a*); it is not clear, however, whether this element of the tool had a functional or aesthetic imperative, but it may have been related to tool prehension.

The study also showed that a series of production stages existed within the manufacturing process, and these were respected to a greater or lesser extent; in particular, the Goodland assemblage, which was dominated by hollow scrapers, provided a wealth of information regarding the production and use of these tools (Nelis 2003b). For the most part, once a trapezoidal flake with a ridged platform was produced, the blank could be modified by:

(a) the application of a concave (or 'hollow') fracture in advance of retouch *(55g:3)*
(b) the application of minimal, fine retouch along the fractured hollow *(55g:4)*, or naturally occurring concave *(55g:2)* and
(c) pressure-faceting of a ridged platform into the classic *chapeau de gendarme* form *(55g:4)*

The Goodland assemblage showed that while combinations of these elements were found on blanks and finished tools, and it seemed acceptable for the morphology of blanks and hollows to range considerably *(55a & c)*, some discernible trends emerged: in general, it seems that concave fractures were produced if the naturally occurring concave was lacking. Beyond this, however, retouch seems to have respected faithfully the form of the concave; these concaves could be highly variable, and so their form effectively determined variability in the size and form of arcs on finished tools. The study also clearly showed that plain ridged platforms on blanks were the basis for the pressure-faceted *chapeau de gendarme* platforms on finished tools. Therefore, this pressure-faceting was effectively a secondary retouch technique, rather than an element of platform preparation prior to flake production.

In a general sense, the dating and phasing of hollow scrapers is an issue which is gradually becoming clearer: they do not seem to be associated with the earliest Neolithic contexts. For instance, none was found in the Early Neolithic assemblage from Thornhill, and only one was recovered from the 25,000 strong assemblage from Donegore Hill. A single, atypical example relates to the house settlement at Ballynagilly. At Lyles Hill, many questions remain regarding the sequencing of archaeological activity, but hollow scrapers do not seem to be associated with the Neolithic palisades which may be the earliest activity on the hill: rather they appear to relate to the activity focused at the cairn, the date of which is unclear (Evans 1953; Sheridan 2001) but at least some of its activity may date to the Middle Neolithic. Hollow scrapers and associated debitage were identified within all court tomb assemblages, and also proved to be the dominant tool type from other Middle Neolithic settlement sites such as Goodland and Windy Ridge. While hollow scrapers continue to appear in some Late Neolithic contexts (such as the Dundrum sandhills; Collins 1952; 1959b), by final Neolithic/Grooved Ware contexts they seem to have become obsolete, as at Ballynahatty and at Donegore Hill. Hollow scrapers, therefore, appear to develop at some later point in the Early Neolithic, achieving their prime during the course of the Middle Neolithic and continuing into the Late Neolithic, declining by the final Neolithic.

As a tool which entirely dominated Middle Neolithic assemblages, hollow scrapers are stunningly simple in form: the extent of retouch is very minimal, and while the application of concave fractures presumably required some level of skill, retouch techniques were quite basic. It is apparent that the technique and skills required were emphatically focused on the production of the blank. The manufacture of hollow scrapers therefore contrasts significantly with the manufacture of tools such as arrowheads, where a considerable level of skill was mainly required for secondary production.

Much more analysis is required in order to clarify in particular the sequence of hollow scraper development, but at this point a word or two may be said of their function. As a tool type viewed as an eccentricity of the Irish Neolithic, hollow scrapers have been imbued with a sense of wonder which has informed their study; as a result, questions as to their function have been expected to provide a spectacularly interesting answer. Recent studies have suggested that they primarily functioned as tools for processing willow fibre (O'Hare 2000), and it would seem that they are well suited for such a purpose, but their ubiquitous presence during the Middle Neolithic and their domination of most chipped stone assemblages at the time suggest that they probably served innumerable purposes where a sharp or serrated cutting tool and/or spoke-shave was required. It is worthy of note that hollow scrapers develop at a time when plano-convex knives and associated types are in decline. It is plausible, then, that hollow scrapers are the knives of the Irish Middle Neolithic, and, in being so, they offered a simply produced, minimally retouched and readily achievable tool. In many ways, it seems that the morphology of the flake and the completion of the tang became a significant element of the tool, while the hollow itself seems to have been deemed acceptable whether its form was regular or slightly irregular, or with a shallow or full arc. Furthermore, the visible damage on many of the tools within a single assemblage (as at Goodland, for example) suggests that a variety of materials were cut or shaved, since working edges vary between smoothed, glossed, polished and chipped. Some use-wear analysis will help to clarify this matter, but it is unlikely that there will be just one reason for their existence, and given the possible development of the tool from less morphologically distinct concave tools, it need not necessarily be the case that a single need was the driving imperative behind its development.

SCRAPERS

Our understanding of scraper function has come some way since the days of antiquarian study, when Irish scrapers were initially considered to have been spoons (e.g. Benn 1865) but it is still over a century since a major study of Irish scrapers has been undertaken (Knowles 1898). Scrapers are certainly the most consistently and prolifically found artefact type throughout Irish Neolithic

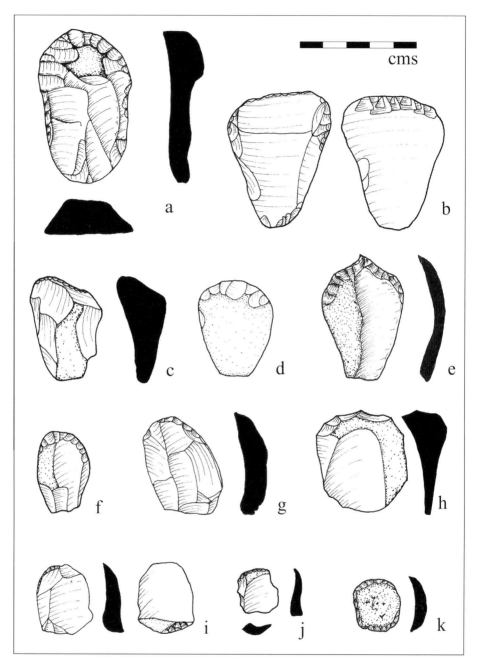

56 Scrapers. a with heavy dorsal reduction, Donegore Hill; b 'pushing' scraper from Goodland;
c heavily worn scraper from Goodland; d Ballymarlagh; e scraper with point or spur, Donegore
Hill; f Goodland; g Lyles Hill; h Ballynahatty; i Lyles Hill; j thumbnail scraper from
Ballynahatty; k thumbnail scraper, Donegore Hill

contexts *(56)*, and within individual assemblages and throughout the period range considerably in size and form, as well as quality and extent of retouch. For the most part, however, they tend to be formed on plunging flakes (with the curving profile assisting in the tool function) and commonly on corticated flint. In some cases, they are noticeably dorsally thinned at their proximal end (a feature which may be related to hafting methods) and this is a particularly common feature on larger scrapers (e.g. Donegore Hill: *56e*). In general, the scraping edge is formed along the distal end of a flake or blade on the dorsal face, but most assemblages have small numbers of exceptions to this norm.

While the morphology of scraping edges tends to be variable within any one assemblage, most are convex in form; while a variety of more angular or irregular edges are found in small numbers at most sites, the Donegore assemblage included a small number of scrapers with a distal spur, and so far this form seems to have been unique to that particular site *(56)*. The variability of scraper morphology need not necessarily be related to tool function, and it is now generally accepted that individual tools, as well as scrapers of similar form, were put to a variety of uses on a variety of materials (e.g. Siegel 1984). The wear and tear evident on the Goodland scrapers, for example, suggests a body of tools that were used on a range of materials in a number of ways: a thorough use-wear analysis of these tools was not undertaken, but at first glance the wear patterns varied from worn and polished scraping edges (e.g. *56c*) to chipped, scaling edge damage (e.g. *56b*), suggesting (in a very general sense) use on soft materials as well as on hard/brittle materials respectively. Furthermore, some scraper assemblages exhibited diversity in the location of edge damage, with dorsal as well as ventral damage being evident *(56b)*. This suggests that while most scrapers were used in a manner that pulled against their scraping edge, some at least were pushed against their scraping edge (Hayden 1986, 66). Such scrapers may have functioned similarly to adzes or chisels, but it is interesting that it was a feature which did not seem to relate to a particular scraper size or morphology.

In general, the study produced little physical evidence for scraper refurbishment: occasional examples of recognisable resharpening flakes were evident within some of larger assemblages, as at Donegore Hill, for example, but most assemblages lacked such evidence. The condition of scrapers at Goodland, where tools were discarded once they became worn or damaged, was an unusual aspect of behaviour and not commonly found at other sites. Most of the scrapers studied, therefore, were found to retain reasonably fresh scraping edges, and therefore it is reasonable to conclude that some level of refurbishment did occur. However, this may have involved such small-scale pressure flaking and trimming that micro-debitage may have been the only result, and in the absence of fine sieving, such small scale material is commonly lost from assemblages.

As with all elements of a lithic assemblage, however, the character of a scraper assemblage will be determined by a number of factors which may or may not be related to function. For example, the extent of curation affecting any one particular site will determine scraper variability within that assemblage: sites such as Lyles Hill and Donegore Hill, which may have witnessed significant movements of people during their occupation, yielded large and variable scraper assemblages, whereas at court tombs, scrapers commonly occur in groups which are similar in terms of raw material, blank selection, retouch methods and scraping edge morphology (e.g. Tamnyrankin West). The ability to discern discrete groups of scrapers was a common feature of court tomb assemblages; such unity within tomb assemblages may reflect a desire to create an aesthetically compatible group of tools for presentation or use at the tomb, but is also an indicator that the scrapers were probably produced at a single sitting, either by one individual, or by a small group working with communal intent. As a consequence, however, such conformist bodies of tools may argue against multiple periods of lithic activity, and therefore perhaps use, at these tombs at least; it seems then that such scraper assemblages were subject to reasonably limited curation prior to deposition.

The study showed that scraper size was at least partly determined by the availability of raw material: at Early Neolithic settlements such as Ballynagilly and Thornhill which seem to have had limited access to flint, the diminutive size of the scrapers reflects the limited availability of large-scale raw material; on the other hand, the large size of many of the Middle Neolithic scrapers from Goodland seems to have been partly determined by the ease of access to large scale raw material in this area. Scraper size and form was variable throughout the entire Neolithic period, to the extent that most assemblages offer a size distribution that spans a continuum of tools ranging from 'large' to 'small' (e.g. *56a & f*). This was also apparent during the Late Neolithic, which saw the emergence of thumbnail scrapers, and it was found that a valid distinction between thumbnail scrapers and simply 'small' scrapers was elusive, and unachievable based on size attributes alone (e.g. *56f & i-k*). The emergence of thumbnail scrapers at this time seems to highlight a dramatic shift in scraper production, perhaps reflecting fundamental changes in their primary function that may be related to changes in the economy at this time (Nelis 2003b).

KNIVES AND OTHER TOOLS

Knives comprise quite a variable group of artefacts *(57)*, being recovered in particular from Early Irish Neolithic contexts at settlement sites such as Thornhill and Donegore Hill. At no point, however, are they particularly dominant, and at all times are less commonly found in assemblages than expediently retouched or utilised cutting tools, which seem to bear most responsibility for cutting functions. In Early Neolithic contexts, however, they are most clearly distinguished as extensively worked plano-convex examples, with those found at Donegore Hill being among the most accomplished (e.g. *57a & g*). Such examples show that plano-convex knives seem to have been frequently refurbished, so that knives may have started as unmodified flakes with sharp edges, and were then resharpened perhaps on multiple occasions until they resembled diminutive 'slug' examples *(57g)*. Knives are also the only tool type of the Irish Neolithic to be predominantly formed on blades (e.g. *57a-d*), but, from a number of clearly refurbished examples, it is evident that their multiple stages of production have rendered them much more blade-like than their original form may have been: that is, while they may have begun their use-lives as broad flakes, in their final state they appear to be long blades. Evidence for this narrowing is mainly readable from the ventral features, which can indicate that the artefact was at one point much broader than its current

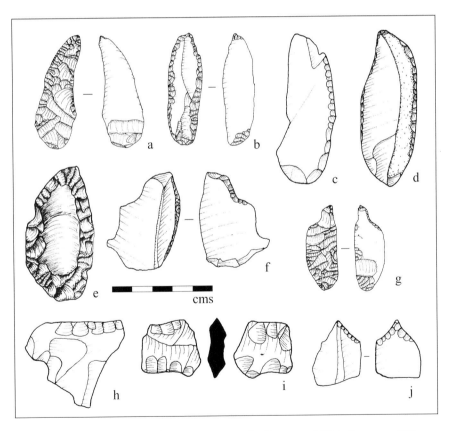

57 Knives and other tools: a plano-convex example, Donegore Hill; b Donegore Hill; c Ballyalton; d Lyles Hill; e Donegore Hill; f minimally worked knife/cutting tool with piercer/borer, Lyles Hill; g plano-convex, with multiple phases of refurbishment, with tang, Donegore Hill; h wedge tool, Ballymarlagh; i wedge tool, Ballynahatty; j piercer, Ballynahatty

state *(57g)*. Such frequent reworking partly explains why the morphology of knives can be so variable, and this can be particularly problematic for analysts as we attempt to isolate the point at which a non-specific 'edge retouched flake' becomes a 'minimally modified knife' *(57a-g)*.

The context and condition of knives is of particular interest, since there seems to be a particular tendency for knives to be burned. This is evident both at settlement sites such as Thornhill and Donegore Hill, for example, and also at court tombs, such as Legland, County Tyrone, for example (Davies 1940). It is possible, then, that the use of knives was in some way related to activities involving fire, or at least that they were commonly disposed of in this way.

Undoubtedly the most neglected elements of modified tool assemblages are those which tend to be among the most significant components at most sites, including settlement and overtly ritual sites. These tools mainly consist of quite minimally and opportunistically worked artefacts, which serve a number of functions. For the most part, they seem to have been used for cutting or piercing/boring (e.g. *57f & g*) and these generally include minimally modified or simply utilised flakes and blades. Such assemblages include tools which retain visible signs of wear, but undoubtedly a further element of debitage assemblages were utilised in a similar way. To these may be added a highly variable body of tools, formed by either retouch or bipolar reduction on flakes and cores, which seemed to function as wedges (e.g. *57h & i*); such tools are found within most assemblages, and while they tend to be of flint, they can also include reworked non-flint debitage resulting from the refurbishment of stone axe-heads (as at Donegore, for example: Mallory *et al.* in press).

Some Conclusions

This paper has sought to present a very brief overview of some results of a recent study which looked at the primary and secondary flint-industry of the Neolithic in the north of Ireland (Nelis 2003b), focusing in this instance on some of the modified tool types of the period. Some general comments may therefore be made regarding the development of the chipped flint industry at this point. It is evident that pressure flaked leaf- and lozenge-shaped arrow-heads and percussion flaked bifaces are a particular feature of Early Neolithic settlement contexts *(54)*; similarly, formal knives (particularly, plano-convex examples) are mainly found in Early Neolithic contexts *(57)*. Highly developed pressure flaking skills, evident on arrowheads and many knives, are elements of the apparently fully developed Early Neolithic technology that we witness in our earliest known contexts; other less extensively worked knives are common, and some may have been borne out of previous, understood techniques, but at the very least the extent of modification is a new departure. The basis of many arrowheads on double ventral flakes is a further indicator of the technical complexity exhibited within most assemblages at this time.

Much more remains to be understood about the development of the new technology within the island, and the external influences which brought the new technology to Ireland's shores need to be explored. It does seem, however, that some elements of Early Neolithic assemblages echo Late Mesolithic technology, and furthermore there appears to be a subtle correlation between the continuance of a broad blade industry and Early Neolithic cache deposits: the Ballyalton cache (which includes the unusual hollow scraper discussed above) *(55d)* includes broad blade artefacts which are entirely at odds with the remainder of material recovered from the court tomb (in fact, the size distribution between cache and non-cache artefacts is mutually exclusive: Nelis 2003b). At Cuilbane, County Derry (Yates 1985; Nelis 2003b), a cache of unfinished bifaces, knives and scrapers (some of which refit) points definitively to Early Neolithic technology, and includes a number of Late Mesolithic butt trimmed forms. Elsewhere, butt trimmed forms were recovered from Early Neolithic sites such as Thornhill, County Derry, Donegore Hill, Lyles Hill and Squires Hill, County Antrim, and there is no real reason to dismiss these as being residual and relating to earlier activity (Nelis 2003b).

By the Middle Neolithic, arrowheads are undoubtedly less evident in settlement contexts. However, they continue to be commonly found at court tombs where lozenge-shaped examples become the dominant form. By this time, knives are in demise, whereas hollow scrapers, which may have developed from more simple forms in the Early Neolithic, become something of an artform *(55)*; their profusion and variable condition suggests that they served a number of functions, and may well have been the 'knives' of the Middle Neolithic. At this stage, there is a general move away from fully invasive pressure flaking, therefore, which appeared during the Early Neolithic, and tool production tends to depend upon more minimalist retouch methods. Scrapers are the most commonly found tool type throughout the Neolithic *(56)*, and there is a significant departure in their morphology in Late Neolithic/Early Bronze Age contexts with the emergence of thumbnail scrapers.

While this study has begun to elaborate upon general chronological trends for some of the more commonly found tool types of the north Irish Neolithic, much work remains to be done in order to establish a tighter chronological framework for developments in the lithic industry across the island. In Irish Neolithic studies, achieving a clearer understanding of these dynamics is particularly timely, in light of recent and ongoing clarification of the sequencing and dating of Irish ceramics (e.g. Sheridan 1995; Brindley 1999). But some distance remains to be covered in chipped stone assemblage analysis in order to 'catch up' with ceramic studies of the period. The aim of such studies, of course, is to use the analysis to inform our understanding of the social, economic and spiritual imperatives that drove the day-to-day activities of those who occupied the sites. While there may always be inherent limitations upon many lithic artefacts as distinct chronological indicators, there is great potential for analytical methods to explore and convey the personality of individual assemblages; all of which bear testimony to processes of tool production and failure, use and re-use, and discard, loss and deposition. The analytical methods deployed, therefore, need to look beyond stock typological groupings which do little to further our understanding of what an assemblage really means. This paper has considered a number of tool types, and as such has focused on only one aspect of lithic assemblage studies. But this reconsideration of recognisable types such as arrowheads and hollow scrapers, for example, has highlighted the importance of understanding the primary reduction strategies in their manufacture, and these manufacturing processes can offer a rich insight into the activities represented by the archaeological remains. At Thornhill, for example, in a context where an Early Neolithic enclosed settlement may have witnessed violent events (Logue 2003 and Moore, this volume), complex and opportunist production methods were deployed in order to produce arrowheads: scrapers and other pieces were reworked in order to yield arrowhead blanks, broken arrowheads were refurbished into new arrowheads, and attempts were made to produce arrowheads from broken knife fragments (Nelis 2003b). Such behaviour hints at strong imperatives behind this almost desperate approach to the production of projectiles. Nuances such as these would be hard pressed to fit with strict typological groupings, but their recognition is critical if we are to understand the mindset and experiences of the inhabitants of such settlements.

It is hoped, therefore, that this paper will encourage a reconsideration of the material culture of many of the north Irish Neolithic sites, particularly in light of ongoing excavations of yet more Neolithic activity, and to highlight the wealth of information regarding the daily lives of Neolithic communities that all too often languishes overlooked in dusty boxes; as such, then, it is very much hoped that the results of the study will regenerate interest in an artefact group sometimes dismissed as a static, unemotional and uninformative medium for the conveyance of social behaviour and interaction.

Acknowledgements

Like many, I am indebted to Derek Simpson for his gracious support and encouragement over the years. Thanks are also due to Libby Mulqueeny, who kindly provided the base-map *(53)*, and to John O'Neill, who read an earlier draft of this paper.

Bibliography

Ahler, S.A., 1971 *Projectile Point Form and Function at Rodgers Shelter, Missouri*. Missouri: Missouri Archaeological Society Research Series 8.

ApSimon, A., 1969 An Early Neolithic house in County Tyrone. *Journal of the Royal Society of Antiquaries of Ireland*, 99, 165-8.

ApSimon, A., 1976 Ballynagilly at the beginning and end of the Irish Neolithic. In de Laet, S.J. (ed.) *Acculturation and Continuity in Atlantic Europe*, 15-38. Bruges: Dissertationes Archaeologicae Gandenses.

Armit, I., Murphy, E., Nelis, E.L. &. Simpson, D.D.A. (eds), 2003 *Neolithic Settlement in Ireland and Western Britain*. Oxford: Oxbow.

Bengtsson, H. & Bergh, S., 1984 The hut sites at Knocknarea North, Co. Sligo. In Burenhult, G. (ed.) *The Archaeology of Carrowmore: Environmental Archaeology and the Megalithic Tradition at Carrowmore, Co. Sligo*, 216-318. Stockholm: Theses & Papers in North European Archaeology, 14.

Benn, E., 1865 Proceedings and papers. *Journal of the Royal Society of Antiquaries of Ireland*, 7.

Bergman, C.A. & Newcomer, M. H., 1983 Flint arrowhead breakage: examples from Ksar Akil, Lebanon. *Journal of Field Archaeology*, 10, 238-43.

Brindley, A.L., 1999 Irish Grooved Ware. In Cleal, R. & MacSween, A. (eds), *Grooved Ware in Britain and Ireland*, 23-35. Neolithic Studies Group Seminar Papers (3). Oxford: Oxbow.

Brown, A.G., 1995 The Mesolithic and later flint artefacts. In Healy, F. (ed.) *Lithics and Landscape: Archaeological Discoveries on the Thames Water Pipeline at Gatehampton Farm, Goring, Oxfordshire 1985-1992*, 65-83. Thames Valley Landscapes Monograph (7). Oxford: Oxford Archaeological Unit.

Case, H., 1973 A ritual site in north-east Ireland. In Daniel, G. & Kjaerum, P. (eds), *Megalithic Graves and Ritual*, 173-96. Copenhagen: Jutland Archaeology Society Publications xi.

Collins, A.E.P., 1952 Excavations in the sandhills at Dundrum, Co. Down, 1950-51. *Ulster Journal of Archaeology*, 15, 2-26.

Collins, A.E.P., 1954 The excavation of a double horned cairn at Audleystown, Co. Down. *Ulster Journal of Archaeology*, 17, 6-56.

Collins, A.E.P., 1959a Further work at Audleystown long cairn, Co. Down. *Ulster Journal of Archaeology*, 22, 23-7.

Collins, A.E.P., 1959b Further investigations in the Dundrum sandhills. *Ulster Journal of Archaeology*, 22, 5-20.

Collins, A.E.P., 1966 Barnes Lower court cairn, Co. Tyrone. *Ulster Journal of Archaeology*, 29, 43-75.

Collins, A.E.P., 1978 Excavations on Ballygalley Hill, County Antrim. *Ulster Journal of Archaeology*, 41, 15-32.

Collins, A.E.P., 1981 The flint javelin heads of Ireland. In O'Corrain, D. (ed.) *Irish Antiquity: Essays and Studies Presented to Prof. M. J. O' Kelly*, 111-31. Cork: Tower Books.

Davies, O., 1940 Excavations at Legland horned cairn. *Proceedings of the Belfast Natural History and Philosopical Society*, 1, 1939/40, 16-24.

Davies, O. & Evans, E.E., 1933 Excavations at Goward, near Hilltown, Co. Down. *Proceedings of the Belfast Natural History and Philosopical Society*, 1932/1933, 90-105.

Eogan, G., 1963 A Neolithic habitation-site and megalithic tomb in Townleyhall townland, Co. Louth. *Journal of the Royal Society of Antiquaries of Ireland*, 93, 37-81.

Evans, E.E., 1938 An Archaeological Miscellany. *Ulster Journal of Archaeology*, 1, 14-5.

Evans, E.E., 1953 *Lyles Hill: a Late Neolithic Site in County Antrim*. Belfast: HMSO.

Evans, E.E. & Davies, O., 1934 Excavation of a chambered horned cairn at Ballyalton, Co. Down. *Proceedings of the Belfast Natural History and Philosopical Society*, 1933/34, 79-104.

Flanagan, L.N.W., 1965 Flint hollow scrapers and the Irish Neolithic. In Sansoni, G.C. (ed.) *Atti del VI Congresso Internazionale delle Scienze Preistoriche e Protostoriche*, 323-8. Rome: Union Internationale des Sciences Préhistoriques et Protohistoriques.

Flanagan, L.N.W., 1966 The petit-tranchet derivative arrowhead and the Irish Neolithic. *Actes du VII Congres International des Sciences Prehistoriques et Protohistoriques, Prague Academia, 1966*, 523-7.

Hartwell, B., 2002 A Neolithic ceremonial timber complex at Ballynahatty, Co. Down. *Antiquity*, 76, 526-32.

Hayden, B., 1986 Use and Misuse: The analysis of endscrapers. *Lithic Technology*, 15, 48-54.

Healey, E. & Robertson-Mackay, R., 1987 The flint industry. In Robertson-Mackay, R. The Neolithic causewayed enclosure at Staines, Surrey: excavations 1961–63. *Proceedings of the Prehistoric Society*, 53, 23-128.

Hedges, J. & Buckley, D., 1978 Excavations at a Neolithic causewayed enclosure, Orsett, Essex, 1975. *Proceedings of the Prehistoric Society*, 44, 219-308.

Herring, I.J., 1941 The Tamnyrankin cairn: west structure. *Journal of the Royal Society of Antiquaries of Ireland*, 11, 31-52.

Jelinek, A., Bradley. B. & Huckell, B., 1971 The production of secondary multiple flakes. *American Antiquity*, 36, 198-200.

Knowles, W. J., 1898 Irish flint scrapers. *Journal of the Royal Society of Antiquaries of Ireland*, 28, 367-90.

Logue, P., 2003 Excavations at Thornhill, Co. Londonderry. In Armit *et al.* (eds), 149-55.

Mallory, J.P., Nelis, E.L. & Hartwell, B., in press. *Donegore Hill, Co. Antrim: a Neolithic Causewayed Enclosure*. Wicklow: Wordwell.

Nelis, E.L., 1998 *Lithic Analysis of Donegore Hill, Co. Antrim: a Neolithic Causewayed Enclosure*. Unpublished MA thesis, Queen's University Belfast.

Nelis, E.L., 2003a Donegore and Lyles Hill, Neolithic enclosed sites in Co. Antrim: the lithic assemblages. In Armit *et al.* (eds), 2003, 203-17.

Nelis, E.L., 2003b *Lithics of the Northern Irish Neolithic*. Unpublished PhD thesis, Queen's University Belfast.

Nelis, E.L., in press. The lithic assemblage. In Mallory, J.P., Nelis, E.L., & Hartwell, B. (eds), in press.

O'Hare, M., 2000 *The Enigmatic Hollow Scraper*. Unpublished BA thesis, Queen's University Belfast.

O'Kelly, M.J., 1982 *Newgrange: Archaeology, Art and Legend*. London: Thames & Hudson.

Saville, A., 2002 Lithic artefacts from Neolithic causewayed enclosures: character and meaning. In Varndell, G. & Topping, P. (eds), *Enclosures in Neolithic Europe*, 91-105. Oxford: Oxbow.

Sheridan, J.A., 1995 Irish Neolithic pottery: the story in 1995. In Kinnes, I.A. & Varndell, G. (eds), *Unbaked Urns of Rudely Shape*, 3-22. Oxbow Monograph (55). Oxford: Oxbow.

Sheridan, J.A., 2001 Donegore Hill and other Irish Neolithic enclosures: a view from outside. In Darvill, T. & Thomas, J. (eds), *Neolithic Enclosures in Atlantic north-west Europe*, 171-89. Neolithic Studies Group: Seminar Papers 6. Oxford: Oxbow.

Siegel, P.E., 1984 Functional variability within an assemblage of endscrapers. *Lithic Technology*, 13, 35-51.

Simpson, D.D.A. & Gibson, A., 1989 Lyle's Hill. *Current Archaeology*, 114, 214-5.

Whittaker, J.C., 1987 Making arrowpoints in a Prehistoric Pueblo. *Lithic Technology*, 16, 1-12.

Woodman, P.C., 1967a Some implement types from Glenarm. *Ulster Journal of Archaeology*, 30, 3-7.

Woodman, P.C., 1967b A flint hoard from Killybeg. *Ulster Journal of Archaeology*, 30, 8-14.

Woodman, P.C., 1992 Excavations at Mad Man's Window, Glenarm, Co. Antrim: Problems of flint exploitation in East Antrim. *Proceedings of the Prehistoric Society,* 58, 77-105.

Woodman, P.C., 1994 Towards a definition of Irish Early Neolithic lithic assemblages. In Ashton, N. & David, A. (eds), *Stories in Stone,* 213-18. Lithic Studies Society Occasional Paper 4. London: British Museum, Lithic Studies Society.

Woodman, P.C., Doggart, R. & Mallory, J.P., 1992 Excavations at Windy Ridge, Co. Antrim. *Ulster Journal of Archaeology,* 54/55, 1991-2, 13-35.

Yates, M.J., 1985 Restoration of the Cuilbane stone circle, Garvagh, County Londonderry, and the discovery of a cache of flints. *Ulster Journal of Archaeology,* 48, 41-50.

12

READING A BURIAL: THE LEGACY OF OVERTON HILL

FRANCES HEALY AND JAN HARDING

INTRODUCTION

The *Guide Catalogue of the Neolithic and Bronze Age Collections in Devizes Museum* (Annable & Simpson 1964) has long been an invaluable resource for those seeking to interpret Early Bronze Age burials, as has Derek Simpson's discussion of Food Vessels and their associated artefacts (1968). New ground was broken in this field by his and Isobel Smith's interpretation of the assemblage from the central burial in an Early Bronze Age round barrow on Overton Hill, near Avebury. They argued convincingly that the artefacts were leather-working tools, and demonstrated that the grave group combined elements of two separate sets of funerary associations, generally buried with male skeletons and stylistically late long-necked Beakers (Smith & Simpson 1966). Since then, Case has defined broad groupings of Beaker burials (1977); Barrett has explored the social context of barrow building and attempted to reconstruct funerary rites, emphasising that they and the deposits which they generated inevitably expressed the concerns of the living rather than the persona of the deceased (1994); Thomas (1991), and Sofaer-Derevenski (2002), among others, have developed the themes of ascribed role and identity, including gender, in Beaker burials; and Woodward has emphasised that objects placed in Early Bronze Age graves were often used, like the slate 'sponge-fingers', antler spatula, flint flake and 'strike-a-light' from Overton Hill, and were some-times already old, incomplete or damaged when they were buried, their histories and associations known to those who placed them in the grave (2002).

This paper examines one burial of the period, the primary grave under Barrow 1 at Raunds, in the Nene valley in Northamptonshire *(58)*, a mound which is best known for the piling over it of the skulls of almost 200 cattle (S. Davis & Payne 1993; S. Davis, forthcoming). The mound was one of several Early Bronze Age round barrows excavated in the 1980s and early 1990s in the course of the Raunds Area Project, undertaken by bodies then known as the Central Excavation Unit of English Heritage, the Northamptonshire Archaeology Unit and the Oxford Archaeological

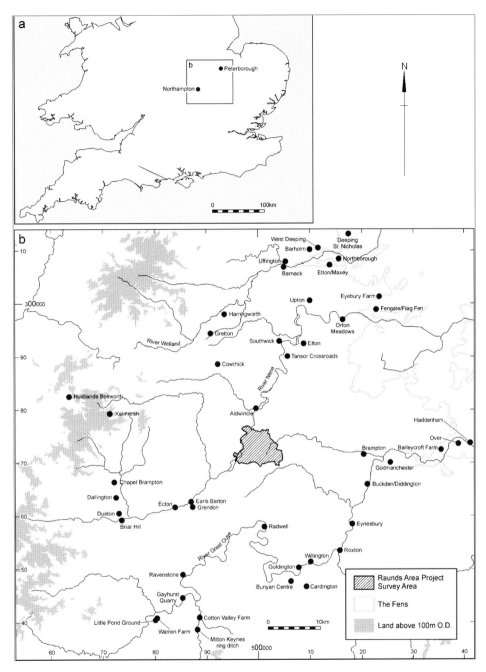

58 Location of the Raunds Area Project, showing selected prehistoric sites. *Copyright and by permission of English Heritage*

Unit. The barrows were built in pasture (Campbell & Robinson forth-coming), some on a low gravel terrace within an existing group of Neolithic monuments, others, including Barrow 1, on an 'island' defined by two arms of the river, where no monuments had been built before *(59)*. This particular burial has been chosen for closer examination because it was by far the most abundantly and diversely furnished of those excavated in the area and thus provides an opportunity to pursue some of the lines of enquiry noted above.

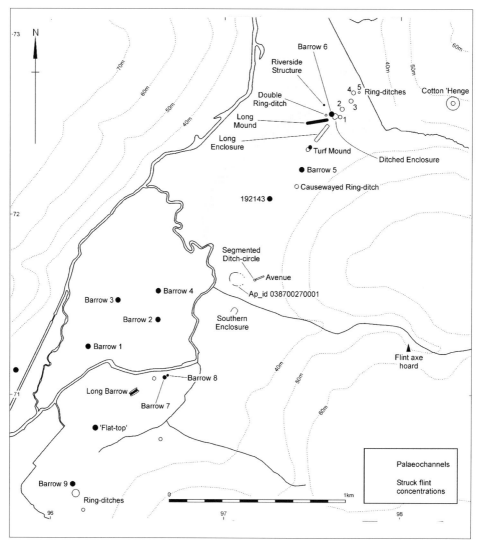

59 The Nene Valley in the Raunds area, showing Neolithic and Bronze Age monuments and main flint concentrations. Palaeochannels which were possibly, but not definitely, active at the time are hatched diagonally. *Copyright and by permission of English Heritage*

THE RAUNDS BARROW 1 BURIAL

A man who had died around the turn of the second and third millennia BC
was buried at the centre of the monument in a chamber built of oak planks
set in a large, deep rectangular grave. The grave had been backfilled around the
sides of the chamber, and a cairn of limestone brought from the valley sides a
kilometre or so away had been built over it. Over this cairn had been piled the
cattle skulls, themselves covered by an earthen mound raised from the first of

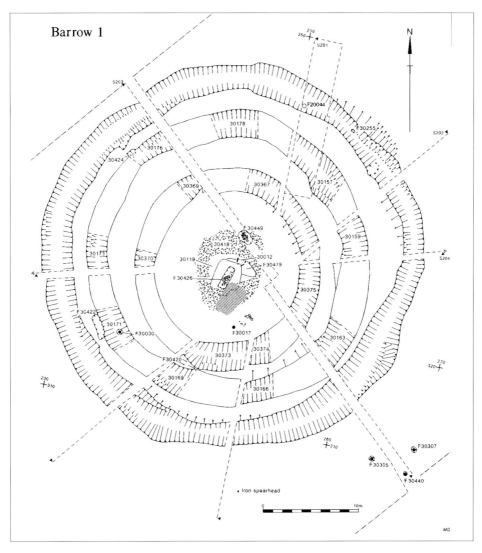

60 Raunds Barrow 1. Overall plan. *Copyright and by permission of English Heritage*

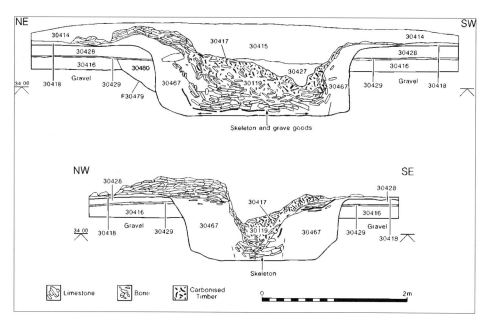

61 Raunds Barrow 1. Sections through primary burial. *Copyright and by permission of English Heritage*

three concentric ditches *(60)*. The eventual collapse of the chamber had precipitated cairn, bone and mound material into the grave, crushing and displacing the burial *(61)*. At the feet of the skeleton were an elaborate Beaker and a heap of 36 other objects, so tightly bunched that they may have been in an organic container *(62-3; Table 6)*. This is an exceptionally large grave group, although it falls well short of the almost 100 objects which accompanied the man now known as the Amesbury archer (Fitzpatrick 2002), buried 200-300 years earlier. Thanks to the work of numerous colleagues, it is possible to suggest some of the connotations which these objects may have had for those who deposited them, whether of known people and recent events, of remote times and places, or of both.

The lower part of the interior of the Beaker was marked by spalling and pitting, as if eroded by its contents (Tomalin forthcoming). High levels of animal fat lipids were detected in a sherd from below the 'tideline' and low levels in one from above it (Copley *et al.* forthcoming). The pot must have contained a meat- or milk-based liquid and have stood upright and intact long enough for the contents to eat into its walls. Both vessel and contents would have been relatively fresh when deposited, perhaps derived from consumption or ceremonies attending the burial. Flint scrapers, knives and flakes, all freshly knapped and freshly used for a variety of tasks and on a variety of materials (*Table 6*; Grace 1990 and forthcoming), would have had an equally recent history. Since these would all have been quickly made and quickly discarded, they may have been a sample of tools used in acts relating directly to the burial, notably wood-working and butchery.

62 Raunds Barrow 1. Some of the grave goods at feet of the primary burial. *Copyright and by permission of English Heritage. Photo courtesy of CfA*

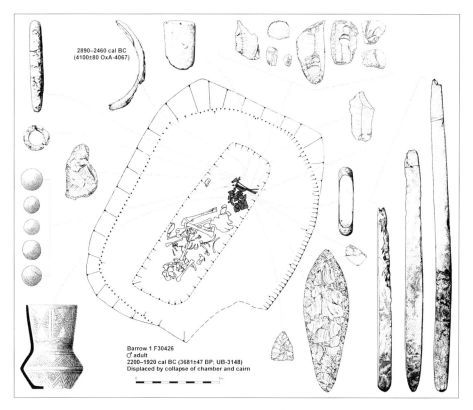

63 Raunds Barrow 1. Primary grave group. Clockwise from top left: elongated chalk object, pig tusk, Group VI bracer/burnisher, flint flakes, knives and scrapers, stone 'sponge-finger', longitudinally split cattle ribs, further flint flake, flint dagger, triangular flint arrowhead, Beaker (shown at half the scale of the other artefacts), jet buttons, flint knife, amber ring. *Copyright and by permission of English Heritage*

Based on the work of Torben Bjärke Ballin, Mark Copley, Mary Davis, Stephanie Dudd, Richard Evershed, Andrew Foxon, Roger Grace, Carl Heron, Jon Humble, Ian Shepherd; David Tomalin and David Williams

Description	Source	Condition
Shell-tempered Beaker	Local ?	Interior pitted and spalled beneath 'tideline' low down in belly of vessel. High levels of degraded animal fat lipids in fabric below 'tideline', low levels above
Dagger, probably of chalk flint	East Anglia? Wessex?	Edges of blade (but not haft) worn by sheathing and unsheathing. No other wear
Triangular flint arrowhead	Local?	Fresh and without wear or hafting traces, point possibly too thick for use
2 flint flake knives	Local?	Fresh. One used for scraping wood or antler, one for cutting soft material on medium material, possibly butchery or skinning
3 flint scrapers	Local?	Fresh. 2 used for scraping wood, 1 for scraping hide
Retouched flint flake	Local?	Fresh. Used for scraping medium material
5 flint flakes	Local?	Fresh. 1 used for butchery, 1 for cutting medium to hard material, 3 smallest unused
Group VI wristguard	Ultimately Cumbria. Could have been made from locally-collected axehead	One perforation broken, ?during manufacture. Opposed end truncated and worn down by use
Slate 'sponge-finger' whetstone	East Midlands? Beyond?	Ends worn
Elongated carved and smoothed chalk object	Surrounding plateau? East Anglia? Wessex? Lincolnshire/Yorkshire?	Broken in antiquity
D-sectioned amber ring with possible trace of V-boring	Ultimately Baltic. Might have been found on east coast of Britain	Too badly preserved for condition on burial to be assessed
5 V-perforated jet buttons	Whitby area of Yorkshire	Varying degrees of wear on perforations, fresh bevel cut on one button after wear already sustained
3 longitudinally split cattle ribs	Local?	No sign of wear
Pig tusk	Local?	Unmodified. Hundreds of years old when buried

Table 6 Grave goods from the primary burial in Raunds Barrow 1

The flint dagger, on the other hand, is the product of much time and skill. Its size and the quality of its raw material mean that it must have been made of flint obtained directly from the chalk, and hence from some distance away. It had been sheathed and hafted, on the evidence of polish on the edges and arrises of both faces in the blade area and of the absence of polish from the tang, but showed no sign of other wear (Grace 1990 and forthcoming). This was an artefact which had been transported and curated. Other flint daggers were similarly treated. There was comparable wear on an example from Barrow 6 at Raunds. A dagger from Ffair Rhos, Ceredigion, had been sheathed and unsheathed many times and retained microscopic traces of the binding which had secured the haft (Green *et al.* 1982). Slight polish on the higher arrises of the blade of one from Shorncote, Gloucestershire, suggests a similar history. On this dagger the distal end of the haft had left a shallow V-shaped outline immediately below the notches, preserved by differential patination (P. Bradley 1995, 23-9, 44-5, fig. 4), like that on one from Ystradfellte, Powys (Green *et al.* 1982, 497-8). Most flint daggers, indeed, seem to have been hafted, since they often have notches for binding and are less carefully flaked on the tangs than on the blades. A hafted, sheathed flint dagger may have appeared little, if at all, different from a hafted, sheathed metal one.

The amber ring was badly preserved. It retains the possible vestige of a V-perforation suggesting that, like better-preserved jet examples, it may have been sewn to a belt and used to fasten it (Shepherd forthcoming; Clarke 1970, 113-4, 262-3, figs 143-4). Its material derives ultimately from the Baltic (Beck & Shennan 1991, 37). The association of amber and jet in this burial foreshadows recurrent associations during the first half of the second millennium, when jet and amber beads were made in identical forms (Shepherd 1985, figs 5.45, 5.48, 5.50; Beck & Shennan 1991, fig. 4.1). Both were also used to make V-perforated buttons. The convergence between materials of different appearance and from different sources may be due in part to similar working properties (Shepherd 1985, 205-10), which could have led to their being shaped by the same hands. They may also have been seen as analogous because of their common electrostatic properties, which have often had magical connotations (Woodward 2002).

Although all the jet buttons were of material from the Whitby area of Yorkshire (M. Davis forthcoming), they did not have a common history. Jet is

64 Raunds Barrow 1. Grave goods from primary burial. *Copyright and by permission of English Heritage. Photo courtesy of CfA*

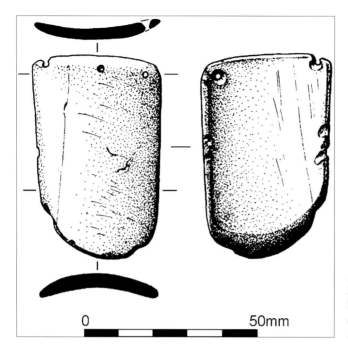

65 Raunds Barrow 1. Detail of stone bracer/burnisher. *Copyright and by permission of English Heritage*

so soft that it readily shows signs of wear. All five buttons had been attached to garments or other items, but their perforations show disparate amounts of wear, suggesting that they were used separately. Furthermore, while all five were bevelled at the junction of base and upper surface *(64)*, the bevel on one was freshly worked, truncating existing wear-marks and suggesting that this button had been modified to match the others immediately before burial (Shepherd forthcoming). This apparent assembly of a set from several sources is akin to that of some necklaces from graves of the following centuries, which were made up of beads of diverse materials in diverse conditions (Barrett 1994, 121-3). Both may have carried connotations of the different individuals and places from which they came.

Another convincing instance of the creation of a set of buttons for burial is provided by an inhumation at Durrington, Wiltshire, which was furnished with, *inter alia*, a V-perforated shale button and two chalk pseudo-buttons, each with a small depression in the centre of the flat face where the perforation would have been on a true button (Annable & Simpson 1964 catalogue nos 86-90; Hoare 1812, 172, pl. xix). The impression here is of the provision of substitutes for objects which should have been placed in a particular grave but could not be. This consideration may extend to a chalk artefact from the Raunds burial. This was carefully carved, ground, and smoothed to a slender, elongated form so fragile that it broke in antiquity (Williams & Humble forthcoming). It cannot have been functional and is likely to be a replica of an implement of more robust material, perhaps a second 'sponge-finger', bearing in mind that these were paired in at least two other burials, at Overton Hill itself and at Winterborne

Stoke G54, also in Wiltshire (Smith & Simpson 1966, fig. 3:3-4, fig. 6: 2-3). The chalk of which the Raunds object was made need not have been brought from far away: it is one of the erratics of the boulder clay which covers the plateau to either side of the valley. The belief that chalk, rather than more readily available limestone, was a suitable material for the task may, however, have emanated from chalkland areas, where there was a long, if occasional, history of carving chalk replicas, the best known of which are chalk axeheads from Woodhenge and Stonehenge (Varndell 1991, 106; Cleal *et al.* 1995, 403-6).

The stone 'sponge-finger' is a used, functional tool, and a carefully made one. Scratch-marks generated during manufacture have largely been removed by polishing, but both bevelled ends carry fine microscopic striations which post-date the polish and would accord with prolonged contact with a resilient material containing minute abrasive grits, such as a hide (Williams & Humble forthcoming). This corresponds to Smith's and Simpson's suggestion that both 'sponge-fingers' and bone and antler spatulae were used to rub fat into leather and to burnish it (1966, 134). Similar wear occurs on another object, this time one with an obvious history *(65)*. The squared, perforated end shows that this was a bracer or wristguard before it was used as a burnishing tool. Lateral chips on the underside may reflect hafting during this secondary use. The bracer may never have been completed: one of the surviving perforations is so close to the edge that it may have broken during manufacture, unless it was damaged on removal from a backing. Manufacture may have preceded the burial by some time. Such objects are usually associated with Beakers of Clarke's Wessex/Middle Rhine and Northern Beaker groups, rather than of his Southern group, as here (Clarke 1970, 448). The object may have been in circulation for a considerable period. Its burial in a re-used state with the 'wrong' Beaker may suggest that it was no longer seen as a bracer, but as a comparable implement to the 'sponge finger'.

This was not the first transformation that it had undergone. It was made of greenish-grey altered basic tuff, probably of petrological group VI from Great Langdale in Cumbria (Williams & Humble forthcoming). Another bracer of this material came from a burial with a Wessex/Middle Rhine Beaker at Dorchester-on-Thames site XII in Oxfordshire (Whittle *et al.* 1992, 179-84). The source was exploited for axehead manufacture in the Neolithic, but seems to have gone out of use by the mid-third millennium BC (R. Bradley & Edmonds 1993, 199). The exceptional curvature of both the Raunds and Dorchester bracers could reflect their manufacture from Neolithic axeheads, which would have been available in both the Nene and Thames valleys (Clough & Cummins 1988, map 6). The material may have been selected because its green colour approached that of some of the schists and slates of which bracers were usually made, but it is difficult to believe that the parent artefacts were not recognised for what they were. The Raunds bracer had not simply been through different uses, perhaps in the hands of different generations, it was also many centuries old, beyond the ambit of an heirloom, and the antiquity of the parent artefact may have contributed to the significance of the object made from it.

It was not the only object in the grave to have an extended history. A pig tusk piled with the other grave goods came from an animal which died between 2890 and 2460 cal BC, hundreds of years before the man with whom it was buried, who died between 2200 and 1920 cal BC (*Table 7 & 66*: UB-3148, OxA-4067; Bayliss *et al.* forthcoming). The tusk may have remained in circulation, passed from generation to generation in a mutating package of traditions, or it may have been recovered from what was already an archaeological context – pig tusks figured in Neolithic burials of Kinnes' stages D–E (1979, figs 3.2-3, 18.5, 18.9).

Of the remaining artefacts in the burial, three longitudinally-split cattle ribs are longer, thinner and more curved than the bone and antler spatulae which recur in Beaker and Early Bronze Age graves, some of them illustrated by Smith and Simpson (1966, fig. 5). The split cattle ribs also show no trace of wear, in contrast to many of the shorter, thicker spatulae (*ibid.*, 147-9). They would have been springy and resilient when fresh, and may have been the

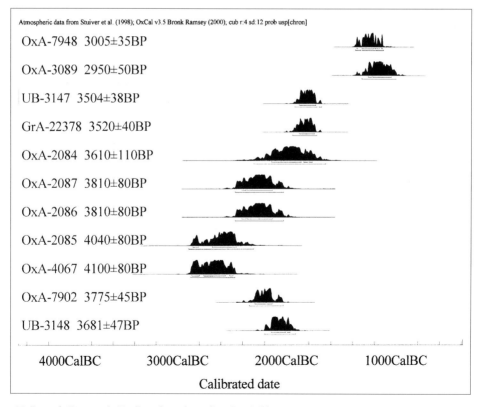

66 Raunds Barrow 1. Radiocarbon dates, listed in *Table 7*

reinforcements of a composite bow (Foxon forthcoming). Unequivocally associated with archery is a triangular arrowhead which is fresh, with no trace of hafting or wear. It may, indeed, have been too thick to complete (Grace 1990, 12) – Green has seen these as blanks for barbed and tanged arrowheads (1980, 142-3, fig. 54).

In other words, of three artefacts certainly or possibly associated with archery, the bracer had been adapted to another use, the bow reinforcements had not been used – indeed they were buried in a bunch, rather than attached to a bow – and the arrowhead was unused or unfinished. The juxtaposition of these to artefacts which *had* been used suggests that their significance was rather different. Perhaps, by this time, when the accoutrements of archery were at their most elaborate, the bow and arrow had almost ceased to be used in inter-personal conflict.

Bows and arrows with single-piece flint tips had been used in Britain since the earliest Neolithic. Leaf-shaped and barbed and tanged arrowheads occur in similarly large numbers across England and Wales (*ibid.*, figs 31, 47); each would have been made and used over about a thousand years; and a dearth of evidence for hunting throughout suggests that both were primarily inter-personal weapons. Yet, while evidence accumulates for death or injury inflicted by arrows with leaf-shaped heads, and for their concerted use in assaults on enclosures, in the fourth millennium (Mercer 1999; Wysocki & Whittle 2000, 599-600), the record of the late third millennium and the second millennium remains scanty. One convincing case is a barbed and tanged arrowhead with an impact fracture at the tip and both barbs broken off which lay next to the spine of a male at Barrow Hills, Radley, Oxfordshire (Barclay & Halpin 1999, 133-8; P. Bradley 1999, 139-40). The most conspicuous instance is a man buried in a grave cut into the silted ditch of Stonehenge, near the entrance. He had been shot at close range by at least three arrows tipped with barbed and tanged points (Evans 1984, 13-22). The unique location and the uniquely large number of arrows strongly suggest that this was an exceptional event. Very few of the usual human burials show any sign of death by arrowshot. The disparity in traces of injury by arrowshot between the two epochs is all the greater because such events should be more readily detectable among the numerous articulated skeletons of the Early Bronze Age than among the largely disarticulated human remains of the Neolithic. The role of archery may have changed. The daggers and battle-axes of the late third and early second millennia may signal an increase in face-to-face, hand-to-hand fighting. Many barbed and tanged arrowheads may have been loosed into the landscape in the course of formalised combat or formalised hunting, the effects of which were as much social as lethal (Gdaniec 1996, 656-7). Elaboration of archery equipment may have been bound up with the demise of the bow and arrow as practical weapons and an expansion of their symbolic value, which may have owed much to their place in the armoury of the past. Such a

Laboratory number	Sample	Radiocarbon age (BP)	Calibrated date range (95% confidence)
UB-3148	Human bone from adult male from primary Beaker burial in grave F30426	3681±47	2200–1920 cal BC
OxA-7902	*Quercus* sp sapwood from chamber enclosing primary Beaker burial in grave F30426	3775±45	2400–2030 cal BC
OxA-4067	Boar's tusk accompanying primary Beaker burial in grave F30426	4100±80	2890–2460 cal BC
OxA-2085	R aurochs M^2 from bone cairn, forming part of same find as sample for OxA-2086, with other teeth and a horncore, all from domestic cattle	4040±80	2880–2340 cal BC
OxA-2086	L aurochs M^2 from bone cairn, forming part of same find as sample for OxA-2085, with other teeth and a horncore, all from domestic cattle	3810±80	2470–1980 cal BC
OxA-2087	R cattle M^2 from badly preserved skull in bone cairn	3810±80	2470–1980 cal BC
OxA-2084	R cattle M^2 from badly preserved skull in bone cairn	3610±110	2290–1680 cal BC
GrA-22378	Cremated bone from secondary deposit F30017, combining ?male of 20–40 yr and child of *c* 13–14 yr, accompanied by early Bronze Age urn, bronze dagger with horn hilt, antler pommel, bone pin	3520±40	1950–1730 cal BC
UB-3147	Human bone of adult male from secondary inhumation F30449	3504±38	1940–1690 cal BC
OxA-3089	Charred *Arrhenatherum* tubers from cremation F30030 cut into silted middle ditch	2950±50	1370–1000 cal BC
OxA-7948	Indet tuber fragments from lower fill of cremation pit F30307, outside outer ditch	3005±35	1390–1120 cal BC

Table 7 Radiocarbon measurements from Raunds Barrow 1

transition may even have had its origin in the early third millennium, given that some of the domestic pigs consumed at Durrington Walls, Wiltshire, had been shot with flint-tipped arrows (Albarella & Serjeantson 2002).

The bag, box, hide or cloth which contained the Barrow 1 grave goods may thus have encapsulated a web of beliefs and allusions encompassing known individuals, events and lineages as well as remote times and distant places. The scale of the group which generated this collective mnemonic may be echoed in the bone deposit overlying the limestone cairn which surmounted the burial. On the cairn were approximately 185 domestic cattle skulls, a much smaller number of cattle mandibles, scapulae and pelves and some aurochs remains. These have been analysed by Simon Davis (S. Davis & Payne 1993; S. Davis forthcoming). The bone was badly preserved, a result of local conditions, and the skulls survived mainly as pairs of intact maxillary tooth rows, which remained the 'right way up'. When complete, the skulls would have to have been stacked in three or four tiers to fit onto the small cairn.

Tooth eruption and wear indicate that most of the beasts were young adults when slaughtered, with few calves and few old animals. They would have been prime beef animals. Cut-marks show that they were butchered. The shortfall of mandibles in relation to crania shows that most of the skulls were already defleshed when placed on the cairn. A further shortfall of maxillary premolars and incisors (the least firmly-rooted teeth and the first to fall out) shows that many of the skulls were not entirely fresh. They had not, on the other hand, been subjected to weathering for long periods: most of the teeth were in good condition and showed little sign of exposure to frost and temperature change. This suggests that the cattle had been dead for a few years at most, and possibly less, and that there was little interval between their installation on the cairn and their protection by the construction of the first mound. Davis' preferred interpretation is that some animals, probably those represented by mandibles, scapulae and pelves as well as skulls, were slaughtered and consumed at the barrow, perhaps in the course of funerary rites, while the majority were brought there already defleshed. If the 35 animals represented by scapulae were slaughtered in a single event, the resulting 7,500kg of meat could, on a distinctly generous ration of 1kg per person per day, have fed a thousand people for a week, with the remaining 32,500kg from the other animals consumed over a period of months or a couple of years in various communities at various locations. Aggregation on this scale, if it occurred, would be a telling indicator of the importance ascribed to the man buried beneath the cairn. Even if all the cattle were slaughtered and consumed in the wider territory, the scale of the slaughter surely reflects the involvement of a relatively large social unit (clan? tribe?), rather than the small (family?) group which is all that would have been needed for the physical labour of digging the grave and constructing the monument. It is on this larger scale that the web of allusions tied up in the grave goods gains social texture. However few saw them go into the grave, their composition reflected the concerns and participation of many. A similar scale of involvement may be reflected by a mass of cattle bone, this time from all parts of the skeleton, placed over the mound covering a large grave with a wooden chamber at Gayhurst Quarry, Buckinghamshire (Chapman *et al.* 1999).

There was another facet to the bone deposit. Among the few aurochs remains were loose teeth, two of which have been radiocarbon-dated. While one was of indistinguishable age from the two dated cattle skulls, the other was older than the other three samples from the cairn, and than the underlying burial. The animal lived at some point between 2880-2340 cal BC and may have been contemporary with the pig whose tusk was placed in that burial beneath (66 & *Table 7*: OxA-2085, -4067). The incorporation of the already old pig tusk and aurochs tooth (and possibly more of the aurochs) into Barrow 1 may have been a deliberate connection to the past, equivalent to the construction of barrows among Neolithic monuments on the nearby terrace. The early third millennium dates of both tusk and tooth correspond to an apparent lull in monument building in this part of the valley (although the record is incomplete and riddled with uncertainty). They may have been brought from elsewhere when ritual use of the area gathered new momentum.

There is another sense in which the cattle skull deposit connects to earlier times. It is highly unlikely to reflect the composition of contemporary living herds, as Davis points out, since, by this time, herds were diversifying and sheep were becoming increasingly important. Most of the bone assemblages from settlements with Beaker and Early Bronze Age pottery around the fenland basin include some pig and substantial, though variable, proportions of caprines, which seem to have increased as the second millennium progressed (Healy 1996, 171-4, 179). Rather later than the Barrow 1 cairn is a large assemblage accumulated at West Row, Mildenhall, Suffolk in the early to mid-second millennium, in which there were slightly more caprines than cattle, although in terms of meat weight beef would have been of greater importance than mutton (Olsen 1994). Caprines were also well represented among the animal bone accumulated in the course of the second millennium at Fengate, although again outnumbered by cattle (Biddick 1980), and the paddocks and droves from which the assemblage was recovered are interpreted as designed for sheep management (Pryor 1998, 89-108). Cattle were the pre-eminent meat and ceremonial species of the Neolithic (Ray & Thomas 2003). Their continued ceremonial role at this time may have been yet another use of the past in the present, reflecting an intertwining of long-lived practice, attachment to tradition, and manipulations of the symbolic value of the past to justify and perpetuate the *status quo* of the present.

The reader may well reject all or any of the interpretations offered here. However they are received, it is hoped that he or she will be convinced of the complexity and capacity for communication of this burial.

ACKNOWLEDGEMENTS

Appreciation is due above all to Derek Simpson, for his own contribution to Neolithic and Bronze Age studies and for his decades of teaching. The frequency with which his former students distinguish themselves in print and at the lectern is testimony to the enthusiasm to which they have been exposed and to the guidance, encouragement and support which they have received. Thanks are given to English Heritage for funding the analysis and writing-up of the pre-Iron Age aspects of the Raunds Area Project, and for permission to reproduce illustrations from the forthcoming publication. Those illustrations are the work of John Vallender and his colleagues in the Graphics Office of the Centre for Archaeology, Fort Cumberland. It would have been impossible to write the paper without the expertise of all the colleagues who are cited here. Particular thanks are owed to Alex Gibson for the invitation to contribute to this volume and for monitoring the project so effectively. Comments from Roger Mercer have worked welcome improvement.

BIBLIOGRAPHY

Albarella, U. & Serjeantson, D., 2002 A passion for pork: meat consumption at the British Late Neolithic site of Durrington Walls. In Miracle, P. & Milner, N. (eds), *Consuming Passions and Patterns of Consumption*, 33-49. Cambridge: McDonald Institute Monographs.

Annable, F.K. & Simpson, D.D.A., 1964 *Guide Catalogue of the Neolithic and Bronze Age Collections in Devizes Museum*. Devizes: Wiltshire Archaeological and Natural History Society.

Barclay, A. & Halpin, C., 1999 *Excavations at Barrow Hills, Radley, Oxfordshire*. Vol.1: *the Neolithic and Bronze Age Monument Complex*. Thames Valley Landscapes Monograph 11. Oxford: Oxford Archaeological Unit.

Barrett, J.C., 1994 *Fragments from Antiquity. An Archaeology of Social Life in Britain, 2900-1200 BC*. Oxford: Blackwell.

Bayliss, A., Healy, F., Bronk Ramsey, C., McCormac, F.G., Cook, G.T. & Harding, J., forthcoming. Absolute chronology. In Healy, F. & Harding, J., forthcoming.

Beck, C. & Shennan, S., 1991 *Amber in Prehistoric Britain*. Monograph 8. Oxford: Oxbow.

Biddick, K., 1980 Appendix 7. Animal bones from the second millennium ditches, Newark Road subsite, Fengate. In Pryor, F. *Excavation at Fengate, Peterborough, England: the Third Report*, 217-32. Northamptonshire Archaeological Society Monograph 1/Royal Ontario Museum Archaeological Monograph 6. Northampton & Toronto: Northamptonshire Archaeological Society & Royal Ontario Museum.

Bradley, P., 1995 Flint. In Barclay, A. & Glass, H. with Parry, C. Excavations of Neolithic and Bronze Age ring ditches, Shorncote Quarry, Somerford Keynes, Gloucestershire. *Transactions of the Bristol & Gloucestershire Archaeological Society*, 113, 25-2, 31, 37, 39, 43-45.

Bradley, P. 1999. Worked Flint. In Barclay, A. & Halpin, C. *Excavations at Barrow Hills, Radley, Oxfordshire*. Vol. 1: *the Neolithic and Bronze Age Monument Complex*. Thames Valley Landscapes Monograph 11. Oxford: Oxford Archaeological Unit/OUCA, 14-15, 25-6, 31, 33-4, 38-40, 45, 49-52, 55, 57, 59-60, 63, 65-7, 71, 73, 77, 85-7, 94, 97, 100-1, 109-10, 114-5, 119, 124, 127-8, 133, 139-40, 145-7, 152, 156-7, 162, 166, 211-28.

Bradley, R. & Edmonds, M., 1993 *Interpreting the Axe Trade*. Cambridge: Cambridge University Press.

Campbell, G. & Robinson, M., forthcoming. Environment and land use in the valley bottom. In Healy, F. & Harding, J. forthcoming.

Case, H.J., 1977 The Beaker culture in Britain and Ireland. In Mercer, R.J. (ed.) *Beakers in Britain and Europe*, 71–101. BAR International Series 26. Oxford: British Archaeological Reports.

Chapman, A., Jones, C., Holmes, M. & Prentice, J., 1999 Gayhurst, Gayhurst Quarry. *South Midlands Archaeology*, 29, 17-20.

Clarke, D.L., 1970 *Beaker Pottery of Great Britain and Ireland*. Cambridge: Cambridge University Press.

Cleal, R.M.J., Walker, K. & Montague, R., 1995 *Stonehenge in its Landscape. Twentieth-century excavations*. Archaeological Report 10. London: English Heritage.

Clough, T.H.McK. & Cummins, W.A. (eds), 1988 *Stone Axe Studies* Vol. 2. Research Report 67. London: Council for British Archaeology.

Copley, M., Dudd, S., Evershed, R. & Heron, C., forthcoming. Residue analysis. In Healy, F. & Harding, J. forthcoming.

Cotton, J., 1991 Prehistory in Greater London. *Current Archaeology*, 124, 151-4.

Davis, M., forthcoming. Analysis of buttons from Irthlingborough and West Cotton. In Healy, F. & Harding, J., forthcoming.

Davis, S., forthcoming. The animal remains from Barrow 1. In Healy, F. & Harding, J. forthcoming.

Davis, S. & Payne, S., 1993 A barrow full of cattle skulls. *Antiquity*, 67, 12-22.

Evans, J.G., 1984 Stonehenge – the environment in the Late Neolithic and Early Bronze Age and a Beaker-age burial. *Wiltshire Archaeological and Natural History Magazine*, 78, 7-30.

Fitzpatrick, A., 2002 The Amesbury archer: 'king of Stonehenge'? *Past*, 41, 1-2.

Foxon, A., forthcoming. The bone spatulae and points from Barrow 1. In Healy, F. & Harding, J. forthcoming.

Gdaniec, K. 1996. A miniature antler bow from a middle Bronze Age site at Isleham (Cambridgeshire), England. *Antiquity*, 70 (269), 652-7.

Grace, R., 1990 The limitations and applications of use wear analysis. In Gräslund, B. Knutsson, H., Knutsson, K. & Taffinder, J. (eds), *The Interpretive Possibilities of Microwear Studies. Proceedings of the International Conference on Lithic Use-Wear Analysis, 15th-17th Febuary 1989* (Aun 14), 9-14. Uppsala.

Grace, R., forthcoming. Usewear analysis of flint grave goods from Barrow 1 and artefacts from treethrow hole F62123. In Healy, F. & Harding, J. forthcoming.

Green, H.S., 1980 *The Flint Arrowheads of the British Isles* BAR British Series 75. Oxford: British Archaeological Reports.

Green, H.S., Houlder, C.H. & Keeley, L.H., 1982 A flint dagger from Ffair Rhos, Ceredigion, Dyfed, Wales. *Proceedings of the Prehistoric Society*, 48, 492-501.

Healy, F. & Harding, J., forthcoming. *Raunds Area Project. The Neolithic and Bronze Age Landscapes of West Cotton, Stanwick and Irthlingborough, Northamptonshire* (English Heritage Archaeological Report).

Healy, F., 1996 *The Fenland Project Number 11: The Wissey Embayment: Evidence for Pre-Iron Age Settlement Accumulated prior to the Fenland Project* East Anglian Archaeology 78. Gressenhall: Field Archaeology Division, Norfolk Museums Services.

Hoare, R.C., 1812 *The Ancient History of South Wiltshire*. London: William Miller.

Kinnes, I., 1979 *Round Barrows and Ring Ditches in the British Neolithic*. Occasional Paper 7, London: Department of Prehistoric and Romano-British Antiquities, British Museum.

Mercer, R.J., 1999 The origins of warfare in the British Isles. In Carman, J. & Harding, A. (eds), *Ancient Warfare*, 143-56. Stroud: Sutton.

Olsen, S.L., 1994 Exploitation of mammals at the Early Bronze Age site of West Row Fen (Mildenhall 165), Suffolk, England. *Annals of Carnegie Museum*, 63(2), 115-53.

Pryor, F., 1998 *Farmers in Prehistoric Britain*. Stroud: Tempus.

Ray, K. & Thomas, J., 2003 In the kinship of cows: the social centrality of cattle in the earlier Neolithic of southern Britain. In Parker Pearson, M. (ed.) *Food, Culture and Identity in the Neolithic and Early Bronze Age*, 37-44. BAR International Series 1117. Oxford: British Archaeological Reports.

Shepherd, I.A.G., 1985 Jet and amber. In Clarke, D.V., Cowie, T.G. & Foxon, A., 1985 *Symbols of Power at the Time of Stonehenge*, 204-16. Edinburgh: National Museum of Antiquities of Scotland.

Shepherd, I., forthcoming. Jet buttons and amber ring from barrows 1 and 6. In Healy, F. & Harding, J., forthcoming.

Simpson, D.D.A., 1968 Food Vessels: associations and chronologies. In Coles, J.M. & Simpson, D.D.A. (eds), *Studies in Ancient Europe. Essays Presented to Stuart Piggott*, 197-212. Leicester: Leicester University Press.

Smith, I.F. & Simpson, D.D.A., 1966 Excavation of a round barrow on Overton Hill, North Wiltshire. *Proceedings of the Prehistoric Society*, 32, 122-55.

Sofaer-Derevenski, J., 2002 Engendering context. Context as gendered practice in the Early Bronze Age of the Upper Thames valley, UK. *European Journal of Archaeology*, 5(2), 191-211.

Thomas, J., 1991 Reading the body: Beaker funerary practice in Britain. In Garwood, P., Jennings, J., Skeates, R. & Toms, J. (eds), Sacred and Profane. Proceedings of a Conference on Archaeology, Ritual and Religion. Oxford, 1989, 33-49. Monograph 32. Oxford: Oxford University Committee for Archaeology.

Tomalin, D.J., forthcoming. Pottery and fired clay from Irthlingborough, West Cotton and Stanwick, with an overview of the ceramic evidence. In Healy, F. & Harding, J., forthcoming.

Varndell, G., 1991 The worked chalk. In Longworth, I., Herne, A., Varndell, G. & Needham, S. *Shaft X: Bronze Age Flint, Chalk and Metal Working. Excavations at Grime's Graves Norfolk 1972-1976*, 94-153. Fasicule 3. London: British Museum Press.

Whittle, A., Atkinson, R.J.C., Chambers, R. & Thomas, N., 1992 Excavations in the Neolithic and Bronze Age complex at Dorchester-on-Thames, Oxfordshire. *Proceedings of the Prehistoric Society*, 58, 143-201.

Williams, D. F., & Humble, J., forthcoming. Catalogue of stone implements. In Healy, F. & Harding, J., forthcoming.

Woodward, A., 2002 Beads and Beakers: heirlooms and relics in the British Early Bronze Age. *Antiquity*, 76(294), 1040-7.

Wysocki, M. & Whittle, A., 2000 Diversity, lifestyles and rites: new biological and archaeological evidence from British earlier Neolithic mortuary assemblages. *Antiquity*, 74(285), 591-601.

13

THE NEOLITHIC POTTERY AND THE BRONZE AGE CIST AT RATH, COUNTY WICKLOW

A.L. BRINDLEY

Derek's work in Ireland has involved revisiting a number of well-known excavations with a view to updating the information that these have provided. This is a very necessary thing to do. It casts no aspersions on the first excavator because it respects the original work as having being done at a time when archaeological data were either limited or were interpreted in another way, and although not regarded by everyone as such, it is in fact a compliment to the original worker if their work can indeed be revisited. Much archaeology remains a question of interpretation and will remain so. Derek's return to Lyles Hill, Island MacHugh and Dun Ruadh have contributed to the understanding of these sites. I offer this very brief piece to him in like spirit.

In 1944, the National Museum of Ireland was asked to investigate the discovery of a grave in a sandpit at Rath, County Wicklow. The late Ellen Prendergast visited the site and found that during sand digging, two men had come across large stones in the face of a quarry. As these started to fall out, they revealed a small bowl. On realising that they had found a grave the men contacted the museum. By the time of Prendergast's visit, the stones surrounding the bowl had fallen into the quarry but the bowl had been retrieved intact. The 'back' stone of the grave was all that remained *in situ*. Prendergast realised that there was a second cavity behind this stone and on excavation discovered an intact small rectangular cist containing a cremation. The grave consisted of four side stones, a floor slab, two capstones and, on the undisturbed sides, some packing stones. Examination of the quarry face suggested that the grave had been dug into the original ground surface and that no artificial mound was present. Prendergast's plan also shows that the cist was neatly made and that at least two of the four side stones (south and east) were probably split boulders with the straight edges to the inside *(72)*. Some distance away, a 'haphazard pile of large stones' (Prendergast 1959, 19)

---

67 Opposite Top: Rath, County Wicklow. *After Prendergast 1959;* Middle: Ballyduff, County Wexford. *After Hartnett & Prendergast 1953;* Bottom: Ballynerrin, County Wicklow. *After Hartnett 1952*

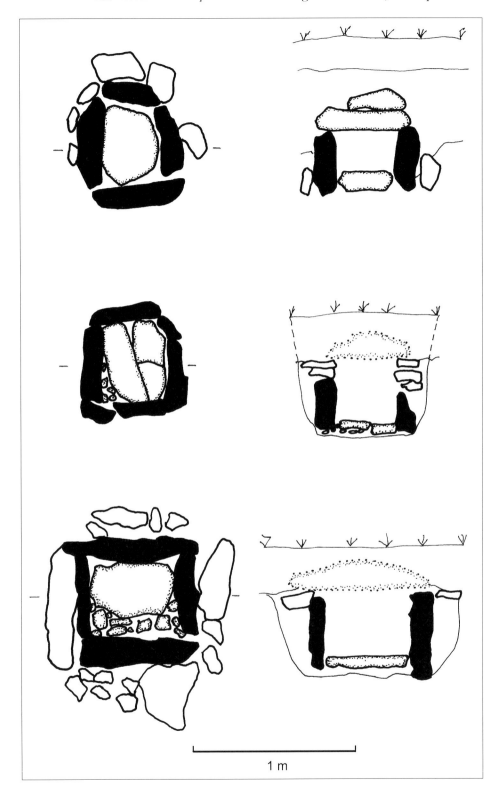

1 m

had also been revealed in the quarry face and these too began to collapse. Underneath these was found a second bowl. Due to the dangerous condition of the quarry face in this area, no further examination of this findspot could be undertaken.

Prendergast recorded the account given to her by the two quarry workers. It appeared that they had only seen the grave from the quarry face while working their way into the centre of the sandpit, which was in a natural sand mound approximately 60m in diameter. They had first seen the large stones in the quarry face and subsequently, as these fell out, a small pot. They reconstructed the grave as having been 'coffin-shaped' and running east–west with capstones but without a floor stone. By the time of Prendergast's arrival the whole of this edifice, except apparently for one stone, had collapsed. Prendergast published an account of her findings in 1959.

At the time of discovery the site attracted interest because of the then new types of pottery discovered (*ibid.*, fig. 2). Prendergast argued that the round bases of the two pots placed them within the Neolithic pottery tradition but that the shape and lugs and the basal decoration of the smaller vessel linked it to the bowl Food Vessels of the Bronze Age in a possible 'fusion of styles' (*ibid.*, 24), while the use of a cist emphasised this connection. Prendergast concluded that the pottery and the compartmented grave (which she compared to wedge tombs) belonged to the end of the Neolithic when the major elements of the Early Bronze Age had already been anticipated.

In the decades following the discovery of the grave at Rath, the tradition of non-megalithic, non-communal burial in the Neolithic began to take on a more clearly defined shape, initially in the Leinster region. These burials most often consisted of a submegalithic polygonal chamber built on the old ground surface, containing one or two male inhumations accompanied by most characteristically a round-based pot, the grave covered by a circular mound.

By 1980, radiocarbon dating had become a routine tool for investigation. Attracted by the large number of well-defined contexts with short-life samples in Ireland (chiefly unburnt bone from graves), Brindley and Lanting initiated a project to provide radiocarbon dates for various prehistoric phenomena. At this time, the only means of dating unburnt bone involved large samples and so the initial thrust of the project became the series of Food Vessels with inhumations from the Early Bronze Age and the smaller series of Neolithic burials.

Not all the Neolithic burials could be dated in the 1980s for a variety of reasons. In some instances the bones were not available, or were in poor condition and did not have sufficient collagen, and in the unique case of Rath, the presence only of cremated bone meant the exclusion of this grave. The anticipated results were expected to confirm the conventional Late Neolithic/Early Bronze Age dating. The actual results placed the graves firmly in the Early Neolithic.

This initially led to excitement in some quarters and mixed horror and disbelief in others. The radiocarbon dates showed that the development of Early Neolithic pottery occurred far more quickly and earlier than had hitherto been believed. Subsequent developments in the technique of radiocarbon dating during the 1980s led to the use of much smaller samples and the possibility of dating graves which had only small amounts of bone preserved. Re-dating of several samples and the inclusion of several recent discoveries of Neolithic graves was also carried out. All re-affirmed the previous results. However, when Brindley and Lanting discussed the results, they did not question the association of the compartmented cist with the two round-based bowls at Rath and their general position within the Neolithic (Brindley & Lanting 1990).

When in 1997 Lanting recognised that it was possible to use the carbonate apatite in bone for radiocarbon dating, it became possible to date burials using carbonate, the most significant application being to cremated bone (Lanting *et al.* 2001). Material from the Irish dating project was used as one of the two sources of samples during the testing stages of the technique. Amongst the earliest samples to which this technique was applied was, at long last and in general for the sake of completeness only, a sample of cremated bone from Rath, County Wicklow.

The sample of cremated bone from Rath produced an unexpected result: 3590±40 BP (GrA-14760) which placed the cremation burial unambiguously in the Early Bronze Age. The context of the sample is secure and there are no indications that the result is anomalous.

When one reconsiders the Rath burial, there are grounds for accepting the date as true and accurate. Firstly, the burial was disturbed before being recorded and indeed one of the chambers of the compartmented cist had collapsed by the time of Prendergast's visit. Her report of this first chamber relies entirely on the memories of the two quarry workers who saw the structure as it fell out of the quarry face. Even a trained observer would have had difficulty recognising the precise configuration of a grave observed only as it collapsed down an exposed quarry face. There is no documentation of the relationship of the two chambers to each other, just as there is no record of the actual form of the first chamber discovered.

SMALL CONSTRUCTIONS OF STONE ASSOCIATED WITH NEOLITHIC POTTERY

Small stone constructions forming graves are known to have been used during the middle Neolithic (Brindley & Lanting 1990, Hartwell 1998). In general, they appear to vary quite considerably in shape but can be recognised by the occurrence of grave goods with the burial. Some examples have been dated which suggests that this practice was probably more widespread than can

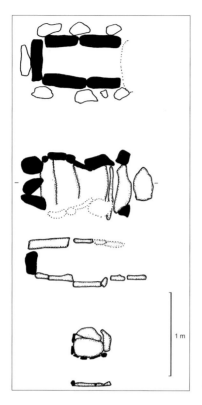

68 Top: Rath. *Reconstruction after Prendergast 1959;*
Others: Ballynahatty, County Down. *After Hartwell 1998*

generally be appreciated where no grave goods are present and without radiocarbon dating. Two examples have been excavated on the perimeter of the Ballynahatty, County Down, enclosure (both dated to 4460±40 BP (Brindley & Lanting, in preparation), with *Carrowkeel Style* bowls) and others have been excavated within and around the periphery of the passage tomb at Tara, County Meath (peripheral burials without pottery, 4550-4440 BP, small cists within passage tomb mound, 4530-4187 BP, Brindley *et al.* forthcoming). A list of non-megalithic burials of the Middle Neolithic was included in the discussion of the dating of Neolithic single burials (Brindley & Lanting 1990, 6). The smaller of the two bowls from Rath is closely parallelled by pottery in two inhumation graves, Ashleypark, County Tipperary (Manning 1985) and Cahirguillamore, County Limerick (Hunt 1967). At the latter site, a communal burial also contained sherds of similar pottery. There are good arguments for an Early/Mid-Neolithic transition date for the Rath graves on the basis of the pottery and the non–megalithic (but clearly protected in some form or another) context. The absence of actual bone may point to the presence of an inhumation originally, as occurred at both Cahirguillamore and Ashleypark. There was a mixed tradition of burial at this time, encompassing small cist-like graves containing cremations and, where pottery is included, *Carrowkeel Style* bowls, and inhumations associated with *Rath Style* bowls and a more eclectic choice of grave type.

There are no reasons therefore to doubt the earlier Neolithic date of the two bowls from Rath. Both Neolithic pots were associated with stone; the smaller pot was clearly protected in a cist-type structure and the larger pot was found in a collapse of stone. Prendergast remarked that the stones used for this second feature were unshaped.

THE RECTANGULAR CIST ASSOCIATED WITH A CREMATION

Waddell has described the salient features of Bronze Age cists on a number of occasions (e.g. Waddell 1979; 1990). The cist which contained the Rath cremation fully conforms to the type and is a well constructed example. Cists, or indeed pits with cremations and no other grave goods, are difficult to date without radiocarbon sampling and it is possible that their use in the later stages of the Early Bronze Age has been underestimated. Several examples of rectangular, almost square, cists with floor slab have been excavated in the Wicklow-Wexford region *(67)*. An excellent parallel for the Rath cist was in fact excavated by Prendergast, together with Hartnett, at Ballyduff, County Wexford, some time later (Hartnett & Prendergast 1953). The small rectangular and symmetric grave contained not only a cremation but also a vase and a faience bead. The cremation has been dated as part of the Early Bronze Age dating programme and the result is similar to the Rath date (3559±50 BP, GrA–14604, Brindley forthcoming). If it is accepted that the grave excavated and planned by Prendergast represents a single-celled cist, there are no archaeological grounds for dismissing the radiocarbon date on the cremation that it contained.

CONCLUSIONS

The compartmented cist apparently recorded by Prendergast in fact consists of a Neolithic structure which can be dated to the earlier Neolithic on the basis of a round-based pot found in it, and a small neatly constructed cist with floor stone, side stones and two capstones which contained cremated bone, carbonate from which has been dated to the Early Bronze Age.

Unfortunately the precise contexts of the two Neolithic pots from Rath must now be regarded as unknown but apparently they both involved some form of stone construction, 10m apart and were possibly originally associated with inhumation burials. The reconstruction published by Prendergast, based on the description by the two quarry workers, appears to be similar to one of the structures excavated by Hartwell at Ballynahatty *(68, middle)* which suggests that it is, in fact, fairly accurate. The small (finger bone sized, they apparently did not say finger bone shaped) hard object which they reported as having been with the bowl may have been the head of an object, variously described as mushroom-headed or barbell-shaped, of a type which has been found with burials of this date, especially at Cahirguillamore (Hunt 1967).

Prendergast suggested that the object was of burnt bone *because* it was described as hard, but in fact bone becomes brittle when exposed to heat. The material used for the mushroom and barbell-headed objects has not been identified but is generally described also as hard. The size of the lost object from Rath does not preclude the possibility that it was part of a similar object.

BIBLIOGRAPHY

Brindley, A.L., forthcoming. *The dating of Food Vessels and Urns in Ireland.* Galway: Galway University Press.

Brindley, A.L. &. Lanting, J.N., 1990 Radiocarbon dates for Neolithic Single Burials. *Journal of Irish Archaeology,* 5, 1989/90, 1-7.

Brindley, A.L. &. Lanting, J.N., forthcoming. Some other radiocarbon dates for the Irish Neolithic.

Brindley, A.L., Lanting, J.N. & van der Plicht, H., forthcoming. Report on a series of radiocarbon dated samples from the Mound of the Hostages, Tara, Co. Meath. In Ó Ríordáin, S.P. & O'Sullivan, M. publication of the excavations at Tara.

Hartnett, P.J., 1952 Bronze Age burials in Co. Wicklow. *Journal of the Royal Society of Antiquaries of Ireland,* 82, 153-62.

Harnett, P.J. & Prendergast, E., 1953 Bronze Age burials, Co. Wexford. *Journal of the Royal Society of Antiquaries of Ireland,* 83, 46-57.

Hartwell, B., 1998 The Ballynahatty Complex. In Gibson, A. & Simpson, D. (eds), *Prehistoric Ritual and Religion,* 32-44. Stroud: Alan Sutton.

Hunt, J., 1967 Prehistoric burials at Cahirguillamore, Co. Limerick. In Rynne, E. (ed.) *North Munster Studies: Essays in Commemoration of Monsignor Michael Moloney,* 20-42. Limerick: Thomond Archaeological Society.

Lanting, J.N., Aerts-Bijma, A.T. & van der Plicht, H., 2001 Dating of cremated bone. In Carmi, I. & Boaretto, E. (eds), *Proceedings of the 17th International Radiocarbon Conference, Jerusalem 2000. Radiocarbon,* 43, 249-54.

Manning, C., 1985 A Neolithic burial mound at Ashleypark, County Tipperary. *Proceedings of the Royal Irish Academy,* 85C, 61-100.

Prendergast, E., 1959 Prehistoric burial at Rath, Co. Wicklow. *Journal of the Royal Society of Antiquaries of Ireland,* 89, 17-29.

Waddell, J., 1979 Bronze Age cists, a survey. *Journal of the Royal Society of Antiquaries of Ireland,* 109, 91-139.

Waddell, J., 1990 *The Bronze Age Burials of Ireland.* Galway: Galway University Press.

14

BELL BEAKER AND CORDED WARE CULTURE BURIAL ASSOCIATIONS: A BOTTOM-UP RATHER THAN TOP-DOWN APPROACH

HUMPHREY CASE

INTRODUCTION

Some thousands of Corded Ware and Bell Beaker burials, taken together extending from the Atlantic coast to deep within central Europe and through the Mediterranean, and current more or less throughout the third millennium BC (with Bell Beakers extending into the second), comprise an exceptionally complex mass of data, which has generally attracted rather simplistic explanations – with so-called battle-axes and daggers for example invoking warfare and conquest, and more recently status and ranking. Such explanations partly involve top-down analogy, a type of argument familiar in prehistory, involving attaching secondary explanations derived directly or sometimes very indirectly from sociological or ethnographic data (or from philosophical speculation) to primary archaeological material culture. A contrasting bottom-up approach, less conspicuous generally in anglophone research, is to infer more emphatically the inherent functional and contextual nature of the primary material culture itself as the major sources of explanation.

The following is an essay in approaching Bell Beaker and Corded Ware burial associations from the bottom up. I offer it to Derek Simpson in appreciation of his thorough and revealing expositions of material culture.

THE BELL BEAKER CULTURE

The most prominent feature of all in Bell Beaker studies, whatever combination of approaches is favoured, has been to focus on the pottery, and within that category virtually only on the beakers themselves. Other material culture has been given less prominence. All this is well known, but it is sometimes overlooked that from an early stage and over a prolonged period and a large part of its geographical range, from the Iberian peninsula in the west to central Europe and prominently in southern Britain,[1] the richest burials display the Bell Beaker as only one component in a recurrent set of burial associations (in a culture in the strictest archaeological sense) comprising Beaker – copper knife – stone wristguard – and arrowhead or other projectile *(69, nos 9-19; 75)*. The importance of this culture is emphasised by its association with rare materials such as gold (e.g. *69, nos 8, 14*), silver, amber; and its concentrated ritual power is further emphasised by its recurrence in single burials, whether in megalithic contexts or not. And the number of eligible graves can be increased, if one takes wristguard and projectile head as interchangeable in representing archery (e.g. *69 nos 1-8, 15-19*) and brings into consideration the characteristically central European bow-pendants; and similarly, if one takes a flint knife as interchangeable with a copper or bronze one (e.g. *case 2004b, 24*).

How can this archaeological culture be explained within the wider meaning of culture as that term is understood by historians of most kinds, by sociologists of various persuasions or by the general public? To describe its components as prestige items, status symbols, counters in a very serious game of peer polity, does not take us very far, since the question then remains: why these particular objects?

To start with, one can argue plausibly on demographic grounds that Bell Beaker burials as represented in the archaeological record in the great majority of regions, represent an elite; and that the richer burials (such as those in question here) represent the most privileged part of that elite. Where skeletons survive, these are predominantly of men. However, components of the burial association in question here have been recorded associated in central Europe with children's burials (Turek 2000, 435 & fig. 7) and at least once with a woman's (Dvořák *et al.* 1992, obr. 8); and the man in Amesbury 1289, Wiltshire, was permanently lame (Fitzpatrick 2003; Andrew Fitzpatrick pers. comm.).

Do these burial associations then represent sets of equipment used by individuals when living? Unlikely in the case of children or possibly a lame man. Do they represent offerings to the deceased by individual mourners of equipment which they themselves possessed, or had made at the time of the funeral (Brodie 1997, 300-1; 1998, 48-9)? Possibly so, but the pan-European recurrence of this set of equipment suggests that more than the emotions of random collections of mourners is represented. Arguably this equipment may not have been regarded as belonging to the deceased, but rather as signifying his or her role within society (e.g. Turek 2000, 432; 2001, 226) or even as belonging to society as a whole rather than to any division within it; but its more or less invariable association with single burials or single burial events,[2] is apparently irrefutable evidence that it was assigned by the living to individuals – dead individuals presumably with promise or eligibility to fulfil the wishes and aspirations of the living, whatever they may have been.

Thus the individual role cannot be ignored. What was it? Why these particular objects? Taken together and in their ritual context as burial offerings, I have suggested (Case 2004a; 2004b) that they are explainable as symbolical hunting equipment: the arrowheads to maim and wound the quarry until it fell, the knife to perform the *coup-de-grâce* by cutting its throat, and the Beaker from which to drink its blood. An equipment suitable for hunting large or medium-sized animals, such as the wild ox (definitely hunted and with arrowheads: e.g. Holloway Lane, west London; Cotton 1991, 153-4, personal information and discussion), the wild boar (I assume some recurrent tusks in richer graves, e.g. Amesbury 1289, Wiltshire, Fitzpatrick 2003, to have been from hunted animals), the red deer (culled but also conserved for antler?), the horse (also culled? Sometimes hunted, e.g. Moncín, Zaragoza, Harrison *et al.* 1994) and man himself (shot in feuding and ambushes, e.g. Stonehenge burial: Cleal *et al.* 1995, 455-6 and references).

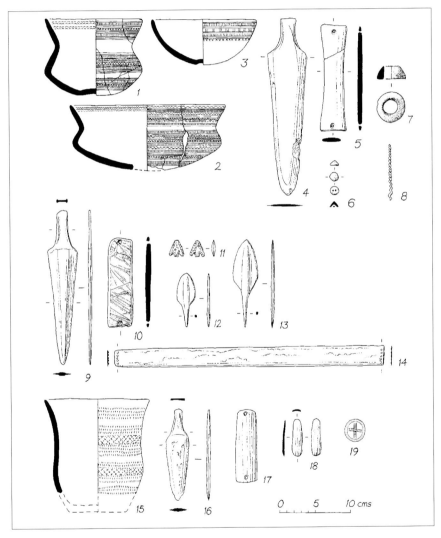

69 Nos 1-8, El Pago de la Peña, Zamora; nos 9-14, Fuente Olmedo, Valladolid (three pots comparable to nos 1-3 and ten other Palmela points not illustrated); nos 15-19, Mere 6a, Wiltshire. Nos 4, 9, 12, 13, 16, copper. Nos 5, 10, 17, stone. No. 11, flint. Nos 8, 14, 19, gold. Nos 6, 7, 18, bone. *Nos 1-8, after Harrison 1977 and Garrido- Pena 2000; nos 9-14, after Garrido-Pena 2000*

I suggest that it was equipment given to the dead for the purpose of furthering the interests of the living in the Otherworld. Why hunting? Since hunting appears little represented overall in the food quest,[3] it can be seen in life as being both a leisure and a ritualised activity: as a recreation appropriate to the privileged, exemplifying and demanding desirable qualities of cunning, courage and endur-ance; and as a means to drink in these qualities from the wild. Thus, assuming a dialogue between the living and the dead, society can be taken to have assigned the privileged few this role in the Otherworld not only out of gratitude and admiration, and to assert their participation in activities desirable for the wellbeing of the group both living and dead, but also to keep powerful potentially interfering spirits diverted into leisure activity while the living occupied themselves undisturbed with food production, resource accumulation and kinship alliances. But just as importantly those few of the dead were sent into the Otherworld in the role of fully armed ancestors, available when entreated to close the ranks and protect the living from malignant Grendel-like spirits, whose incursions from the Otherworld may always have been a threat.

I argue that this symbolism and related set of beliefs were near the core of ethos and mythology associated with the Bell Beaker's pan-European range. But this should not be taken to assert that it illustrates other than a single aspect (albeit important) of that complex manifestation which is Bell Beaker burial practice (Case 2004a for summary account: Gibson 2004). For instance, less well-furnished graves of men and of women and children can plausibly be taken to reflect different roles (Case 1998, 406-10; 2004a) in a putative interaction with the Otherworld; and mutilated, fragmentary and rearranged burials invite other explanations. Nor, taking the question more widely, can this symbolism or its related beliefs reasonably be seen as other than aspects of a series of major beliefs (including for examples, creation myths), in which the sun may have figured prominently as in the Later Neolithic generally: note interpretations of gold so-called sun-discs (*69, no. 19*; e.g. Darvill 1997, 187, 190); a tendency for burials in north Britain to face the southern hemisphere and the general direction of the sunrise in southern Britain (Case 2004a; and recently excavated Amesbury 1289, Wiltshire, inf. Andrew Fitzpatrick); and an apparent representation of the sun (rising or setting?) on a Bell Beaker period stela at Petit-Chasseur, Sion, Valais (North stela, Dolmen M.I: Bocksberger 1978. I am grateful to Volker Heyd for this reference).

A RANGE OF FUNCTIONS

BELL BEAKERS

Emphasis on ritual explanation should not be surprising since Bell Beaker evidence is conspicuously funerary. But it would be wholly mistaken to read into the argument presented here an assertion that the individual components of the Beaker–knife–wristguard–projectile set possessed solely or even predominantly ritual significance.

Take first the Bell Beaker itself. The potential ritual significance of potting and pottery in non-industrial societies is well known, where the boundary between ritual and mundane may appear shifting and porous. But the view that the Bell Beaker was a specialised grave pot is no longer tenable. It appears rather as the fine ware aspect (commonly chosen for burial) within a varied repertoire of settlement pottery throughout which the beaker shape was a recurrent feature (Case 1995; Besse 2003, pls 21-4, *passim*). Its form suggests that it sometimes functioned as a drinking pot, but there is no convincing evidence that that was its special use.

COPPER TANGED KNIVES

It can be argued that the Beaker shape and some basic elements of its decoration derived from widespread imitation of pottery developed early in the third millennium BC around the Tagus estuary (Case 2004b). An Iberian Chalcolithic inspiration can similarly be argued for the copper tanged knives *(loc cit)*. These have been generally classified as daggers, on account presumably of their sometimes pointed shape (e.g. *70, no. 18*). However these thin blades would have been quite unsuitable for stabbing. Moreover, well-preserved and apparently mint-fresh specimens have a linguate shape (e.g. *69, no. 4; 70, no. 2*)[4] suggesting that the points may have been the result of repeated whetting down and resharpening of the edges.[5] These were knives with potentially razor-sharp edges. In hostile encounters, they might have threatened an unpleasant superficial wound but were incapable of the knock-out blow to a vital organ precluding retaliation or further resistance, which is characteristic of a true dagger or a well-aimed salvo of arrows.

MULTIPLE USE; LIMITED EXPLANATIONS

It is likely, if only for comparative rarity, that copper knives had a greater symbolical value than flint ones. Sharp knives would have had many potential uses besides giving the *coup-de-grâce*: for instance cutting up the quarry for gifts to favoured kin or clients. And, besides surgery, razor-sharp knives have potential applications in hairdressing ('razor cuts'), shaving, ritual mutilation, and production of scar tissue. Such conspicuous features of personal appearance may (along with clothing and other material culture or practices such as body painting not generally surviving in the archaeological record) have been more subtle and precise indicators of affilation, status and regional diversity than pottery or other surviving material culture. In these directions, accepting that potting was women's speciality (following Brodie 1997, 300-01; 1998, 48-9),[6] then the regional groupings ascertainable from pottery distributions may refer to little more specific than the ability of women to maintain contact with each other over varying distances through exogamy and seasonal meetings. Similarly the distributions of rarer objects and exotic substances such as copper, gold and foreign rock (and including possibly some exceptional Beakers) may show little more than the ability of men to range further afield or receive gifts from afar. Useful but rather generalised patterns of behaviour are indeed inferrable from such data; but excessive expectations may provide a reason why the so-called Bell Beaker phenomenom has sometimes been termed enigmatic.

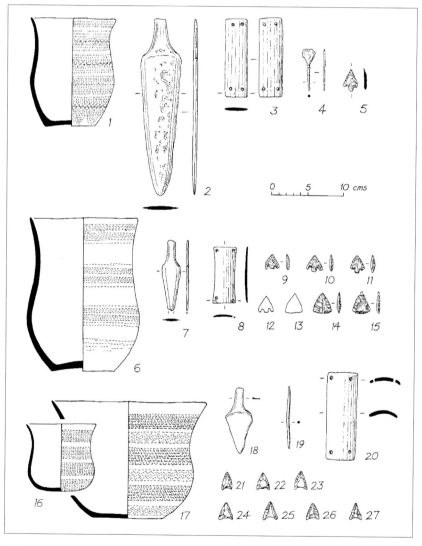

70 Nos 1-5, Roundway 8, Wiltshire; nos 6-15, Ede, Ginkelse Heide; nos 16-27, Smolín 1-13/51, Moravia. Nos 1, 4, 7, 18, copper. Nos 3, 8, 20, stone. Nos 5, 9-15, 21-7, flint. (*Nos 6-15, after Lanting & van der Waals 1976; nos 16-27, after Dvořák et al, 1996*

WRISTGUARDS AND PROJECTILE HEADS

(Wristguards: 69, nos 5, 10, 17; 70, nos 3, 8, 20. Projectile heads: 69, nos 11, 12, 13; 70, nos 5, 9-15, 21-27; 71, nos 11-13, 27, 28)

Returning to the components of the Beaker culture as defined above, I take the stone wristguard to be another Iberian innovation. Often highly polished, and in developed forms sometimes embellished with copper and gold, I take stone wristguards to be symbolical renderings of more comfortable workaday leather ones – to have been badges placed or worn sometimes in a non-functional position outside the wrist (Whittle *et al.* 1992, 176) and worn by the living as well as the dead,[7] being occasionally found in settlement contexts.[8] In graves, the wristguard can be taken as interchangeable with the flint arrowhead (or other projectiles) in symbolising hunting or feuding. Clarke (1970, 438-48) recorded arrowheads in twice as many graves as wristguards, but they are by no means ever-present. Statistics are far from comprehensive, but the general impression given is that arrowheads are not especially numerous in settlements on a European range.[9] Taken together the evidence suggests that archery was not a weapon for the population as a whole, but a restricted pursuit even among the elite whose burials survive.

CORDED WARE CULTURE

The relationship between Corded Ware and the later emerging Bell Beakers has often been debated. A direct derivation of one from the other was for long the consensus view; but in my opinion the derivation was partial and indirect (Case 2004b), and their strongly contrasting grave furniture is consistent with this view. This contrast is all the more significant in view of their considerable chronological overlap and their spatial separation in central Europe. Corded Ware grave furniture varies over its great geographical extent, but I am mainly concerned here with its northwestern branches, the Single Grave Cultures of Denmark (mainly Jutland) and the Lower Rhine. In Denmark the characteristic spectrum in apparently men's graves in descending order of frequency appears to be: so-called battle-axe – flint knife – flint axe – Beaker or other pot – arrowhead (Glob 1944, 173, 176). The main components of the Single Grave Culture of the Netherlands are generally similar (e.g. *71, nos 1-4*) although it is possible that the beaker was relatively more frequent.

Corded Ware men's and women's grave furniture appears generally to show strong positive divergence in central Europe (e.g. Turek 2001, fig. 5); this contrasts apparently with more negative divergence in Bell Beaker contexts generally throughout western Europe (e.g. in Britain, where women's graves tend empha-tically to be poorer than men's: Clarke 1970, 448; Case 2004a) – although this is not necessarily the case in central Europe nearer the Corded Ware heartland.

Bottom-up analysis of male Corded Ware grave furniture reveals a symbolical emphasis on food production, contrasting strongly with the Bell Beaker situation discussed above.

BATTLE-AXES AND AXE-HAMMERS

Stone battle-axes and axe-hammers represent a very long European tradition of Neolithic shafthole implements extending into the insular Bronze Age (Roe 1966 for later chronological range in Britain). I take battle-axes as a

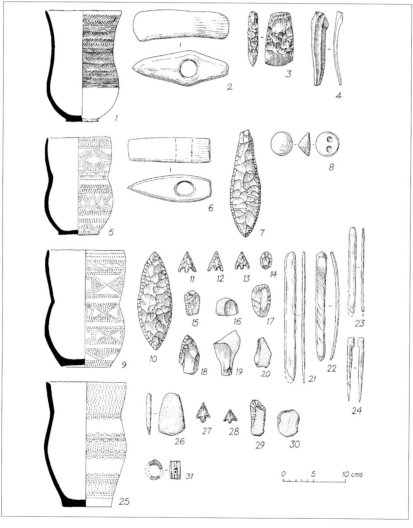

71 Nos 1-4, Balloo, Drenthe; nos 5-8, Garton Slack 37, east Yorkshire; nos 9-24, Alsop Moor, Derbyshire; nos 25-31, Clinterty, Aberdeen. Nos 2, 6, 26, stone; nos 3, 4, 7, 10-20, 27-30, flint; nos 21-4, bone; no 8, shale or jet. *Nos 1-4, after Glasbergen 1971. Nos 5-24, after Case 2001. Nos 25-31, after Clarke 1970*

general class usually to be symbolical grave versions of the functional axe-hammers, which are not normally recognised in graves. If both classes of implement were generally made from cobbles, as Fenton (1984) argued for the great majority of Scottish examples, shafthole diameters would have been constrained. Roe (1966, 200-1) provided metrical data including shafthole diameters for battle-axes ranging from about 12mm to 28mm[10] and axe-hammers from about 20mm to 40mm. In a sample of 34 British battle-axes illustrated by Roe (1966), almost half had diameters of about 20mm. Cursory inspection suggests that many continental battle-axes (e.g. *76, no. 2*) are generally similar in this respect. A Dutch axe-hammer with shafthole diameter of about 25mm was accompanied by its wooden haft somewhat over 700mm long (of Bell Beaker date: Brinkkemper & Drenth 2002).

Judging by these shafthole diameters, the hafts of battle-axes and some axe-hammers would have been about as thick as those of a modern light hammer; they would have been slight for a modern hoe and considerably slighter than those for a modern felling axe, mattock, pick or heavy hammer. This appears confirmed by the range of weights published by Roe (1966, 201), although some heavier axe-hammers (up to about 4.5kg) would have been suitable for heavy work.

Not all battle-axes were made of stones which would stand up to heavy use; but rocks with hard fracture toughness seem to have been used recurrently (e.g. Fenton 1984, 231). No systematic studies are available of marks of use on these classes of implements. However a battle-axe in a Food Vessel burial association at Dalgety, Fife (Shepherd in Watkins 1982, 107-8) showed emphatic marks of use; and use damage appears to be represented on Dutch battle-axes (Lanting 1973, figs 7a, 8). I suggest that axe-hammers, with hafts such as the Dutch example discussed above (Brinkkemper & Drenth 2002) or longer, would have been useful in agriculture in the economically essential, laborious and symbolically important task of breaking up into a fine tilth the soil already turned over by the spade or plough,[11] for teasing away fragments of roots or rhizomes and small stones and trenching an accurate seed bed. And with similar or shorter hafts, they would have been suitable for innumerable hammering tasks. Serving as weapons, they would have been useful perhaps for threatening at boundary disputes and other confrontations.

A well-polished dolerite axe-hammer, intrusive in sub-Boreal peat at Cleethorpes, South Humberside, showed striation consistent with the use in tillage as suggested above (Leahy 1986, 148-9 and supporting arguments). Its wooden haft (probably poplar) was about 30mm in diameter, wedged in place, and about 760mm long, comparable in length to the aforementioned example from Emmer-Compasum, the Netherlands (Brinkkemper & Drenth 2002).

Fragments could have resulted from determined use, as in Single Grave contexts at Vorbasse, central Jutland (Hvass 1977, 227) and at Aartswoud, north Holland, in a pit with a pottery, an arrowhead, a quern stone, rubbers and hammerstones (Iterson Scholten & Vries-Metz 1981, 131-2). Arrowheads and fragmentary battle-axes occurred at Zeewijk, north Holland; elsewhere in north Holland a concentrated surface scatter of battle-axe fragments is suggestive (Find location 29: Heeringen & Theunissen 2001, 2: 279-83).[12] Roe reported no fewer than 74 stray finds of battle-axe fragments from Britain (1966, 214).

FLAKE KNIVES, BEAKERS AND ARROWHEADS

Flake knives (e.g. *71, no. 4*) can be taken as symbolising a great range of cutting and shaping tasks (their curved profiles precluding consideration as daggers), axes *(71, no. 3)* as symbolical of felling and trimming, Beakers *(71, no. 1)* as celebrating well-earned refreshment; and the arrowheads representing hunting in marginal environments, such as those of the Single Grave settlements in north Holland. Arrowheads were recorded at Zeewijk and Aartswoud, and the great importance of hunting (including large mammals), fishing and gathering has been reported at these and other Single Grave settlement sites in north Holland: Hogestijn 1992, 200-2; Gehasse 2001, Table 14 for comparative mammalian evidence, and fig. 5 for seasonality). And local variations should not be at all surprising: note the importance of hunting of red deer at the Swiss Lake settlements (Whittle 1996, 221).

WOMEN'S GRAVES

Characteristic women's graves give a complementary picture.[13] Ovoid pots and so-called amphorae can be taken to symbolise the storing of produce, and beads or pendants made from the teeth of wild animals (including wolf) may reflect both the community's enjoyment of hunting and the procurement of furs as special gifts. In some contrast to Beaker Culture practice, ornaments and exotic materials tend to be concentrated in women's graves. Women were the recipients of long- and short-range exchanges, which may suggest that they therefore had the prominent roles in devising and inspiring kinship alliances. The elite were thus celebrated as the creators, founders and exploiters of the community's land holding and alliances. Both sexes were encouraged as benign ancestors to continue their influence and protection from the Otherworld.

EPILOGUE

It can be argued that the apparent emphasis on the individual in both Corded Ware and Bell Beaker burial practice represents an increasingly open kinship system with shorter lines of descent (Whittle 1996, 287) and more fragmented, which both inspired concentration on more individual and more intensely farmed land holdings, and encouraged wide contacts with more distant kin in a more accessible landscape.

Corded Ware and Bell Beaker burial customs may thus represent two versions of a similar social system, which were evolved independently but which both gave greater importance to the individual in life and as an agent in the Otherworld: a western version which emphasised more the privileges of the exceptionally qualified, generally men; and an eastern one which stressed more strongly the collaboration of men and women in a common task. Whatever the sequel, it is noteworthy that in northwest Europe the western (Bell Beaker) symbolism had generally faded away by the end of the third millennium BC after its infiltration quite early by the eastern (Corded Ware) equivalent, which itself persisted into the second millennium. These trends can be seen for example in the presence of battle-axes in Veluwe and other late Bell Beaker associations in the Netherlands and northwest Germany (Lanting 1973; Lanting & van der Waals 1976, fig. 26-9); in battle-axes, and tool kits and an adze in Group B Bell Beaker association in Britain *(71, nos 6, 1–20, 26)*; in the presence of axes in the Breton Barrow Grave assemblages and in the early Wessex Series grave at Wilsford 5, Wiltshire (discussed in Case 2003); in the presence of rich women's graves in the Wessex Series and the minimal occurrence of arrow-heads *(loc. cit.)*, and in the persistence of Intermediate and Variant battle-axes in British second millennium BC associations (Roe 1966, Table IV, 224-7).

FOOTNOTES

[1] Where the recently excavated Amesbury 1289, Wiltshire, is an outstanding example: Fitzpatrick 2003 and pers. comm.

[2] In the Iberian homeland and generally in the Atlantic world, Bell Beaker burials in collective tombs appear invariably individualised where ascertainable (Salanova 2003, 165 and references; Ireland, Case 2004a). In earlier Neolithic tombs, they can be taken as terminating the sequence of deposits – in similar fashion to the two individual Bell Beaker-associated individual houses (E.N. and F.M.: Cardoso 2000, 131-6; 2001, figs 5-9) on the margins of a long sequence of earlier Neolithic and Chalcolithic collective building at Leceia, Oeiras, Portugal.

[3] Judging from the absence or rarity of detritus from wild animals in deposits of all kinds. This should be only partly explainable by the rarity of well-preserved settlement sites such as those of the Single Grave Culture in north Holland discussed below. Systematic hunting of the horse inferred in Bell Beaker context at Moncín, Zaragoza appears exceptional: Harrison *et al.* 1994.

[4] And e.g. Winterslow JSS 1, Clarke 1970, figs 132, 134; and around half of those from the Spanish Meseta illustrated in Garrido-Pena 2000.

[5] Unusually small blades which occur sometimes in graves (e.g. Amesbury 1289, Wilts., inf. Andrew Fitzpatrick; Spanish Meseta, Garrido-Pena 2000, fig. 28, no. 3) could also have been produced in this way. True intentional minatures however (symbolic tokens?) do appear to have existed (e.g. Dorchester XII, Oxon: Clarke 1970, fig. 127).

[6] Although ethnography and archaeology do not provide entirely unambiguous analogies, I take them to favour this assertion: Barley 1994, 61ff.; Barnett & Hoopes (eds), 1995, 5-6, 101, 247-9, 278.

[7] Clarke 1970, 438-48 recorded them in only eight British graves (all men's), the fifth most frequent grave association.

[8] Pit BB 12, Ben Bridge, Chew Valley Lake, Somerset; Rahtz & Greenfield 1977, 187-90; Hockwold-cum-Wilton, Norfolk, Bamford 1982, 18; Myrhøj, Jutland, Jensen 1972, fig. 16; an unbored example, Boritov VII, Moravia, Turek *et al.* 2003, fig. 1 no. 26.

[9] For example, described as rare at Noir-Bois and recorded as just over 4% of retouched flints at Derrière-le-Château (Bailly 2002) and under 3% at Myrhøj (Jensen 1972).

[10] Oval shaftholes may partly exceed these dimensions (e.g. *76, no. 6*).

[11] Ard marks were recorded at the north Holland settlement complex: Hogestijn 1992, 200.

[12] Battle-axe fragments: also Lanting 1973, figs 38 & 39a.

[13] But note Wierman's arguments (1998) that some Corded Ware grave furniture was determined by age and status, producing ill-defined or reversed gender roles.

ACKNOWLEDGEMENTS

I am grateful to Maxence Bailly, Zita van der Beek, Jonathan Cotton, Erik Drenth, Andrew Fitzpatrick, Volker Heyd, Alison Sheridan and Jan Turek for generously providing information. Nick Griffiths drew the illustrations.

BIBLIOGRAPHY

Bailly, M., 2002 *La Fleche et l'éclat. Production et Consommation des Outillages Taillés de la Fin du Néolithique au Début de l'Age du Bronze entre Saône et Rhône (2600-2000 av. J.-C)*. Unpublished PhD. Thesis: Université de Franche-Comté, Besançon.

Bamford, H.M., 1982 *Beaker Domestic Sites in the Fen Edge and East Anglia*. Report 16. Dereham: East Anglian Archaeology.

Barley, N., 1994 *Smashing Pots: Feats of clay from Africa*. London: British Museum.

Barnett, W.K. & Hoopes, J.W., 1995 *The Emergence of Pottery: Technology and Innovation in Ancient Societies*. Washington & London: Smithsonian Institution.

Benz, M. & Willigen, S. van (eds), 1998 *Some New Approaches to the Bell Beaker 'Phenomenon'. Lost Paradise?* BAR International Series 690. Oxford: British Archaeological Reports.

Besse, M., 2003 *L'Europe du 3e Millennaire avant notre ère: Les Céramiques Communes du Campaniforme*. Lausanne: Cahiers d'archéologie Romande 94.

Bocksberger, O.J., 1978 *Le Site Préhistorique du Petit-Chasseur (Sion, Valais), 3, 4: Horizon Supérieur Secteur Occidentale, et Tombes Bronze Ancien*. Lausanne: Cahiers d'Archéologie Romande 13, 14.

Brinkkemper, O. & Drenth, E., 2002 De gesteelde hammerbijl van Emmer-Compascum: C14-gedateerd. *Nieuwe Drentse Volksalmanak*, 2002, 123-7.

Brodie, N., 1997 New perspectives on the Bell-Beaker culture. *Oxford Journal of Archaeology*, 16, 297-314.

Brodie, N., 1998 British Bell Beakers: Twenty five years of theory and practice. In Benz, M. & van Willigen, S. (eds), 43-56.

Buchvaldek, M. & Strahm, Ch. (eds), 1992 *Die Kontinentaleuropäischen Gruppen der Kultur mit Schnurkeramik*. Prague: Praehistorica XIX.

Cardoso, J.L., 2000 *Sítios, Pedras e Homens: Trinta anos de Arquelogia em Oeiras*. Oeiras: Câmara Municipal.

Cardoso, J.L., 2001 La phénomène campaniforme dans les basses vallées du Tage et du Sado (Portugal). In Nicolis, F. (ed.), 139-154.

Case, H.J., 1995 Beakers: loosening a stereotype. In Kinnes, I.A. & Varndell, G. (eds), '*Unbaked Urns of Rudely Shape*'. *Essays on British and Irish Pottery for Ian Longworth*, 55-67. Oxford: Oxbow.

Case, H.J., 1998 Où en sont les Campaniformes de l'autre côté de la Manche ? *Bulletin de la Société Préhistorique Française,* 95, 403-11.

Case, H.J., 2001 The Beaker Culture in Britain and Ireland: groups, European contacts and chronology. In Nicolis, F. (ed.) 361-77.

Case, H.J., 2003 Beaker presence at Wilsford 7. *Wiltshire Archaeological and Natural History Magazine,* 96, 161-94.

Case, H.J., 2004a. Beaker burial in Britain and Ireland: A role for the dead. In Besse, M. & Desidesi, J. (eds), *Graves & Funerary Rituals during the Late Neolithic & Early Bronze Age in Europe (2700-2000 BC),* 195-201. BAR International Series 1284. Oxford: Archaeopress.

Case, H.J., 2004b. Beakers and the Beaker Culture. In Czebresuk, J. (ed.), *Similar But Different: Bell Beakers in Europe,* 195-201. Poznan: Adam Mickiewicz University.

Clarke, D.L., 1970 *Beaker Pottery of Great Britain and Ireland,* Cambridge: Cambridge University Press.

Cleal, R.M.J., Walker, K.E. & Montague, R., 1995 *Stonehenge in its Landscape; Twentieth Century Excavations.* London: English Heritage.

Cotton, J., 1991 Prehistory in Greater London. *Current Archaeology,* 124, 151-4.

Darvill, T., 1997 Ever increasing circles: the sacred geographies of Stonehenge in its landscape. In Cunliffe, B.W. & Renfrew, A.C. (eds), *Science and Stonehenge,* 167-202. London: Proceedings of the British Academy 92.

Dvořák, P., Matéjícková, A., Pěska, J. & Rakovský I., 1996 *Gräberfelder der Glockenbecherkultur in Mähren II.* Brno-Olomouc: Petr Dvořák.

Dvořák, P., Rakovský, I. & Stuchlíková, J., 1992 Pohřebistě Lidu s Kulyurou se Zvoncovitymi Pohary Záhlinic, Pkr Kromeríz. *Pravek* Nr 2, 215-32.

Fenton, M.B., 1984 The nature of the source and manufacture of Scottish battle-axes and axe-hammers. *Proceedings of the Prehistoric Society,* 50, 217-43.

Fitzpatrick, A.P. 2003. The Amesbury Archer: a well-furnished Early Bronze Age burial in southern England. *Antiquity,* 76, 629-30.

Garrido-Pena, R., 2000 *El Campaniforme en la Meseta Central de la Península Ibérica.* BAR International Series 892. Oxford: British Archaeological Reports.

Gehasse, E., 2001 Aartswoud: an environmental approach at a Late Neolithic site. In van Heeringen, R.M. & Theunissen, E.M., 3: 161-201.

Gibson, A., 2004. Burials and Beakers: seeing beneath the veneer in Late Neolithic Britain. In Czebresuk, J. (ed.), *Similar But Different: Bell Beakers in Europe,* 173-192. Poznan: Adam Mickiewicz University.

Glasbergen, W., 1971 Graves containing Beakers with Protruding Foot. *Inventaria Archaeologica,* NL 1-10. Bonn: Habelt.

Glob, P.V., 1944 Studier over den Jysk Enkeltgravskultur. *Aarbøger,* 1944.

Harrison, R.J., 1977 *The Bell Beaker Cultures of Spain and Portugal.* Harvard: American School of Prehistoric Research, Bulletin 35.

Harrison, R.J., Moreno López, G.C. & Legge, A.J., 1994 *Moncín: Un Poblado de la Edad del Bronce (Zaragoza)*. Zaragoza: Collección Arquelogia, 16.

Heeringen, R.M. van & Theunissen, E.M. (eds), 2001 *Kwaliteitsbalend Onderzoek ten Behoeve van Duurzaam Behoud van Neolithische Terreinen in West Friesland en de Kop van Noord-Holland, 23*. Amersfoort: ROB.

Hogestijn, J.W.H., 1992 Functional differences between some settlements of the Single Grave Culture in the northwestern coastal area of the Netherlands. In Buchvaldek, M., & Strahm, Ch. (eds), 199-205.

Hvass, S., 1977 A house of the Single-Grave Culture at Vorbasse in central Jutland. *Acta Archaeologica,* 48, 219-32.

Iterson Scholten, F.R. van & Vries-Metz, W.H. de, 1981 A Late Neolithic Settlement at Aartswoud I. *Helinium,* 21, 105-35.

Jensen, J.A., 1972 Bopladsen Myrhøj, 3 hustomter med klokkebaegerkeramik. *Kuml,* 1972, 61-122.

Lanting, J.N., 1973 Laat Neolithikum en Vroege Bronstid in Nederland en N.W.-Duitsland: Continue Ontwikkelingen. *Palaeohistoria,* 15, 215-317.

Lanting, J.N. & Waals, J.D. van der, 1976 Beaker Culture relations in the Lower Rhine Basin. In Lanting, J.N & Waals, J.D. van der (eds), *Glockenbechersymposion: Oberried 1974,* 1-80. Bussum: Uniboek n.v.

Leahy, K., 1986 A dated axe-hammer from Cleethorpes, South Humberside. *Proceedings of the Prehistoric Society,* 52, 143-152.

Nicolis, F. (ed.), 2001 *Bell Beakers Today: Pottery, People, Culture, Symbols in Prehistoric Europe.* Trento: Servizio Bení Culturali.

Rahtz, P.A. & Greenfield, E., 1977 *Excavations at Chew Valley Lake.* London: HMSO.

Roe, F.E.S., 1966. the Battle-Axe series in Britain. *Proceedings of the Prehistoric Society*, 32, 199-245.

Salanova, L., 2003 Heads north: Analysis of Bell Beaker graves in western Europe. *Journal of Iberian Archaeology,* 5, 163-9.

Turek, J., 2000 Being a Beaker child: the position of children in Late Eneolithic society. *Památky Archeologické,* supplementum, 13, 424-38.

Turek, J., 2001 Late Eneolithic mortuary practices and their social significance. In Biehl, P.F., Bertemes, F. & Meller, H. (eds), *The Archaeology of Cult and Religion,* 219-34. Budapest: Archaeolingua, 11.

Turek, J., Dvořák, P. & Pěska, J., 2003 Archaeology of Beaker settlements in Bohemia and Moravia: an outline of the current state of knowledge. In Czebreszuk, J. and Szmyt, M. (eds), *The North-East Frontier of Bell Beakers*, 183-208. BAR International Series 1155. Oxford: British Archaeological Reports.

Watkins, T., 1982 The excavation of an Early Bronze Age cemetery at Barns Farm, Dalgety, Fife. *Proceedings of the Society of Antiquaries of Scotland,* 112, 48-141.

Whittle, A., 1996 *Europe in the Neolithic: the Creation of New Worlds.* Cambridge: Cambridge University Press.

Whittle, A., Atkinson, R.J.C., Chambers, R. & Thomas, N., 1992 Excavations in the Neolithic and Bronze Age Complex at Dorchester-on-Thames, Oxfordshire, 1947-1952 and 1981. *Proceedings of the Prehistoric Society,* 58, 143-201.

Wierman, R.R., 1998 An Anthropological Approach to Burial Customs of the Corded Ware Culture in Bohemia. In Benz, M. & Willigen, S. van (eds), 129-40.

15
FOOD VESSELS
WITH HANDLES

T.G. MANBY

INTRODUCTION

This consideration of handled Food Vessels is offered in appreciation of Derek Simpson's Bronze Age research. Derek's analysis of the burial associations and chronology of the wide range of accessory vessel types termed Food Vessels (Simpson 1968) made untenable the traditional concept of a chronologically and culturally exclusive 'Food Vessel Period' within the Bronze Age of Britain and Ireland. The Food Vessel types and other ceramic classes were soon to become contemporary strands within richly diverse schemes of monuments, practices and material associations which made up the burial traditions of the earlier second millennium BC (Clarke 1970, 270-5; Burgess 1980, 79-131; Longworth 1984, 19-24).

Handled Food Vessels are a rare class within the overall Food Vessel tradition, constituting less than 1% of all Northern Food Vessels (see below) in their distributional range (72). They were noticed by Abercromby, who placed them within his category of 'English Cups' in his great corpus (Abercromby 1912, I, 44-5, pl. xxii, figs 296a-301 bis). They attracted no further attention until David Clarke's seminal Beaker corpus considered handled Food Vessels to be derivatives, by way of some hybrid vessels – 'H(FV)' – of the handled Beakers of his Southern British Beaker Group (Clarke 1970, 252). A further element was brought into the equation by Sabine Gerloff's research into the handled vessels of amber, shale and gold found in Wessex 2 series graves (Gerloff 1975). The relative size of all these various handled vessels is presented in (73).

This contribution will re-examine the question of origins. But first, some background information about the Food Vessel tradition in general and its dating and origins is required.

THE OVERALL FOOD VESSEL TRADITION

A history of research into the vessel types brought together under the later nineteenth century 'Food Vessel' designation has been provided by Ó Ríordáin

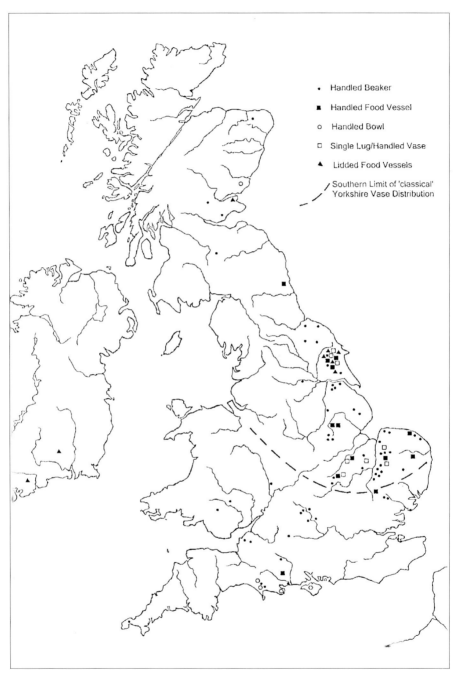

72 Distribution in the British Isles of handled Beakers, handled Food Vessels and Bowls; and lidded Food Vessels

and Waddell (1993, 1-4), in their corpus of Bowls and Vases in Ireland. This covers two of the four geographical-cum-stylistic groupings that have been identified within the overall Food Vessel tradition, namely:

i Irish-Scottish Bowls – concentrated in Ireland and western Scotland, extending to eastern Scotland and the Isle of Man; and

ii Irish-Scottish Vases – distribution as above. These are complemented, in Britain, by:

iii Northern Vases, including the 'Yorkshire Vase' series – concentrated in Yorkshire, Northumberland, the East Midlands, southern and eastern Scotland, extending into North Wales and East Anglia; and

iv Southern English Vases – concentrated in Dorset and Wiltshire, extending into Cornwall, the Thames Valley, the southern Midlands and Wales.

Within each of these stylistic traditions (Burgess 1980, 86-9, fig. 3.1-3) there is considerable regional variability in size and in predominant decorative motifs and techniques. As in Ireland (Ó Ríordáin & Waddell 1993, 5-36), taxonomy-inspired considerations are apparent in all the regional corpus studies: south-west Scotland (Simpson 1965), Northumberland and Durham (Gibson 1978), the Peak District (Manby 1957), Wales (Savory 1957) and Cornwall (Patchett 1944; 1951). The inter-regional diversity across northern England and Scotland in shapes, decorative treatment and associations provided the basis for Stephen Pierpoint's wide-ranging factor analysis and his sociology-inspired interpretative approach (Pierpoint 1980). Pierpoint's database was founded on the densest regional Vase concentration from the eastern Yorkshire barrow excavations, totalling 411 Vases plus 39 miniatures and Food Vessel Urns. The predominantly plainer Southern English group apart (see below), there is a strong element of individuality displayed in the production of many of the finer Vases and Bowls, especially in decorative treatment. This offers the potential for discerning the work of a particular potter or workshop – more so than is the case with Beaker pottery. Several pairings or linkages have been recognised in vessels from the same and adjoining barrows, or from more distant findspots. Most are separated by no more than 20-30km, although a few inter-regional pairings are as much as 145km apart (*ibid.*, 119-21; Sheridan 1993, 51-7; Manby 1994). This phenomenon suggests either the long-distance transmission of finished goods, or the activities of itinerant potters.

Much has been written about Northern and Irish-Scottish types of Food Vessel; the southern English tradition, represented by far fewer examples and greatly outnumbered by Beakers and Collared Urns, has received less attention. Here the predominant vessel forms are Abercromby's Types 3 and 4 – bipartite and biconical Vases (Abercromby 1912; cf. Ashbee 1957, 158-9, 165-6). Moving southwards from the East Midlands, the southern

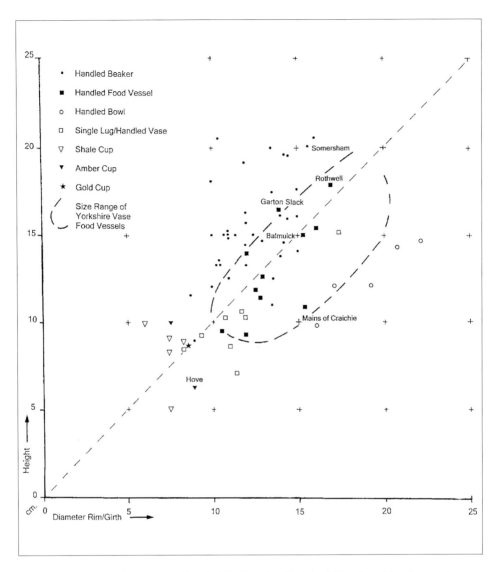

73 Scatter Diagram. Size range of handled Beakers, handled Food Vessels and Bowls; and Cups in shale, amber and gold

English Food Vessels become increasingly common in the West Midlands and the upper Thames valley, where typical southern-style Vases accompany inhumation graves at Barrow Hills, Radley, Oxfordshire (Barclay & Halpin 1999, 121-7, fig. 4, 63-4). The main concentration, as indicated above, is in Dorset and Wiltshire, where small numbers of tripartite and ridged-profile vessel forms are also found (Tomalin 1984, 73-5). A few further examples are scattered westward in Devon and Cornwall. Generally slenderer than Yorkshire Vases, southern English Food Vessels are usually plain or have their decoration limited to simple stab, incised or cord-impressed designs confined to the rim and shoulder or ridge *(ibid.)*. Complex ornamentation in the style of the Northern Food Vessel tradition is scarce; the rare examples include the zonal triangular patterning on the large bipartite Vases from Bishop Waltham, Hampshire (Ashbee 1957, fig. 9) and Sutton Veny, Wiltshire; these two vessels seem closely related by the use of cord-impressed zonal motifs.

As regards the chronology of the overall Food Vessel tradition, the grave associations demonstrate that this pottery was concurrent with developing Beaker and other ceramic traditions (Simpson 1968) extending across Stuart Needham's Periods 2 and 3 (and possibly extending into Period 4) of his Bronze Age periodisation scheme spanning the late third and early second millennia BC (Needham 1996, 124-33, fig. 2). Absolute dating leaves much to be desired, however: sampling has been geographically disparate and older determinations often have unacceptably large standard deviations and are mostly based on charcoal that is subject to the problems of old wood, contamination by downwash in the soil profile etc. Only Ireland has had an intensive dating programme for Food Vessels, undertaken by Anna Brindley and Jan Lanting and focusing on unburnt and cremated human remains (Brindley forthcoming). There, Bowl and Vase types are strongly associated with a 3770-3470 BP radiocarbon range (Bridndley pers. comm.), indicating the development of Irish-Scottish bowls during Period 2, *c.*2300-2050 BC. There are very few high quality determinations supportive of a typo-chronology for the Northern and southern English tradition Food Vessels (although see Sheridan this volume for current developments in Scotland), but the earliest examples probably appeared before the beginning of Period 3 (*c.*2050-1700 BC). The extent of their continuation into Period 4 (*c.*1700-1500 BC) is not well defined.

Within the Northern Food Vessel tradition there are clusters of dates from two regional concentrations, the first being eastern Scotland's Fife-Tayside area and the second being eastern Yorkshire, arising from the Heslerton landscape project's excavated flat graves and barrow cemetery (Powlesland *et al.* 1986, 25-7). Within the former cluster, the dates for the recently excavated flat cist cemetery at Leven, Fife provide two useful determinations for 'classic' Yorkshire Vases, combining the narrow shoulder groove with lugs and all-over herringbone decoration: 3560±60 BP and 3520±60 BP (GrA-22107, 22106), calibrating to 2020–1770 and 1920-1740 cal BC respectively at 1σ, and 2120-1730 and 2020-1680 cal BC respectively at 2σ. (Sheridan, pers. comm.)

As for the Heslerton dates, preliminary results indicate that Yorkshire Vase type Food Vessels were being deposited before the end of the third millennium BC, their use being concurrent with that of late Beakers and continuing into the early centuries of the second millennium. Of the two context sequences, the earliest series of small barrows and graves has produced a date range of 3730 to 3510 BP (2100-2050 cal BC at 1σ, 2200-2000 cal BC at 2σ). Finds include a lugged Food Vessel with a lined bar chevron among comb impressed motifs and an S1(W)/Step 5 Beaker with bar chevron and pendant triangle motifs (Haughton & Powlesland 1999, 42-4 and 64, figs 22-4, 31, 35). A second series from Barrow 1R has a 3659 to 3470 BP range (2140-1700 cal BC at 1σ, 2280-1670 cal BC at 2σ) for Food Vessels including a boss-handled jar *(81.1)* and an N/NR/Step 4 Beaker (Powlesland *et al.* 1986, 98-104, figs 30-9).

Of the previous Yorkshire determinations (Manby *et al.* 2003, 62) Garton Slack Site 7 (3550±70 BP, HAR-1236) came from 'timbers of large size', for a cremation with a multi-lugged vase; Gnipe Howe, Hawsker has two widely distant datings on charcoal of 3240±80 BP (HAR-4993) and 3500±90 BP (HAR-8787) for cremated remains in a cist. For the East Midlands, the Food Vessel dates of 3700±150 BP (BM-210) and 3440±150 BP (BM-178) from Harland Edge, Derbyshire, and of 3410±165 BP (UB-450) from Tallington, Lincolnshire, are low value dates with unacceptably large standard deviations. Similarly unreliable dates are the Northumberland determinations of 3700±80 BP (HAR-1199) from Milfield and 3635±120 BP (GU-1340) from Well House Farm, both from stratigraphically-linked charcoal.

Regarding the question of Food Vessel origins, for most of the twentieth century the ancestral source of the Northern or 'Yorkshire Vase' tradition has been seen to lie in Later Neolithic Peterborough Ware. Of its parallel styles, Mortlake had the heavy-rimmed shouldered bowls and a strong use of horizontal incised and twist cord-impressed decoration, while the Rudston style of northern England (Manby 1975, 59), and the Scottish Meldon Bridge style and Impressed Wares (Burgess 1980, 91) had the internally bevelled everted and T-profiled rims and flat bases, and also a similar distribution to northern Food Vessels. In the 1990s, however, the application of radiocarbon dating has taken the chronological range of Peterborough Ware back to the mid-fourth millennium BC for its designated styles of Fengate (Gibson & Kinnes 1997), Rudston (Manby *et al.* 2003) and Meldon Bridge and Scottish Impressed Wares (MacSween 2001, 79). The higher precision of determinations using short-life materials such as hazel nuts suggests a duration of the Peterborough styles ending in the early third millennium BC. This distances the northern Peterborough Ware styles from having an immediate formative role in Food Vessel development, a situation parallel to that of the Fengate style in relation to Collared Urns (Gibson & Kinnes 1997). A possible half-millennium chronological gap would call into question typo-chronological schemes that propose the Peterborough shouldered bowl as being the prototype for the heavy-rimmed bipartite form, Type 3 of Abercromby's classification (1912, I, 94 & 112), and, through that, for subsequent Northern Vase developments (Manby 1957, 3-4, fig. 1; Gibson 1978, 7, fig. 1). The ceramic tradition spanning most of the third millennium BC in radiocarbon chronology is Grooved Ware, joined by Beaker grave associations from the middle of the millennium (Garwood 1999, 159-77, illus. 15.7). In southern England it is the Woodlands style Grooved Ware that is associated with most third millennium determinations. In eastern and central Yorkshire, however, it is the Durrington Walls style, from pit contexts, that has been associated with dates from short-life materials in the 3350–2250 cal BC range (Manby *et al.* 2003, 55, 115).

An alternative origin for all four Food Vessel traditions lies in the speculative area of the organic containers, utilising wood, basketry, bark or leather, that were probably in use during the later third to early second millennium BC. The obvious reminder of this material culture element is the twisted cord impressions, using cordage of animal or plant fibre, so very commonly used to produce patterns on funerary pottery. The number of contemporary wooden containers recovered from wetland contexts in Britain and Ireland is disappointingly small and the vessels are plain in character (Earwood 1993, 38-45). Organic vessels have long been suggested as a source of inspiration for Early Bronze Age ceramics, with Clarke proposing wooden prototypes for handled Beakers, for example. Recent discussion has focused on Irish-Scottish Bowls (Sheridan 1993, 42), the Footed Food Vessel class (Manby 1995, 83-4) and some accessory cup forms (Allen & Hopkins 2000) as ceramic imitations of carved wood, basketry and leather vessels.

Unfortunately, the free-draining soils preferred for Early Bronze Age graves do not favour the survival of organic materials. The extent of organic materials used in furnishing a burial of Needham's Period 3 is provided by the 1834 excavation of the Gristhorpe barrow on the Yorkshire coastal till, south of Scarborough, where waterlogging preserved intact a split oak tree trunk coffin (Williamson 1872). The basic techniques of the time recognised lichen, leaves, seeds and fruits, animal skin, wooden pins or points, horn bindings, a whale bone pommel and bronze dagger, 'a *dish composed of pieces of bark, stitched together with strips of skin or sinew… of round form, rather more than six inches in diameter*' [my italics], along with flint flakes and the accompanying human skeleton. In dry, free-draining, soil conditions survival would have been limited to a skeleton accompanied by flint flakes and the bronze blade, with soil stains and the slumped filling of the grave pit as the only indication of the organic component. Comparison must be made with the similar waterlogged Danish tree trunk coffin burials of Montelius II date; not only are the coffins preserved, but there is also a range of carved wooden bowls and cups, sewn bark containers, textiles and skins (Glob 1973). The simple round-based wooden cups, some with loop handles, were enhanced to quality status at Lille Dragshoj and Guldhoj by inlaying small tin nails (Glob 1973, pls. 5, 34) – a phenomenon also found in contemporary graves in Lower Saxony such as Heerstedt, Kreis Wesermunde (Jacob-Friesen 1963, 298, abb. 276).

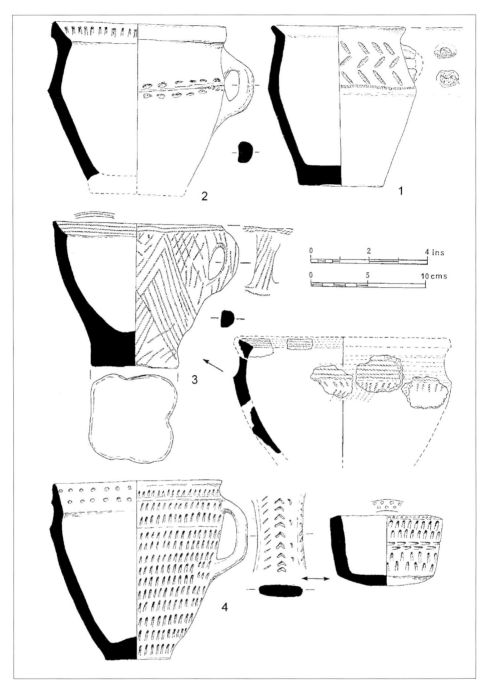

74 Handled Food Vessels: 1 Simonside; 2.Garrowby 104; 3 Blanch 265 and fragmentary Food Vessel associated with primary burial; 4 Garton Slack 141 with associated bowl.

Of other organic material there is a strong resemblance to basketry to be seen in the complex patterning of many Irish-Scottish bowls, and in Irish lidded Food Vessels. However, basketry frames could be embellished with other pliable materials such as reeds, straw or cord. Such a combination, featuring interlaced viburnum, spruce and reed, was used in the conical hat with narrow brim from Fiavè, Italy (Coles 2001, 34, fig. 17), preserved in a Bronze Age wetland context. The stitching on sewn containers of bark or leather, possibly reinforced by wooden rings, may be the inspiration for the limited stroke and jab ornamentation confined to the rim necks and ridges of the handled Vase from Garrowby, East Riding of Yorkshire *(74.2)* and seen also on southern English Food Vessels. A sewn box can be proposed as an organic prototype for the lidded cup from Goodmanham, East Riding of Yorkshire (Kinnes & Longworth 1985, no. 98).

HANDLED FOOD VESSELS

Handled Food Vessels *(74-5)* are characterised as having a single loop handle superimposed on one of the basic Yorkshire Vase type profiles (Abercromby 1912, I, 114-5). Applied loop handles on Northern Food Vessels are relatively scarce; more common are lugs – clay pellets that may or may not be perforated after their application and modelling onto the pot profile. Equally spaced lugs around the girth are usually four in number, but instances of five, six, eight and up to 18 occur. Evenly-spaced small multiple strap handles are rare and confined to globular vessel shapes from Doddington, Northumberland (Greenwell 1877, fig. 78; Gibson 1978, 61, no. 67; Kinnes & Longworth 1985, 111, no. 189.1) and Wetton, Staffordshire (Manby 1957, 29, fig. 7.C5; Vine 1982, 253, no. 598). Such loop handles are not a feature of the Irish-Scottish Vase series except for a tripartite bowl from Keenoge, County Meath (Ó Ríordáin & Waddell 1993, 125, no. 177), with its pair of opposed strap handles.

From Northumberland, east Yorkshire, the East Midlands and East Anglia comes a small series of basic, mostly bipartite Yorkshire Vases (Abercromby's Type 3) with a single large handle, rounded or D-shaped in cross section, variably applied to the neck, neck and shoulder or neck and body profile. The exceptions are the tripartite Vases from Great Chesterford, Essex *(75.9)* and Garton Slack, East Riding of Yorkshire *(74.4)*, the latter having a flattish oval strap handle characteristic of the Beaker series. The quality of craftsmanship and decoration is not of the finest quality. The handled vessel from Simonside, Northumberland *(74.1)* is tall in proportion to its girth; its handle, with its whipped cord 'maggot' decoration, had been applied to the neck but is mostly broken off. Of the examples from the East Riding of Yorkshire Garrowby *(74.2)* has its handle extending from the neck to below the shoulder. The heavy rim of the Garrowby vessel has strokes of a square-tipped tool on its internal bevel, and jabs made by a broken ended stick along the shoulder.

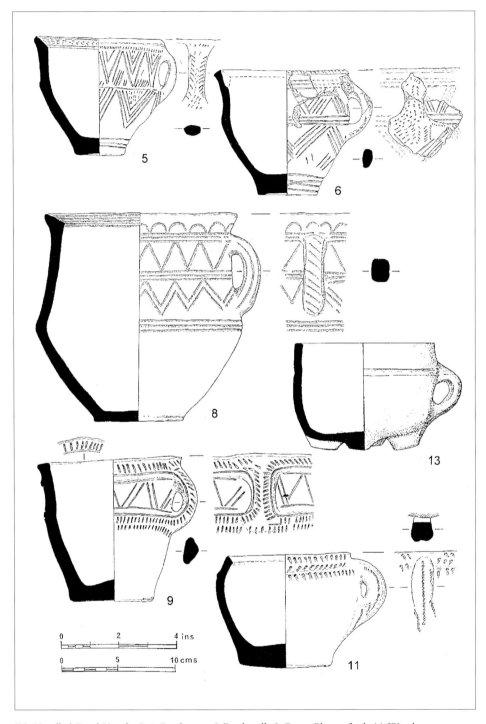

75 Handled Food Vessels: 5-6 Caythorpe; 8 Rothwell; 9 Great Chesterford; 11 Wereham;
13 Wimbourne St Giles

Blanch *(74.3)*, an open cup-shaped vessel with a lobate foot, has complex all-over cord impression forming a multi-lined bar chevron, on a background infilled with diagonals and, in places, a lattice design. Garton Slack *(74.4)* has all-over rows of short vertical stroke decoration on the exterior; a broken-ended tool was used on the deep internal bevel below a simple lip. In terms of its modelling, finish and decoration this is the finest handled Food Vessel in east Yorkshire. A similarly-decorated small cup was found with it.

From the East Midlands, of the two vessels found at Caythorpe, southern Lincolnshire, one *(75.5)* has incised line chevrons and pendant triangles infilled with point jabs, while the second, fragmentary, vessel *(75.6)* has lined chevrons. The similarities in treatment, especially the point jabbing on and below the handles, suggest these pots had the same maker. From the western edge of the Fen Basin at Orton Longueville, Cambridgeshire, is a vessel (not illustrated) with similar profile to that from Blanch *(74.3)*. Unfortunately the base is damaged, and decoration limited to a row of spatula-tip imprints under the lip. The cup from Rothwell, Northamptonshire *(75.8)*, related by Gerloff to the Wessex biconical cup series (Gerloff 1975, 178), stands out by its size, low shouldered biconical profile and its squarish sectioned handle, applied to the deep neck. It has an everted, internally bevelled rim, and open zonal decorative motifs of a large running chevron, a zigzag and horseshoe hoops, all of whipped cord impressions.

South and east of the Fenland Basin, Great Chesterford, Essex *(75.9)* has a weak tripartite profile. A deep zone of incised paired diagonal gives the impression of a running chevron, the zone outlined by rows of short vertical strokes linked down the back of the handle. In Norfolk, the vessel from Wereham *(75.11)* is of globular bipartite shape, with cord-impressed herring-bone decoration; its handle is out of proportion to its aperture and to the body. The marks of a broken-off handle appear on the neck of the similarly-decorated vessel fragment from Bixley (not illustrated); the limited extent of the surviving rim circuit leaves some uncertainty that this was its only handle. Included by reason of its round-sectioned handle is the Hockwold mug (not illustrated) that lacks a datable context; its absence of decoration and coarseness of fabric excludes this vessel from being classified as a handled Beaker, and so it is tentatively included here.

A distant outlier to the distribution of handled Food Vessels is that from Wimbourne St Giles, Dorset *(75.13)*. This is a plain, footed, cup-shaped vessel divided by a horizontal groove, and it combines diagnostic features of both the handled and the footed Food Vessel classes (Manby 1995, 87).

In terms of the relationship between these vessels and the main Food Vessel traditions, only those examples from Blanch *(74.3)*, Garton Slack *(74.4)* and Caythorpe *(75.5-6)* have the all-over decoration that is common to Northern Food Vessels; on the Simonside *(74.1)*, Rothwell *(75.8)*, Great Chesterford *(75.9)*, Wereham *(75.11)* and Bixley (not illustrated) vessels the decorative

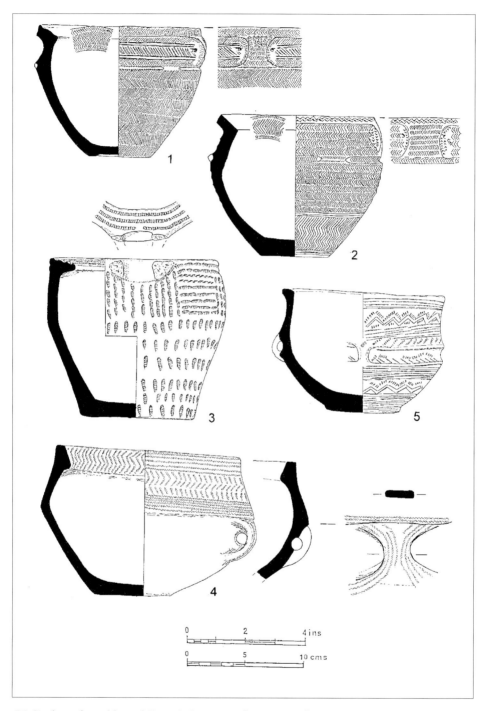

76 Single perforated lugged Vases: 1 Cropton, Fall Rigg; 2 Folkton 243; 3 Blanch; 4. Roystone Grange; 5. Colwell

motifs have been applied only to the upper half of the profile. The decorative techniques and motif range are common to the Northern Food Vessel tradition; apart from horizontal lines, there is a recurrence of the bar-chevron motif, either open (75.*8-11;* cf. Monquhitter, *79.2),* or multi-lined *(74.3, 75.5 -6).* Short strokes made with a point, and other kinds of jabbed decoration, are the simplest of techniques, and these are found combined at Garton Slack *(74.4)* and Garrowby *(74.2).* The sparse decoration on the Garrowby vessel, like that seen on the Orton Longueville example (not illustrated), under the lip, echoes the restrained embellishment of southern English Food Vessels.

There are no examples of a strap or round-sectioned handle applied to a 'classic' Yorkshire Vase, that is a bipartite Vase with lugs in the shoulder groove (Abercromby's Type 1a: 1912, I, 93-4), although such lugs may be the inspiration for the large single perforated lugs in the necks of the Cropton and Folkton vessels *(76.1-2)* considered below.

The handles' functional role is debatable; it is unclear whether they would support the weight of the vessel (whether full or empty) if it were to be picked up solely by the handle. Furthermore, the handle apertures do not permit a closed hand grip: at best only one or two fingers could be passed between the handle and the body to manipulate the vessel. Indeed, in most cases, particularly Simonside *(74.1)* and Wereham *(75.11),* the aperture is too small to admit a finger; only a finger and thumb hold on the sides is possible. Alternative interpretations of the handles are as an aid to suspension (for hanging the vessels up, or for lifting them out of a container), or a way to secure a cover in a hinge-like arrangement. The former purpose has also been suggested for the perforations through the feet of some of the Footed Bowl series (Manby 1969, fig. 3.1, 4 & 6; 1995, fig. 8.4); and the shoulder-groove lugs seen on Yorkshire Vases have been ascribed the 'cover-fixture' function. However, many of the groove lugs are in fact imperforate.

SINGLE-LUGGED FOOD VESSELS

This type of handled Food Vessel is represented by three examples from eastern Yorkshire and single examples from Northumberland and the Peak District *(75).* The single lug is large and perforated, and its position on the profile varies; all five vessels are individualistic products. Two, of the classic Yorkshire Vase type, come from Cropton and Folkton *(76.1-2).* They have a large perforated lug spanning the neck between rim and shoulder, and a narrow shoulder groove. They are fine quality products from sites 30km apart on opposite sides of the Vale of Pickering and their unique combination of features and decorative treatment is indicative of their having been made by the same potter. The large lug in the neck of these vessels is close enough to the rim to have provided a hinge-point for a lid or cover but there is no evidence of wear to confirm such a function. The absence of

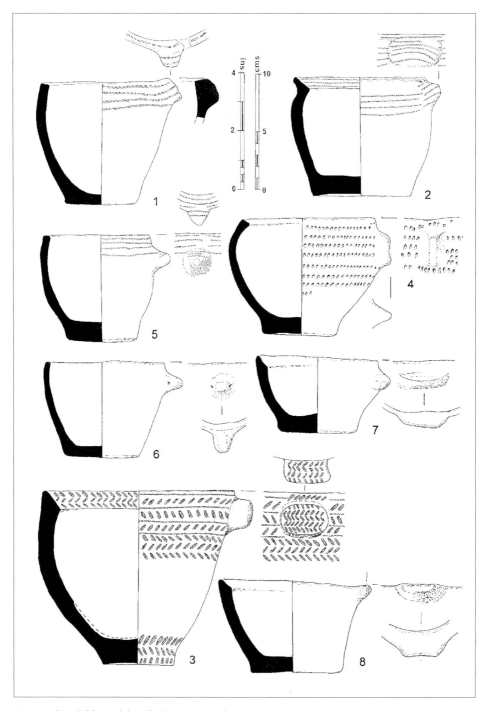

77 Single solid lugged/handled Vases: 1 Heslerton 1R.; 2 Sunderlandwick; 3 Towthorpe 21; 4 Rothwell Woods; 5 Elton; 6 Manea; 7 Upper Hare Park; 8 Warren Hill

perforations on the shoulder-groove lugs rules out their use to secure or tie down a cover.

Better placed to have acted as a hinge-point for a cover are the broken springings of a horizontal, vertically perforated lug on the exterior of the rim of a slack-profile bipartite Vase from a barrow on the Yorkshire Wolds at Blanch *(76.3)*. The rim is of a usual broad internal ledge type.

The single-lugged bowl from Colwell *(76.5)* stands out among Food Vessels from Northumberland as a vessel in the Irish-Scottish Bowl tradition. It is comparable in its basic profile to Irish bowls from Glenariff, County Antrim; Sliguff, County Carlow; Kilcattan, County Derry and Crouck, County Tyrone; some of these have four lugs, others none (Ó Ríordáin & Waddell 1993, nos 109, 124, 133, 190). The bar chevron motifs frequently appearing in false-relief on these Irish bowls are also imitated at Colwell by using incision; this technique is also seen, along with flanking maggot impressions, on a simple bowl of unlocated provenance in Ireland *(ibid.,* no. 23). This Colwell bowl is not the only representative of the Irish-Scottish Bowl tradition from a region dominated by the Northern Vase tradition: simple Bowls are also known from from Alnwick, Moor Lodge and Jesmond, all in Northumberland (Gibson 1978, nos 70, 72; Abercromby 1912, fig. 227). A similarly distinctive vessel among the Peak District regional Food Vessels is the bipartite Bowl from Roystone Grange, Derbyshire *(76.4)*. Its deep, internally bevelled rim has a flat lip, and under a slight shoulder there is a modelled lug of hourglass shape outlined by parallel cord lines. This fine quality Bowl has a lop-sided appearance after reconstruction, probably resulting from distorting pressure during the settling of the cairn structure. For both Roystone Grange and Colwell the lugs are set close to mid-height; this is probably too low for a cover hinge function and any hinging movement would be obstructed by the waisted profile of the Roystone Grange lug.

VESSELS WITH SOLID BOSS HANDLES

There is a small group of vessels from barrow contexts in Eastern Yorkshire and East Anglia that have bodies sufficiently complete to be certain they did not have more than a single applied projection. There are three vessel forms to consider *(77)*:

i Cylindrical jars with simple rims and projecting conical boss: Manea *(77.6)* is plain and has an uncompleted perforation. Heslerton *(77.1)* and Elton *(77.5)* both have a zone of cord line impressions below the rim;

ii Globular vases with internally bevelled rims: Sunderlandwick *(77.2)* has a rounded shoulder, an applied oval boss in the neck and horizontal cord-impressed lines on the exterior and on its moulded bevel; Towthorpe *(77.3)* has a most substantial oval boss and lines and 'maggots' of whipped cord impressions; Rothwell *(77.4)* has a vertical rectangular boss and rows of jab imprints;

iii Shallow bowls, plain with a ledge handle: Upper Hare Park *(77.7)* and Warren Hill *(77.8)* from East Anglia. These have no direct association with other classes of Food Vessel in a burial or other context. This form may be related to the small 'drainer', with perforated base and a small applied ledge on one side that accompanied a deposit of cremated remains in an enlarged Bipartite Food Vessel Urn at Spong Hill, Norfolk. Charcoal from this burial provided a C14 date of 3810±70 BP (BM-1532), 2470-2030 cal BC at 2σ (Healy 1988, 102, 104, P224, 226).

The boss and ledge handles of the above vessels allow only a finger and thumb hold for tilting and turning; they are not a means of lifting vessels of such weight. However, the Heslerton and Sunderlandwick vases could be gripped by putting the fingers inside the rim and placing the thumb under the lug. The Food Vessel grave context is firmly established at Heslerton *(77.1)*, with a determination on human bone having a mean of 3647±26 BP, 2140-1920 cal BC at 2σ. Without an accompanying burial at Sunderlandwick *(77.2)* the vase was enclosed in a decayed wooden 'cist', no dimensions recorded, without an accompanying burial.

Before considering the question of the origin of these various handled and lugged forms of Food Vessel, it is necessary to comment on some Beaker and Beaker-related handled vessels – Clarke's Handled Food Vessel hybrids H(FV).

HANDLED BEAKERS AND BEAKER-RELATED VESSELS

Clarke's category of handled Food Vessel hybrids H(FV) comprises S-profiled vessels, tall in proportion, with strap handles and Beaker-style motifs and decorative techniques *(78-84)*. From this author's point of view, a designation of such vessels as 'Food Vessel hybrid' is contentious, since they lack the heavy internally bevelled and moulded rim that is such a major characteristic of the Northern Food Vessel tradition. Be that as it may, these vessels are relevant to the question of the relationship between the Beaker and Food Vessel traditions and deserve to be described here.

From eastern Scotland, between the Firth of Forth and the Moray Firth – the area with the greatest concentration of Beaker- and Food Vessel-accompanied burials – there are three handled vessels: those from Balmuick, Perth & Kinross *(78)* and Monquhitter, Aberdeenshire *(79.1)*, previously the only handled Beakers in the Scottish Beaker series (Creighton-Mitchell 1934, 152) and designated as Handled Food Vessels by Clarke (1970, 245); and one from Mains of Craichie, Angus *(79.2)*, excavated after Clarke's corpus was compiled. Subsequently, indisputable vessels of Clarke's SH(3) and SH(2) handled Beaker classes have come from excavations at Balfarg, Fife (Mercer 1981, 133-4, fig. 45) and Biggar Common, South Lanarkshire (Sheridan in

78 The Balmuick Handled Beaker.
Photo courtesy of the National Museums of Scotland

Johnston 1997, 212-3, illus. 22), thereby confirming the northern extent of the handled Beaker distributional province (*72*) in southern and eastern Scotland.

Regarding the Balmuick vessel, Clarke argued that it was 'a Food Vessel clearly based on a metal prototype', the latter being the gold cup from Rillaton, Cornwall (Clarke 1970, 252; vol. II frontispiece & fig. 1081). Its horizontal grooving recalls the Rillaton cup's corrugated profile (and indeed that of a further, recently-excavated example from Ringlemere, Kent: Varndell & Needham 2002). This corrugation would have provided rigidity for the thin beaten sheet gold. Although this 'gold cup skeuomorphism' interpretation was perceptive, Mercer subsequently commented that the exclusion of this vessel from Clarke's 'Beaker' category seemed 'a little perverse' (Mercer 1981, 135). Among eastern Scottish Beakers there are close parallels for Balmuick's body shape, collared rim and horizontal line decoration from Kilcoy, Highland (Ross and Cromarty); Pityot, Aberdeenshire; and Forglen, Moray (Clarke 1970, nos 1757 (E); 1689 (N/MR) & 1582 (AOC) respectively). Furthermore, in discussing the sources of inspiration for handled Beakers, Clarke identified the collared rim, the cordons, and the splayed ends of the handle merging into the cordon and shoulder as aspects deriving from a wooden prototype (*ibid.*, 246). These features are all present at Balmuick. The 'wooden prototype' idea can arguably be taken a step further, since the broad concentric grooves on its rim, like those on its base, would be consistent with patterns produced by applying the tip of a pointed tool to a vessel roughout during wood-turning. Further skeuomorphism of turned wooden vessels has

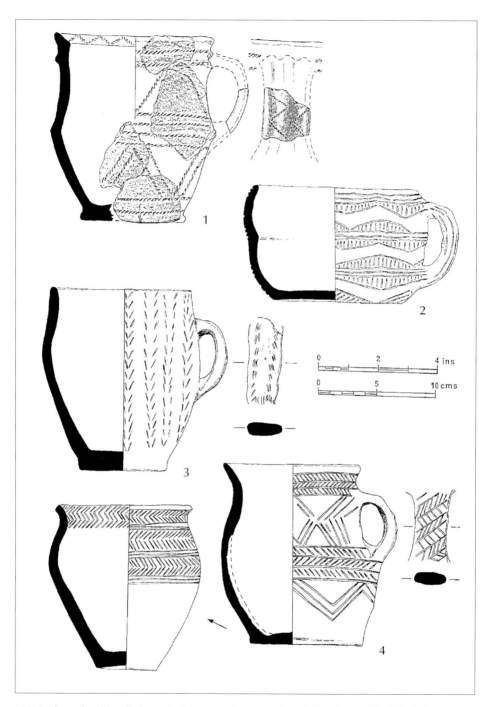

79 Beaker-related handled vessels: 1 Monquhitter; 2 Mains of Craichie; 3 Slip Gill; 4 Huggate and Warter 264 and jar accompanying secondary burial

been claimed for the basal decorative motifs found on some Irish Bowls (Ó Ríordáin & Waddell 1993, 42, nos 3, 26, 39, 100, 130).

The fragmentary Monquhitter vessel *(79.1)* has a tall biconical profile, internally bevelled rim, a cordon, protruding foot, and grooved strap handle; its twisted cord-impressed decoration consists of large bar chevrons in deep zones on body and neck, and zigzags on the rim bevel and handle. As the most northern handled Beaker, it is included in Step 7 of Ian Shepherd's North-east Scotland regional sequence, based on Lanting and van der Waals' Beaker typological developmental steps (Lanting & van der Waals 1972; Shepherd 1986, 26, illus. 19). Except for the handle and the protruding foot, most of its features (including the cord impressed motifs) appear again across the Moray Firth at Dornoch, Sutherland, on a 'sub-Beaker Food Vessel' (Clarke 1970, fig. 1012). Indeed, had the Monquitter and Dornoch vessel motifs been executed by comb impression or incision, these pots would surely have been classified as Beakers. However, the Monquhitter arrangement of cord-impresssed bar chevron zones bounded by horizontal lines does appear on a bipartite Food Vessel from Balcalk, Angus (Abercromby 1912, fig. 269).

The Mains of Craichie *(79.2)* handled Bowl is a squat vessel with a simple lip. It is decorated with a reserve bar chevron motif in three bands across the body, a motif characteristic of Developed and Late stages of Clarke's Southern British Beaker group (Clarke 1970, 210, 225; Lanting & van der Waals' Step 6:1972, 26-7; Case's Southern Group B3: Case 2001). The reserve bar chevron is uncommon on Beakers north of Yorkshire but does appear in eastern Scotland. A round-section handle is not a feature of handled Beakers; and if one discounts 'Dorset bowls' as a likely source of design influence (Gerloff 1975, 62; Mercer 1981, 134), the most likely source of inspiration would seem to be the Irish-Scottish Bowls series, as its constricted-waist profile is that of the Bipartite Bowls, a class represented in western Scotland at Barsloisnoch and Dunchraigaig, Argyll & Bute (Abercromby 1912, figs 306 & 236-7; Kinnes & Longworth 1985, 151, UN135). Irish-Scottish Bowl varieties have a strong element of Southern Beaker-like reserve motifs. Comparable to Mains of Craichie in Ireland are the bar chevron motifs on Bipartite Bowls from Loughloughan, County Antrim; Grange, County Roscommon; and Crouck, County Tyrone (Ó Ríordáin & Waddell 1993, 32-45, nos 3, 49, 59).

ORIGINS: HANDLED BEAKERS TO HANDLED FOOD VESSELS

As noted above, Clarke regarded handled Food Vessels to be derived from the more abundant handled Beakers of his Southern British Beaker Group *(fig. 72*; Clarke 1970, 252). Looking to the Middle Rhine Bell Beaker Group as the source of British handled Beakers, Clarke argued that the strap handles, cylindrical and barrel-shaped profiles and basal decoration of his typologically earliest handled Beaker class had been based on long-lasting wooden prototypes (*ibid.*, 245-47); in the absence of surviving wooden Beakers, he provided ethnographic parallels (*ibid.*, pls 7, 8). From the earliest pottery imitations – cylindrical and barrel-shaped mugs locally restricted to the Fen Basin – handles also appear on typologically successive Beaker S2 to S4 shapes in a wider eastern and southern English distribution (*ibid.*, map 10). As derivative developmental strands from his handled Beakers, by way of some hybrid vessels, came handled Food Vessels, Dorset Bowls and, ultimately, Wessex cups in non-ceramic materials; all of these he seamlessly integrated into a sweep of ceramic developments spanning the Early Bronze Age (*ibid.*, 245-52).

The taxonomic groupings of David Clarke's Beaker classification are retained here for their stylistic characterisations. Handled Beakers, like all Clarke's Southern British Beakers in their Developed (S2), Late (S3) and Final (S4) Stages, were brought into Lanting & van der Waals' developmental Steps 5 to 7 (Lanting and Van der Waals 1972, 36–40), and are included in Humphrey Case's Late style Beakers of geographical Group B (Case 1993, 254-9), more specifically in his late Group B3, distributed in eastern and southern England (Case 2001, fig. 8).

The continental European background to handled Beakers provided by Clarke (1970, 250-1) was enlarged by Sabine Gerloff, who distinguished between handled Beakers and Bell Beaker cups of the Reinecke A1 period and a second, later, tradition of handled vessels including biconical-profiled cups. These date to the Reinecke A2 and early B periods and are distributed in the Aunjetitz-Straubing-Adlerberg complex areas in Bohemia and Southern Germany, and the Rhône-Alpine groupings in Switzerland and eastern France (*ibid.*, 177-89). The round and pointed-based Adlerberg handled biconical cups of metal provide the closest parallels for the Wessex biconical cups in gold, amber and shale (*ibid.*, 178, pls. 49, 57).

There is no reason to dispute Clarke's handled Beakers as the general source of inspiration for the appearance of handles on Food Vessels (although his derivation of 'Dorset Bowls' from this source is debatable)[1]. His Beaker motif group 4 is also a source for their zigzag/chevron patterns; and in Scotland a link to the southern Beaker 'province' is offered by the handled Beaker from Balfarg. Handles as a novel design element were, like the other kinds of handling device as outlined above, absorbed into the Food Vessel tradition, with the variety in vessel forms and decorative schemes echoing the variability within the overall tradition. For example, the restraint in decorative treatment common to many southern English Food Vessels is shared by the handled footed bowl from Wimbourne St Giles, Dorset (*75.13*), whose four pad feet provide a link to the pair of footed bowls with incised herringbone decoration and opposed perforated lugs from Gallibury Down, Isle of Wight (Tomalin 1979; Sheridan 1993, 51, fig. 16). The sharing of design ideas on an inter-regional scale also seems to have occurred: it is suggested, for example, by the relative simplicity and sparseness of the decoration on the Garrowby (B2) and Orton Longueville

(B7) handled Food Vessels, which is more characteristic of the southern English tradition than of Food Vessels in Yorkshire and the East Midlands (see Manby 1957, figs 5.A7 & 6.A30, 35, for other southern English-like bipartite and tripartite Vases in these areas). Such inter-regional sharing is echoed in funerary practices too: evidence for what has been described as the 'Yorkshire/Fife axis' (Shepherd 1982) is particularly manifest by the buttons and necklaces of imported Whitby jet found in Fife (Sheridan & Davis 2002).

How does the available radiocarbon (and other) dating evidence square with Clarke's suggestion of handled Beakers and handled Food Vessels as being broadly concurrent ceramic classes?

Unfortunately, neither ceramic class is securely dated. The date for the handled Beaker from Wattisfield, Suffolk, for example, has far too large a standard deviation to be of any use (3520±150 BP, BM-77). As far as handled and single-lugged Food Vessels are concerned, some indirect dating evidence exists for the Mains of Craichie vessel, inasmuch as it comes from a dagger grave (Henshall 1968). The flat bronze dagger has a triangular blade of Type Masterton and an omega-shaped hiltmark of Type Butterwick (Gerloff 1975, 60) – an unusual combination that occurs again in eastern Scotland at Collessie, Fife, in a dagger with a gold hiltband (*ibid.*, no. 84). The associated cremated bone and ox-hide scabbard from Collessie have been dated to 3693±45 BP (GrA-10054) and 3690±80 BP (OxA-4510), calibrating to around 2200-1950 cal BC (Sheridan 2002, 795). This dating range has support among the Irish-Scottish Bowl series in Ireland, where the Mains of Craichie bowl's parallels have consistent determinations of 3660 BP, calibrating to within 2050-1950 BC (inf. A. Brindley; Brindley forthcoming). Such a date fits comfortably within the overall date span for Beaker pottery, but until more (and more reliable) dates are available for handled Beakers, the chronological relationship between the two classes of pottery must remain an open question.

Relative stratigraphy offers some clues in this regard, however. Most of our dating evidence for handled and single-lugged Food Vessels comes from the barrows of eastern Yorkshire, where a notable feature is the use of some graves for successive inhumation burials, Beakers preceding Food Vessels where ceramic associations are present (Burgess 1980, 297-9, fig. 7.1). The chronological span represented by such sequenced interments are difficult to refine in terms of years, decades or centuries, especially where our evidence is based on limited nineteenth-century recording. Handled Food Vessels accompany adult and child inhumations in successional relationships in the following examples:

Garrowby 104 *(74.2)* was in a grave inserted into the mound covering a central grave, whose upper burial was accompanied by an S2(W) Beaker;

Blanch 265 *(74.3)* overlay a disturbed interment on the grave floor with a cord-decorated bipartite Food Vessel;

Garton Slack *(74.4)* succeeded an unassociated inhumation at the bottom of a grave. These three inhumations followed a common east–west alignment of regional Beaker and Food Vessel burials, with the ceramic container placed at the head or the feet.

The boss-handled Vase from **Towthorpe** *(77.3)* succeeded an S2(W) Beaker-associated inhumation. Here, as at Garrowby 104, the Developed Southern British (Step 5) Beaker pre-dates the handled Food Vessel.

Finally, as for the question of whether the non-ceramic Wessex 2 biconical cups could have provided the inspiration for any of the handled ceramic vessels, this seems a possibility in only a tiny minority of cases, mostly within their Wessex distribution area. The plain cup with flattened base from Collingbourne Ducis, Wiltshire (Annable & Simpson 1964, no. 499) falls into this category; outside Wessex, the cup from Rothwell, Northamptonshire, has already been mentioned. Otherwise, the Wessex biconical cups can be ruled out on the grounds of their small size and their relatively late date in comparison with the estimated date of handled ceramic vessels. As for Clarke's claim that the Balmuick vessel is a skeuomorph of the Rillaton cup, this is brought into question if one accepts the possibility that it is actually a skeuomorph of a turned wooden vessel.

FOOTNOTE

[1] A more convincing source of inspiration for 'Dorset Bowls' is the Armorican *vases à anse,* single-handled jars and multi-handled carinated bowls with arched strip handles (Piggott 1938, 98-9, fig. 23; Briard 1984, 120-4), which have been found in Dorset and Wiltshire burials of the Wessex 2 series (Tomalin 1988, 212-19) and which provide graphic evidence for Breton-Wessex links. A particularly interesting find of such a vessel comes from Gallibury Down, Isle of Wight, where a *vase à anse* was found inside an inverted Vase Urn and within a smaller Vase Urn, the whole associated with cremated remains *(ibid.,* 208-9, fig. 5).

APPENDIX

Bibliographic references and museum registration numbers relating to the pots discussed in this paper.

Key to museum abbreviations: BM: British Museum; CUMAA: Cambridge University Museum of Archaeology & Anthropology; HM: Hull Museum; NMA: Museum of Antiquities, Newcastle-upon-Tyne; NMS: National Museums of Scotland.

HANDLED FOOD VESSELS

Simonside, Spital Hill, Northumberland *(74.1)*: NMA 1881.23.1. Gibson 1978, 75, no. 68; Annable 1987, 569, no. 558.

Garrowby barrow 104, Kirby Underdale, East Riding of Yorkshire *(74.2)*: HM 435.42. Mortimer 1905, 136, fig. 353; Abercromby 1912, I, 45, 91, fig. 296a; Sheppard 1929, 48, no. 42.

Blanch barrow 265, North Dalton, East Riding of Yorkshire *(74.3)*: HM 506.42. Mortimer 1905, 330, fig. 990; Abercromby 1912, I, 159, fig. 224; Sheppard 1929, 103, no. 990; Manby 1969, 281, no. 2, fig. 3; 1995, 88.

Garton Slack barrow 141, East Riding of Yorkshire *(74.4)*: HM 489.42. Mortimer 1905, 259, fig. 725; Abercromby 1912, I, 157, fig. 60; Sheppard 1929, 87, no. 725; Clarke 1970, I, 248, no. 1305, fig. 1083.

Caythorpe, Lincolnshire *(75.5 & 6)*: Grantham Museum EBP 15-16. Phillips 1933, 126-7, pl. viii; A. Clarke 1970, 507, fig. 1082; May 1976, 85, fig. 48.3.

Orton Longueville, Cambridgeshire (not illustrated): Taylor 1981, 114; Mackreth, D.F. & Bamford, H.M. unpublished report.

Rothwell, Northamptonshire *(75.8)*: Northampton Museum D42/1954-5. Abercromby 1912, I, 91 & 45, fig. 286 bis; Gerloff 1975, 178.

Great Chesterford, Essex *(75.9)*: Saffron Walden Museum 1884.205. Fox 1923, 32.

Bixley, Norfolk (not illustrated): Norwich Castle Museum. Ashwin & Bates 2000, 43, P10, fig. 37.

Wereham, Norfolk *(75.11)*: CUMAA 1892.82; AR 1892.3. Abercromby 1912, I, pl. xxii, 297; Fox 1923, 38, pl. VI B; Lawson 1984, fig. 6, 2C.

Hockwold Fen, Norfolk (not illustrated): Norwich Castle Museum 44.493. Healy 1996, 152, P363, fig. 102.

Wimbourne St. Giles, Dorset *(75.13)*: Devizes Museum 186. Abercromby 1912, fig. 21 bis; Annable & Simpson 1964, 24 & 60, no. 463; Manby 1969, 282, no. 14.

SINGLE-LUGGED FOOD VESSELS

Cropton, Fall Rigg, North Yorkshire *(76.1)*: Yorkshire Museum 1184.47. Pierpoint 1980, 119, pl. VIII (wrongly attributed to Cawthorn!).

Folkton barrow 243, North Yorkshire *(76.2)*: BM 89.2-2.41. Greenwell 1890, fig. 12, fig. 4; Abercromby 1912, I, fig. 152; Pierpoint 1980, 119; Kinnes & Longworth 1985, 115, 245:1.

Blanch, Warter Parish, East Riding of Yorkshire *(76.3)*: BM 79.12-9.1998. Kinnes & Longworth 1985, 42, UN 68:5.

Roystone Grange, Ballidon, Derbyshire *(76.4)*: Sheffield City Mus 1981.460. Marsden 1982, 27-9, fig. 4; Vine 1982, 219, (597).

Colwell, Northumberland *(76.5)*: NMA 1856.37. Abercromby 1912, I, fig. 185; Gibson 1978, 60, no. 66; Annable 1987, 550, fig. 93.169.

See also (not illustrated): Somersham, Huntingdonshire: CUMAA 23.1215. Fox 1922, appendix 1; *Antiq J*, 4, 131-2; Clarke 1970, 484, no. 372, fig. 1086.

VESSELS WITH SOLID BOSS HANDLES

Heslerton barrow 1R, North Yorkshire *(77.1)*: Powlesland *et al.* 1986, 104 & 123, figs 38-9, 224K.

Sunderlandwick, Hutton Cranswick, East Riding of Yorkshire *(77.2)*: HM 493.42. Mortimer 1905, 296, fig. 895; Sheppard 1929, 89, no. 895.

Towthorpe barrow 21, North Yorkshire *(77.3)*: HM 404.42. Mortimer 1905, 12, fig. 26; Sheppard 1929, 4 & 126, no. 26; Clarke 1970, 509, no. 1400-1400F, fig. 828.

Rothwell Woods, Northamptonshire *(77.4)*: CUMAA 1918.206. Fox 1923, 38, pl. vi, A.

Elton, Cambridgeshire *(77.5)*: Peterborough Museum L.10. Gibson 1979, 89, fig. 1.

Manea, Cambridgeshire *(77.6)*: CUMAA Z.15240. Fox 1923, 35 (a vessel with a single lug is referred to but site not given).

Upper Hare Park, Swaffham, Norfolk *(77.7)*: CUMAA Z.14984. Fox 1923, 35.

Warren Hill, Three Hills, Suffolk *(77.8)*: BM 79.12-9.1899. Fox 1923, 327.

HANDLED BEAKERS & BEAKER-RELATED VESSELS

Balmuick, Comrie, Perth & Kinross *(78)*: NMS X.EH 8. Boston 1884; Anderson 1902, 684, fig. 12; Abercromby 1912, I, 45; Creighton-Mitchell 1934, 152 & 187, no. 253; Clarke 1970, 248 & 417, fig. 1081; Clarke *et al.* 1985, 282-3, no. 106, illus. 4.

Monquhitter, Cairnhill, Aberdeenshire *(79.1)*: NMS X.EQ 335. Anderson 1902, 682-4, fig. 10-11; Creighton-Mitchell 1934, 152 & 177, no. 62; Shepherd 1986, 34, illus. 19.

Mains of Craichie, Dunnichen, Angus *(79.2)*: Dundee Museum 1971.169-1.Coutts 1971, 46, no. 83; Gerloff 1975, 60-1, pl. 44, D2.

Slip Gill, Scawton, N. Yorkshire *(79.3)*: Scarborough Museum 652.52. Hayes & Rutter 1955, fig. 1, pl. xxxvia; Hayes 1963, 18 & 356, fig. 4.5; Clarke 1970, 509, no. 1388, fig. 1085.

Huggate & Warter, barrow 264, East Riding of Yorkshire *(79.4)*: HM 215.42. Mortimer 1905, 317, fig. 944; Abercromby 1912, I, fig. 296a; Sheppard 1929, 96, no. 944; Clarke 1970, 248 & 508, no.1337, fig. 1087.

ACKNOWLEDGMENTS

For facilities to study material in their care the writer wishes to record his gratitude to Martin Foreman, Hull and East Riding Museum, Hull; Elizabeth Hartley, Yorkshire Museum, York; Dr Alison Sheridan, National Museums of Scotland, Edinburgh; Anne Taylor, Cambridge University Museum of Archaeology & Anthropology; Carolyn Wingfield, Saffron Walden Museum. Grateful thanks are expressed for discussion, advice, background information and literature to Dr Helen Bamford, Norwich; Pauline Beswick, Froggatt; Anna Brindley, Groningen; Humphrey Case, Oxford; Dr Frances Healy; Oxford; Donald Mackreth, Peterborough; Ian Shepherd, Aberdeenshire Council; Dr David Tomalin, Isle of Wight Council; John Waddell, Galway University; and Adrian Zealand, Dundee Museum. Recent radiocarbon dating results were kindly made available by Dominic Powlesland, Yedingham, and Alison Sheridan who also advised on Scottish Food Vessel topics. Thanks are offered to Northamptonshire Archaeology and H.A. Jacklin for drawing the Rothwell Handled Food Vessel.

BIBLIOGRAPHY

Abercromby, J., 1912 *A Study of Bronze Age Pottery of Great Britain and Ireland and its Associated Grave Goods.* (2 vols) Oxford: Clarendon Press.

Allen, C. & Hopkins, D., 2000 Accessory cups from Lincolnshire: Early Bronze Age Pot? *Proceedings of the Prehistoric Society*, 66, 297-318.

Anderson, J., 1902 Notices of Cists discovered in a cairn at Cairnhill, Parish of Monquhitter, Aberdeenshire, and at Doune, Perthshire. *Proceedings of the Society of Antiquaries of Scotland*, 36 (1901-02), 675-88.

Annable, F.K. & Simpson, D.D.A., 1964 *Guide Catalogue of the Neolithic and Bronze Age Collections in the Devizes Museum*. Devizes: Wiltshire Archaeological & Natural History Society.

Annable, R., 1987 *The Later Prehistory of Northern England*. BAR British Series 160. Oxford: British Archaeological Reports.

Ashbee, P., 1957 Excavation of a Barrow at Bishop's Waltham, Hampshire. *Proceedings of the Prehistoric Society*, 23, 124-37.

Ashwin, T. & Bates, S., 2000 *Norwich Southern Bypass, Part I: Excavations at Bixley, Caistor St. Edmund, Trowse*. East Anglian Archaeology 91. Dereham: Norfolk Museums Service.

Barclay, A. & Halpin, C., 1999 *Excavations at Barrow Hills, Radley, Oxfordshire*. Vol. I: *The Neolithic and Bronze Age Monument Complex*. Oxford: Oxford Archaeological Unit.

Boston, T., 1884 Notes on three sepulchral mounds on the farm of Balmuick (the property of Col. Williamson of Lawers), near Comrie, Perthshire. *Proceedings of the Society of Antiquaries of Scotland*, 18 (1883-4), 306-08.

Briard, J., 1984 *Les Tumulus d'Armorique. L' age du Bronze en France 3*. Paris: Picard.

Brindley, A., forthcoming. *The Dating of Food Vessels and Urns in Ireland*. Galway: University of Galway Press.

Burgess, C., 1980 *The Age of Stonehenge*. London, Toronto & Melbourne: Dent.

Case, H., 1993 Beakers: deconstruction and after. *Proceedings of the Prehistoric Society*, 59, 241-68.

Case, H., 2001 The Beaker Cultures in Britain and Ireland: groups, European contacts and chronology. In Nicolis, F. (ed.) *Bell Beakers Today: Pottery, People, Culture, Symbols in Prehistoric Europe*, 361-77. Trento: Servizio Bení Culturali.

Clarke, D.L., 1970 *Beaker Pottery of Great Britain and Ireland*. Cambridge: Cambridge University Press.

Clarke, D.V., Cowie, T.G. & Foxon, A., 1985 *Symbols of Power at the Time of Stonehenge*. Edinburgh: Her Majesty's Stationery Office.

Coles, J., 2001 Energetic activities. *Proceedings of the Prehistoric Society*, 67, 19-48.

Coles, J.M. & Simpson, D.D.A., (eds), 1968 *Studies in Ancient Europe: Essays Presented to Stuart Piggott*. Leicester: Leicester University Press.

Coutts, H., 1971 *Tayside Before History: A guide-catalogue of the collection of Antiquities in Dundee Museum*. Dundee: Dundee Museum Service.

Cowie, T.G., 1983 The pottery from the henge monument at North Mains. In Barclay, G.J. Sites of the third millennium BC to the first millennium AD at North Mains, Strathallan, Perthshire, *Proceedings of the Society of Antiquaries of Scotland*, 113, 155-63.

Creighton-Mitchell, M.E. 1934. A new analysis of the Early Bronze Age Beaker pottery of Scotland. *Proceedings of the Society of Antiquaries of Scotland*, 68 (1933-4), 132-89.

Earwood, C., 1993 *Domestic Wooden Artefacts in Britain and Ireland from Neolithic to Viking Times*. Exeter: Exeter University Press.

Fox, C., 1923 *The Archaeology of the Cambridge Region*. Cambridge: Cambridge University Press.

Garwood, P., 1999 Grooved Ware in southern Britain: chronology and interpretation. In Cleal, R. & MacSween, A. (eds), *Grooved Ware in Britain and Ireland*, 145-76. Oxford: Oxbow.

Gerloff, S., 1975 *The Early Bronze Age Daggers in Great Britain and a Reconsideration of The Wessex Culture*. Prähistorische Bronzefunde VI/2. München: Beck'sche.

Gibson, A.M., 1978 *Bronze Age Pottery in the North-east of England*. BAR British Series 56. Oxford: British Archaeological Reports.

Gibson, A.M., 1979 Bronze Age pottery from the collections of the City Museum and Art Gallery, Peterborough. *Northamptonshire Archaeology*, 14, 89-91.

Gibson, A.M. & Kinnes, I.A., 1997 'On the Urns of a Dilemma': radiocarbon and the Peterborough Problem. *Oxford Journal of Archaeology*, 16(1), 65-72.

Glob, P.V., 1973 *The Mound People: Danish Bronze-Age Man Preserved*. London: Book Club Associates.

Greenwell, W., 1877 *British Barrows*. Oxford: Clarendon Press.

Greenwell, W., 1890 Recent researches in barrows in Yorkshire, Wiltshire, Berkshire, etc. *Archaeologia*, 52, 1-72.

Hayes, R.H., 1963 Archaeology 2-4. In McDonnell, J. (ed.) *A History of Helmsley, Rievaulx and District*, 31-53, 335-403. York: Yorkshire Archaeological Society.

Hayes, R.H. & Rutter, J.G., 1955 The discovery of a Handled Beaker in a fissure near Helmsley, Yorkshire. *Antiquaries Journal*, 35, 223-5.

Healy, F.M., 1988 *The Anglo-Saxon Cemetery at Spong Hill, North Elmam, Part VI. Occupation During the Seventh to Second Millennia BC*. Report 39. Norwich: East Anglian Archaeology.

Healy, F. M., 1996 *The Fenland Project No. 11: The Wissey Embayment: Evidence for preIron Age Occupation*. East Anglian Archaeology 78. Dereham: Norfolk Museums Service.

Henshall, A.S., 1968 Scottish dagger graves. In Coles, J.M. and Simpson, D.D.A. (eds), 173-95.

Jacob-Friesen, K.H., 1963 *Einführung in Niedersachens Urgeschichte, II. Teil. Bronzezeit*. Hildesheim.

Jewitt, L., 1864 Notice of the discovery of some Celtic remains at Stancliffe Hall, Darley Dale. *Reliquary*, 4, 204-6.

Johnston, D.A., 1997 Biggar Common, 1987-93: an early prehistoric and domestic landscape in Clydesdale, South Lanarkshire. *Proceedings of the Society of Antiquaries of Scotland*, 127, 185-253.

Kinnes, I.A. & Longworth, I.H., 1985 *Catalogue of the Excavated Prehistoric and Romano-British Material in the Greenwell Collection*. London: British Museum Press.

Kinnes, I.A. & Varndell, G. (eds), 1995 *'Unbaked Urns of Rudely shape': Essays on British and Irish Pottery for Ian Longworth*. Oxbow Monograph 55. Oxford: Oxbow.

Lanting, J.N. & van der Waals, J.D., 1972 British Beakers as seen from the Continent. *Helinium*, 12, 20-4.

Lawson, A., 1984 The Bronze Age in East Anglia with Particular Reference to Norfolk. In Barringer, G. (ed.) *Aspects of East Anglian Prehistory*, 141-77. Norwich: Geo Books.

Longworth, I.H. 1984. *Collared Urns of the Bronze Age in Great Britain and Ireland*. Cambridge: Cambridge University Press.

MacSween, A., 2001 Scottish Impressed Wares. In Barclay, G.J., Carter, S.P., Dalland, M.M., Hastie, M., Holden, T.G., MacSween, A. & Whickam-Jones, C.R. A possible Neolithic settlement at Kinbeachie, Black Isle, Highland. *Proceedings of the Society of Antiquaries of Scotland*, 131, 57-85.

Manby, T.G., 1957 Food Vessels from the Peak District. *Derbyshire Archaeological Journal*, 78, 1-29.

Manby, T.G., 1969 Bronze Age pottery from Pule Hill, Marsden, W.R. Yorkshire and Footed Bowls of the Early Bronze Age from England. *Yorkshire Archaeological Journal*, 42 (1967-70), 237-82.

Manby, T.G., 1975 Neolithic Occupation Sites on the Yorkshire Wolds. *Yorkshire Archaeological Journal*, 47, 23-9.

Manby, T.G., 1994 Type 1 Food Vessels. In Coombs, D. The Excavation of Two Bronze Age Round Barrows on Irton Moor, Yorks. 1973. *Yorkshire Archaeological Journal*, 66, 36-40.

Manby, T.G., 1995 Skeuomorphism: some reflections of leather, wood and basketry in Early Bronze Age Pottery. In Kinnes, I. & Varndell, G. (eds), 81-8.

Manby, T.G., King, A. & Vyner, B., 2003 The Neolithic and Bronze Ages: a time of early agriculture. In Manby, T.G. Moorhouse, S. & Ottaway, P. (eds), *The Archaeology of Yorkshire. A Assessment at the Beginning of the 21st Century*, 35-116, Occasional Paper no. 3. Leeds: Yorkshire Archaeological Society.

Marsden, B., 1982 The Excavation of the Roystone Grange round cairn (Ballidon 12), Derbyshire. *Derbyshire Archaeological Journal* 102, 23-32.

May, J., 1976 *Prehistoric Lincolnshire*. Lincoln: Lincolnshire Archaeological Society.

Mercer, R.J., 1981 The excavation of a Late Neolithic henge-type enclosure at Balfarg, Markinch, Fife, Scotland. *Proceedings of the Society of Antiquaries of Scotland*, 111, 63-171.

Mortimer, J.R., 1905 *Forty Years' Researches in British and Saxon Burial Mounds of East Yorkshire*. London & Hull: Brown & Co.

Needham, S.P., 1996 Chronology and Periodisation in the British Bronze Age. *Acta Archaeologica*, 67, 121-40.

Ó Ríordáin, B. & and Waddell, J., 1993. *The Funerary Bowls and Vases of the Irish Bronze Age*. Galway: Galway University Press.

Patchett, F.M., 1944 Cornish Bronze Age Pottery. *Archaeological Journal*, 101, 17-49.

Patchett, F.M., 1951 Cornish Bronze Age Pottery: Part II. *Archaeological Journal*, 107, 44-65.

Phillips, C.W., 1933 The Present State of Archaeology in Lincolnshire: Part 1. *Archaeological Journal*, 90, 106-49.

Pierpoint, S., 1980 *Social Patterns in Yorkshire Prehistory 3500-750 BC*. BAR British Series 74. Oxford: British Archaeological Reports.

Piggott, S., 1938 The Early Bronze Age in Wessex. *Proceedings of the Prehistoric Society*, 23, 124-37.

Powlesland, D., Haughton, C. & Hanson, J., 1986 Excavations at Heslerton, North Yorkshire 1978-82. *Archaeological Journal*, 143, 53-173.

Savory, H.N., 1957 A Corpus of Welsh Bronze Age pottery: II. Food-vessels and enlarged Food-vessels. *Bulletin of the Board of Celtic Studies*, 17 (1955-8), 196-233.

Shepherd, I.A.G., 1982 Comparative background: the assemblage. In Watkins, T. The excavation of an Early Bronze Age cemetery at Barns Farm, Dalgety, Fife. *Proceedings of the Society of Antiquaries of Scotland*, 112, 129-32.

Shepherd, I.A.G., 1986 *Powerful Pots: Beakers in North-east Prehistory*. Aberdeen: Anthropological Museum, University of Aberdeen.

Sheppard, T., 1929 *Catalogue of the Mortimer Collection of Prehistoric Remains from East Yorkshire Barrows*. Hull: A. Brown & Sons.

Sheridan, J.A., 1993 The manufacture, production and use of Irish Bowls and Vases. In O Ríordáin, B. & Waddell, J. (eds), 45-75.

Sheridan, J.A., 2002 The radiocarbon dating programmes of the National Museums of Scotland. *Antiquity*, 76, 794-6.

Sheridan, J.A. & Davis, M., 2002 Investigating jet and jet-like artefacts from prehistoric Scotland: the National Museums of Scotland project. *Antiquity*, 76, 812-25.

Simpson, D.D.A., 1965 Food Vessels in South-West Scotland. *Transactions of the Dumfries & Galloway Natural History & Antiquarian Society*, 42, 25-50.

Simpson, D.D.A., 1968 Food Vessels: associations and chronology. In Coles, J.M. & Simpson, D.D.A. (eds), 197-211.

Taylor, A., 1981 The barrows of Cambridgeshire. In Lawson, A.J., Martin, E.A. & Priddy, D. (eds), *The Barrows of East Anglia*, 108-20. East Anglian Archaeology 12. Dereham: Norfolk Museums Service.

Thurnam, J., 1871 On Ancient British Barrows especially those of Wiltshire and adjoining counties. Part II. Round Barrows. *Archaeologia*, 43, 285-544.

Tomalin, D.J., 1979 Barrow excavations in the Isle of Wight. *Current Archaeology*, 68, 273-6.

Tomalin, D.J., 1984 The pottery. In Greenfield, E. The excavation of three round barrows at Puncknowle, Dorset 1959. *Proceedings of the Dorset Natural History & Archaeology* Society, 106, 72-5.

Tomalin, D.J., 1988 Armorican *vases à anse* and their occurrence in southern Britain. *Proceedings of the Prehistoric Society*, 54, 203-22.

Varndell, G. & Needham, S.P., 2002 New Gold Cup from Kent. *Past*, 41, 2-4.

Vine, P., 1982 The *Neolithic and Bronze Age Cultures of the Middle and Upper Trent Basin*. BAR British Series 105. Oxford: British Archaeological Reports.

Williamson, W.C., 1872 *Description of the Tumulus Opened at Gristhorpe, near Scarborough. Third Edition (Scarborough)*. Reprinted 1976 as: *The Bronze Age Tree Trunk Coffin Burial Found at Gristhorpe, near Scarborough*. Leeds: Yorkshire Archaeological Society.

16

Scottish
Food Vessel Chronology
Revisited

Alison Sheridan

Preface

Derek: Exactly 20 years ago, at the Queen's University of Belfast Institute of Irish Studies, you gamely sat through my execrable seminar on Irish Food Vessels. You were patient and encouraging then, as ever, and luckily things have since moved on a little on the Food Vessel front! This contribution is offered with my thanks and warmest wishes, and in the hope that you will enjoy this freshly-picked posy of Scottish Food Vessel dates.

Introduction

In his 1968 paper 'Food Vessels: associations and chronology', Derek Simpson reported that only a single radiocarbon date existed for this kind of pottery, from Harland Edge in Derbyshire (Simpson 1968). His discussion of Food Vessel chronology had therefore to rely on comparative dating, based largely on associated artefacts and on the then-current belief that the 'Wessex Culture' (against which many of these artefacts were assessed) dated to 1650–1400 BC.

Today, some 36 years later, we are in a happier position to review Food Vessel chronology. There are now over 50 radiocarbon dates relating to Food Vessels in Britain (of which some 34 are from Scotland), and a further 74 dates for Irish examples,[1] the latter mostly obtained as part of Anna Brindley's groundbreaking systematic programme for dating Irish Bronze Age pottery (undertaken in collaboration with Jan Lanting: Brindley 1995; forthcoming; Lanting & Brindley 1998). In addition, we know more about the dating of some of the associated artefact types, such as daggers (Brindley 2001; Sheridan in press a) and faience (Sheridan 2004a); the date range of the rich Wessex graves has been re-assessed as c.1950–1450 BC (Garwood & Barclay 1999, 285; Needham 2000); and it has been established that many Food Vessels are likely to have been in use before the emergence of this particular series of graves.

However, the news on dating is not uniformly good. While the Irish radiocarbon dates can be regarded as reliable, having been determined recently and with scrupulous care as to their evaluation, many of the British dates were

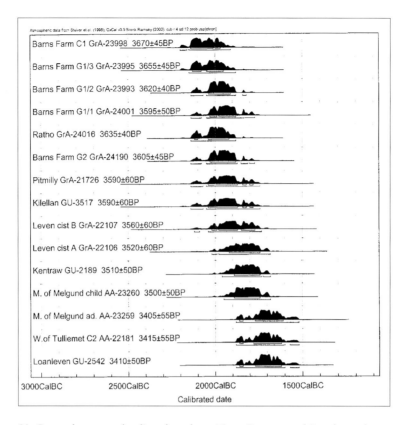

Atmospheric data from Stuiver et al. (1998); OxCal v3.9 Bronk Ramsey (2003); cub r:4 sd:12 prob usp[chron]

Barns Farm C1 GrA-23998 3670±45BP

Barns Farm G1/3 GrA-23995 3655±45BP

Barns Farm G1/2 GrA-23993 3620±40BP

Barns Farm G1/1 GrA-24001 3595±50BP

Ratho GrA-24016 3635±40BP

Barns Farm G2 GrA-24190 3605±45BP

Pitmilly GrA-21726 3590±60BP

Kilellan GU-3517 3590±60BP

Leven cist B GrA-22107 3560±60BP

Leven cist A GrA-22106 3520±60BP

Kentraw GU-2189 3510±50BP

M. of Melgund child AA-23260 3500±50BP

M. of Melgund ad. AA-23259 3405±55BP

W.of Tulliemet C2 AA-22181 3415±55BP

Loanleven GU-2542 3410±50BP

3000CalBC   2500CalBC   2000CalBC   1500CalBC

Calibrated date

80 Currently-accepted radiocarbon dates. Note: Kentraw and Loanleven dates are *tpq*; Kilellan date just gives general indication of date of midden with Food Vessels. See Appendix for details

obtained a considerable time ago and/or would not meet current standards as to acceptability. As far as the 34 Scottish dates are concerned, just over half fall into the latter category. With the old determinations, standard deviations have had to be adjusted to ±110 or over (see Ashmore *et al.* 2000 for details). A few dates are obviously anomalous, for various reasons. For example, in the case of the female skeleton associated with a Food Vessel and a spacer–plate necklace of jet and cannel coal at Mount Stuart, Bute (Bryce 1904, 63-8), two late and widely-spaced dates obtained from two bones can be explained in terms of (invisible) contamination from an animal-based consolidant that must have been applied to them shortly after their discovery in 1887 (Sheridan *et al.* 2002, 56). Details of these and the other Scottish Food Vessel dates can be found in the Appendix.

The 15 ostensibly reliable Scottish dates, which form the main subject of this contribution, include six obtained as part of a current National Museums of Scotland (NMS) initiative to improve the dating of Scottish Bronze Age pottery in general (Sheridan 2001; 2002; 2003a; 2003b; 2004a;

in press a). A further seven samples – including one from the famous cist at Doune, Perth & Kinross, where a miniature battle-axe and a large and a small Food Vessel were buried with a child (Hamilton 1957; cf. Simpson 1968, 210 and McLaren, this volume) – are currently being dated as part of the Food Vessel section of the NMS dating programme, and an eighth is being re-dated, to check the reliability of its initial determination.[2] The overall NMS initiative, supported by the Society of Antiquaries of Scotland, Historic Scotland, the Natural Environment Research Council, Aberdeenshire Archaeology and the University of Groningen, features the AMS dating of human bone, both unburnt and cremated. The latter – which in Scotland constitutes a significant minority of the human remains associated with Food Vessels – can now be dated reliably thanks to the work of Jan Lanting and Dr Johannes van der Plicht at Groningen University (Lanting *et al.* 2001). While previous attempts to date charred or burnt bone on the basis of its organic carbonate content had produced highly unreliable results, the new technique focuses on the structural carbonate that recrystallises in bone when it reaches 600°C (Aerts *et al.* 2001). This technique, which is well-tried and tested, produces results that are accurate and fairly precise, and are not susceptible to the sources of bias or contamination that can affect unburnt bone (e.g. the marine effect from the individual's diet; groundwater leaching; or the use of organic consolidants). The development of this technique has allowed an entire class of hitherto undatable material to yield important chronological information.

The principal aim of this contribution is to present the 15 Scottish dates along with images of the pots to which they relate (except in the case of the unpublished Kilellan assemblage, where only selected pots are reproduced), and to discuss their significance in terms of our understanding of Food Vessel development, both within Scotland and in Britain and Ireland in general. An additional aim is to understand where Food Vessels fit into the broader picture of Copper and Early Bronze Age ceramic developments in Scotland (cf. Sheridan 2003b; in press a), and how Food Vessel use relates to the changing pattern of funerary practice in Early Bronze Age Scotland. Given the relatively small number of dates involved, and the various qualifications that must be borne in mind in using them (as outlined below), the conclusions can only be regarded as provisional.

A comment on the vexed question of terminology is required at this point. Although our Irish colleagues generally (and wisely) eschew the use of the archaic term 'Food Vessel', preferring to use the more function-neutral 'Bowl' and 'Vase' (e.g. Waddell 1976), the term will be retained here purely as a convenient catch-all label; no functional significance should be read into it. As for defining sub-types, a considerable amount of ink has already been spilt on this issue, and a plethora of classificatory schemes of varying degrees of complexity proposed (e.g. Abercromby 1912; ApSimon 1958;

1969; Burgess 1974; 1980; Cowe 1983; Gibson 1978; 2002, 94-6; Simpson 1965; 1968; Waddell 1976; 1998, 140-9; Ó Ríordáin & Waddell 1993). Definitions have often lacked clarity and precision, and there has been variability and subjectivity in the application of terms so that, for example, 'there is a broad, grey area comprising vessels which can be described either as tall bowls or squat vases' (Burgess 1980, 86). Given that these vessels were not designed for the convenience of twenty-first-century ceramic classification, and that Brindley's Irish dating project has demonstrated that diverse vessel forms and decorative schemes were in broadly contemporary use (Brindley pers. comm.), the intention here is to take a minimalist approach to classification, and to let the pots speak for themselves as far as possible.

THE CURRENTLY-ACCEPTED SCOTTISH FOOD VESSEL DATES

The 15 dates in question are summarised in *(80)* and listed fully, with bibliographic references, in the Appendix; the pots in question are illustrated in *(81-8)*. All but three of the dates are Accelerator Mass Spectrometry (AMS) determinations obtained from cremated (in seven cases) or unburnt human

81 Dated Food Vessels from Barns Farm: 1: cist 1; 2: grave 2; 3: grave 1 *(from Watkins 1982)*

bone. Nine of these AMS dates have been obtained within the last year, mostly for the NMS dating programme, but with three commissioned by Fife Council. These AMS dates can arguably be regarded as the most reliable and useful dates. The non-AMS determinations consist of: i) a hazel charcoal date from Loanleven, Perth & Kinross (GU-2542), obtained in 1988, which gives a *terminus post quem (tpq)* for a cist with a fragmentary Food Vessel; ii) a date (GU-3517), obtained in 1993, for mixed charcoal from short-lived species, sealed in an undisturbed domestic midden at Kilellan, Islay and therefore giving a *general* date for Food Vessel sherds from the midden; and iii) a date (GU-2189), obtained in 1987 from an unburnt femur from a cist at Kentraw, Islay, providing a *tpq* for a burial with a Food Vessel and accessory vessel.[3]

As for the closeness of association between the AMS-dated samples and the Food Vessels in question, in most cases the contemporaneity of the dated human remains and the pot is not in question. However, in a few cases, some qualification is required. In Grave 1 at Barns Farm, Fife, a tripartite lugged Food Vessel had been buried in an organic coffin, together with a stone battle-axe, as grave goods for a flexed unburnt corpse. Three sets of cremated remains, representing three individuals, were also deposited in the coffin, and the excavator argued convincingly that these must have been buried simultaneously with the unburnt corpse. The three dates obtained from the three sets of cremated remains all overlap at the 1σ level and suggest that the individuals died between 2100–1900 cal BC. Unless these remains had been curated for a significant time before burial, it is assumed that they are broadly contemporary with the inhumed individual and hence the pot. The same can be said of the cremated remains found with unburnt remains in grave 2 and cist 2 from the same cemetery. At Ratho, Midlothian, the cremated remains were allegedly found inside the Food Vessel, in a cist that had also originally housed a crouched, unburnt corpse. If it is assumed that the pot had originally been deposited as an offering of drink or food for the unburnt individual's journey into the Afterlife, and that the cremated remains had been deposited in it at a later date, the date obtained from the latter must be regarded as a *terminus ante quem* for the pot. (It should be noted, however, that the cist was uncovered before 1863 and the account of the disposition of finds in it may not be wholly accurate.) This cist is also of interest as it had evidently been revisited during the Iron Age when a set of bronze items, including a penannular bangle and button-and-loop fastener, was deposited in it. Despite previous assumptions about the Bronze Age date of these objects (e.g. Simpson 1968, 198), they can confidently be ascribed to the Roman Iron Age (Hunter pers. comm.). Finally, at Pitmilly, Fife, the physical association between the dated cremated remains and the pot (and indeed the cist with which they are believed to be associated) is not as close as one would have liked, as all were found during drainage operations (Sheridan in 2004b). It is not known

82 Dated Food Vessels from Ratho (left) and Pitmilly (right), and accessory vessel in the form of a miniature Food Vessel from Craigdhu. *Photo courtesy of NMS*

whether the cist had originally also contained an unburnt corpse, for whom the pot had been a grave gift, but this is a possibility.

In addition to these various *caveats*, it must be emphasised that the set of 15 dates does not purport to cover the full range of Food Vessel forms and decorative schemes found in Scotland. It is particularly unfortunate that a recently-discovered classic bipartite 'Irish Bowl' from Seafield West, Highland produced an anomalous date (see Appendix), since this pot – one of two recent finds of this type from the north-east, representing outliers of an otherwise south-west Scottish cluster with strong Irish connections – ought to date within the early part of the Scottish sequence (Cressey & Sheridan 2003; the second find is from near Elgin). Nor are the dated vessels geographically evenly distributed, with all but the two Islay assemblages coming from Tayside and Fife. This is due partly to the uneven availability of datable human remains; partly to the 'happenstance' of fieldwork; and partly to the fact that the systematic dating programme is still in its early stages. There are yet further pitfalls for the unwary: as others have noted (e.g. Brindley 1995; forthcoming), the radiocarbon calibration curve has plateaux around 3700-3500 BP, which can produce a false impression of contemporaneity for clusters of C14 dates; and, with the determinations made on unburnt bone, one must always be alert to the possibility of groundwater leaching affecting collagen content (Hedges 2002).

The Results: A Scottish Food Vessel Sequence?

Notwithstanding all these constraints on our interpretation, the set of 15 dates provides a useful starting point from which to build. What can we learn from it?

The overall date range appears to span the period *c.*3700-3400 BP, with 1σ and 2σ calibrated ranges for the earliest and latest dates of 2140–1970 (2200-1910) cal BC and 1860–1620 (1880-1520) cal BC respectively. (It should be remembered, however, that the Loanleven date is a *tpq*, predating the pot by an unknown length of time.) It may be that, through wiggle-matching (cf. Brindley forthcoming) or statistical analysis of the data, a slightly tighter date range may be arrived at; the current author claims no expertise in such matters. Since not all varieties of Food Vessel have been dated, it is currently impossible to tell whether the original date span exceeded this; however, the Irish dates, which do cover all (or virtually all) of the variant forms found there, have produced a comparable, although somewhat shorter, date range (3770-3470 BP, *c.*2180-1725 cal BC: Brindley, pers. comm.). Some support, albeit indirect and tenuous, for the idea of Food Vessel use in Scotland continuing until *c.*3300 BP (seventeenth to the fifteenth/fourteenth century BC) is offered by AMS dates of 3295±50 BP and 3300±50 BP (AA-23258, 23261) from human bone from associated with flint knives in 'crouched inhumation' cists at East Campsie and West Scryne, Angus, respectively (Rideout & Cowie 1998, 65). As the authors note, such knives tend elsewhere to be associated with Food Vessels. A further, admittedly provisional, indication of a late use of Food Vessels in Scotland is offered by the AMS date from cremated bone associated with a pot from cist 3, Balbirnie, Fife (GrA-24860, 3335±40 BP; fig. 90.4); this is the date that is currently being re-checked at Groningen.[6]

Can any trends be perceived? In terms of form, it appears that the undifferentiated globular vessels from Mains of Melgund, Angus, and cist 2, Westhaugh of Tulliemet, Perth & Kinross, fall at the end of the date range. It may be noted that the aforementioned Balbirnie cist 3 pot is of similar shape to the Mains of Melgund example. The tall Kentraw vessel (which would be classed as a vase in anyone's terminology, although opinions would differ over whether it is a bipartite or tripartite vase!) and its accessory vessel also fall towards the end of our set of dates; the fact that the Kentraw date is a *tpq* for the pottery should also be borne in mind.

Setting aside for a moment the Kilellan assemblage, the other dated Food Vessels are bi- or tripartite vessels, most of which – to revert briefly to traditional typology – would happily fit within the category of 'Yorkshire Vase' Food Vessels. They include examples with narrow (Ratho, Leven cists A & B) and broad (Barns Farm grave 1) stop-ridges. Their apparent date span is *c.*3670-3520 BP (*c.*2150-1750 cal BC at 1σ; *c.*2200-1700 cal BC at 2s). The two examples from Leven, Fife are sufficiently similar to each other (and to another vessel from the same cemetery) as to appear to have been made by the same

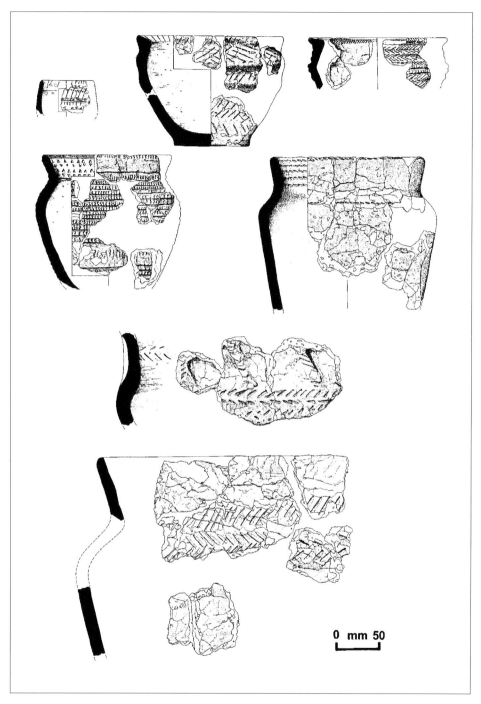

83 *Above* Selection of pottery from the Food Vessel domestic assemblage from Kilellan, including large encrusted pot; largest pot size omitted. *By Alan Braby, reproduced courtesy of Anna Ritchie*

84 *Opposite* Dated Food Vessels from Holly Road, Leven; 1: cist B; 2: cist A. *By Marion O'Neil, reproduced courtesy of Douglas Speirs*

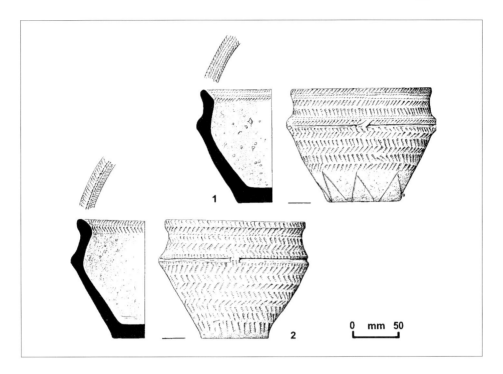

potter; the two dates obtained for them could well be contemporary. Although one hesitates to read too much into the data, it is not inconceivable that family or community members died within a short time of each other, and that the incised zigzag pattern at the bottom of the cist B pot indicates that it was finished off in a hurry. (Further examples of pairs or groups of Food Vessels suspected to have been made by the same potters are discussed in Sheridan 2004c).

The remaining pot, a bipartite vase from Barns Farm (grave 2), Fife, was considered in the excavation report as a possible example of a 'Beaker/Food Vessel hybrid' (Shepherd 1982, 110, citing Clarke 1970, 236). The relationship between Food Vessel and Beaker design – another terminological minefield, open to subjective assessments – is a topic that deserves closer attention and is touched on further below, and in Manby, this volume. That the two ceramic traditions overlapped in currency is beyond doubt (see below) and the Barns Farm date of 3605±45 BP lies well within that overlap period. Another vessel that might be considered in this context is the Beaker from North Mains henge (burial F), Perth & Kinross (Cowie, T.G. 1983, fig. 30). The cremated remains associated with this pot have just been dated to 3670±35 BP (GrA–24863, 2140-1970 cal BC at 1σ, 2150-1940 cal BC at 2σ). While this vessel might be felt to lie on the 'Beaker' side of the divide, it is worth noting that it was found close to cists containing Food Vessels, including one (SF 18: *ibid.*, fig. 29) super-ficially similar in shape to it.

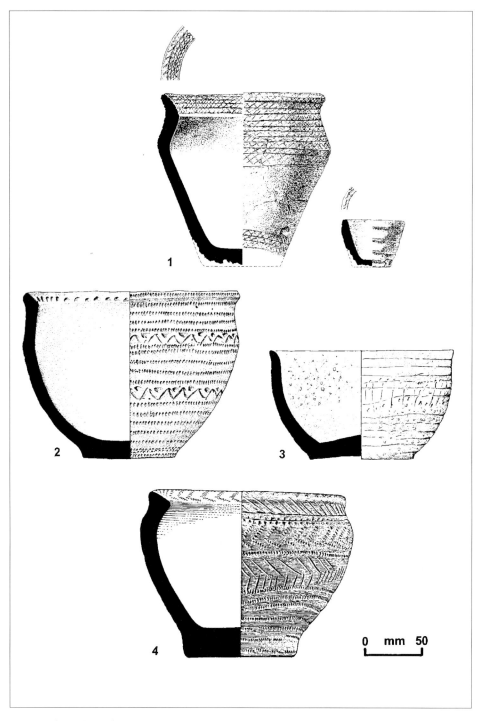

85 Dated Food Vessels: 1 Kentraw (with accessory vessel); 2 Mains of Melgund; 3 Westhaugh of Tulliemet cist 2; 4 Balbirnie cist 3 (date for this currently being re-determined). Note: Loanleven sherds not illustrated. For sources of images, see Appendix

The large domestic assemblage of over 100 pots from Kilellan, Islay (Ritchie forthcoming and see *(83)* is of crucial importance in demonstrating the wide range of forms in broadly contemporary use, and it is unfortunate that the midden in which it was found is dated by just a single date (owing to the lack of other datable material). However, Burgess' suspicion that the midden may have accumulated over a relatively short time (Burgess 1976, 196) seems to be borne out by subsequent research on the assemblage by Rosemary Cowie (Cowie, R., forthcoming). The assemblage shares many features in common with that from Ardnave settlement, just 2.5km away *(87)*; Ritchie & Welfare 1983), and both include elements readily comparable among Food Vessel pottery in Ireland. In their unmodified form, the radiocarbon dates from Ardnave suggest contemporaneity with Kilellan; unfortunately, the standard deviations of these dates have had to be increased as a result of Patrick Ashmore's critical reappraisal of 'old' dates. If one accepts that the Kilellan assemblage is likely to date within the range 2150-1750 BC, this makes it comparable in date to the aforementioned 'Yorkshire Vase' and Barns Farm grave 2 bipartite vase pots. The assemblage comprises small, medium-sized and large pots; the medium-sized pots include bi- and tripartite vases/bowls, and the large pots include examples which, as Cowie observes, would be called 'Vase Urns' (including 'Encrusted' examples) within a funerary context. Given the dating evidence currently available for Scottish Vase Urns (see below), their presence at Kilellan at this time is not exceptional.

So much for form: are there trends in the nature or style of decoration? The use of a comb to effect impressed decoration is only represented on one or two of the Kilellan pots; in every other dated pot, decoration has been made by impression (most often with twisted or whipped cord) or incision. The use of comb-impression is uncommon on Scottish Food Vessels in general and, as others have observed (e.g. Abercromby 1912; Cowe 1983, Simpson 1965; Young 1951), appears on pots which most resemble their counterparts in Ireland, where comb decoration is more common (at least as far as the Bowl tradition is concerned). Perhaps not surprisingly, most examples have been found in south-west Scotland (e.g. tripartite vessels from Glenramskill, Argyll & Bute and Logan, Dumfries & Galloway: Young 1951, pl. 6; bipartite vessel from Duncraigaig, Argyll & Bute: Clarke *et al.* 1985, fig. 4.87).

There is a general tendency, among the dated pots, for the decoration to occupy the whole of the exterior surface and to extend over the rim bevel; the exceptions to the 'all over external' pattern are the Kentraw vase and some of the large pots from Kilellan. Perhaps of greatest interest in terms of comparisons with Food Vessels outside Scotland is the all-over herringbone pattern as seen on the Ratho and Leven vessels; the associated dates indicate a date within the range *c*.2150-1700 BC (at 2σ).

Finally, it should be noted that the overall pattern described here is echoed among those other Scottish Food Vessels with not obviously anomalous dates,

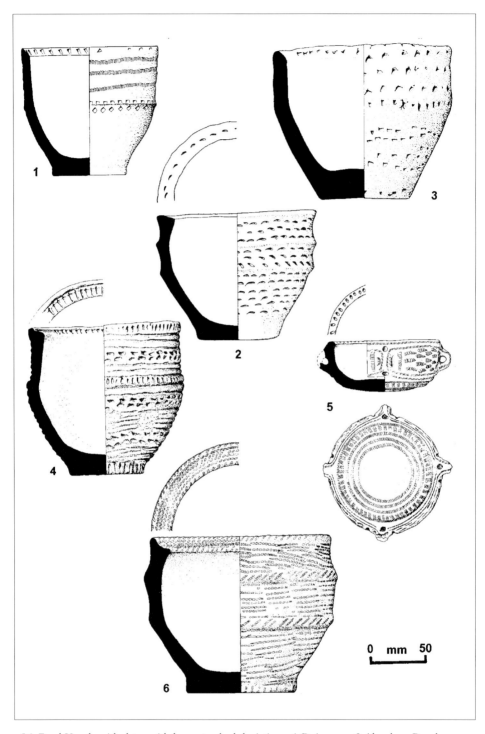

86 Food Vessels with dates with large standard deviations: 1 Raigmore; 2 Aberdour Road, Dunfermline cist 3; 3 Almondbank cist 2; 4 North Mains henge burial B; 5-6: Gairneybank cists 1 & 2 respectively. For sources of images, see Appendix

whose standard deviations have had to be increased as the determinations were undertaken a considerable time ago (see Appendix and *86-8*). Furthermore, it can be predicted that the aforementioned assemblage from Doune, with its large and small bipartite vessels and miniature battle-axe, will produce a date in the latter half of the Scottish Food Vessel sequence: a full-sized battle-axe of similar shape from Oban, found in a Cordoned Urn, has recently been dated (from associated cremated bone) to 3400±40 BP (GrA-24017, 1750-1620 cal BC at 1σ, 1880-1530 cal BC at 2σ: Sheridan in press a).[6]

COMPARISON WITH FOOD VESSELS ELSEWHERE

The pioneering work by Anna Brindley and Jan Lanting on Food Vessels in Ireland has produced a complex typochronological sequence which, when it is published (in 2005), will offer many valuable indicators of relevance to Scottish Food Vessels, especially as far as Irish-like pots are concerned. It would not be appropriate to discuss this unpublished work in detail, however. Suffice it to say that, in addition to the aforementioned observation that in both Ireland and Scotland the earliest dated Food Vessels appeared towards the end of the third millennium BC, the use of the all-over herringbone design seems to be a feature of the early stages in the Irish sequence. At Carrowntober East, County Galway, for example, a bipartite vase with stopridge (in other words, a 'Yorkshire Vase': cf. Goodmanham CXV, East Riding of Yorkshire: Simpson 1968, fig. 45.1) with all-over herringbone decoration has been dated to 3755±30 BP (GrN-11354, unburnt bone, 2270-2060 cal BC at 1σ, 2290-2030 cal BC at 2σ: Ó Ríordáin & Waddell 1993, 37, 263, pl. 24 no. 516).

As indicated above, the radiocarbon dating evidence for England and Wales is woefully inadequate (though it must be stressed that there are few Food Vessels at all in Wales (Lynch 2000, 117-9), and that one of the few Welsh Food Vessel dates known to the author was obtained by this volume's co-Editor, for a small plain bipartite vessel from Sarn-y-bryn-caled: Gibson 1994, 171, 177, fig. 25.P4, BM-2809, charcoal, 3660±40 BP, 2140-1950 cal BC at 1σ, 2200-1910 cal BC at 2σ). In northern England, the results recently obtained from unburnt human bone samples from Dominic Powlesland *et al.* excavations at West Heslerton have demonstrated that 'Yorkshire Vases' with herringbone design were in use there by *c.*3730 BP (*c.*2280-1980 cal BC at 2s: Haughton & Powlesland 1999, figs 24, 31; Manby pers. comm.; cf. Manby *et al.* 2003, 61-2) – roughly contemporary with Irish examples, and marginally earlier than the dated Scottish examples. The West Heslerton dates also demonstrate that diverse kinds of Food Vessel were in use in the *c.*3730–3500 BP (*c.*2280-1670 cal BC at 2σ) date range, including globular vessels, and that Beakers were in contemporary use in the immediate vicinity.

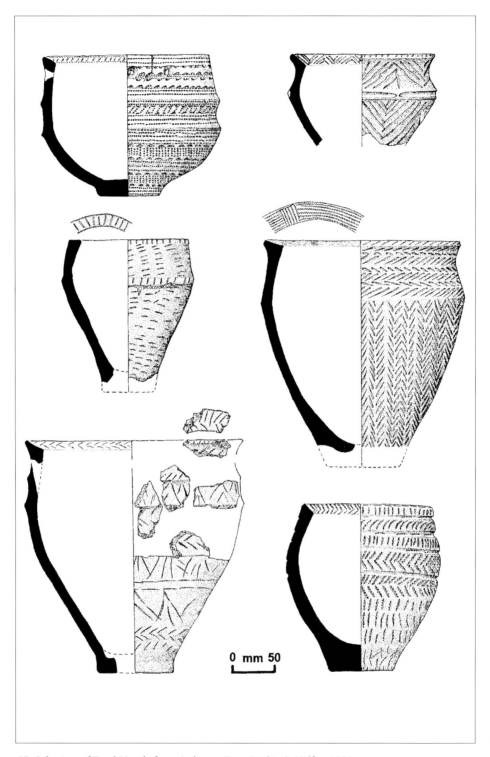

87 Selection of Food Vessels from Ardnave. *From Ritchie & Welfare 1983*

In southern England, where Food Vessels are markedly scarcer (Burgess 1980, 86) and often plainer than their northern counterparts, dates obtained from unburnt human bone from the Barrow Hills, Radley, complex in Oxfordshire have demonstrated that this type of pottery was in use there by *c.*3670 BP (OxA-1884, 3670±80 BP, 2200–1930 cal BC at 1σ, 2300-1750 cal BC at 2σ), continuing until at least *c.*3500 BP (BM-2698, 3500±50 BP, 1890–1740 cal BC at 1σ, 1950-1680 cal BC at 2σ) and overlapping with the use of Beaker pottery (Cleal 1999, 208). The two dated Barrow Hills vessels are slack-profiled bipartite vases, the division between the two sections marked by an applied cordon; the earlier of the two has oblique slashes on its cordon and immediately below the rim (Barclay & Halpin 1999, 112 Pot 51, 126 Pot 68). A further date, just obtained from cremated bone associated with a plain bipartite vase with everted rim and a necklace of segmented faience beads from Long Ash Lane, Frampton, Dorset (Forde-Johnston 1958, pot G) has demonstrated that Food Vessel use in southern England continued at least as late as *c.*3300 BP (GrA-24867, 3315±35 BP, 1680–1520 cal BC at 1σ, 1690–1510 cal BC at 2σ).

Little more can be said about the dating of Food Vessels in England, given that so many of the other available dates would not stand up to current criteria for acceptability. The dating evidence reviewed briefly here is in broad agreement with Stuart Needham's 1996 assessment of the currency of British Food Vessels, which he estimated at between the twenty-second/twenty-first century BC and *c.*1700 BC or perhaps slightly later (Needham 1996, 128–32); the Long Ash Lane provides the high-quality evidence that he said would be needed to demonstrate post-1700 BC use.

SCOTTISH FOOD VESSELS WITHIN THE BROADER CONTEXT OF EARLY BRONZE AGE SCOTTISH POTTERY

In Scotland, as elsewhere, the various types of Early Bronze Age pottery have tended to be studied in isolation from each other; and yet, with the dating evidence now available to us, it is clear that several kinds of pottery were in contemporary use (as previous commentators such as Simpson (1968) had argued). This section summarises the currently-available evidence.

Although the dating of Scottish Beaker pottery is bedevilled by the same problems that face Food Vessel dating (i.e. many dates were obtained a considerable time ago; some dates are clearly anomalous; some others do not meet current standards of acceptability), it is nevertheless clear that there was a significant chronological overlap in the two pottery traditions from around the twenty-second century BC. In his latest assessment of the evidence for Beaker dating in Britain, Stuart Needham argues that the currency established by the British Museum Beaker Dating Programme in 1989 (Kinnes *et al.* 1991) is broadly correct, at *c.*2500/2400-1700 BC, with Beakers starting to be used in

Scotland as early as elsewhere (Needham forthcoming). In view of this potentially half-millennium-long overlap – and of the fact that the geographical distributions of Beakers and Food Vessels also overlaps, and that the two kinds of pottery are sometimes found in the same cemeteries – it is perhaps surprising that there was not more sharing of design features than is witnessed by the relatively few 'Beaker-Food Vessel hybrid' pots in Scotland. Others have sought to rationalise the relationship in terms of overarching Beaker-Food Vessel typo-chronologies, with the hybrid forms falling at the end of the Beaker sequence (Ritchie & Shepherd 1973, fig. 2, for south-west Scotland; Shepherd 1986, illus 19-20 for north-east Scotland). It remains to be seen whether these proposed sequences are borne out by radiocarbon dating; some doubt on the lateness of 'hybrids' has been cast by Needham who prefers to view them as one element from a developing domestic-cum-funerary repertoire (Needham forthcoming and pers. comm.). Apropos this question, it is worth noting that, in several cemeteries where Beaker and Food

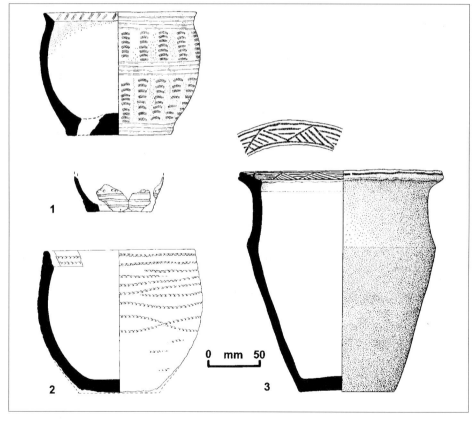

88 Food Vessels with dates with large standard deviations: 1 Ord North; 2 Reswallie Mains; 3 Traigh Bhan cist 1. For sources of images, see Appendix

Vessel pottery has been found together, the former has been of a kind traditionally regarded as typologically 'late', or of 'Beaker-Food Vessel hybrid' type. Examples include Barns Farm, Fife (Shepherd 1982); North Mains henge, Perth & Kinross (Cowie, T.G., 1983 – see above for the date of *c.*2000 BC from burial F); Limefield, South Lanarkshire (MacLaren 1984); Slaterich, Kerrera, Argyll & Bute (Ritchie & Shepherd 1973, 24 & fig. 2); and West Water Reservoir, Scottish Borders (Sheridan 2000; typologically earlier Beaker also present, seemingly pre-dating the cists in question). There is clearly much more to be learned and understood about the relationship between the two ceramic traditions; unfortunately space does not permit a lengthy discussion here.

As for other kinds of Early Bronze Age pottery, a fairly clear picture of their currency of use is emerging, thanks mainly to the current NMS radiocarbon dating initiative (Sheridan 2003b; in press a) and to the dating of two cemeteries in north-east Scotland by the Centre for Field Archaeology (Johnson & Sheridan 2004). As in Ireland, there is a substantial overlap between the currency of use of Food Vessels and of Vase (including Encrusted)[4] Urns, which is not surprising in view of the formal and decorative similarities between some Food Vessels and some Urns; their distributional similarity (Sheridan 2003b, fig. 13.3); and their association, in domestic contexts, at Killelan and Ardnave. The earliest dated urn of this tradition is from Aberdour Road, Dunfermline, Fife (3680±45 BP, GrA-19422, 2140-1970 cal BC at 1σ, 2200-1920 cal BC at 2σ) and the latest is from Tayport, Fife (3490±60 BP, GrA-21745, 1890–1690 cal BC at 1σ, 1960-1630 cal BC at 2σ, both dates from cremated bone: Sheridan 2003b)[5]. This suggests that Vase Urns started to be used almost as early – if not at roughly the same time – as Food Vessels, and continued for nearly as long as Food Vessels.

It also appears that Collared Urns were also in use over much of the period when Food Vessels were current, although their initial use in Scotland may have post-dated that of Vase Urns by at least a century. The earliest dated Scottish example is from Grandtully, Perth & Kinross (GrA-21743, 3580±60 BP, 2030-1770 cal BC at 1σ, 2130-1740 cal BC at 2σ) and the latest is from Gilchorn, Angus (GrA-18693, 3370±60 BP, 1740-1530 cal BC at 1σ, 1880-1510 cal BC at 2σ, both dates from cremated bone: Sheridan 2003b). As argued elsewhere (*ibid.*, Sheridan in press a), it seems likely that this particular style of cinerary urn was adopted from England, as Longworth and Burgess had previously argued (Longworth 1984; Burgess 1986). Its geographical distribution is not dissimilar to that of Food Vessels (Sheridan 2003b, fig. 13.2).

Cordoned Urns – which appear to be a north British and Irish adaptation of the Collared Urn form – also started to be used while Food Vessels were still current, but then continued to be used after Food Vessel use ceased. The earliest dated Scottish example is from Seggiecrook,

Aberdeenshire (GrA-19427, cremated bone, 3495±45 BP, 1880-1740 cal BC at 1s, 1940-1680 cal BC at 2s) and the latest is from Benderloch, Argyll & Bute (AA-26980, charcoal, 1600–1430 cal BC at 1s, 1680-1410 cal BC at 2s: Sheridan 2003b). Once again, a degree of geographical coincidence is apparent (*ibid.*, fig. 13.2).

The currency of the small vessels that have been variously labelled as 'pigmy cups', 'accessory vessels' or simply 'cups' (see Gibson this volume), and which are usually found in association with urns of various kinds, also overlaps with that of Food Vessels. The earliest dated Scottish example – and the one of greatest relevance to the current discussion – was found with an Encrusted Urn at Craigdhu, Fife, and is a miniature bipartite vase Food Vessel with stop-ridge (*81*; GrA-23991, 3600±40 BP, 2020-1880 cal BC at 1σ, 2130-1770 cal BC at 2σ: Sheridan in press a). The latest dated example, associated with a Bucket Urn at Balloch Hill, Argyll & Bute, dates to 3360±70 BP, 1740-1520 cal BC at 1s, 1880-1490 cal BC at 2s, both dates from cremated bone: Sheridan 2003b). The aforementioned Food Vessel-associated example from Kentraw, unusually associated with the rite of inhumation, fits within this date range. Also contemporary with Food Vessels, but geographically remote, are the regionally-distinctive urns of the Northern Isles (*ibid.*).

The overall chronological picture is summarised in (*89*). In exploring its significance, one must also consider what this evidence tells us about funerary practices.

SCOTTISH FOOD VESSELS AND EARLY BRONZE AGE FUNERARY PRACTICES

The picture that emerges is one of a diversity of contemporary funerary practices. Whereas earlier accounts of Scottish prehistory had envisaged a clear sequence from crouched inhumation in cists or pits to the deposition of cremated remains within cinerary urns (and sometimes just on their own), it now appears that there was a considerable overlap of these practices, even though stratigraphic evidence from cemeteries tends to support the traditional view. It is also clear – and has been known for some time (e.g. McAdam 1982, Table 3) – that cremation was also practised by some people who deposited Beakers and Food Vessels. The cremated remains may be deposited alongside inhumed remains, as contemporary or successive burials (as at Barns Farm and Ratho, for instance), or on their own with a Beaker or Food Vessel. Opinions still differ about what prompted the widespread adoption of the practice of depositing cremated remains in cinerary urns from the end of the third millennium BC; it may be a fashion that started in southern England (with the early use of Collared Urns there) and was emulated elsewhere, using Vase Urns in northern Britain and Ireland until (and after) Collared Urns themselves were adopted (Sheridan 2003b).

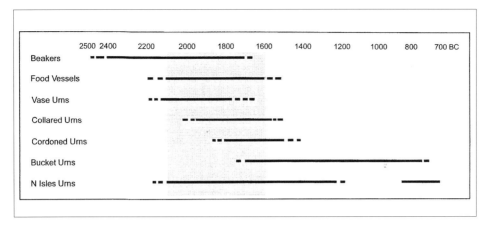

89 Currency of ceramic types in Scotland during the late third and second millennia BC; shaded area indicates key overlap period concerning Food Vessel use

It seems likely that a degree of regional variation existed regarding the choice of funerary rite, as Ashmore had previously argued (1996, 90-101). In southern Scotland, several Early Bronze Age 'enclosed cremation cemeteries' are known (e.g. Camps Reservoir and Cloburn Quarry, South Lanarkshire, the former associated with Beaker, the latter with a Food Vessel: Ward 1993, 1994, forthcoming; Lelong & Pollard 1998) and this may reflect a relatively early, localised preference for the practice of cremation (but not in-urned cremation in this case). The Camps cemetery has produced dates that lie mostly between *c.*2100 cal BC and *c.*1700 cal BC (at 2σ Ward 1996). At the other end of the chronological scale, radiocarbon dates for crouched inhumations in cists in Tayside and East Lothian suggest that this funerary tradition persisted for several centuries after the practice of cremating the dead then burying them in urns had become popular. In addition to the aforementioned examples from Mains of Melgund, Westhaugh of Tulliemet, Loanleven, East Campsie and West Scryne (and cf. Rescobie – see Appendix), one could cite the short cist from Grainfoot, East Lothian (Dalland 1991). Here, two unburned individuals had been buried with a joint of pork, and a sample from one of the bodies produced a date of 2930±50 BP (GU-2762, 1260-1040 cal BC at 1σ, 1310-970 cal BC at 2σ). Indeed, an even later short cist was excavated at Kingsbarns, Fife (James 2001). This was found to date to 2250±60 BP (GU-8219, 390-200 cal BC at 1σ, 410-160 cal BC at 2σ); but whether this indicates an unbroken local tradition of short cist burial is a moot point.

CONCLUSION

The small but important assemblage of 'reliable' radiocarbon dates for Scottish Food Vessels has served to set their chronological position on firmer grounds, even if our conclusions about typochronological sequencing are necessarily provisional at this stage. This brief review of the currently-available evidence makes it easy to set an agenda for future research. A revisiting of the material that had previously been used for non-AMS radiocarbon dating, this time in order to obtain AMS dates, would usefully enlarge our information base, as would the continuation of the NMS' dating programme, targeting kinds of Food Vessel and areas of Scotland that are poor or lacking in dates. A critical review of the stratigraphic and associational data would properly update Derek's 1968 work; but most importantly, a nationwide *corpus*, along with a substantial number of radiocarbon determinations, would help to tease out regional variability (cf. Simpson 1965; Cowe 1983). The significance of the Irish and Yorkshire links could then be explored properly, and set in the context of what we already know about such connections (e.g. the early metalwork and metallurgy link with Ireland, featuring south-west Scotland but extending to the north-east: Cressey & Sheridan 2003; the Yorkshire jet jewellery connection: Sheridan & Davis 2002).

One of the most significant discoveries to emerge from the dating of Scottish Food Vessels and other kinds of Early Bronze Age pottery is the confirmation that diverse ceramic and funerary traditions were in contemporary use during the early second millennium BC (cf. Burgess 1974; Ashmore 1996). This demands explanation, and once again it may be that a finer-grained picture of regional and chronological developments may help us to disentangle the somewhat confusing picture. So, too, might additional domestic assemblages; the Kilellan and Ardnave material serves to remind us that some of our funerary ceramic categories may not have been discrete in everyday life. One key question still outstanding is: why and how did Food Vessels begin to be used in Scotland? Do they simply represent the adoption of Irish and/or English pottery traditions which themselves had originated as a kind of response to Beaker pottery? To answer this, many more dates from both English and Scottish vessels are required.

It is hoped that this collection of new and nearly-new dates will please you, Derek. As you can see, there is still much to do!

FOOTNOTES

General note: all the radiocarbon dates cited here have been calibrated using OxCal v3.9 (Bronk Ramsey 2003), with atmospheric data from Stuiver *et al.* 1998).

[1] Several additional Irish dates exist but have been rejected, for good reasons, by Brindley & Lanting.

[2] This is from Balbirnie cist 3: see Appendix.

[3] Graham Ritchie had published this date as a *taq* for the pottery (Ritchie 1987), but agrees that *tpq* was meant (Ritchie pers. comm.). Gordon Cook, who

undertook the dating, has confirmed that only one bone was used for the dating, although four samples (probably from more than one individual) had been submitted.

[4] Irish writers (e.g. Waddell 1976, 1998) tend to regard Vase Urns and Encrusted Urns as distinct, but related, pottery types whereas they tend to be discussed as a single, broad type in Scotland (e.g. Cowie, T.G., 1978).

[5] See Sheridan in press a on why some apparently later examples can now be excluded.

[6] The additional new dates have now been received and confim the overall picture presented here. That of 3400±35 BP (SUERC-2869, 1750-1630 cal BC at 1σ, 1870-1530 cal BC at 2σ) for the Doune burial as predicted, while that for Balbirnie cist 3 confirms the date but invites a re-evaluation of burial activities.

ACKNOWLEDGEMENTS

The following are thanked for their advice and assistance (which, in some cases, included granting access to unpublished material): Anna Brindley & Jan Lanting; Anna & Graham Ritchie; Terry Manby; Trevor & Rosemary Cowie; Patrick Ashmore; Gordon Cook; Stuart Needham; and Douglas Speirs. Thanks are also extended to all the funders of the NMS dating project, especially Historic Scotland (*per* Patrick Ashmore); and, for permission to reproduce illustrations, to the Society of Antiquaries of Scotland, the Prehistoric Society, the Tayside & Fife Archaeological Committee and individual illustrators and authors. Finally, Alex Gibson is thanked for his saint-like patience as co-Editor.

BIBLIOGRAPHY

Abercromby, J., 1912 *A Study of the Bronze Age Pottery of Great Britain and Ireland and its Associated Grave Goods*. Oxford: Clarendon Press.

Aerts, A.T., Brindley, A.L., Lanting, J.N. & van der Plicht, J., 2001 Radiocarbon dates on cremated bone from Sanaigmhor Warren, Islay. *Antiquity*, 75, 485-6.

ApSimon, A.J., 1958 Food Vessels. *University of London Institute of Archaeology Annual Reports*, 1, 24-36.

ApSimon, A.J., 1969 The earlier Bronze Age in the north of Ireland. *Ulster Journal of Archaeology*, 32, 28-72.

Ashmore, P.J., 1996 *Neolithic and Bronze Age Scotland*. London: Batsford.

Ashmore, P.J., Cook, G.T. & Harkness, D.D., 2000 A radiocarbon database for Scottish archaeological samples. *Radiocarbon*, 42 (1), 41-8.

Barclay, A. & Halpin, C., 1999 *Excavations at Barrow Hills, Radley, Oxfordshire*. Vol. I: *the Neolithic and Bronze Age Monument Complex*. Oxford: Oxford Archaeological Unit (Thames Valley Landscapes, Vol. 11).

Barclay, G.J., 1983 Sites of the third millennium BC to the first millennium AD at North Mains, Strathallan, Perthshire. *Proceedings of the Society of Antiquaries of Scotland*, 113, 122-281.

Brindley, A.L., 1995 Radiocarbon, chronology and the Bronze Age. In Waddell, J. & Shee, E. Twohig (eds), *Ireland in the Bronze Age*, 4-13. Dublin: Stationery Office.

Brindley, A.L., 2001 Tomorrow is another day: some radiocarbon dates for Irish Bronze Age artefacts. In Metz, W.H., van Beek, B.L. & Steegstra, H. (eds), *Patina:*

Essays Presented to Jay Jordan Butler on the Occasion of his 80th Birthday, 145-60. Groningen & Amsterdam: privately published.

Brindley, A.L., forthcoming. *The Dating of Food Vessels and Urns in Ireland*. Galway: Galway University Press.

Bronk Ramsey, C., 2003 *OxCal Version 3.9*. Oxford: Oxford Radiocarbon Accelerator Unit.

Bryce, T.H., 1904 On the cairns and tumuli of the Island of Bute. A record of explorations during the season of 1903. *Proceedings of the Society of Antiquaries of Scotland*, 38 (1903-4), 17-81.

Burgess, C.B., 1974 The Bronze Age. In Renfrew, A.C. (ed.) *British Prehistory – a New Outline*, 165-232, 291-329. London: Duckworth.

Burgess, C.B., 1976 An Early Bronze Age settlement at Kilellan Farm, Islay, Argyll. In Burgess, C.B. & Miket, R. (eds), *Settlement and Economy in the Third and Second Millennia BC*, 181-207. Oxford: British Archaeological Reports (British Series 33).

Burgess, C.B., 1980 *The Age of Stonehenge*. London: Dent.

Burgess, C.B., 1986 'Urnes of no small variety': Collared Urns revisited. *Proceedings of the Prehistoric Society*, 52, 339-51.

Clarke, D.L., 1970 *Beaker Pottery of Great Britain and Ireland*. Cambridge: Cambridge University Press.

Clarke, D.V., Cowie, T.G. & Foxon, A., 1985 *Symbols of Power at the Time of Stonehenge*. Edinburgh: Her Majesty's Stationery Office.

Cleal, R., 1999 Prehistoric pottery. In Barclay, A. & Halpin, C. *Excavations at Barrow Hills, Radley, Oxfordshire*. Vol. I: *the Neolithic and Bronze Age Monument Complex*, 195-211. Oxford: Oxford Archaeological Unit (Thames Valley Landscapes, Vol. 11).

Close-Brooks, J., Norgate, M. & Ritchie, J.N.G., 1972 A Bronze Age cemetery at Aberdour Road, Dunfermline, Fife. *Proceedings of the Society of Antiquaries of Scotland*, 104 (1971-2), 121-36.

Coutts, H., 1971 *Tayside Before History*. Dundee: Dundee Museum & Art Gallery.

Cowe, D.L., 1983 *Food Vessels of South East Scotland*. Unpublished MA dissertation, University of Edinburgh.

Cowie, R., forthcoming. The Pottery. In Ritchie, A. (ed.).

Cowie, T.G., 1978 *Bronze Age Food Vessel Urns*. BAR British Series 55. Oxford: British Archaeological Reports.

Cowie, T.G., 1983 The pottery from the henge monument at North Mains. In Barclay, G.J. Sites of the third millennium BC to the first millennium AD at North Mains, Strathallan, Perthshire. *Proceedings of the Society of Antiquaries of Scotland,* 113, 155-63.

Cowie, T.G. & Ritchie, J.N.G., 1991 Bronze Age burials at Gairneybank, Kinross-shire. *Proceedings of the Society of Antiquaries of Scotland*, 121, 95-109.

Cressey, M. & Sheridan, J.A., 2003. The excavation of a Bronze Age cemetery at Seafield West, near Inverness, Highland. *Proceedings of the Society of Antiquaries of Scotland,* 133, 47-84.

Dalland, M., 1991 A short cist at Grainfoot, Longniddry, East Lothian. *Proceedings of the Society of Antiquaries of Scotland*, 121, 111-5.

Forde-Johnson, J., 1958 The excavation of two barrows at Frampton in Dorset. *Proceedings of the Dorset Natural History & Antiquarian Society*, 80, 111-32.

Garwood, P. & Barclay, A., 1999 The chronology of depositional contexts and monuments. In A. Barclay & C. Halpin *Excavations at Barrow Hills, Radley, Oxfordshire*. Vol. I: *The Neolithic and Bronze Age Monument Complex*, 275-93. Oxford: Oxford Archaeological Unit (Thames Valley Landscapes, Vol. 11).

Gibson, A.M., 1978 *Bronze Age Pottery in the North-east of England*. BAR British Series 56. Oxford: British Archaeological Reports.

Gibson, A.M., 1994 Excavations at the Sarn-y-bryn-caled cursus complex, Welshpool, Powys, and the timber circles of Great Britain and Ireland. *Proceedings of the Prehistoric Society*, 60, 143-223.

Gibson, A.M., 2002 *Prehistoric Pottery in Britain and Ireland*. Stroud: Tempus.

Hamilton, J.R.C., 1957 Food Vessel cist at Doune, Perthshire. *Proceedings of the Society of Antiquaries of Scotland,* 90 (1956-7), 231-4.

Haughton, C. & Powlesland, D., 1999 *West Heslerton: the Anglian Cemetery.* Vol. 1: *The Excavation and Discussion of the Evidence*. Yedingham: Landscape Research Centre.

Hedges, R.E.M., 2002 Bone diagenesis: an overview of processes. *Radiocarbon*, 44 (3), 319-28.

James, H., 2001 Excavations at Kingsbarns, Fife, in 1997-8: an Iron Age short cist burial, prehistoric pits and a buried eighteenth century bridge within the designed landscape of Cambo. *Tayside & Fife Archaeological Journal*, 7, 16-26.

Johnson, M. & Sheridan, J.A., 2004 Skilmafilly: a well-dated Bronze Age cremation cemetery. *Scottish Archaeological News*, 44, 12-13.

Kinnes, I.A., Gibson, A.M., Ambers, J., Bowman, S. & Boast, R., 1991 Radiocarbon dating and British Beakers: the British Museum programme. *Scottish Archaeological Review*, 8, 35-68.

Lanting, J.N. & Brindley, A.L., 1998 Dating cremated bone: the dawn of a new era. *Journal of Irish Archaeology*, 9, 1-8.

Lanting, J.N., Aerts-Bijma, A.T. & van der Plicht, J., 2001 Dating of cremated bones. *Radiocarbon* 43 (2), 249-54.

Lelong, O. & Pollard, A., 1998 Excavation of a Bronze Age ring cairn at Cloburn Quarry, Cairngryffe Hill, Lanarkshire. *Proceedings of the Society of Antiquaries of Scotland* , 128, 105-42.

Longworth, I. H., 1984 *Collared Urns of the Bronze Age in Great Britain and Ireland*. Cambridge: Cambridge University Press.

Lynch, F.M. 2000. The Later Neolithic and Earlier Bronze Age. In Lynch, F.M., Aldhouse-Green, S. & Davies, J.L. *Prehistoric Wales*, 79-138. Stroud: Sutton Publishing Ltd.

MacLaren, A., 1984 A Bronze Age cairn at Limefield, Lanarkshire. In Miket, R. & Burgess, C.B. (eds), *Between and Beyond the Walls*, 97-115. Edinburgh: John Donald.

Manby, T.G., King, A. & Vyner, B.E., 2003 The Neolithic and Bronze Ages: a time of early agriculture. In Manby, T.G., Moorhouse, S. & Ottaway, P. (eds), *The Archaeology of Yorkshire: an Assessment at the Beginning of the 21st Century*, 35-116. Leeds: Yorkshire Arch. Soc. (Occasional Paper 3).

McAdam, E., 1982 Comparative background: the cemetery. In Watkins, T. The excavation of an Early Bronze Age cemetery at Barns Farm, Dalgety, Fife. *Proceedings of the Society of Antiquaries of Scotland*, 112, 120-9.

Needham, S.P., 1996 Chronology and periodisation in the British Bronze Age. *Acta Archaeologica*, 67, 121-40.

Needham, S.P., 2000 Power pulses across a cultural divide: cosmologically driven acquisition between Armorica and Wessex. *Proceedings of the Prehistoric Society*, 66, 151-207.

Needham, S.P., forthcoming. Transforming Beaker culture in north-west Europe: processes of fusion and fission.

Ó Ríordáin, B. & Waddell, J., 1993 *The Funerary Bowls and Vases of the Irish Bronze Age*. Galway: Galway University Press.

Rideout, J.S. & Cowie, T.G., 1998 Discussion. In. Taylor, D.B., Rideout, J.S., Russell-White, C.J. & Cowie, T.G. Prehistoric burials from Angus: some finds old and new. *Tayside & Fife Archaeological Journal*, 4, 60-6.

Rideout, J.S. & Russell-White, C.J., 1998 Four cists excavated in Angus 1986-1994. In Taylor, D.B., Rideout, J.S., Russell-White, C.J. & Cowie, T.G., Prehistoric burials from Angus: some finds old and new. *Tayside & Fife Archaeological Journal*, 4, 49-60.

Ritchie, A. (ed.), forthcoming. *Kilellan Farm, Ardnave, Islay: Excavations of a Prehistoric to Early Medieval Site by Colin Burgess and Others 1954-76*. Edinburgh: Society of Antiquaries of Scotland.

Ritchie, J.N.G., 1974 Excavation of the stone circle and cairn at Balbirnie, Fife. *Archaeological Journal*, 131, 1-32.

Ritchie, J.N.G., 1987 A cist from Kentraw, Islay. *Proceedings of the Society of Antiquaries of Scotland*, 117, 41-5.

Ritchie, J.N.G. & Shepherd, I.A.G., 1973 Beaker pottery and associated artefacts in south-west Scotland. *Transactions of the Dumfriesshire & Galloway Natural History & Antiquarian Society*, 50, 18-36.

Ritchie, J.N.G. & Stevenson, J.B., 1982 Cists at Traigh Bhan, Islay, Argyll. *Proceedings of the Society of Antiquaries of Scotland*, 112, 550-9.

Ritchie, J.N.G. & Welfare, A., 1983 Excavations at Ardnave, Islay. *Proceedings of the Society of Antiquaries of Scotland*, 113, 302-66.

Russell-White, C.J., Lowe, C.E. & McCullagh, R.P.J., 1992 Excavations at three Early Bronze Age monuments in Scotland. *Proceedings of the Prehistoric Society*, 58, 285-323.

Sharples, N.M., 1981 The excavation of a chambered cairn, the Ord North, at Lairg, Sutherland by Corcoran, J.X.W.P. *Proceedings of the Society of Antiquaries of Scotland*, 111, 21-62.

Shepherd, I.A.G., 1982 The artefacts. In Watkins, T. The excavation of an Early Bronze Age cemetery at Barns Farm, Dalgety, Fife. *Proceedings of the Society of Antiquaries of Scotland*, 112, 99-113.

Shepherd, I.A.G., 1986 *Powerful Pots: Beakers in North-east Prehistory*. Aberdeen: Anthropological Museum, University of Aberdeen.

Sheridan, J.A., 2000 Pottery. In Hunter, F.J. Excavation of an Early Bronze Age cemetery and other sites at West Water Reservoir, West Linton, Scottish Borders. *Proceedings of the Society of Antiquaries of Scotland*, 130, 141-6.

Sheridan, J.A., 2001 The National Museums' of Scotland *Dating Cremated Bones Project*. *Discovery & Excavation in Scotland*, 2, 129.

Sheridan, J.A., 2002 The radiocarbon dating programmes of the National Museums of Scotland. *Antiquity*, 76, 794-6.

Sheridan, J.A., 2003a The National Museums' of Scotland dating programmes: results obtained during 2001/2. *Discovery & Excavation in Scotland*, 3, 154-5.

Sheridan, J.A., 2003b New dates for Scottish cinerary urns: results from the National Museums' of Scotland *Dating Cremated Bones Project*. In Gibson, A. (ed.) *Prehistoric Pottery: People, Pattern & Purpose*, 201-26. BAR International Series 1156. Oxford: British Archaeological Reports.

Sheridan, J.A., 2004a The National Museums' of Scotland *Dating Cremated Bones Project*: results obtained during 2002/3. *Discovery & Excavation in Scotland*, 4, 167-9.

Sheridan, J.A., 2004b Pitmilly (Kingsbarns Parish). *Discovery & Excavation in Scotland*, 4, 77-8.

Sheridan, J.A., in press a. Dating the Scottish Bronze Age: 'There is clearly much that the material can still tell us'. In Burgess, C. (ed.) *In the Shadow of the Age of Stonehenge*. Oxford: Oxbow.

Sheridan, J.A., 2004c. The pottery. In Lewis, J. & Terry, J. Excavation of an Early Bronze Age cemetery at Holly Road, Leven, Fife. *Tayside & Fife Archaeological Journal*, 10, 34-40.

Sheridan, J.A. & Davis, M., 2002 Investigating jet and jet-like artefacts from prehistoric Scotland: the National Museums of Scotland project. *Antiquity*, 76, 812-25.

Sheridan, J.A., Cowie, T.G. & Hunter, F.J., 2002 National Museums of Scotland dating programme: 1994–98. In Bronk Ramsey, C., Higham, T.F.G., Owen, D.C.,

Pike, A.W.G. & Hedges, R.E.M. Radiocarbon dates from the Oxford AMS system: *Archaeometry* date list 31, 55-61. *Radiocarbon*, 44 (3), Supplement 1.

Simpson, D.D.A., 1965 Food Vessels in south-west Scotland, *Transactions of the Dumfriesshire & Galloway Natural History & Antiquarian Society*, 42, 25-50.

Simpson, D.D.A. 1968 Food Vessels: associations and chronology. In Coles, J.M. & Simpson, D.D.A. (eds), *Studies in Ancient Europe: Essays Presented to Stuart Piggott*, 197-211.

Simpson, D.D.A., 1996 Excavation of a kerbed funerary monument at Stoneyfield, Raigmore, Inverness, Highland, 1972-3. *Proceedings of the Society of Antiquaries of Scotland*, 126, 53-86.

Stevenson, S., 1995 The excavation of a kerbed cairn at Beech Hill House, Coupar Angus, Perthshire. *Proceedings of the Society of Antiquaries of Scotland*, 125, 197-235.

Stewart, M.E.C. & Barclay, G.J., 1997 Excavations in burial and ceremonial sites of the Bronze Age in Tayside. *Tayside & Fife Archaeological Journal*, 3, 22-54.

Stuiver, M., Reimer, P.J., Bard, E., Beck, J., Burr, G.S., Hughen, K.A., Kromer, B., McCormac, G., van der Plicht, J. & Spurk, M., 1998 INTCAL98 radiocarbon age calibration, 24000–0 cal BP. *Radiocarbon*, 40 (3), 1041-83.

Waddell, J., 1976 Cultural interaction in the insular Early Bronze Age: some ceramic evidence. In Laet, S.J. de (ed.) *Acculturation and Continuity in Atlantic Europe*, 284-95. Bruges: de Tempel. (Dissertationes Archaeologicae Gandenses Vol. 16).

Waddell, J., 1998 *The Prehistoric Archaeology of Ireland*. Galway: Galway University Press.

Ward, T., 1993 Camps Reservoir. *Discovery & Excavation in Scotland 1993*, 89.

Ward, T., 1994 Camps Reservoir. *Discovery & Excavation in Scotland 1994*, 73.

Ward, T., 1996 Camps Reservoir & Camps Reservoir 1994. In Ashmore, P.J. A list of Historic Scotland archaeological radiocarbon dates, *Discovery & Excavation in Scotland 1996*, 140-1.

Ward, T., forthcoming. Survey and excavation of a Bronze Age and later landscape at Camps Reservoir, near Crawford, South Lanarkshire.

Watkins, T., 1982 The excavation of an Early Bronze Age cemetery at Barns Farm, Dalgety, Fife. *Proceedings of the Society of Antiquaries of Scotland*, 112, 48-141.

Wilson, D., 1863 *Prehistoric Annals of Scotland* (Vol. 1). London & Cambridge: Macmillan & Co.

Young, A., 1951 A tripartite bowl from Kintyre. *Proceedings of the Society of Antiquaries of Scotland*, 85 (1950-1), 38-51.

Appendix

Radiocarbon Dates for Scottish Food Vessels: The Good, the Bad and the Ugly

Dates currently accepted as reliable

For illustrations of pots, see FIGS 86—93. 'FV' = Food Vessel

Findspot	Material dated; AMS?	Lab no.	Date BP	Date cal BC (1σ values in bold; 2σ values plain)	Associations; comments	References
Barns Farm, Fife (cist 1)	Cremated human bone, AMS	GrA-23998	3670±45	2140–2010 (56.2%) 2000–1970 (12.0%) 2200–2160 (4.3%) 2150–1910 (91.1%)	Cremated remains deposited shortly before unburnt crouched corpse; latter assoc. with FV, antler frag. & animal hide 'pillow'. Unburnt human bone from this cist had produced an obviously anomalous date of 4696±85 BP (SRR-700)	Shepherd 1982, 99–100, fig 14; Watkins 1982, 137
Barns Farm, Fife (grave 2)	Cremated human bone, AMS	GrA-24190	3605±45	2030–1880 (68.2%) 2140–2080 (7.4%) 2050–1870 (82.2%) 1850–1810 (3.8%) 1800–1770 (2.0%)	Coffin probably a coracle. Cremated remains deposited simultaneously with unburnt crouched corpse; latter assoc. with FV. Deposit of fish bones in upper fill of grave	Shepherd 1982, 109–10, fig 20
Barns Farm, Fife (grave 1): i) deposit 3 ii) deposit 2 iii) deposit 1	Cremated human bone, AMS (all)	i) GrA-23995 ii) GrA-23993 iii) GrA-24001	i) 3655±45 ii) 3620±40 iii) 3595±50	2130–2080 (22.2%) 2050–1950 (46.0%) 2150–1880 (95.4%) 2040–1910 (68.2%) 2140–2070 (10.5%) 2050–1880 (83.8%) 1840–1820 (1.0%) 2030–1990 (14.2%) 1980–1880 (54.0%) 2140–2080 (6.4%) 2050–1770 (89.0%)	Cremated remains deposited simultaneously with unburnt flexed corpse, latter assoc. with FV & stone battle axehead. Deposit 2 of crem. bone assoc. with burnt bone bead	Shepherd 1982, 106, Fig 19; Watkins 1982, 70–4
Ratho, Midlothian	Cremated human bone, AMS	GrA-24016	3635±40	2120–2100 (5.4%) 2040–1920 (62.8%) 2140–1880 (95.4%)	Found pre-1863, crem bones allegedly found in FV, in cist with crouched inhumation & FV, therefore faq for latter. Roman Iron Age metal objects also present in cist	Wilson 1863, 270–1, 427, 454; Hunter pers comm
Pitmilly, Fife	Cremated human bone, AMS	GrA-21728	3590±60	2040–1870 (62.4%) 1840–1820 (3.7%) 1800–1780 (2.1%) 2140–2070 (7.6%) 2050–1740 (87.8%)	FV and crem. bones found outside cist during pipe laying, but had prob. originally been assoc. Unknown whether cist had also contained inhumation but seems likely	Sheridan in press c
Kilellan, Islay, Argyll & Bute	Charcoal, non-AMS	GU-3517	3590±60	2040–1870 (62.4%) 1840–1820 (3.7%) 1800–1780 (2.1%) 2140–2070 (7.6%) 2050–1740 (87.8%)	In midden which is thought to have accumulated fairly rapidly	Cowie, R. forthcoming
Holly Rd., Leven, Fife (cist B)	Unburnt human bone, AMS	GrA-22107	3560±60	2020–1980 (3.5%) 1980–1870 (43.8%) 1850–1770 (20.9%) 2120–2090 (1.5%) 2040–1730 (93.9%)	-	Sheridan 2004c
Holly Rd., Leven, Fife (cist A)	Unburnt human bone, AMS	GrA-22106	3520±60	1920–1740 (68.2%) 2020–1990 (2.4%) 1980–1680 (93.0%)	Fossil crinoid used as bead; flint knife	Sheridan in 2004c
Kentraw, Islay, Argyll & Bute	Unburnt human bone, non-AMS	GU-2189	3510±50	1890–1740 (68.2%) 1960–1730 (90.6%) 1720–1680 (4.8%)	Tpq for inhumation accompanied by FV & accessory vessel, in cist with remains of 4, possibly 6 individuals	Ritchie 1987
Mains of Melgund, Angus: i) child skel. ii) adult skel.	Unburnt human bone (both), AMS	i) AA-23260 ii) AA-23259	i) 3500±50 ii) 3405±55	1890–1740 (68.2%) 1950–1680 (95.4%) 1860–1840 (3.0%) 1770–1610 (65.2%) 1880–1520 (95.4%)	Bodies must have been buried simultaneously, back to back, may well have been bound into tightly crouched position	Rideout & Russell-White 1998, 49–54
Westhaugh of Tulliemet, Perth & Kinross (cist 2)	Unburnt human bone, AMS	AA-22181	3415±55	1860–1840 (5.8%) 1780–1620 (62.4%) 1880–1600 (90.6%) 1570–1520 (4.6%)	Cremated bone also present in cist	Stewart & Barclay 1997, 34–41
Loanleven, Perth & Kinross (cist 2)	Charcoal, non-AMS	GU-2542	3410±50	1860–1840 (3.1%) 1770–1620 (65.1%) 1880–1600 (90.9%) 1570–1520 (4.5%)	Tpq for cist containing Food Vessel sherds. Cist probably disturbed in antiquity; a few frags crem. human bone, & unburnt bone frags of a med-lg bird present. Cist lg enough to have held crouched inhum. originally	Russell-White et al 1992, 301–12

Date currently being re-determined

Findspot	Material dated	Lab no.	Date BP	Date cal BC (1σ values in bold; 2σ values plain)	Associations; comments	References
Balbirnie, Fife (cist 3)	Cremated human bone	GrA-24860	3335±40	1690–1580 (46.2%) 1570–1520 (22.0%) 1740–1710 (3.6%) 1700–1520 (91.8%)	Flint knife. Cremated remains are those of young adult female & child c 6. Date being re-determined because initially suspected to be too young	Ritchie 1974

Dates determined over 10 years ago, whose standard deviations have had to be increased (see Ashmore et al. 2000)

Note: none of these is an AMS date. Calibrated using adjusted standard deviation; details of probability ranges within the 1σ and 2σ ranges not given. Ideally these dated using AMS

Findspot	Material	Lab no.	Date BP	Date cal BC	Associations; comments	Reference
	dated		(adjusted ± in brackets)	(1σ values in bold; 2σ values plain)		
Stoneyfield, Raigmore, Highland (cist 1)	Charcoal	SRR-430	3723±100 (140)	2340–1910 2550–1700	-	Simpson 1996, 56–8, illus 18.1
Ardnave, Islay, Argyll & Bute	Charcoal (all)	i)GU-1439 ii) GU-1371 iii) GU-1440 iv) GU-1272	i) 3680±65 (110) ii) 3610±85 (120) iii) 3687±60 (110) iv) 3230±120 (170)	2210–1880 2300–1700 2140–1770 2350–1600 2280–1910 2500–1750 1740–1260 1950–1000	i) & ii) either contemporary with, or tpq for, tripartite vessel (no 1); iii) may be contemporary with that vessel; iv) from midden containing most of the FV assemblage	Ritchie & Welfare 1983
Aberdour Rd., Dunfermline, Fife (cist 3)	Unburnt human bone	SRR-292	3581±40 (110)	2130–1740 2300–1600	Flint knife, flint strike-a-light, iron ore nodule	Close-Brooks et al 1972, 123, 127–8, illus 3
Almondbank, Perth & Kinross (cist II)	Unburnt human bone	SRR-590	3556±80 (110)	2040–1740 2250–1600	Bronze awl frag., 2 pieces ?calcined mollusc shell	Stewart & Barclay 1997, 24–6
North Mains henge, Perth & Kinross (burial B)	Unburnt human bone	GU-1381	3490±65 (110)	1960–1640 2150–1500	-	Cowie 1983, fig 29a; Barclay 1983,136
Gairneybank, Perth & Kinross (cist 1)	Unburnt human bone	GU-1118	3470±80 (110)	1940–1630 2150–1500	Small, unusually-shaped vessel but in general FV tradition, knife-dagger	Cowie,T.G & Ritchie 1991, 95–6, 100–3, illus 3.2, 6
Gairneybank, Perth & Kinross (cist 2)	Unburnt human bone	GU-1119	3460±70 (110)	1920–1620 2150–1500	-	Cowie,T.G & Ritchie 1991, 96–8, 103, illus 3.3
Ord North, Highland	Charcoal	GU-1167	3435±65 (110)	1890–1600 2050–1450	Although not directly associated with deposit of cremated bone above collapsed roof of chamber tomb, had probably been	Sharples 1981, 36, 54, illus 10
Reswallie Mains, Angus	Unburnt human bone	N-1238	3160±70 (110)	1600–1260 1700–1100	Retouched flint flake	*Discov Excav Scot* 1967, 3; Coutts 1971, no 97a
Traigh Bhan, Islay, Argyll & Bute (cist 1, body 2)	Unburnt human bone	GU-1379	3005±105 (145)	1410–1040 1550–800	Anomalously late? Cist also contained disarticulated remains of a second body, dating to 3330±95 (135) BP, GU-1378	Ritchie & Stevenson 1982

Obviously anomalous dates

Note: dates not worth calibrating

Findspot	Material dated	Lab no.	Date BP	Associations; comments	References
Barns Farm, Fife (cist 1)	Unburnt human bone	SRR-700	4696±85 (120)	See above for details & date from cremation from this cist	Shepherd 1982, 99–100, illus 14; Watkins 1982, 137
Beech Hill House, Coupar Angus,	Charcoal	GU-2739	2880±120	Crouched inhumation.	Stevenson 1995 226–8, illus 12

Perth & Kinross (cist 5)			(not adj.)	fragments of bone pin and bronze 'pin'	
Mount Stuart, Bute	Unburnt human bone. i) ulna ii) femur	i) OxA-6130 ii) OxA-6579	i) 2645±50 ii) 2955±55 (not adj.)	Crouched inhumation; jet & cannel coal spacer plate necklace, 'some burnt stuff' 'remains of pins or skewers', 'corrupt piece of bronze'. AMS dates, both from same skeleton. Bones contaminated by consolidant	Bryce 1904, 63–8, Sheridan et al 2002, 56
Seafield West, Highland	Organic encrustation inside pot	AA-29063	2625±45	Probably crouched or flexed inhumation in wooden coffin, flint knife, scraper, flake & 4th flint item, lost. Expected date for this type of FV: c2200–1950 BC by analogy with Irish finds	Cressey & Sheridan 2003; Brindley pers comm

17

SMALL, BUT PERFECTLY FORMED? SOME OBSERVATIONS ON THE BRONZE AGE CUPS OF SCOTLAND

ALEX GIBSON

INTRODUCTION

Scotland has long had a tradition of the study of Bronze Age ceramics. This may largely be due to the earlier emphasis on funerary archaeology resulting in a considerable amount of material in museum collections throughout Scotland, as well as to the paucity and conservatism of the pottery from later periods, particularly on the mainland. Equally, the Neolithic ceramic corpus for Scotland, other than from the Western and Northern Isles, has generally been slow in coming forward, especially in the Middle and Later Neolithic. Derek Simpson, like the present writer, published a treatise on Scottish Bronze Age pottery after he had left Scotland and was in residence at Leicester University (Derek as a lecturer and the present writer, some (considerable!) time afterwards, as a PhD student: Simpson 1965; Gibson 1984). It is a great pleasure for me to return to Scotland and offer this small contribution in honour of Derek; a fellow 'ex-pat', teacher, colleague and, above all, friend.

'WE'LL TAK' A CUP'

Small pottery vessels are an important part of the Bronze Age ceramic repertoire not just in Scotland but in the whole of Britain, Ireland and indeed continental Europe (though less well studied). Normally found with burials, the British and Irish cups can take a variety of forms from simple undecorated 'thumb pots' to exotic forms such as the Grape Cups of Wessex or the more widely distributed Fenestrated (or Perforated Wall) Cups (Longworth 1983). In addition there are miniature forms of vessels normally encountered in a larger variant, namely Food Vessels and Collared Urns. These pots were formally ascribed the generic names of Incense Cups or Pigmy Cups (90). The former was a function inferred from the occasional sooting reported within some vessels as well as multiple wall perforations (whether 'windows' or piercings) which led the early antiquaries to believe that they were used for the burning of incense at the funeral rituals. This term cannot be widely applied, however, for most vessels have neither sooting nor multi-perforated walls. In 1912, Abercromby commented that the label 'has nothing to recommend it' (Abercromby, 1912, II, 24). Earlier, Greenwell, who, for his day, had a sound knowledge of prehistoric ceramics, had wrestled with the functions of these small pots and failed to find a practically convincing interpretation (1877, 74-83). The latter term, Pigmy Cup, referred simply to their diminutive size but has somewhat gone out of fashion in the wake of our fixation with political over-correctness.

The term 'Accessory Vessel' has often been, incorrectly, substituted for Pigmy Cup. I say incorrectly because not all of these vessels act in an accessory (i.e. extra or additional) capacity while larger Beakers, Food Vessels and Urns may also serve this role. The term Miniature Cups has also been used but is again inaccurate because some forms, such as the Grape Cup, Fenestrated Wall Cup and Aldbourne Cup are not miniatures: they cannot be because they do not manifest themselves in larger forms.

Pigmy Cup, the term favoured by Abercromby, may still be the preferred term for, like 'Food Vessel', 'Henge' and even 'Carp's Tongue' (I have been reliably informed that carp do NOT have tongues!) it is a term that is now well established in the archaeological literature and conveys immediate meaning to members of the wider archaeological community. Nor is the term Pigmy Cup politically incorrect any more than the Pigmy Shrew or Pigmy Hippopotamus. But even this poses problems for the purist. 'Pigmy' is from the Greek 'pygmaios' meaning 'dwarf' and so its adjectival use in the context with which we are concerned implies that these are dwarf cups or in other words dwarf versions of a larger form. In short, and to be deliberately pedantic, it suffers from the same inaccuracy as does 'miniature'.

So what is wrong with 'Cup'? In its most basic definition as a small container, 'cup' would seem to fit the archaeological evidence perfectly and inoffensively. While the pedant might argue that those with multi-perforated walls could scarcely contain anything, this assumes that only liquids needed containing. Cup will be used here generically while sub-categories will be used for greater description and when referring to individual vessels.

TYPOLOGY

Here is not the place for a *resumé* of the previous typologies of these vessels save to say that the most recent, and arguably the most comprehensive, is that advocated by Ian Longworth who, furthermore, very rightly, observes that 'the variation in type of cup is considerable' (1984, 51). This is exemplified by the fact that all of Longworth's 11 cup types have sub-types, sometimes up to seven internal variations or sub-divisions. I think that the reason for this is the over-rigorous classification of hand-built ceramics especially when every variable such as rim form or neck concavity is considered to have been

90 Bronze Age cups from (left to right) Ronaldsay, Old Penrith and Dunbar. *From Smith 1872.*
By kind permission of the Society of Antiquaries of Scotland

important. Observation of hand-built Neolithic pottery from Lyles Hill, County Antrim, Donegore Hill, County Antrim, and, especially, Ballygalley, County Antrim, where whole rim diameters are reconstructable with minimal infill, indicates that several rim forms may be found on a single vessel. The same can be said for base diameters, bevel forms and shoulders on most hand-built ceramics.

The Scottish material that is the subject of this study suggests a simpler basic classification *(91)*.

1. Thumb cups with rounded bases similar in form to crucibles (Longworth's type 11)
2. Splayed cups with flaring sides and comparatively narrow bases (Longworth's types 7 & 8)
3. Vertical-sided cups (Longworth's type 6)
4. Globular hemispherical or closed cups (Longworth's type 9)
5. Distinctly shouldered biconical cups (Longworth's types 5 & 10)
6. Miniature vase Food Vessels (Longworth's type 3)
7. Miniature Collared Urns (Longworth's type 4)
8. Fenestrated wall cups (Longworth's type 2)

In addition, outside Scotland, there are:

9. Grape cups (Longworth's type 1)
10. Aldbourne cups

Nevertheless, ten basic types are still an indication of the variety of cups and Longworth is quite correct to point out that there is variation within each group and there are also vessels which seem to fall between two types, particularly the more simple or basic types. However, there are some distinct grammatical rules associated with the various types and to which we will return.

MINIATURISATION

Many small objects appear in the archaeological record during the Neolithic and Bronze Age and the reasons for this have rarely been discussed. In early metalwork, it is often easy to understand. There would, for example, appear to be a trinket phase at the start of the Bronze Age when both the raw material was rare and the technical skills were being learned. This resulted not just in small artefacts, but also in small composite artefacts such as the gold and copper-alloy halberd pendant from the Manton Barrow, Wiltshire (Annable & Simpson 1964, 101). Accompanying the primary female inhumation, this item was associated with a Grape Cup (type 9) and a Splayed Wall Cup (type 2) as well as a small knife, awls and a variety of beads and ear studs. This composite item, like a similar artefact from Wilsford G8, Wiltshire, is easily interpreted as an item of jewellery, a 'charm' even, and some of these miniature items seem to have been perforated for suspension, presumably on a thong around the neck.

Other artefacts are less easy to explain. The variety of sizes within polished stone axes, for example, is often considerable. This is especially true in France and Ireland but by no means restricted to those areas. Even within the pages of the *Devizes Catalogue* (Annable & Simpson 1964), no. 18 is a small chalk axe from Woodhenge, Wiltshire, measuring some 86mm while item 20 is a miniature polished axe from Enford, Wiltshire, measuring only 40mm. From almost the other end of Britain, a battle-axe from Doune, Perth & Kinross, measures a paltry 70mm long and Fenton (1988, fig. 23) classifies anything below 80mm long as miniature (see also McLaren, this volume). In French museums, such small artefacts are usually described as 'toys' but surely this cannot be entirely the case; indeed some of these miniature items may have taken longer to produce than the larger variants given their small size, the need for more careful handling and their inherent fragility. While the small polished axes may be considered to have had a role as chisels, particularly if set within an antler or wooden sleeve, or to have been used in the finer aspects of wood-working, the smaller battle-axes are less easily explained. The small amber beads in the shape of pestle maceheads from Wilsford G8 (Annable & Simpson, 1964, nos 183-7) may also be relevant in this context (see McLaren this volume).

In ceramic terms, small vessels may also be part of a manifestation of experiment. People new to potting often create a range of small vessels, and anthropomorphic or zoomorphic forms (see Gibson 2002; 2003). While these

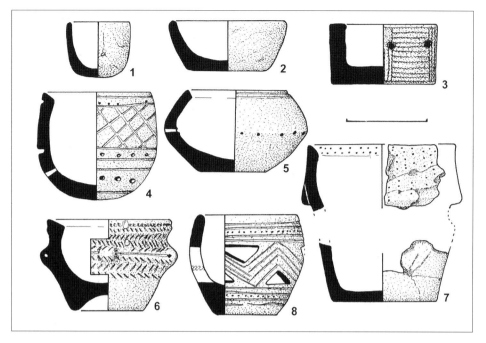

91 Suggested typology for Scottish cups. 1 Brackmont Mill, 2 Bankfoot, Glenluce, 3 Kirk Park, Musselbur, 4 Carlochan, 5 Muirkirk, 6 West Skichen, 7 Green Knowe, 8 Unprovenanced (Dundee Museum). Scale = 5cm.

figurative items do not presently survive in the British archaeological record, nevertheless small pinch-pots and smaller, simple vessels are to be found throughout British prehistory. There is, for example, a variety of small bowls from the Neolithic assemblage at Staines, Surrey (Robertson-Mackay 1987, 75) and from Windmill Hill, Wiltshire (Smith 1965, fig. 15). These may have functioned perfectly well as cups in a domestic repertoire.

Perhaps the earliest 'non-functional' miniature ceramic known to the present writer is a small Impressed Ware bowl from the Dublin area in Ireland (Kavanagh 1977, no. 26). Unfortunately this vessel is a stray find but the rounded and expanded rim, the sharply concave neck and the rounded base clearly indicate Peterborough Ware, or at least Impressed Ware, rather than Early Bronze Age affinities. This diminutive vessel, presumably pinch-formed, measures a tiny 40mm high. Interestingly, this vessel is imperfect and has a small firing spall near the base *(92)*.

Within a Grooved Ware environment, the small cups from Woodlands, Wiltshire, are well known (Stone 1949) and measure only about 55mm high. There are also some small Grooved Ware vessels in the Balfarg, Fife, assemblage and vessel 41, for example, measures only 60mm high (Barclay & Russell-White 1993). The small vessel from the Unival chambered tomb, N. Uist, is also a classic example of a Grooved Ware cup (Henshall 1972, 309 & 533). The small square Grooved Ware vessels from the Links of Noltland and Skara Brae, Orkney (Sheridan 1999, 116), have been likened to the stone ochre grinding pots from Skara Brae and Sheridan's scatter diagram (*ibid.*, illus. 12.5) indicates several vessels with a diameter of between 50mm and 100mm suggesting a cup element in the assemblage.

Humphrey Case (1995) has admirably demonstrated the range in vessel capacities for Beakers and has identified small pots with volumes of up to 500cc, a middle range from 500cc to 2 litres and a large group of over 2 litres. The medium-sized group is most frequently associated with burials though the smaller and larger vessels are by no means excluded from graves. At Northton on Harris, the site with which Derek is, perhaps, most associated, there is also considerable variation within the Beaker assemblage. We must await the final publication of this assemblage before full quantification can be made but a preliminary study has suggested that the capacity of these Beaker vessels ranges from some 300cc to 7 litres; the small Beakers may be less than 120mm high (Gibson 2002, fig. 43).

The smallness of some vessels throughout the British and Irish Neolithic makes some of the Bronze Age vessels easier to understand. The variation in Collared Urn sizes, for example, has been clearly demonstrated (Barclay 2002, fig. 9.3b: Gibson 2002, fig. 47). While it might be easy to think of this size variation in terms of vessel utilities within domestic assemblages, the particularly diminutive Collared Urns, such as that from Broadstairs, Kent, at 68mm high or that from Roxby cum Risby, East Riding of Yorkshire, at 60mm high, are more difficult to explain in terms of logical functions (Longworth 1984, nos 793 & 755 respectively).

The same variation can be found within the Food Vessel repertoire, particularly when Food Vessel Urns are taken into consideration. Unfortunately there is as yet no national corpus for Food Vessels. I remember seeing the beginnings of one in Derek's office just as flares were going out of fashion. Unfortunately David Clarke's *Beakers*, Joan Taylor's *Goldwork* and Ian Longworth's *Collared Urns* proved such expensive books to produce in those days of high inflation that Cambridge 'pulled the plug' on Food Vessels. Trevor Cowie, however, analysed the size range of both Food Vessels and Food Vessel Urns for Scotland and the North of England (Cowie 1978, fig. 2). There appeared to be a break at about 200mm when defining Food Vessels and their Urn variants. Food Vessels were generally considered to be over 10cm high and if this is the case, as indeed it seems to be, then the smaller vessels may justifiably be termed 'miniature'. Once again the tiny Food Vessels such as the miniature vases from Craigdhu, North Queensferry, Fife, at 56mm high (Smith 1872 & see Sheridan this volume) or Loanhead of Daviot, Aberdeenshire, at 46mm high (Kilbride-Jones 1935) or the miniature Yorkshire Vase from Hill of Keir, Aberdeenshire, at 46mm high (Reid 1912, no. 228) are, like the diminutive Urns, more difficult to explain logically, at

92 Miniature Impressed Ware bowl from the Dublin area. *By kind permission of the Trustees of the National Museum and Galleries of Northern Ireland (Ulster Museum): copyright reserved*

least in a secular environment. This said, however, one must remember the domestic context of the small cylindrical cup from the house site at Ardnave, Islay. This small vessel measures only 80mm high and a narrow 24mm at the mouth (Ritchie & Welfare 1983, fig. 10, no. 26).

Perhaps, as mentioned above, these pots are the result of experiment. Perhaps they represent the works of new potters experimenting with their new medium. We might call them 'apprentice pieces' and this might explain their diminutive form and the often elaborate, if sometimes careless, decoration (see below). It might also explain the forming traces seen inside some cups; however it does not explain the strict grammatical rules adhering to the various forms.

FUNCTION

Small may be beautiful but small need not be purely decorative and diminutive vessels certainly should not be considered useless or non-functional. Small vessels are, of course, known from many societies including our own. In Chinese and Japanese cultures, tea is drunk from small cups despite the abundance of the herb and the weakness of the brew. In the Mediterranean regions sweet tea is taken from small glasses while pungent, strong ground-laden coffee is leisurely sipped from small cups with impractically minute handles. In our own culture, small 'cups' of plastic or glass may be used for special drinks such as medicine or strong alcohol and, in a religious context, very small glasses are used to drink symbolic blood, as part of 'a foretaste of the heavenly banquet'.

Did the Biconical Cup from Garton Slack Barrow 40, East Yorkshire, contain some potent, magical or even medicinal brew? This cup is reported to have contained bones from 'some small animal' and brings to mind the cauldron contents of Macbeth's witches. More importantly, the cup was found inverted into the mouth of the skeleton (*93*: Mortimer 1905, 229). It certainly gives a whole new meaning to 'toad in the hole'. If the contents of the cup (whether solid or liquid) were medicinal, then the administers of this remedy were too late: they had to remove the lower jaw of the individual in order to insert the cup. While the origins of the small animal bones must, of course, remain uncertain, it nevertheless seems likely that the burial is one of a number of instances where the grave had been revisited once the body had decayed or where the burial had been made when the body was in an advanced cadaverous state (Woodward 2000, 36-42: Gibson 2004). Whatever scenario is correct, it is certain that the cup had been deliberately placed and even though the text of the ritual may not be translatable, the deep symbolism of this act cannot be denied.

Since the nineteenth century, speculations have been made for the uses to which these vessels were put. Incense burning has already been mentioned and may be particularly relevant to the multi-perforated varieties. The perforations have been used to suggest that the vessels were suspended and lamps, cups, receptacles for taking flame to the pyre and tokens have all been suggested. But in looking for comfortable, single functions we are in danger of uniting these vessels in a single class simply because of their smallness. This is exactly the difficulty faced by Greenwell and his predecessors. As mentioned above, these vessels have a distinct grammar particular to their type. Grape Cups, Aldbourne Cups and Fenestrated Wall cups, for example, are all readily identifiable and are well-defined 'types'. Miniature Urns, Food Vessels and the distinctly Biconical Cups are similarly so. Such recognisable grammars, the strict languages of traditions, must have conveyed some meaning to the makers and users of the pots. While, archaeologically, we are generally happy acknowledging the distinctions of the larger ceramic traditions (Beakers, Food Vessels, Collared Urns) while respecting 'grey' vessels that seem to combine elements from more than one type, we seem to have been less willing to do so with the Cups and instead have been content to group them together purely on the basis of their diminutive size with little consideration of their recognisable forms. Furthermore, pure logic will tell us that Grape Cups, Fenestrated Wall Cups and other multi-perforated cups could not have held liquid while others would have been perfectly capable of doing so.

Andrew Sherratt has made a case for the use of mind-altering substances in the Later Neolithic (Sherratt 1991; 1997) and perhaps the multi-perforated varieties could have been used in this context. The paired perforations of the Biconical Cups may well have been intended as outlets for the inhalation of fumes and vapours and, being usually sited on the shoulders of biconical vessels, these perforations are well suited to oral inhalation.

This does not preclude the non-perforated examples from use as burners for aromatic and/or narcotic substances. However it has also been suggested that the smaller simpler non-perforated cups may have been used as lamps. Perhaps potent or magical brews may even have been symbolically and ritually imbibed from the non-perforated types as has been suggested for Garton Slack (surely a clear argument in favour of a connection with oral ingestion).

With regard to suspension, this is highly possible but, I think, unlikely. The majority of the perforations noted on the Scottish examples were formed while the clay was still wet and so the holes were clearly part of the initial design. Indeed, in the case of a Biconical Cup from near Dunbar, East Lothian, (Lowe & Anderson 1894), the perforations had been made before the pot was decorated as the incised lines bend to avoid the holes *(94)*. These features therefore appear to have been integral to the *raison d'être* of the vessel. However most of these Biconical Cups have only a single pair of perforations so, if suspended, the pots would have hung at an angle and their contents, if liquid, would have been spilled. Also, the shape of most of these pots, widening from the base upwards to a shoulder or rim, means that perforations would have been unnecessary as a means of suspension. The cups would have been perfectly suited to being held within a cord cradle.

If, however, the Biconical cups with a single pair of perforations were suspended as decorations, charms or talismen, then this would have been irrelevant: they would not have needed to have been suspended level. Indeed Greenwell (1877, 82) commented on the frequency with which decoration is found on the bases of cups when compared with the larger Bronze Age pots

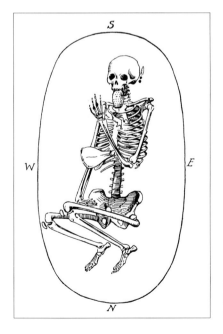

93 The burial from Garton Slack Barrow 40. Note Biconical Cup in the mouth and the dislodged jaw on the chest of the skeleton *From Mortimer 1905*

and suggested that the decoration was designed to be seen. This would have been possible if the cups had been hanging. The subjectivity of this argument is, however, fully acknowledged and it must be noted that few cups exhibit (at least macroscopically) any real wear at these perforations: there is no abrasion or smoothing around them as one might expect had the cups been suspended for any length of time.

With these ideas in mind a programme of absorbed residue analysis was undertaken on Bronze Age cups at the University of Bradford. No carbonaceous residues were encountered in any of the cups whether recently excavated or not and so small samples were taken from underneath the inside surfaces of the ceramic itself. This is the area where one might expect to see high levels of organic material (Stern *et al.* 2000). The samples were analysed using gas chromatography and, where lipids were recognised, by gas chromatography-mass spectrometry but the results were very disappointing. Of the 25 cups analysed, only four contained traces of lipids and none of these are conclusively ancient in origin nor do they necessarily result from the vessel's use. An exception may be the cup from Whitford, Flintshire (Savory 1980, no. 466) which has a series of five wax esters and $C28:0$, $C30:0$ and $C32:0$ alcohols (with some underivatised components). This *may* be indicative of the former presence of beeswax but the material was too degraded to be certain.

The undecorated Biconical Cup from Amesbury 61a, Wiltshire (Ashbee 1985), shows a range of fatty acids ($C12:0$, $C14:0$, $C15:0$, $C16:0$, $C17:0$, $C18:0$, $C20:0$) with significant abundances of $C16:0$ and $C18:0$. The remainder occur at low levels, therefore it is also difficult to ascribe an origin to these lipids. Although the $C16:0$ abundance is a little higher than the $C18:0$ little inference can be drawn from this.

The small round-based thumb pot from Lenton, Lincolnshire (Allen & Hopkins 2000, no. 16) had higher levels of fatty acids than the other samples and these may well represent the former presence of a fat or oil though the material is once again so degraded that the source of this lipid cannot be determined.

The recently excavated Fenestrated Cup from Dowsby, Lincolnshire (Allen & Hopkins 2000, no. 1) provided the best suite of samples in the series. No significant lipids were recovered from the pot itself but wax esters were recovered from the soil samples from both inside and outside of the pot and though the internal sample is more complex with a number of peaks including alcohols and alkanes, these may still be derived from modern contamination; they could also be plant or fossil fuel derived. While the presence of wax must remain a possibility, these peaks may also stem from soil-absorbed lipids. The external soil sample also shows wax esters and fatty acids though the chromatogram is not as complex as the internal data. Wax esters outside as well as inside might suggest soil bacterial contamination although, being a Fenestrated Wall Cup, leakage caused through biodegradation is to be expected.

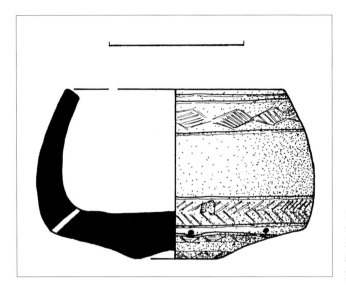

94 Biconical Cup from near Dunbar. Note how the incised decoration curves to avoid the left hand perforation. Scale = 5cm

The results of these analyses are disappointing and suggest that molecular analysis has little to offer in the study of these enigmatic vessels. The largely negative results do not mean that these pots were never used, however. They do not mean that the pots were always empty. They simply mean that traces of the contents could not be detected or, if detected, identified.

DECORATION

No attempt will be made here to form a comprehensive catalogue of the decorative repertoire of these vessels. This form of description is more in keeping with a corpus than with the overview presented here. But needless to say the decoration varies considerably. Both highly decorated and totally undecorated vessels are present with a range of decorative complexity in between. Interesting from the point of view of this writer is some of the carelessness of the decoration.

A Biconical Cup from Wester Bucklyvie, Fife (Smith 1872, 189-91), at first sight appears to be very ornate, and indeed it is, but a miscalculation has been made on the upper portion. The incised rectangular panels are filled with diagonal incisions alternatively in the top left half and bottom left half of the rectangle but the miscalculation has resulted in two adjacent panels having their bottom left corners filled. Thus the geometry of the design is interrupted. The unprovenanced Biconical Cup from either North or South Ronaldsay, Orkney (Anon 1859, 485), exhibits a 'crowding' of the decoration on the belly of the vessel where the alternating filled chevrons do not quite fit the circumference of the pot *(95.2)*. Another Biconical Cup, from Ross-shire, Highland, (unpublished, Hunterian 1926.2), has incised chevrons on the body below the shoulder but again the points have been miscalculated to the extent that the 'star-like' pattern has not been closed *(95.1)*. The decoration is less complex but equally careless on the underside of another unprovenanced Biconical Cup (Smith 1872, 189-207). Here the carelessness of the design seems to have been unimportant because it could easily have been erased and redone. Instead, it was left sloppy. Why was the accuracy of the geometrical decoration so unimportant in these cases? Was the grammar of the form or shape of the pot more important than the decoration? These questions must remain hypothetical for the time being.

Traces of inlay within the decoration have been noted on four vessels. The Biconical Cup from Crailing Hall, Jedburgh, Scottish Borders, is poorly preserved and decorated on the upper portion with a single zone of herringbone twisted cord impressions (Smith 1872, 198). Traces of what appears to have been a red inlay are visible in some of the impressions. The rim fragment from what appears to have been a Globular Cup from Cauldchapel, South Lanarkshire (Scott 1951, 8, fig. 2.33) is decorated with opposed dot-filled triangles and there are traces of white inlay within the dots. The vessel with the imperfectly geometrical decoration from either North or South Ronaldsay already mentioned above also has traces of white inlay in the incisions. The small Miniature Vase from Hill of Skene, Aberdeenshire (Reid, 1912, no. 228) may also have traces of similar inlay in the incisions. None of these pigments (if such they are) have been analysed and they may, of course, result from the burial environment. More work needs to be done on these issues.

TECHNOLOGY

Little attention has been paid to the technology of these cups. They look very similar when seen on the pages of an archaeological publication; however this belies the truth and there is as much variation in the quality of these small vessels as there is in the larger elements of the Bronze Age ceramic repertoire.

Of the 72 Scottish vessels so far examined by the present writer, the majority contain crushed stone inclusions *(96)*. Occasionally this stone is not at all well crushed or sorted and in the case of a small vase from Newport, Fife, (unpublished, NMS no. XEA 64) the stone inclusions reach 11mm across and in an unprovenanced vessel from Ross-shire (unpublished, Hunterian A.1926.2) they are not much smaller at 10mm. Generally speaking, however, the stone inclusions measure between 2mm and 6mm across. But even amongst these smaller fractioned fabrics, the stone can often protrude through both surfaces giving the pot a gritty and uneven texture.

Grog forms the next most frequent inclusion and this tends to result in better, smoother fabrics. The organic tempered sherds have a much more open appearance, with voids within the fabric of the pot and a pitted surface. The pots also feel more friable though they have been equally well-fired. Shell has only been detected in two vessels and, unusually, bone was noticed in the intricately decorated cup from Bennachie Hill, Aberdeenshire (Smith 1872, 193). No attempt has yet been made to determine whether the bone is animal or human.

The majority of the pots seem to have been pinched. Only five of the Scottish cups so far examined exhibit the tell-tale traces of coil building. That from Arnbathie, Perth & Kinross, has, in fact, broken along a coil and it may even be the base portion of a much larger vessel (Scott 1951, 80, fig. 2.17). The Biconical Cup from Coulter, South Lanarkshire, has also broken along the coil, this time above the shoulder (*ibid.*, 82 fig. 2.31). In the case of the remaining vessels, the coils are only visible on the inside surface while the outer is more perfectly smoothed.

Very unusual finishing marks are the profuse fingernail impressions on the inside of the cups from Balnakettle, Aberdeenshire (Cowie & Ritchie 1991) and Blairgowrie, Perth & Kinross (Fraser 1878). No attempt seems to have been made to eradicate these imperfections and indeed there should really have been no need for them. They appear to be careless and unimportant. The curvature of the impressions suggests the thumb of a right-handed potter.

One aspect of these cups which has not been commented upon or indeed, to the writer's knowledge, recognised before is the number of firing wasters amongst these vessels. The wasters noted are as follows:

1. Crailing Hall, Jedburgh *(97.4 & 98.3)* has a severely spalled surface and indeed appears to have been a catastrophic waster (i.e. some spalls result in holes in both surfaces rendering the cup useless as a container).

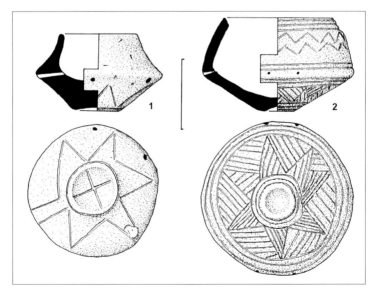

95 Careless decoration on Biconical Cups from Rosshire (1) and North or South Ronaldsay (2). Scale = 5cm

2. The globular bowl from Greystone Park, Dumfries & Galloway (Morrison 1968, no. 94) has a large spall on the outer surface.
3. A small hemispherical cup from Kirkburn, Dumfries & Galloway (Cormack 1963, fig. 7) is also a catastrophic waster being heavily spalled on the lower part of the body *(97.3 & 98.6)*.
4. The Globular Cup from Brackmont Mill, Fife, while not spalled, is nevertheless bloated and sintered at the rim *(97.2 & 98.4)*. This represents the initial stages of vitrification and is indicative of over-firing, an observation made at the time of discovery (Childe & Waterston 1942).
5. The Biconical Cup with the poorly judged geometric decoration from Wester Bucklyvie, discussed above, also has a large spall on the outer lower surface *(98.1)*.
6. The Globular Cup from Dighty Water, City of Dundee (Scott 1951, 82, fig. 2.18) is spalled on the lower surface *(98.5)*.
7. The similar cup from Hill of Culsh, Aberdeenshire, has a spall on the upper outer surface (Scott 1951, 80, fig. 2.11).
8. An unprovenanced Biconical Cup (presumably from Scotland, Smith 1872, 189-207) has a firing spall on the upper surface.
9. The outer surface of both the upper and lower body of the Biconical Cup from Carnousie, Aberdeenshire, is heavily spalled (Longworth 1984, no. 1903) and the base too is damaged *(97.1)*.
10. The remains of the Biconical Cup, also discussed above, from Coulter is another catastrophic waster with severe spalling on the outer surface *(102.5 & 103.2)*.

These ten vessels are firing wasters: that is to say that they result from the initial firing of the clay vessel. The spalling on the majority of these pots has been caused by either the remnant water of plasticity or, more probably, the water of chemical composition turning to steam during firing. This water vapour has been unable to escape through the vessel wall (Gibson & Woods 1997, 156). The resulting explosion has blown off discs of clay leaving corresponding scars on the pot. Catastrophic spalling is where the whole thickness of the body has been affected and a hole has been left in the vessel wall. Spalling of this highly diagnostic nature only occurs in the initial firing. It is not caused by reheating or 'burning' pottery because it results from water turning to steam, expanding and, finding that it cannot escape through the pores of the clay, blowing its way out. Once fired, however, any water permeating the vessel wall (from soaking, from its contents or even from absorption from the ambient atmosphere) will be able to escape from the very routes it used to enter the fabric and so spalling would not result.

Some of these vessels (e.g. Crailing Hall and Kirkburn) would not have been serviceable as containers. All are 'imperfect'. Yet they end up accompanying burials; presumably prestigious vessels or vessels obtaining

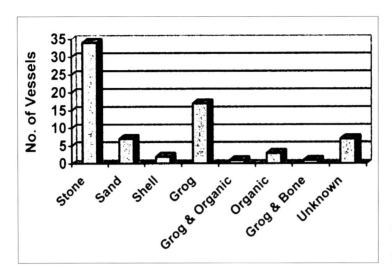

96 Frequency of inclusions in Scottish Cup fabrics

prestige by virtue of their deposition. They may have been made specifically for the burial and fired with the cremation. This may explain why traces of their use have not been found and it may explain why fragmentary vessels are also found.

CONCLUSION

There are various problems with the interpretation of these enigmatic vessels and the imperfections in some of the vessels add to our problems. It must remain a possibility that these cups, particularly perhaps, the Biconical Cups, may have been made by inexperienced potters specifically for the burial. They may also have been fired in the flames of the 'pyre'. I have decided to put the word 'pyre' in inverted commas to enable us to consider all cremation fires. Pyres are generally considered to have been large constructions for the combustion of a whole body while a case has been made elsewhere for the combustion of disarticulated and de-fleshed bone in the Bronze Age, sometimes in pits (Gibson 1993; 2004, 186-8). These cups may have been fired in any of these environments. Some cups also appear grey and soft and may have been burnt if not actually fired in these 'pyres'. This may also explain the lack of lipid residues in the ceramics: the residues may have been burnt out or the vessels may have been fired and immediately buried. Once more we must be careful not to group all these vessels under the same interpretive umbrella.

Many cups are also incomplete. Restoration makes the quantification of this difficult and the retrieval strategies of earlier excavations may account for much of the incompleteness of some vessels. Nevertheless it would appear that many of the cups that accompanied burials were incomplete or otherwise imperfect. Were they deliberately 'killed' or 'cremated'? This may have been a necessity to ensure that they were suitable for the accompanying of the dead.

More work needs to be done on the contexts and associations of these vessels. A re-analysis of the associated cremated remains is now due. A re-assessment of other accompanying vessels is also needed. As archaeologists we record pots in drawings as if they were complete. We draw the 'best view'. Excavation reports rarely mention what proportion of the vessel was recovered. Were all pots broken or rendered imperfect when accompanying burials? Is there a difference in completeness between vessels from inhumations and cremations? Between large vessels and cups? Despite the large amount of excellent research that has taken place on Bronze Age ceramics over recent years, it seems time for a re-assessment from a technological rather than typological viewpoint.

The fate of the second cup from Gilchorn, Angus, teaches us a salutary lesson. Alexander Hutcheson records the discovery of urns and cups from Mr Bell's farm at Gilchorn near Arbroath (Hutcheson 1891). Hutcheson illustrated the Collared Urn and the small Biconical Cup recovered by the farmer but 'on making enquiries… subsequently learned that another small urn of a different shape was also found in the larger urn'. They went to the farmhouse kitchen to retrieve the cup but discovered that Mrs Bell 'dreading a visit of the spirit of the "craetur" at wis buried there seekin' its cuppie' had thrown the 'cuppie' into the fire as the best means known to her of preventing the advent of such a very undesirable visitor' (*ibid.*, 451-2). Fragments of the second vessel, which was plainly seen to have 'passed through the fire', were recovered from the farm midden. How very archaeological!

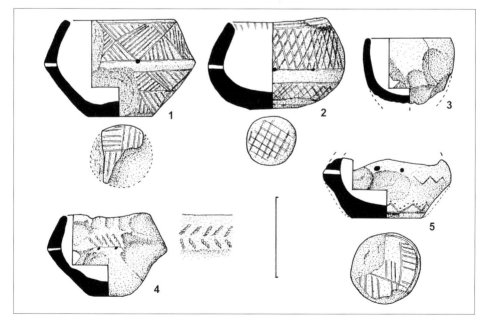

97 Firing wasters amongst Scottish Cups. 1 Carnousie, 2 Brackmont Mill, 3 Kirkburn, 4 Crailing Hall, 5 Coulter. Scale = 5cm

98 Firing wasters amongst Scottish cups. 1 Wester Bucklyvie, 2 Coulter, 3 Crailing Hall, 4 Brackmont Mill, 5 Dighty Water, 6 Kirkburn. Scales in cms. *Photos by kind permission of the Trustees of the National Museums of Scotland: copyright reserved*

ACKNOWLEDGEMENTS

Sincere thanks are due to Ian Longworth who, with characteristic kindness and grace, allowed me free access to his corpus of cups. This corpus forms the underlying database for this study. The Society of Antiquaries of Scotland generously grant-aided costs involved in museum visits throughout Scotland and I am grateful to the regional museum curators of Scotland for answering queries and for their helpfulness during my visits. Dr Ben Stern of the Department of Archaeological Sciences at the University of Bradford undertook the residue analysis which was funded by the British Academy. I have also benefited from discussions with Ole Stilborg (University of Lund), Carol Allen and members of the *Prehistoric Ceramics Research Group*. Special thanks go to my fellow editor, Alison Sheridan, for not only freely supplying her ideas on these vessels, radiocarbon dates and photographs, but also facilitating access to the collections of the National Museums of Scotland and pointing out the Gilchorn quotation.

BIBLIOGRAPHY

Abercromby, J., 1912 *A Study of the Bronze Age Pottery of Great Britain and Ireland and its Associated Grave Goods.* Oxford: Clarendon Press.

Allen C. & Hopkins, D., 2000 Bronze Age accessory cups from Lincolnshire: Early Bronze Age pot? *Proceedings of the Prehistoric Society*, 66, 297–318.

Annable, K. & Simpson, D.D.A., 1964 *Guide Catalogue of the Neolithic and Bronze Age Collections in Devizes Museum.* Devizes: Wiltshire Archaeological and Natural History Society.

Anon., 1859 Donations to the Museum. *Proceedings of the Society of Antiquaries of Scotland*, 3 (1857-9), 185.

Ashbee, P., 1985 The excavation of Amesbury Barrows 58, 61a, 61 and 72. *Wiltshire Archaeological and Natural History Magazine*, 79, 39-91.

Barclay, A., 2002 Ceramic Lives. In Hill, J.D. & Woodward, A. (eds), *Prehistoric Britain: The Ceramic Basis*, 85-95. Oxford: Oxbow & The Prehistoric Ceramics Research Group.

Barclay, G. & Russell-White, C.J., 1993 Excavations in the ceremonial complex of the fourth to second millennium BC at Balfarg/Balbirnie, Glenrothes, Fife. *Proceedings of the Society of Antiquaries of Scotland*, 123, 43-210.

Case, H.J., 1995 Beakers: Loosening a Stereotype. In Kinnes, I. & Varndell, G. (eds), *'Unbaked Urns of Rudely Shape': Essays on British and Irish Pottery for Ian Longworth*, 55-67. Oxford: Oxbow.

Childe, V.G. & Waterston, D., 1942 Further Urns and cremation burials from Brackmont Mill, near Leuchars, Fife. *Proceedings of the Society of Antiquaries of Scotland,* 76 (1941-2), 84-93.

Cormack, W.F., 1963 Burial site at Kirkburn. *Proceedings of the Society of Antiquaries of Scotland*, 96 (1962-3), 107-35.

Cowie, T., 1978 *Bronze Age Food Vessel Urns.* BAR British Series 55. Oxford: British Archaeological Reports.

Cowie, T. & Ritchie, G., 1991 Bronze Age burials at Gairneybank, Kinross-shire. *Proceedings of the Society of Antiquaries of Scotland*, 121, 95-110.

Fenton, M.B., 1988 The petrological identification of stone battle-axes and axe-hammers from Scotland. In Clough, T.H. McK. & Cummins, W.A. (eds), *Stone Axe Studies* Vol. 2, 92-132. Research Report 67. London: Council for British Archaeology.

Fraser, W., 1878 Notice of a small urn of the so-called 'Incense Cup' type found within a large urn at Blairgowrie in March last and now presented to the Museum. *Proceedings of the Society of Antiquaries of Scotland,* 12 (1876-8), 624.

Gibson, A.M., 1984 Problems of Beaker ceramic assemblages: the North British material. In Miket, R. & Burgess, C.B. (eds), *Between and Beyond the Walls. Essays on the Prehistory and History of North Britain in Honour of George Jobey*, 74-96. Edinburgh: John Donald.

Gibson, A.M., 1993 The excavation of two cairns and associated features at Carneddau, Carno, Powys, 1989-90. *Archaeological Journal*, 150, 1-45.

Gibson, A.M., 2002 *Prehistoric Pottery in Great Britain and Ireland*. Stroud: Tempus.

Gibson, A.M., 2003 Prehistoric pottery: people, pattern and purpose. Some observations, questions and speculations. In Gibson, A.M. (ed.) *Prehistoric Pottery: People, Pattern and Purpose,* v-xii. BAR International Series 1156 and PCRG Occasional Publication 4. Oxford: British Archaeological Reports & Prehistoric Ceramics Research Group.

Gibson, A.M., 2004. Burials and Beakers: seeing beneath the veneer in Late Neo-lithic Britain. In Czebreszuk, J. (ed.) *Similar But Different. Bell Beakers in Europe.*, 173-192. Poznan: Adam Mickiewicz University.

Gibson, A.M. & Woods, A.J., 1997 *Prehistoric Pottery for the Archaeologist* (2nd edition). London: Leicester University Press.

Greenwell, W., 1877 *British Barrows.* Oxford: Clarendon Press.

Henshall, A.S., 1972 *The Chambered Tombs of Scotland* Vol. 2. Edinburgh: Edinburgh University Press.

Hutcheson, A., 1891 Notice of the discovery and examination of a burial cairn of the Bronze Age at the farm of Gilchorn, near Arbroath. *Proceedings of the Society of Antiquaries of Scotland,* 25 (1890-1), 447-63.

Kavanagh, R.M., 1977 Pygmy cups in Ireland. *Journal of the Royal Society of Antiquaries of Ireland*, 107, 61-5.

Kilbride-Jones, H.E., 1935 Account of the excavation of the stone circle at Loanhead of Daviot, and of the standing stones at Cullerlie, Echt, both in Aberdeenshire, on behalf of H.M. Office of Works. *Proceedings of the Society of Antiquaries of Scotland*, 69 (1934-5), 168-193.

Longworth, I.H., 1983 The Whinny Liggate perforated wall cup and its affinities. In O'Connor, A.C. & Clarke, D.V. (eds), *From the Stone Age to the 'Forty-five*, 65-86. Edinburgh: John Donald.

Longworth, I.H., 1984 *Collared Urns of the Bronze Age in Great Britain and Ireland*. Cambridge: Cambridge University Press.

Lowe, G. & Anderson, J., 1894 Notice of a cemetery of graves and Cinerary Urns of the Bronze Age Recently Discovered at Kirkpark, Musselburgh. *Proceedings of the Society of Antiquaries of Scotland,* 28, 62-78.

Morrison, A., 1968 Cinerary Urns and Pygmy Vessels in South-west Scotland. *Transactions of the Dumfriesshire and Galloway Natural History & Antiquarian Society*, 45, 80-140.

Mortimer, J.R., 1905 *Forty Years' Researches in British and Saxon Burial Mounds of East Yorkshire*. London, Hull & York: A. Brown & Sons.

Reid, R.W., 1912 *Illustrated Catalogue of the Anthropological Museum, Marischal College, University of Aberdeen*. Aberdeen: The University Press.

Ritchie, G. & Welfare, H., 1983 Excavations at Ardnave, Islay. *Proceedings of the Society of Antiquaries of Scotland*, 113, 302-66.

Robertson-Mackay, R., 1987 The Neolithic causewayed enclosure at Staines, Surrey: excavations 1961-63. *Proceedings of the Prehistoric Society,* 53, 23-128.

Savory, H.N., 1980 *Guide Catalogue of the Bronze Age Collections.* Cardiff: National Museum of Wales.

Scott, L., 1951 The Colonisation of Scotland in the Second Millennium BC. *Proceedings of the Prehistoric Society*, 17(1), 16-82.

Sheridan, J.A., 1999 Grooved Ware from the Links of Noltland, Westray, Orkney. In Cleal, R. & MacSween, A. (eds), *Grooved Ware in Britain and Ireland*, 112-24. Oxford: Oxbow.

Sherratt, A., 1991 Sacred and profane substances: The ritual use of narcotics in Later Neolithic Europe. In Garwood, P., Jennings, D., Skeats, R. & Toms, J. (eds), *Sacred and Profane. Procedings of a Conference on Archaeology, Ritual and Religion, Oxford, 1989.* 50-64. Monograph 22. Oxford: Oxford Committee for Archaeology.

Sherratt, A., 1997 Sacred and profane substances: The ritual use of narcotics in Later Neolithic Europe. Reprinted with additions in Sherratt, *Economy and Society in Prehistoric Europe: Changing Perspectives*, 403-30. Edinburgh: Edinburgh University Press.

Simpson, D.D.A., 1965 Food Vessels in South-west Scotland. *Transactions of the Dumfriesshire and Galloway Natural History & Antiquarian Society*, 42, 25-50.

Smith, I.F., 1965 *Windmill Hill and Avebury.* Oxford: Clarendon Press.

Smith, J.A., 1872 Notice of a Cinerary Urn, containing a small-sized urn (in which there were the bones of a child), discovered in Fifeshire; with notes of similar small and cup-like vessels, in the Museum of the Society of Antiquaries of Scotland. *Proceedings of the Society of Antiquaries of Scotland*, 9 (1870-2), 189-207.

Stern, B., Heron, C., Serpico, M. & Bourriau, J., 2000 A comparison of methods for establishing fatty acid concentration gradients across potsherds: a case study using Late Bronze Age Canaanite amphorae. *Archaeometry*, 42(2), 399-414.

Stone, J.F.S., 1949 Some Grooved-Ware Pottery from the Woodhenge area. *Proceedings of the Prehistoric Society*, 15, 122-7.

Woodward, A., 2000 *British Barrows: A Matter of Life and Death.* Stroud: Tempus.

POSTSCRIPT

Since writing this article another catastrophic firing waster has been recognised in the Kelvingrove collections, Glasgow.

18

AN IMPORTANT CHILD'S BURIAL
FROM DOUNE, PERTH AND KINROSS,
SCOTLAND

DAWN McLAREN

INTRODUCTION

In 1957 a short note (Hamilton 1957) was published recording the discovery of a short cist at Doune in Perth & Kinross *(99)*. The cist contained an inhumation burial of a child accompanied by a miniature battle-axe, a small Food Vessel and a fragment of a second, larger Food Vessel *(100 & 101)*. This article was, however, little more than a note reporting the circumstances of the find. It did not attempt any discussion of the significance of the burial assemblage nor of its wider implications. Nearly 50 years after it was first reported analysis of the grave assemblage has shown that it is unusual in several respects. This piece is an attempt to situate this important grave in its wider context.

Preliminary study of battle-axes, based on the lists of Roe (1966) and Simpson (1990) and focused largely on size and find location, indicates the existence of regional differences. It suggests that miniature battle-axes are a distinct and significant variant of this important Bronze Age artefact. Despite the reduction in scale, the miniature battle-axes can still be seen to retain a symbolic function indicative of the status and wealth of the individual. The association of a miniature battle-axe with the child at Doune suggests that this individual was considered to be a significant member of the community. This is reinforced by the identification of the fragmentary Food Vessel as a relic or 'special pot' with an extended biography and special significance. Its inclusion within this mortuary context, the burial of the child, represented an opportunity for lineage ties and social boundaries to be reaffirmed by the living community. This fragment was recovered from the damaged end of the cist and the adjacent scree. These circumstances raise the possibility that this represents what was once a complete pot in the cist. Such a view would not materially alter the interpretations of it offered here.

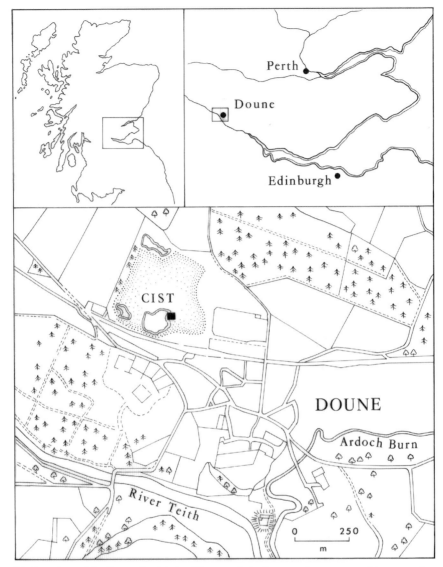

99 Location of the Doune burial site. The actual site has now been removed by quarrying. *Map drawn by Marion O'Neil*

IDENTIFYING THE CHILD'S WORLD

Interest in identifying the world of children in the archaeological record has dramatically increased since Lillehammer's (1989) pioneering article. This new concern with the archaeology of children can be seen to stem from the growing influence of feminist thinking on archaeological interpretations. It has formed part of wider attempts at making visible the social groups that had previously been ignored, overlooked or considered unrecognisable within the archaeological record (Sofaer-Derevenski 1997).

The apparent invisibility of children in the archaeological record was previously attributed to problems of preservation or failure to identify the remains of children during excavation. Certainly, the conspicuous absence of children from the archaeological burial record was formerly assumed to mean that children were not considered important enough to their society to be afforded formal burial. But to state that remnants of the child's world are too difficult to identify in an already fragmentary archaeological record or that factors of preservation have meant that children have all but disappeared from view can now be seen as attempts to over-simplify and dismiss the problem. Scott believes that our marginalisation of the prehistoric child is the result of 'our own cultural association of infants with the female and the domestic [which] has effectively rendered them unworthy of serious academic study' (1992, 82). Despite this recent increase in interest, children remain peripheral to most archaeological interpretations.

The culturally constructed qualities of the terms 'child' and 'childhood' have been extensively discussed by Sofaer-Derevenski (1994; 1997; 2000). Children, in our modern, socially constructed, westernised view, are seen to embody our hopes and expectations for the future. But Mizoguchi reminds us 'that the position of a particular child within a group hierarchy may be constituted by reference to that of their parents and ancestors' (2000, 142) and can, therefore, also be regarded as an embodiment of the past. This means that children can be viewed as potent symbols for the life of the community in general, representing links to the past, present and future. When these powerful symbols are removed by death, a unique occasion when 'social roles are publicly renewed and reinforced' (Sofaer-Derevenski 1994, 23) is created. It can be expected that these key symbolic issues will be brought to the forefront in mortuary rituals. These concerns may then be addressed and communicated through mortuary practice and the treatment of the child in a burial context. The way that children were buried, and what grave goods were interred with them, was deliberately selected by the adult community. Such burials will hold valuable information about the social attitudes of the adult population to children in society.

A recent re-assessment of the skeletal remains from the Doune burial (Koon & McCulloch 2003, 50-2) has confirmed that it was the inhumation of a child of 7 years ± 24 months, and a bone from this burial has just been dated to 3400 ± 35 BP (SUERC-2869, 1870-1530 cal BC at 2σ: Sheridan, A., pers. com.) This confirmation of the deceased's age, together with the unusual grave goods, suggests that we have here a grave with potential wider implications.

Miniature Battle-Axes

The miniature battle-axe from Doune is of Roe's 'intermediary' type (1966, 207) with a rounded butt. It is made of quartz-rich sandstone (S. Miller pers.

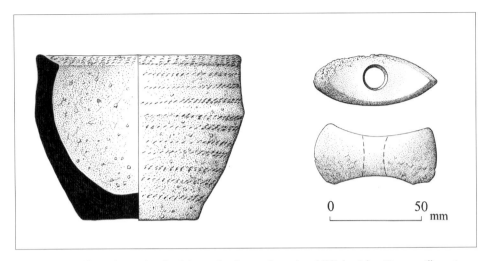

100 The small Food Vessel and miniature battle-axe from the child's burial at Doune. *Illustration by Marion O'Neil*

comm.) with polish remaining on one side of the battle-axe and on the upper surface. The stone itself is characteristic of the region so is most likely to be locally derived. The calcite cement that binds together the quartz inclusions is very poorly consolidated, indicating that the stone would always have been too fragile to be put to any vigorous use. One side of the object is severely eroded, most likely as the result of slightly acidic rainwater percolating into the cist. It is 66mm in length, 31mm wide at the rounded ends, and 21mm wide at the perforation. It has a thickness of 3mm at the cutting edge, 27mm at the rounded butt and 27mm at the perforation. The central cylindrical perforation is 14mm in diameter. Although this battle-axe is frequently referred to and quoted in the literature (e.g. Sharman 2000, 86) its miniature nature and the significance of this has passed without comment.

WHAT DEFINES A MINIATURE BATTLE-AXE?

A distinction needs to be drawn between small battle-axes and those that can be considered miniatures. Roe's article (1966, 201) described battle-axes being between 3.1in (79mm) and 7in (178mm) in length although several examples within her catalogue are smaller than this. Because Roe was concerned with creating a typology using a classification based on shape, the size of particularly small examples was not commented on. A preliminary reanalysis of Roe's (1966) and Simpson's (1990) catalogues based on size and find location has shown that distinct clusters of miniature battle-axes, ranging in length from 60-85 mm, exist in Scotland and Wales. There is no equivalent evidence of miniaturisation of battle-axes in Ireland. In England, the majority of battle-axes are between 100-160mm in length. But there are several examples smaller than

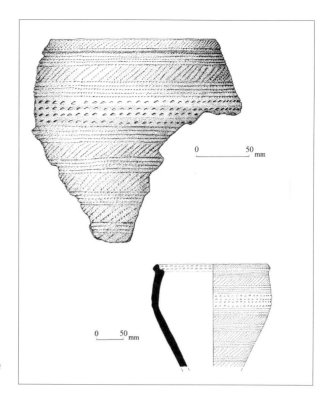

101 The fragment of Food Vessel from the child's burial at Doune, with reconstruction of the probable form of the vessel in an unbroken state. *Illustration by Marion O'Neil*

this although there is no indication of the distinct miniature groups seen in Scotland and Wales. (*102 & 103*) demonstrate the existence of distinct groupings of miniature battle-axes, with lengths between 60 and 85mm, among the finds from Scotland and Wales.

A Review of Miniature Battle-Axes and their Contexts

Examples are listed by country, in order of size.

Scotland

Sumburgh, Shetland (Sharman 2000, 67, fig. 29 no. 723). 34mm. Settlement. The excavators suggest that this is an Early/Middle Bronze Age type but was found in Late Bronze Age levels. Sharman suggested that it is a possible heirloom and that it could have functioned as an amulet, ornament or toy (2000, 86).

Ness of Gruting, Shetland (Calder 1956, 392). 57mm. Unperforated. Settlement.

Doune, Perth & Kinross. 66mm. Inhumation of between five- and eight-year-old child with two Food Vessels, one small and the larger represented only by a fragment when found. Discussed in this article.

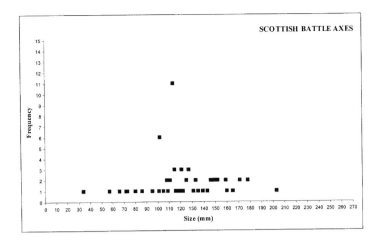

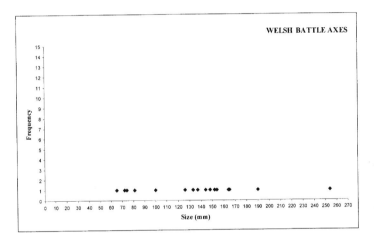

102 Scottish and Welsh battle-axes. The positions on the graph indicate length and frequency

Broken example from Ness of Gruting, Shetland (Calder 1956, 392). This axe was broken in half across the central perforation but symmetry may reasonably be assumed: estimated length is 72mm. Settlement.

Kirkcolm, Low Glengyre, Dumfries & Galloway (Mann 1923, 98-103, fig. 2; Longworth 1984, 297, no. 1800 & pl. 244b). 73mm. Found near to, but not directly associated with, a disturbed cremation burial of a child. The miniature battle-axe was found in 1907 as a stray find but further investigation of the area at a later date revealed a disturbed cremation burial. Mann believed the battle-axe was associated with this burial (1923, 98). A small stone-lined pit with an upright Collared Urn was found containing the cremated remains of a child 'certainly over eight, probably over 12 years of age' (Mann 1923, 101). The Cinerary Urn had been damaged by ploughing. Beside it was an accessory vessel (58mm high), also containing cremated remains. A thumbnail scraper of flint and two small flint flakes were also found; all were fire damaged. The

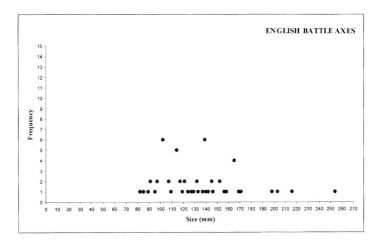

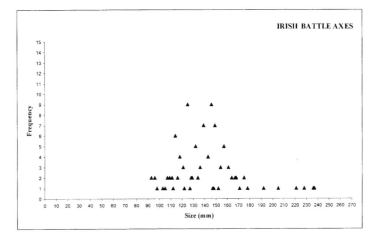

103 English and
Irish battle-axes.
The positions on
the graph indicate
length and
frequency

battle-axe is reported to have been found 31ft (9.45m) from the centre of the
larger urn (Mann 1923, 100) and Longworth (1984, 297) does not accept the
association.

Near Skara Brae, Orkney. (Unpublished: NMS X.HA 702). 80mm. Unperforated. Stray find.

Skoonan, Evie, Orkney. (Purchases for the museum, *Proceedings of the Society
of Antiquaries of Scotland*, 68 (1933-4), 19). Approximately 60% of the length
remains (43mm) but symmetry may be assumed suggesting full length would
not have exceeded 80mm. Stray find.

PoltallochEstate, Argyll. (NMSX.HP026) 86mm. Stray find.

An interesting aspect of the settlement finds of miniature battle-axes is that the
majority are from Shetland and, with the notable exception of the example
from Sumburgh, are broken or unfinished. Finds of broken stone maceheads

from Orkney have previously been noted by Callander (1931, 91-5) who dismissed the possibility of breakage in use because of the lack of any evidence of wear suggesting that they were functional pieces. But he noted that if they were found in a mortuary context in this condition it would be assumed that they had been broken deliberately with ritual significance. His emphasis on context as a frame for explanation enabled him to avoid the key question. In the absence of evidence of use, how are we to explain the breakage of such solid stone pieces? Sharman's suggestion (2000, 86) that the miniature battle-axe from Sumburgh was an heirloom raises the possibility that other examples were also heirlooms or relics for in such circumstances the fact that they were broken would not necessarily have impaired their continuing significance. The unfinished and broken examples from Ness of Gruting (Calder 1956, 392) could equally well introduce the possibility of damage during manufacture.

WALES

Wrexham, Denbighshire (Savory 1980, 94). 72mm. Perforation was not fully completed. Found in the River Clywedog.

Llanrhian, Pembrokeshire (Allen 1903). 74mm. It was found amongst debris thrown out from a large cist under a barrow. The cist contained an inhumation burial. Allen suggested that it was 'too small, and the edge too blunt to be used as a warlike weapon, and was most likely worn as an amulet or an ornament' (1903, 229).

Teifiside, Ceredigion (Peate 1925, 206). Although it is 81mm in length, it is included here because it appears to form part of the group of miniatures even though lying strictly outside the size range. Stray find.

In this context it is worth noting the battle-axe from Garthbeibio, Powys (Wheeler 1923). Although it falls just outside the miniature cluster (being 99mm in length), the find circumstances of this battle-axe are of interest. It was found during the excavation of Foel Cairn, Caeerwyd, Garthbeibio in a cist associated with the primary burial, a cremation of a nine-year-old child. Associated with the burial was this small battle-axe, a hammerstone and three flint flakes. The cist itself was of an unusual form being 6ft (1.83m) long and made up of several small flagstones and river boulders (Wheeler 1923, 280-1).

WHAT IS THE SIGNIFICANCE OF A MINIATURE BATTLE-AXE?

Park (1998, 275) indicates that miniature representations of symbolic items formed an integral part of the Inuit shaman's kit, suggesting the possible magico-religious significance of miniature items. Ethnographic examples from Inuit societies in Greenland (Park 1998, 275) and burial evidence from Bronze Age Scandinavia show that there are instances of specially manufactured, small-scale objects that are interred in a grave as the representation of a full-scale object (Lillehammer 1989). Similarly, miniature versions of pots and battle-axes have been noted within burial assemblages in Late Neolithic Corded Ware burials in Bohemia (Turek 2000). In such contexts these miniatures can be seen to be specially produced funerary objects. However, the presence of miniature battle-axes in Scottish settlement contexts (Calder 1956) suggests that British examples may have served a wider range of functions. Certainly, they appear to require a more complex interpretation than just that of representational items.

Further, most battle-axes in Scotland in burial contexts are associated with cremation burials. The inclusion of one with the inhumation burial of a child at Doune is, therefore, unusual. It provides more of an echo of the common association of elaborate battle-axes and Food Vessels with inhumation burials in the rich barrow burials of Wessex (Case 2003, 177).

There is no evidence in the form of observed wear patterns to suggest that these were functional items (Callander 1931, 94) and the miniature battle-axe from Doune was made from a stone that would be too soft and fragile to withstand being put to any practical use. Although designed for display, it is clear from their size that these miniatures were too large to be considered beads or pendants. One exception to this is the example from the barrow Wilsford G7 (Case 2003, 177). Here a large collection of various types of beads and pendants were found associated with the central primary inhumation. Among them was a pendant made from jet in the shape of a battle-axe. Being less than 80mm in length it conforms to the criteria suggested here as the definition of miniature battle-axes. But its extremely small size (30mm in length) and the use of jet suggests that this example is more likely to have been intended as a pendant or bead. It should, therefore, not be considered as part of the miniature battle-axe group.

Full-sized battle-axes have an accepted ceremonial and ritual use acting as a powerful symbol of wealth, power and social status. These easily recognisable objects reflect the power of the individual having them but could also have been a means whereby that power was legitimised. These small-scale versions must inevitably contain resonances of the meanings inherent in the larger examples. But at the same time they could take on a meaning of their own if they are regarded as a charm as well as a symbol. Perhaps the situation was similar to children from Inuit societies in Greenland who were seen to be vulnerable to malign supernatural forces and wore amulets in an attempt to counter these evil powers (Park 1998, 273). The frequent association of quartz stones with Bronze Age burial contexts (e.g. West Water Reservoir, Scottish Borders (Hunter 2000, 124-5), Beech Hill House, Perth & Kinross (Stevenson 1995, 204)) clearly implies a symbolic purpose. Could it be that the deliberate selection of a stone with a high white quartz content imbued the battle-axe from Doune with a further symbolic quality?

Sharman suggested that the miniature battle-axe from Sumburgh, Shetland could have been a child's toy (2000, 86). This, and the association of the Doune example with a young child, make it easy to assume that all miniature battle-axes were children's toys. We should be aware that our modern, westernised notion of the purpose of a 'toy' should not be considered universal, loaded as it is with preconceived notions. The *Oxford English Dictionary* defines a toy as:

> Toy 1. n. thing to play with, especially for children; trinket or curiosity, trifling thing or thing meant only for amusement. 2.a. that is a toy; (of dog) of diminutive breed; hardly deserving the name, not meant for serious use. 3. v. i. Play or fiddle or dally with (thing, or idea etc.).

This definition rather ignores the potential educational attributes of such an item. As Lillehammer reminds us 'a child's plaything[s] must not necessarily be restricted to objects which do not function in the adult world' (1989, 100). Our modern conception of toys as means of distraction for children limits our understanding of the role that play can have in socialising children and familiarising them with skills that will be fundamental in adult life. Describing objects as toys runs the real risk, then, that we create an image dominated by play as distraction. But we cannot see the miniature battle-axe as a 'toy' if that means that we detach it from the significance of the full-sized object. If these miniature battle-axes were toys, what would be learnt through interaction with such an object? Sillar notes that 'children frequently learn through imitating aspects of the adult world in play; in doing so, they learn the limitations of the physical world but they may also try modifications of the techniques or ideas used by their parents. Thus children's play is potentially a time and place for generating new cultural and material forms as they learn to reproduce and re-create society' (Sillar 1994, 49). All of this suggests that the definition of these objects as toys is too simple an explanation for miniature battle-axes. It is important to note in this context that battle-axes small enough to be viewed as possible toys have been found associated with adult burials, for example at Thirkel Low, Derbyshire (Ward 1897, 263-6) where the battle-axe was some 85mm in length.

Miniature stone implements are not restricted to battle-axes. Miniature axes and maceheads have also been found. Two are particularly worthy of note. At Glenhead, also at Doune but on the southern side of the Ardoch Burn, a miniature macehead was recovered from a burial. It was associated with a Food Vessel containing the inhumed remains of a female aged between 15 and 21 years (Koon & McCulloch 2003, 75-6) and at Brownstone Farm, Kingswear, Devon, a miniature greenstone axe was found within a cist at the centre of a barrow. Close by was the cremation burial of a ten-year-old child (Rogers 1947).

THE POTTERY

Instances of inhumation burials with multiple vessels are well known, for example Balblair, Highland (Hanley & Sheridan 1994) and Little Gonerby, Lincolnshire (Phillips 1933, 128). Some of these burials involve children. But the fragmentary nature of the larger Food Vessel in the burial at Doune suggests that we should not necessarily consider this as two *complete* pots. Rather we could see the burial as having one small Food Vessel and one relic in the form of a fragment of a pot. This opens out two points for discussion: the presence of small pots in the burials of children and the significance of the possible 'heirloom'.

SMALL POTS

The inclusion of small pots is a common feature of the inhumation burial of children, especially in Scotland, for example at Broomend of Crichie (Davidson 1868; Ritchie 1920) and Nether Criggie, both Aberdeenshire (Kirk & McKenzie 1955), and Ireland (O'Donnabháin & Brindley 1990). Although it would be convenient to interpret the small pots in many of these graves as children's toys or as an item designed specifically with children in mind, this fails to explain their presence within the adult graves (e.g. Gairneybank, Perth & Kinross: Cowie & Ritchie 1991, 105). Although their occurrence within adult inhumation burials does not seem to occur with the frequency we see in the children's graves, their presence emphasises that assumptions that these diminutive pots are to be associated with the material culture of children alone should treated with caution. They may not be children's toys but it seems as though, in some instances at least, they were of a size considered appropriate to be included in the burial of a child. Correlation between size of pot and age of individual has been identified at the large Bronze Age cremation cemetery at Pasture Lodge, Lincolnshire (Allen *et al.* 1987). Here it was shown that children were interred within pots, the size of which seemed to reflect the age of the child with the youngest child interred within the smallest pot (Allen *et al.* 1987, 187).

HEIRLOOMS

In Hamilton's original report (1957) he commented that a large fragmentary Food Vessel was associated with the grave. In keeping with the practice of the time, this fragment was presented in a reconstruction drawing showing it as complete vessel. But recent analysis by Woodward, such as her consideration of the 'special pots' within the Lockington hoard (2000a), and grave goods associated with Wessex barrow burials (2000b) suggests heirlooms or relics are a more common feature of Bronze Age material culture than has previously been acknowledged (Woodward 2002). In light of these ideas, a re-analysis of the significance of the fragmentary Food Vessel within the burial at Doune is now possible.

Woodward notes several examples of special pots being associated with burials (2000, 59-60). These pots are often broken and damaged and suggested an extended biography prior to deposition within the grave context. The significance of the inclusion of an heirloom within a mortuary context is emphasised by Lillios' suggestion that 'heirlooms serve to objectify memories and histories, acting as mnemonics to remind the living of their link to a distant, ancestral past' (1999, 236).

The fragmentary pot from Doune may not necessarily have been that ancient when it was incorporated into the burial so that the terms heirloom and relic need to be used in this context with caution. Even if it was not particularly old, it must have been considered special to have been retained in a fragmentary condition and deposited in a burial. A pot only a couple of generations removed from the burial itself may nevertheless have been considered a relic and a link to the past. The fragment may well be an attempt to legitimise and emphasise the status of the individual it was buried with. By burying this special pot within this grave it does suggest that the community was acknowledging the child's lineage and using the pot to delineate social relations. Perhaps, the significance of the pot is not related directly to the child itself but to the remaining living family members and community. Burials are often seen as an opportunity to re-establish and re-affirm social ties and boundaries. By acknowledging the child as part of the community through the interment of a special relic of social significance an opportunity is created for community bonds to be strengthened. If the child was of powerful lineage the interment of the special pot in the grave may have created an opportunity for kin members to acknowledge their connection to the child and as a result re-affirm their claim to that lineage. The potential symbolic value of the association of a relic with an individual in a burial context should not be undervalued in light of the suggestion that 'Our ancient ancestors may have discovered that, in defending territorial claims or legitimating unequal rights to land or other critical resources, heirlooms, as tangible links to their ancestors were their most powerful weapon of all' (Lillios 1999, 258).

The burial of a child at Beckhampton, Wiltshire (Young 1950) shows that the association of children and relics is not restricted to the burial assemblage at Doune. But it is far from common. This burial had an inhumation of a child associated with a severely damaged beaker, a single sherd from another pot, two flints placed directly under each side of the pelvis and a unique carved chalk plaque. It is interesting to note that no attempt was made to hide the obviously damaged condition of the pot when it was placed within the grave as it positioned with the broken surface facing outwards (Young 1950, 314), almost as though deliberately displaying its fragmentary state. The abraded and worn fractured edges imply that this pot had been in circulation for some time prior to deposition. This confirms that the practice of interring 'special pots' within funerary deposits was not restricted to adults only but extended to funerary rites involving children.

The cremation burial of an adult and child at Noranbank, Tannadice (Taylor 1998, 38) shows that the phenomenon of using 'special pots' can be restricted to the single special vessel. Here the cremated remains were contained within a broken Cinerary Urn and, again, the focus seems to have been on the broken condition of the vessel. The base of the Collared Urn in which the calcined bones were contained was broken prior to deposition. A small slab of stone had been placed over the break to seal and protect it. Such treatment suggests that this pot was not a simple and convenient repository for burial but was considered special prior to deposition. It must have been recognised as such when interred as part of the burial.

CONCLUSION

The inclusion of a battle-axe and Food Vessel in the burial at Doune is consistent with the treatment afforded to adult burials but with several specific differences. The small pot and miniature battle-axe found in this child's grave seems to reflect the adult world but in miniature. This special consideration suggests that the child was seen as distinct, but not separate, from the adult world. Although some of the items with this inhumation were perhaps specifically chosen for the child because of their size and form, children do not appear to have had a defined material culture of their own. The overall lack of evidence for toys within the surviving material culture of the Bronze Age emphasises that childhood in prehistory was not defined in terms that we would recognise today. It would be easy to interpret the small Food Vessel and miniature stone implement associated with this grave as the child's toys or as items designed specifically with the child in mind. But to do so would fail to explain the presence of comparable forms in adult graves nor give sufficient recognition of the battle-axe's role as an acknowledged symbolic object. The inclusion of the heirloom, an item whose importance and significance would have been recognisable to the community, confirms the wealth and status that the battle-axe indicates. It appears to have been used as a material representation of the child's important lineage and its addition to the grave may have created an opportunity for kin-members to re-affirm and legitimise their position in society by reference to the child as the focus of the mortuary rituals. This evidence of ascribed status suggests that Hertz' observation that 'the death of a stranger, a slave or a child will go almost unnoticed; it will arouse no emotion, occasion no ritual' (1960, 76) cannot be applicable to Bronze Age children in Britain and Ireland.

ACKNOWLEDGEMENTS

The research for this article was made possible by the financial assistance of the A.R. and K.M. MacLaren Trust, to whom I am especially grateful. My particular thanks go to David Clarke for his support and encouragement. Special thanks go to

Marion O'Neil for illustrations 99-101 and to Suzanne Miller for the geological identification of the miniature battle-axe from Doune. I would also like to thank Alison Sheridan, Trevor Cowie, Fraser Hunter, Ian Ralston and Craig Angus for their help and support.

BIBLIOGRAPHY

Allen, C.S.M., Harman, M. & Wheeler, H., 1987 Bronze Age cremation cemeteries in the East Midlands. *Proceedings of the Prehistoric Society*, 53, 187-221.

Allen, J.R., 1903 Note on a perforated stone axe-hammer found in Pembrokeshire. *Archaeologia Cambrensis*, 6 ser, 3, 224-38.

Calder, C.S.T., 1956 Report on the discovery of numerous Stone Age house-sites in Shetland. *Proceedings of the Society of Antiquaries of Scotland*, 89 (1955-6), 340-97.

Callander, J.G., 1931 Notes on (1) certain prehistoric relics from Orkney, and (2) Skara Brae: its culture and its period. *Proceedings of the Society of Antiquaries of Scotland*, 65 (1930-1), 78-14.

Case, H., 2003 Beaker presence at Wilsford 7. *Wiltshire Archaeological & Natural History Magazine*, 96, 161-94.

Cowie, T. & Ritchie, G., 1991 Bronze Age burials at Gairneybank, Kinross-shire. *Proceedings of the Society of Antiquaries of Scotland*, 121, 95-109.

Davidson, C.B., 1868 Notice of further stone kists found at Broomend, near the Inverurie papermills. *Proceedings of the Society of Antiquaries of Scotland*, 7 (1866-8), 115-18.

Hamilton, J.R.C., 1957 Food Vessel cist at Doune, Perthshire. *Proceedings of the Society of Antiquaries of Scotland*, 90 (1956-7), 231-4.

Hanley, R. & Sheridan, J.A., 1994 A Beaker cist from Balblair, near Beauly, Inverness District. *Proceedings of the Society of Antiquaries of Scotland*, 124, 129-39.

Hertz, R., 1960 *Death and the Right Hand*. London: Cohen & West.

Hughes, G., (ed.) 2000 *The Lockington Gold Hoard. An Early Bronze Age Barrow Cemetery at Lockington, Leicestershire*. Oxford: Oxbow.

Hunter, F.J., 2000 Excavation of an Early Bronze Age cemetery and other sites at West Water Reservoir, West Linton, Scottish Borders. *Proceedings of the Society of Antiquaries of Scotland*, 130, 115-82.

Kirk, W. & McKenzie, J., 1955 Three Bronze Age cist burials in north-east Scotland. *Proceedings of the Society of Antiquaries of Scotland*, 88 (1953-5), 1-14.

Koon, H. & McCulloch, T., 2003 *An Evaluation of Bronze Age Human Remains held by the National Museums of Scotland*. Unpublished Ms held in Department of Archaeology, National Museums of Scotland.

Lillehammer, G., 1989 A child is born. The child's world in an archaeological perspective. *Norwegian Archaeological Review*, 22(2), 89-105.

Lillios, K.T., 1999 Objects of Memory: The ethnography and archaeology of heirlooms. *Journal of Archaeological Method & Theory*, 6, 235-62.

Longworth, I.H., 1984 *Collared Urns of the Bronze Age in Great Britain and Ireland*. Cambridge: Cambridge University Press.

Mann, L. McL., 1923 Discoveries in north-western Wigtownshire: cinerary urn and incense-cup and perforated axe-hammer: mould for bronze winged chisel: whetstone for stone axes: cup-marked rocks and boulder: apron of moss fibres. *Proceedings of the Society of Antiquaries of Scotland*, 57 (1922-3), 98-107.

Mizoguchi, K., 2000 The child as a node of past, present and future. In Derevenski, J.S. (ed.), 141-50.

Moore, J. & Scott, E., (eds), 1997 *Invisible People and Processes. Writing Gender and Childhood into European Archaeology*. London: Leicester University Press.

O'Donnabháin, B. & Brindley, A.L., 1990 The status of children in a sample of Bronze Age burials containing pygmy cups. *Journal of Irish Archaeology*, 5 (1989-90), 19-24.

Park, R.W., 1998 Size counts: the miniature archaeology of childhood in Inuit societies. *Antiquity*, 72, 269-81.

Peate, I.C., 1925 Some Teifiside holed stones. *Archaeol Cambrensis*, 7 ser., 5, 205-6.

Phillips, C.W., 1933 The present state of archaeology in Lincolnshire: part 1. *Archaeological Journal*, 90, 106-49.

Ritchie, J., 1920 The Stone Circle at Broomend of Crichie, Aberdeenshire. *Proceedings of the Society of Antiquaries of Scotland*, 54, 154-72.

Roe, F.E.S., 1966 The battle-axe series in Britain. *Proceedings of the Prehistoric Society*, 32, 199-245.

Rogers, E.H., 1947 The excavation of a barrow on Brownstone Farm, Kingswear. *Proceedings of the Devon Archaeological Exploration Society*, 3 (1937-47), 164-6.

Savory, H.N., 1980 *Guide Catalogue of the Bronze Age Collection, National Museum of Wales.* Cardiff: National Museum of Wales.

Scott, E., 1992 Images and contexts of infants and infant burials: some thoughts on some cross-cultural evidence. *Archaeological Review from Cambridge*, 11(1), 77-92.

Sharman, P., 2000 Steatite and other fine stone objects. In Downes, J. & Lamb, R. *Prehistoric Houses at Sumburgh in Shetland: Excavations at Sumburgh Airport 1964-74*, 65-8, 82-7. Oxford: Oxbow.

Sillar, B. 1994 Playing with God: Cultural perceptions of children, play and miniatures in the Andes. *Archaeological Review from Cambridge*, 13(2), 47-63.

Simpson, D.D.A. 1968 Food Vessels: associations and chronology. In Coles, J.M. & Simpson, D.D.A. (eds), *Studies in Ancient Europe: Essays Dedicated to Stuart Piggott*, 197-211. Leicester: Leicester University Press.

Simpson, D.D.A., 1990 The stone battle-axes of Ireland. *Journal of the Royal Society of Antiquaries of Ireland*, 120, 5-40.

Sofaer-Derevenski, J.S., 1994 Where are the children? Accessing children in the past. *Archaeological Review from Cambridge*, 13(2), 7-20.

Sofaer-Derevenski, J.S., 1997 Engendering children, engendering archaeology. In Moore, J. & Scott, E. (eds), 192-202.

Sofaer-Derevenski, J.S. (ed.), 2000 *Children and Material Culture*. London: Routledge.

Sofaer-Derevenski, J.S., 2000 Material culture shock. Confronting expectations in the material culture of children. In Derevenski, J.S. (ed.), 3-16.

Stevenson, S., 1995 The excavation of a kerbed cairn at Beech Hill House, Coupar Angus, Perthshire. *Proceedings of the Society of Antiquaries of Scotland*, 125, 197-235.

Taylor, D.B., 1998 Some previously unpublished prehistoric burials from Angus. *Tayside & Fife Archaeological Journal*, 4, 31-9.

Turek, J., 2000 Being a beaker child. The position of children in Late Eneolithic society. *Památky Archeologické, Supplementum 13– In memoriam Jan Rulf*, 424-38.

Ward, J., 1897 Further excavations in Barrows in the neighbourhood of Buxton, Derbyshire. *Proceedings of the Society of Antiquaries*, 2 Ser, 16 (1895-97), 261-7.

Wheeler, R.E.M., 1923 A tumulus at Garthbeibio, Montgomeryshire. *Archaeologia Cambrensis*, 7 Ser, 3, 279-90.

Woodward, A., 2000a The prehistoric pottery. In Hughes, G. *The Lockington Gold Hoard. An Early Bronze Age Barrow Cemetery at Lockington, Leicestershire*, 48-61. Oxford: Oxbow.

Woodward, A., 2000b *British Barrows: A Matter of Life and Death*. Stroud: Tempus.

Woodward, A., 2002 Beads and Beakers: heirlooms and relics in the British Early Bronze Age. *Antiquity*, 76, 1040-7.

Young, W.E.V., 1950 A Beaker interment at Beckhampton. *Wiltshire Archaeological & Natural History Magazine*, 53 (1949-50), 311-27.

19

A Landscape Analysis of the Topped Mountain Region, County Fermanagh, Northern Ireland

Ronan McHugh, Eileen Murphy and Barrie Hartwell

Introduction

The upland region of north-east County Fermanagh has long been recognised as an area rich in archaeological heritage. The area is characterised by a wide array of Neolithic and Bronze Age megalithic tombs, stone circles and mounds. At the heart of this region lies Mullyknock or Topped Mountain with its well-known burial cairn, which was investigated in 1897 by Thomas Plunkett and George Coffey (Plunkett & Coffey 1898). The richness of the archaeological remains in this area has already attracted official recognition and the Department of the Environment for Northern Ireland has designated a specific part of the region as an Area of Significant Archaeological Importance (ASAI). In spite of this, however, there has been little archaeological work carried out in the area in recent years. Our knowledge concerning the archaeology of the Topped Mountain region has mostly been derived from earlier work, mainly undertaken during the late nineteenth and early twentieth centuries. In general, however, this has centred on individual monuments (e.g. Wakeman 1875; 1878; Plunkett & Coffey 1898), and has taken little cognisance of the landscape as a whole. This realisation resulted in the development of a programme of collaborative work undertaken by members of the School of Archaeology and Palaeoecology, Queen's University Belfast, with the Topped Mountain Historical Society. The initial phase of this research has resulted in the detailed topographical survey, by total station, of the major monuments contained within the townland of Mountdrum. In addition, a further programme of research was undertaken during 2003, as part of a Masters programme, which attempted to gain a clearer understanding of the complex Neolithic-Bronze Age landscape of the Topped Mountain region (McHugh 2003). The objective of the paper is to provide a summary of the recent research that has been undertaken on the Topped Mountain landscape.

DEFINITION AND METHODOLOGY

At the onset of the study it was necessary to define its physical boundaries. The ASAI as defined by the Department of the Environment identifies the concentration of archaeological sites in the area. However, it is defined by modern boundaries, which would have had no significance in earlier times. The Northern Ireland Sites and Monuments Record (NISMR), maintained by the Environment and Heritage Service (EHS), contains a facility whereby a square vector can be described around a specific point in the landscape and

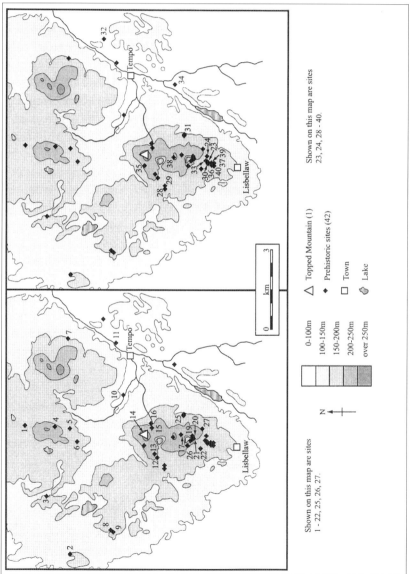

104 Opposite Distribution maps of the sites located within the Topped Mountain study area

the listed archaeological sites within the landscape can be identified. An area of 100km² was selected for the landscape survey, the centre point of which corresponded to the peak of Topped Mountain (OS grid ref H3114 4575). While it is acknowledged that this boundary is entirely notional, it nonetheless contains the main concentration of prehistoric archaeological sites in north-east Fermanagh and provides sufficient topographical diversity to ascertain whether this was a genuine factor in the location of monuments *(104)*. Within the area, 40 sites dating to the prehistoric period were recorded and these form the anthropogenic element of the Topped Mountain prehistoric landscape *(Table 8)*.

The survey also required a set methodology so that meaningful datasets could be accumulated and analysed. Although no particular methodology has been defined for the study of prehistoric landscapes, Cooney (1990, 742) has codified a series of criteria which have been used elsewhere in Ireland to analyse archaeological landscapes *(Table 9)*. These criteria were adopted for the purpose of this study.

Where some or all of these criteria have been employed in previous studies, such as by O'Brien (1999, 200), they have been supplemented by excavation work and dating evidence. Consequently, since the current research was based solely on topographical survey, it was decided to bolster these basic criteria. Thus, Tilley's (1996, 131) suggestion, that tombs situated within 500m of each other should constitute a cluster, was employed in the interpretation of the distance data. Equally, it was recognised that Criterion 6 – 'Distinct topographical location' – was relatively broad, and it was divided into a number of sub-criteria – altitude, soil type, view of the surrounding landscape, type of topographical setting and proximity to water source.

Soil and altitude have been used widely in the study of tomb siting and these aspects of the location were specifically addressed. Cooney (1979) recognised five topographical types of setting for megalithic tombs in County Leitrim. His approach was adopted for the current topographical analysis and the settings were classed either as hilltops, slopes, level plateaux or valley floors. In order to assess whether view was important to the monument builders, a visibility index was created *(Table 10)*.

All of the criteria discussed above were then applied to each site located within the study area and the results were combined so that a comprehensive and integrated impression of the Topped Mountain landscape could be gained.

INTERPRETATION AND DISCUSSION

From the outset, certain limitations were recognised. The NISMR is not designed to provide an exhaustive interpretation of the sites it records. Therefore it was necessary for a number of the sites to be reinterpreted in the field during the course of the survey (see *Table 8*). In addition, a proportion of the

NISMR NO.	Survey classification	Probable Period	Designation in Figure 109
FER 193:019	Court tomb	Neolithic	1
FER 193:021	Unclassified Megalithic tomb	Prehistoric	2
FER 193:024	Court tomb	Neolithic	3
FER 193:025	Round cairn	Bronze Age	4
FER 193:026	Stone Alignment	Bronze Age	5
FER 193:032	Standing stone	Bronze Age	6
FER 193:037	Standing stone	Prehistoric	7
FER 212:001	Court tomb	Neolithic	8
FER 212:002	Court tomb	Neolithic	9
FER 212:010	Stone Alignment	Bronze Age	10
FER 212:017	Standing stone	Bronze Age	11
FER 212:025	Standing stone	Bronze Age	12
FER 212:026	Standing stone	Bronze Age	13
FER 212:028	Round cairn	Bronze Age	14
FER 212:029	Round cairn	Bronze Age	15
FER 212:030	Stone circle	Bronze Age	16
FER 212:047	Round cairn	Bronze Age	17
FER 212:048	Standing stone	Bronze Age	18
FER 212:049	Round cairn	Bronze Age	19
FER 212:050	Round cairn	Bronze Age	20
FER 212:051	Wedge tomb	Bronze Age	21
FER 212:052	Unclassified megalith tomb	Prehistoric	22
FER 212:054	Wedge tomb	Bronze Age	23
FER 212:060	Court tomb	Neolithic	24
FER 212:077	Wedge tomb	Bronze Age	25
FER 212:080	Cairn	Prehistoric	26
FER 212:083	Stone circle	Bronze Age	27
FER 212:086	Alignment	Bronze Age	28
FER 212:087	Round Cairn	Bronze Age	29
FER 212:089	Unclassified megalithic tomb	Prehistoric	30
FER 212:101	Unclassified megalithic tomb	Prehistoric	31
FER 212:102	Fulacht fiadh	Bronze Age	32
FER 212:103	Fulacht fiadh	Bronze Age	33
FER 212:105	Cist burial	Bronze Age	34
FER 212:106	Stone circle	Bronze Age	35
FER 212:111	Stone circle and alignment	Bronze Age	36
FER 212:112	Stone circle and alignment	Bronze Age	37
FER 212:114	Round cairn	Bronze Age	38
FER 212:115	Wedge tomb	Bronze Age	39
FER 212:117	Stone circle and alignment	Bronze Age	40

Table 8 The Neolithic and Early Bronze Age sites of the Topped Mountain region

recorded sites are either no longer visible in the landscape or are in such a poor state of preservation as to defy accurate interpretation. The intervisibility criterion was problematic for the same reason and was also hampered by a dearth of information concerning the extent and nature of environment change that has occurred since the monuments were originally constructed and utilised.

What the survey does produce is an outline imprint of the landscape as it was when the final stone of the last of the prehistoric site was laid, probably during the Late Bronze Age. As is the situation today, there is no doubt that the region would have been dominated by the Topped Mountain uplands. This natural landform of hills and glacial hollows in the centre of the study area completely controls the way its immediate hinterland is viewed. The surviving archaeology suggests that the monument builders recognised this and perhaps capitalised on the natural terrain in order to reinforce the significance of the landscape. A cursory glance at *(104)* reveals a landscape dotted with archaeological sites, but with a large concentration located in a relatively small area to the south of Topped Mountain. The survey revealed that the monuments were not randomly distributed, but rather that there was a great degree of organisation and deliberate structuring of the landscape. This conscious organisation of space can be noted at different scales within the landscape as a whole.

The Micro-Scale – Individual Monuments

The smallest scale of anthropogenic activity is represented by the individual monuments themselves. As with similar monuments throughout the country, each of the individual sites no doubt represented a significant place, both as a

	Criterion
1	Distance between tombs
2	Orientation on a focal point
3	Presence of focal tomb/tombs
4	Intervisibility between tombs
5	Defined area
6	Distinct topographical location
7	Tombs of the same typological class

Table 9 Criteria used to recognise ritual landscapes in Ireland (cf. Cooney 1990)

Visibility Index	View	General guidelines for awarding visibility index value
4	Excellent	Where the monument was situated on a high peak with an uninterrupted panoramic view of the wider landscape.
3	Good	Where the immediate hinterland of the monument was visible, and there was also a view beyond the immediate locale.
2	Fair	Where the immediate topographical hinterland, such as a valley basin or a hilltop plateau was clear, but there was no view beyond this.
1	Poor	Where a slope or permanent landscape feature in immediate proximity to the monument obscured the view from the site.

Table 10 Visibility index used in the assessment of the view from the different monuments (cf. McHugh 2003, 52)

feat of construction and, more importantly, as a focus for individual rituals, ceremonies or meanings. The objective of the current paper is to address the landscape in its entirety, however, and a detailed analysis of the archaeology of these sites will not be presented. These individual sites represent the anthropogenic components of the landscape and therefore a broad understanding of each of the different elements is essential to the interpretation of the landscape as a whole.

The monuments listed in *Table 8* represent human activity in the Topped Mountain region for around 4,000 years of prehistory. On the one hand the presence of five court tombs suggests that the area was a centre of activity in the Early Neolithic, possibly as early as the fourth millennium BC (ApSimon 1986, 6). The occurrence of two *fulachta fiadh* (mounds of burnt stone), on the other hand, may indicate human activity as late as the early first millennium BC (Waddell 2000, 177) if not even later (see O'Neill forthcoming on examples from the historic period).

Unfortunately, few of the monuments in the region have been excavated so it is impossible to build up a clear picture of the precise developmental sequence within the landscape. However, excavations of two of the monuments in the region have revealed evidence which suggests longevity of use for the Topped Mountain sites. The Topped Mountain cairn (FER 212:028) is ostensibly Bronze Age, but produced finds which Williams and Gormley (2002, 100-01) considered to be Neolithic, while the Neolithic dual court tomb at Ballyreagh (FER 193:019) produced a possible Bronze Age urn which was considered to be indicative of 'later reoccupation' (Davies 1942, 88).

The Topped Mountain court tombs are characteristically dispersed and situated on thin, well-drained soils. It can therefore be surmised that the factors that motivated their construction mirrored those which drove the building of similar sites throughout the country. Beyond this, the story is less clear. Stone circles, alignments and wedge tombs are all monuments that characterise the Late Neolithic and Early Bronze Age, but there is no clear indication as to which came first in the area. This is clearly a problem as the site types indicate that this was the period of most intense activity. The waters are further muddied by the occurrence of round cairns, which are the most common site-type in the region. However, 'round cairns' are not even recognised as a particular monument type in Irish archaeology, and these could represent a diverse range of monuments from Neolithic passage tombs to Bronze Age burial mounds or even later constructions. Without a clearer understanding of these monuments, it is impossible to understand the precise chronology of this landscape.

Whatever part these sites played within the wider landscape, they may also have retained the individual ritual purposes associated with similar monuments throughout the country. Although they are in a relatively poor state of preservation, each of the four wedge tombs in the area, for example, exhibits dimensions consistent with wedge tombs throughout the country, while the orientation of each is within the 'remarkably consistent' west–north–west to south orientation discussed by Waddell (2000, 96). Equally, the three stone circles and alignments are constructed of many small stones as is typical of mid-Ulster sites, while the orientations of the alignments are broadly consistent with each other (Burl 1976). Again, this recalls other stone circle complexes (e.g. Beaghmore, County Tyrone and Drumskinny, County Fermanagh), where there is an inter-site consistency in orientation, even if no such pattern is evident on a wider scale (McConkey 1987, 8).

The area is host to two particular sites, however, which are worthy of discussion in their own right. The Topped Mountain cairn is well known in Irish archaeology. This monument is situated on the peak of Topped Mountain, some 277m above sea level. It is set in a conspicuous location and is visible for many kilometres in all directions. The cairn itself is sub-circular in form, measuring 31.5m north–south by 34m east–west and stands over 3m in height at its northern end. The significance of the monument is not confined to its physical aspect in the landscape and Plunkett and Coffey's excavations (1898) unearthed a number of finds. Two deposits of cremated bone were found in the body of the cairn, together with an array of flint scrapers and flakes. However, the most significant finds were from a stone cist situated in the south of the cairn. Here, the skeleton of a man was found with a decorated Vase Food Vessel, a bronze dagger with gold hilt-band and a deposit of cremated human bone. The latter has been dated to 3570±40 BP (GrA-14761, 2029-1773 cal BC at 2σ); it is unclear, however, whether the cremated remains were buried at the same time as the skeleton and the grave goods (Brindley 2001, 146-7). The importance of this site can be gauged from the fact that Topped Mountain is one of only four Irish Bronze Age burial sites which has produced gold artefacts and is the only such site north of County Kildare (Waddell 1990, 21).

Almost within the shadow of the site stands another monument that may also prove to be significant on a broader scale. Site FER 212:111, located in the townland of Mountdrum, consists of three concentric stone circles with two associated stone alignments *(105)*. While concentric stone circles are relatively common, with a possible twelve sites being recorded in Ulster alone (Burl 2000, 137), it is extremely rare to find examples with more than two concentric rings. A four-ringed concentric circle is recorded in the NISMR at Culvacullion, County Tyrone, but this monument is in poor preservation and does not present a clear parallel. At Mountdrum, although damaged and partially covered with peat, a number of radial stones can be seen aligned between the two inner rings to form a series of cist-like compartments.

While cists are known to be associated with Irish stone circles, they are usually found within the perimeter of the circle (e.g. Gortcorbies, County Londonderry), and the Mountdrum arrangement is difficult to parallel in this respect. However, an unusual monument at Meayll (Mull) Hill on the Isle of Man offers a tentative parallel to the Mountdrum circle.

This monument comprises an arrangement of 12 small chambers arranged as six opposed pairs with their side walls aligned concentrically and set within an outer circle of stones *(105)*. Thus, like the Mountdrum circle, it could be argued that the site has been set out on three concentric circles with the inner two taking the form of a series of compartmentalised stone boxes.

There are, however, a number of differences in the Meayll arrangement. The line of cists is discontinuous; each pair is associated with a short, radial, central passage; there is evidence of cairn material – possibly in the form of a ring bank – in which case the outer circle can be interpreted as a revetment; the associated pottery would place it in the Early and Middle Neolithic, considerably earlier than the dates conventionally associated with stone circles in mid-Ulster; and lastly, it has been argued that the Meayll Hill site falls within the passage grave tradition (Gale *et al.* 1997). At Mountdrum, the remnant peat shows no evidence of a previous cairn or cultural material so the comparison must remain tenuous.

Clearly, the Mountdrum stone circle is an unusual monument within an Irish context and one which demands further study in its own right. If a correlation between novelty and prestige is accepted, the presence of the triple-ring stone circle together with the discovery of the gold-pommelled dagger during the excavations at the Topped Mountain cairn may indicate that the landscape was of some significance in terms of its individual monuments as well as for the sheer density of their distribution.

Clustered Monuments and an Upland Cathedral?

The setting of a number of sites in such close proximity would, by itself, suggest that the Topped Mountain area was host to a prehistoric complex of some significance. The survey has endorsed this view and confirms that the distribution of sites on the landscape is not a random phenomenon. The second scale of structuring of the landscape is evident in the way that the concentration of sites is organised, both in relation to the other sites in the area and also to the natural landscape.

As stated above, Tilley's 500m criterion (1996, 131) was used to define apparent clusters of sites within the area. A cluster of sites was taken to include three or more monuments. The other sites in the area occurred either singly or in pairs. Three distinct clusters were identified using this measurement and these were investigated during the field survey. In the field, however, the arbitrary nature of the 500m criterion became clear; while it takes account of proximity, it ignores the actuality of the setting and the way in which the physicality of the landscape dictates how it is perceived. At Topped Mountain, the clustering of sites appears to be governed by the relationship of the monuments to the natural landscape features and, in particular, to three successive glacial basins. Two of these contain lakes – Topped Mountain Lake

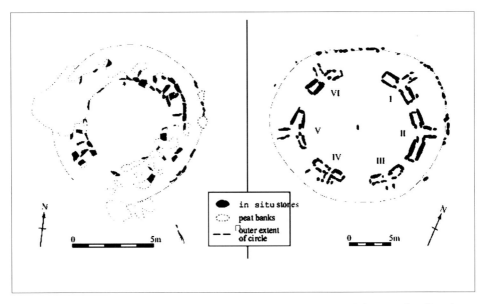

105 Plan of triple-ringed stone circle at Mountdrum (FER 212:111) and the Meayll Hill circle, Isle of Man. *After J. Chartrand as included in Gale* et al. *1997*

and Lough Skale – while the third, southernmost basin occupies a hillside farm in the townland of Mountdrum *(106)*.

THE TOPPED MOUNTAIN CLUSTER

The Topped Mountain cluster consists of six recorded sites, two standing stones, three round cairns and a stone circle *(107)*. The sites in this complex are all recorded as being situated in an undulating series of hollows between the largest peak in the region – Topped Mountain – and Topped Mountain Lough. However, round cairns FER 212:030 and FER 212:106 have been destroyed, while the stone circle FER 212:029 is identified by five apparently extant but partly buried stones and is difficult to define. Of the surviving sites, the most impressive is clearly the round cairn FER 212:028 on Topped Mountain. It is significantly the largest site and is prominently set in the landscape with wide visibility in the surrounding area. As discussed above excavation of the site in 1897 unearthed a number of burials and artefacts that have dated the site to the Bronze Age (Plunkett & Coffey 1898).

The two standing stones, FER 212:025 and FER 212:026, appear to have been erected to acknowledge the eminence of this site. These are set 100m apart on opposite sides of a small valley and appear to be orientated on the peak of Topped Mountain. The NISMR reports that they are part of a three-stone alignment running north-east to south-west from the mountain. Today, there is no longer any trace of a third stone.

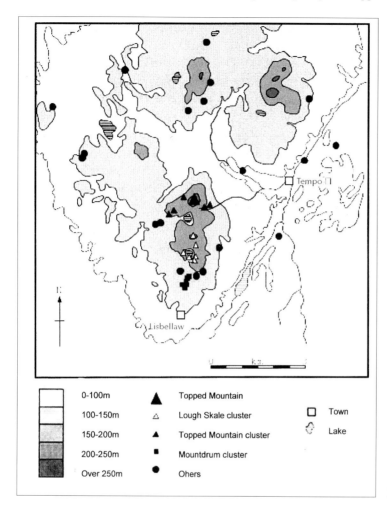

106 Map showing the three clusters of monuments evident in the Topped Mountain landscape

Legend:
- 0-100m
- 100-150m
- 150-200m
- 200-250m
- Over 250m
- ▲ Topped Mountain
- △ Lough Skale cluster
- ▲ Topped Mountain cluster
- ■ Mountdrum cluster
- ● Ohers
- ☐ Town
- ◇ Lake

The condition of the other sites makes it difficult to interpret the archaeology of this complex. However, all of the surviving sites are low set and somewhat concealed from one another so it is unlikely that intervisibility between the sites was important.

What appears to be decisive in the siting of the monuments is the relationship with Topped Mountain Lough. The lake is situated at the foot of Topped Mountain to the south-west in a low but well-defined basin. Although the sites in the cluster are all situated within 200m of the waters' edge, none has been placed within the confines of the basin itself. Indeed, the waters of the lake exist in almost preternatural solitude from the surrounding world. This impression appears to have been emphasised by the siting of the monuments. The standing stones FER 212:025 and FER 212:026 to the west, the stone circle FER 212:029 and the disappeared round cairn FER 212:030, both to the east, are situated at the foot of the outer slopes of the basin. This proximity, coupled with the fact that there are no sites within it, suggests that the absence of sites from the actual basin itself is significant. The impression conveyed is that the basin was somehow off-limits, even to these ritualised sites, and this feeling is heightened by the fact that, with the exception of the round cairn on the peak of Topped Mountain itself, none of the sites has even a visual relationship with the lake. This aspect of the Topped Mountain cluster is quite dramatic and it may be that Topped Mountain Lough represents a conceptualised component in the landscape of the type envisaged by Ashmore and Knapp (1999, 11). The fact that only the burial cairn on Topped Mountain itself has visibility of the lake might indicate that, to the monument builders, the lake basin shared equal significance with the mountain.

THE LOUGH SKALE CLUSTER

Lough Skale is situated at the foot of the south-east slope of Cloghtogle Mountain *(106)*. A ridge of hillocks runs from the foot of the mountain along the eastern shores of Lough Skale before gradually flattening and forming a gentler slope to the south. The Lough Skale basin is defined by these features to the north and east and by more gradual slopes to the south and west. Cloghtogle Mountain itself provides the boundary between the Lough Skale sites and the Topped Mountain basin. The two areas are contiguous but, because of the nature of the topography, the lands to the north are completely obscured from the Cloghtogle basin.

There are seven registered sites in this cluster. Again, a number of them have either been removed or are in poor condition. The cairn FER 212:080 has disappeared while round cairns FER 212:047 and FER 212:050 survive only as circular impressions in the ground. The other sites comprise two round cairns (FER 212:049 and FER 212:114), a wedge tomb (FER 212:051) and a standing stone (FER 212:048).

The presence of four round cairns suggests that this site type was central to whatever purpose the complex served. However, without excavation, it is difficult to ascertain the purpose or even the period of activity they represent. The presence of the wedge tomb suggests a Late Neolithic/Early Bronze Age aspect of this complex and, if the Lough Skale round cairns are dealt with as being broadly con-temporaneous with the Topped Mountain round cairn, then the complex might represent a period of sustained activity during the early part of the Bronze Age.

Geographically, the relationship between Cloghtogle Mountain and Lough Skale replicates that of Topped Mountain and Topped Mountain Lough. The relationship between the archaeology and the natural landscape, however, could not be more different. The Lough Skale complex appears to have been built so that a direct relationship with Lough Skale was manifested in the monuments themselves. The standing stone FER 212:048 is situated on the lake-shore, while a similar situation is suggested by the grid reference for the site of the cairn FER 212:080. Just over 100m to the east, along the line of hillocks, the wedge tomb FER 212:051 and round cairn FER 212:049 have excellent views of the lake and its basin. All of these sites have been placed on a slope or position that encourages a view of the lake. Only the round cairn FER 212:047 is situated in a low-set location facing away from Lough Skale, with an aspect more similar to the sites in the Topped Mountain cluster.

The final round cairn, FER 212:114, is situated on Cloghtogle Mountain and is badly damaged. The surviving dimensions suggest that it is significantly smaller than the Topped Mountain cairn, and in its present condition, it is impossible to verify whether a visual relationship with the lake existed. Indeed, within the Lough Skale complex, the cairn might even have been smaller than the round cairns FER 212:047 and FER 212:050. Therefore, any suggestion of the pre-eminence of this site within the cluster is solely based on its situation on Cloghtogle Mountain, which is admittedly very dominant within the context of the immediate landscape.

The contrast between the locations of sites in this cluster with that of Topped Mountain is striking and must have been intentional. If the current remains represent the totality of the sites that originally populated these basins, then it is surely not a coincidence that one basin seems to attract monuments while the other can be seen almost to repel them. A connection between the ritual meanings of these two basins can be tentatively inferred on the basis of this contrast.

The Mountdrum Cluster

Topographically, Mountdrum is characterised by the intersection of two very gradual slopes, one facing north-east and the other south. The area is further delineated to the west by a low rise. To the east, the terrain slopes down quite dramatically to a small valley containing a stream. Immediately to the east of the stream is Slieve Hill, which rises sharply to provide a barrier to the world beyond. Unlike the other basins, there is no surviving lake feature to provide a focus for the monument building. The local topography, however, suggests that a lake might have existed in the small valley to the east so that, in earlier times, Mountdrum might have mirrored the other basins.

The Mountdrum cluster consists of seven sites: two wedge tombs, three stone circles with associated alignments, a ruined megalith and a *fulacht fiadh (106)*. Two other sites, a damaged megalith to the north and a court tomb on the peak of Slieve Hill, are within Tilley's 500m limit (1996, 131) of the Mountdrum complex, but are separated from the cluster by ridges surrounding the basin. With the exception of the *fulacht fiadh*, all of the Mountdrum sites are set on the north-east facing slope, and they are all situated on plateaux. This location type was the most appropriate to facilitate both the construction of the sites and gatherings around each monument. There appears to be a definite order to the structuring of the Mountdrum sites and the cluster can be seen as being divided into two separate provinces.

The stone circles with their alignments are situated at the southern, more elevated, end of the complex. Two of these in particular, the triple-ringed circle FER 212:111 and the damaged circle and alignment FER 212:117, occupy a more elevated plateau within the complex and indeed are the most southern monuments within the entire study area. The third stone circle is situated some 70m to the north-east and shares a plateau with the remains of wedge tomb FER 212:115. The northern part of the Mountdrum complex can be seen as the province of chambered tombs. Two wedge tombs, FER 212:115 and FER 212:054, survive albeit in relatively poor condition while a third megalithic tomb, FER 212:089, is represented by a single extant stone set in a trapezoidal cut. The Mountdrum basin is the most level of the three and it is possible that all of the sites were intervisible with each other. Their positions also suggest that, if a lake did exist to the east of the cluster, all of the sites would have had some view of it.

Unlike the other clusters, the Mountdrum cluster does not suffer from the uncertainty surrounding the round cairns or by the recent destruction of recorded sites. Most of the sites are of a type most usually associated with the Late Neolithic or Early Bronze Age and, although no excavation work has been carried out, Williams and Gormley (2002, 99) note that coarse pottery sherds were found at wedge tomb FER 212:054, suggesting an Early Bronze Age use. The destroyed tomb FER 212:089, however, might have represented the original element in the complex and may have been the focus of the Bronze Age activity. Certainly, the nearby Slieve Hill court tomb is indicative of an earlier presence in the immediate locale. As Mitchell and Ryan have noted (2001, 196), wedge tombs are often associated with earlier tombs. O'Brien (1999, 202) suggests that wedge tombs were built rapidly, in a single event, so it is possible that the two wedge tombs were added in quick succession. While it is impossible to verify the temporal relationship of the wedge tombs with the stone circle and alignment sites, the seemingly deliberate division of the complex suggests that, if these were not contemporary constructions the location of the later phase of development certainly respected the earlier sites. The *fulacht fiadh* is somewhat isolated from the remainder of the complex, but it does *prima facie* suggest that the complex remained in use at least into the first millennium BC (Waddell 2000, 177). Therefore, the Mountdrum complex might have been of some significance for four millennia. Interestingly, this is paralleled in other more thoroughly studied complexes in Northern Ireland such as Beaghmore in County Tyrone, which contain comparable assemblages of cairns, stone circles and alignments, and enjoyed a similar period of usage (Pilcher 1969, 89–90).

THE BROADER PICTURE

The three clusters at the heart of the Topped Mountain landscape would certainly be worthy of classification as a 'ritual complex' by themselves. The upland table that houses these basins is a distinctive topographical location, and the density of concentration (there are 23 prehistoric sites within an area of approximately 3km^2) compares favourably with monument complexes at Wardhouse and Fenagh, both in County Leitrim, and with Roughan Hill and the Burren, both in County Clare, which have been recognised by Cooney (2000, 146). To limit the definition of the landscape to this area, however, would be to ignore the more outlying sites of the study area. Indeed, there is intriguing evidence that some of these monuments might have played a significant role in the organisation of the area as a whole.

(107) shows the sites within the Topped Mountain study area that were either intervisible with, or orientated on, Topped Mountain. Significantly, this relationship is proportionately higher in sites situated beyond the clusters described above. These outlying sites are generally prominently located in the landscape and, in the main, are situated more than 2km from Topped Mountain. In the case of the round cairn FER 193:025, stone alignments FER 193:026 and FER 212:010, the unclassified megalith FER 193:021 and the court tomb FER 212:001, they were probably visible for miles around when originally constructed. The visibility indices for these sites indicated that the view to the south was disproportionately high (a mean south-facing view of 3 was recorded for these sites as opposed to 1.6 for the monuments in the area as a whole). It can therefore be suggested that view was more important to the builders of the more isolated, outlying monuments than it was in the case of the clustered sites. It also seems that the area to the south, which is dominated by the Topped Mountain uplands, held most importance to the people who constructed these monuments.

The clustered sites to the south of Topped Mountain do not, in the main, exhibit an intervisibility relationship with Topped Mountain. Equally, an orientation on Topped Mountain appears to be more important in sites which were situated at greater distances from the Topped Mountain landform. This suggests that the outlying sites did not function in isolation. Rather, their situation and orientation can be seen as an effort to influence the perception of the landscape by the use of a network of pointers and visual relations orientated towards Topped Mountain. This function was not required of the sites situated within the Topped Mountain landform itself.

Standing alone, these relationships might be regarded as somewhat inconclusive. The dataset is, after all, relatively small and the perceived contrast between the outlying sites and the clustered sites might be attributed to the nature of the topography in the area. However, this 'signposting' of the Topped Mountain upland table is further suggested by an analysis of the altitude data obtained during the survey. The three highest sites within the area are the round cairns of Ballyreagh Hill (FER 193:025), Topped Mountain (FER 212:028) and Cloghtogle Mountain (FER 212:114). There are other peaks within the study area of comparable altitude and view, but which do not host similar monuments. It is therefore likely that these three peaks were specifically

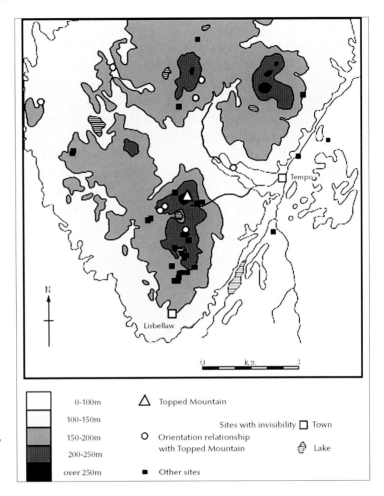

107 Map showing sites with a view to, or intervisibility with, Topped Mountain

0-100m	△ Topped Mountain
100-150m	
150-200m	Sites with invisibility ☐ Town
200-250m	○ Orientation relationship with Topped Mountain
over 250m	⬭ Lake
	■ Other sites

chosen. *(108)* shows the situation of these particular sites within the landscape and it is evident that the three cairns appear to be situated in a linear north–south axis running through the centre of the study area. This axis coincides almost exactly with the glacial water sources; Topped Mountain Lough and Lough Skale are situated directly along this axis, while the Mountdrum basin can be seen as the southernmost point of the axis. The position of the possible lake at Mountdrum is indicated on the map. This axis of highly visible sites extends from Ballyreagh Hill in the north and terminates in the glacial hollows which host the major concentration of archaeological sites in the landscape.

The location of the Ballyreagh site (FER 193:025) at the most northern point on the axis is interesting. It is situated at some distance to the north of the study area in an upland area that is quite separate from the Topped Mountain uplands. Although it commands extensive views in most directions, the view to the north is conspicuously obscured. Given what has already been said about the seeming importance of the Topped Mountain uplands, particularly when viewed from the north, there is a temptation to see the siting of the Ballyreagh monument as deliberate. It can be postulated that a view to the north was unnecessary because the focal point for the building of the monument was situated to the south towards Topped Mountain. A more courageous interpretation might even suggest that the deliberate situation on a south-facing slope is an indication that the monument forms the northern extreme of this ritual landscape and that the significant area for the peoples of this time lay to the south, within the Topped Mountain landform.

Whether the significance lay in the complexes themselves, or whether these were built to affirm an already significant area within the natural landscape, is a question that cannot at present be answered. The relationship between the upland area and a number of sites within the wider environment, however, may suggest that the Topped Mountain landscape was of significance far beyond its immediate locale.

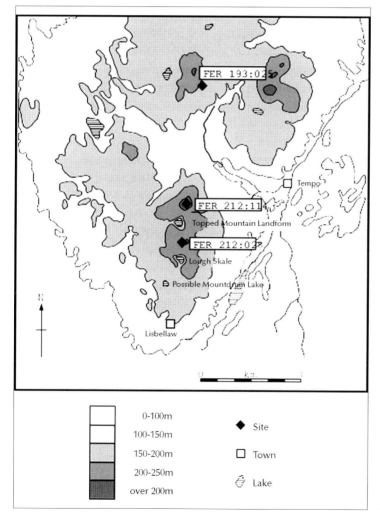

108 Map showing the apparent linear axis of round cairns and lakes which runs in a north–south alignment

Conclusion

The amount of organisation and labour required to create the intricate web of relationships between the archaeological sites in the Topped Mountain region indicates that the region was of considerable significance to the monument builders. The majority of the monuments, which form the anthropogenic constituents of the landscape, are of types considered to have had at least a partly ritual function. It is therefore probable that the Topped Mountain area in general, and the upland axis of lakeland basins in particular, represented a sacred place to the monument builders. This paper has tried to demonstrate that the various elements of the landscape were interwoven. While many of the sites are typical throughout Ireland, some additional factor led to their being situated so closely together. It would be surprising if this proximity did not provide an additional significance to the ritual nature of the monuments. This relationship is most evident in the three complexes discussed above and it is suggested here that it was the specific topography that attracted human attention. Even today, the basin area exists in serene solitude like some great natural cathedral. Although not genuinely mountainous, the elevation of the place lifts it above the surrounding lakes and valleys, while Topped Mountain to the north towers over it, marking the place in the wider landscape while, at the same time, providing a barrier from the outside world. In this regard, the Topped Mountain cairn itself can be seen as a prehistoric analogy to a church bell-tower. The cairn has been placed on the highest peak in the region and is visible from far and wide, demonstrably so from other significant places which have been marked with monuments. However, the ritual centre is further to the south amid the clustered sites of the lakeland basins. The monuments here seem to pay little attention to Topped Mountain. Perhaps the role of the Topped Mountain cairn within this landscape was to beckon people from far and wide to this sacred place, but it had no more active or significant role in the rituals that took place in its shadow.

The largest, and probably most contentious, scale of activity in the landscape lends itself to this notion. The seemingly stronger visual relationships between Topped Mountain and the more distant sites, together with the axis of topographically dominant round cairns, seem to influence the perception of the landscape and to focus attention, firstly on the Topped Mountain uplands and then further into the heart of the landform at the centre of the archaeological activity. The results of the current survey have presented the possibility that the relationship was an intentional one; it is surely unlikely that the builders and users of the monuments were oblivious to this situation.

We know little beyond what is physically evident in the landscape. As such, the development of a reliable chronology for the region is essential so that a more refined idea of its development can be gained. It seems likely that the Topped Mountain landscape was formally ritualised by the Early Bronze Age, but we do not know exactly when it became so significant. At present, for example, it is impossible to ascertain whether it was the monuments that made this place sacred or whether they were built to formalise an already significant landscape. It is also notable that there is no obvious habitation evidence, a situation which probably overemphasises the ceremonial aspect of the landscape. It would be useful to ascertain whether Mountdrum did, indeed, contain a third lake as this would strengthen the hypothesis that it was these water features that were the focus of monument construction. There are tantalising glimpses in the Topped Mountain landscape of a continuously evolving centre of prehistoric ceremonial activity. Given the results of the current topographical research further study, including small-scale excavation and palaeoenvironmental analyses, might enable us to understand not only more about this fascinating place but, in a broader context, about the nature of Late Neolithic and Early Bronze Age ceremonial sites and ritual landscapes throughout Ireland.

Acknowledgements

We are extremely grateful to Ann Orr and Eamon Cox and all the other members of the vibrant Topped Mountain Historical Society who encouraged and supported our research in Mountdrum and the Topped Mountain landscape. We would also like to thank Libby Mulqueeny, School of Archaeology and Palaeoecology, Queen's University Belfast, for producing the illustrations.

Bibliography

ApSimon, A., 1986 Chronological contexts for Irish megalithic tombs. *Journal of Irish Archaeology*, 3, 5-15.

Ashmore, W. & Knapp, A.B., 1999 Archaeological landscapes: constructed, conceptualised, ideational. In Ashmore, W. & Knapp, A.B. (eds), *Archaeologies of Landscape – Contemporary Perspectives*, 1-30. London: Blackwell.

Brindley, A.L., 2001 Tomorrow is another day: some radiocarbon dates for Irish bronze artefacts. In Metz, W.H., van Beek, B.L. & Steegstra, H. (eds), *Patina: Essays Presented to Jay Jordan Butler on the Occasion of his 80th Birthday*, 145-60, Groningen: Privately Published.

Burl, A., 1976 *The Stone Circles of the British Isles.* London & New Haven: Yale University Press.

Burl, A., 2000 *The Stone Circles of the Britain, Ireland and Brittany.* London & New Haven: Yale University Press.

Cooney, G., 1979 Some aspects of the siting of megalithic tombs in County Leitrim. *Journal of the Royal Society of Antiquaries of Ireland*, 109, 74-91.

Cooney, G., 1990 The place of megalithic tomb cemeteries in Ireland. *Antiquity*, 64, 741-53.

Cooney, G., 2000 *Landscapes of Neolithic Ireland.* London: Routledge.

Davies, O., 1942 Excavations at Ballyreagh, Co. Fermanagh. *Ulster Journal of Archaeology*, 5, 78-89.

Gale, J., Chartrand, J., Fulton, A., Laughlin, B. & Darvill, T., 1997 The Mull Hill tomb. In Darvill, T. *Billown Neolithic Landscape Project, Isle of Man, 1996*, 52-60.

Research Report 3. Bournemouth & Douglas: Bournemouth University School of Conservation Sciences.

McConkey, R., 1987 *The Stone Circles of Ulster*. Unpublished MA dissertation: Queen's University Belfast.

McHugh, R., 2003 *The Prehistoric Landscape of the Topped Mountain Area, Co. Fermanagh*. Unpublished MSc dissertation: Queen's University Belfast.

Mitchell, F. & Ryan, M., 2001 *Reading the Irish Landscape*. Dublin: Town House Publishers.

O'Brien, W., 1999 *Sacred Ground: Megalithic Tombs in Coastal South-West Ireland*. Galway: Clodoiri Lurgan Teo.

O'Néill, J., forthcoming. *Lapidibus in Igne Calefactis Coquebatur*: the historical burnt mound tradition.

Pilcher, J.R., 1969 Archaeology, Palaeoecology and 14C dating of the Beaghmore Stone Circle Site. *Ulster Journal of Archaeology*, 32, 91-93.

Plunkett, T. & Coffey, G., 1898 Report on the excavation of Topped Mountain cairn. *Proceedings of the Royal Irish Academy*, 4, 651-8.

Tilley, C., 1996 *An Ethnography of the Neolithic: Early Prehistoric Societies in Southern Scandinavia*. Cambridge: Cambridge University Press.

Waddell, J., 1990 *The Bronze Age Burials of Ireland*. Galway: Galway University Press.

Waddell, J., 2000 *The Prehistoric Archaeology of Ireland*. Bray: Wordwell.

Wakeman, W.F., 1875 On certain markings on rocks, pillar-stones and other monuments observed chiefly in the County Fermanagh. *Journal of the Royal Society of Antiquaries of Ireland,* 13, 445-74.

Wakeman, W.F., 1878 On certain lines of stones and other antiquities at Cavancarragh, Co. Fermanagh. *Journal of the Royal Society of Antiquaries of Ireland*, 14, 499-512.

Williams, B. & Gormley, S., 2002 *Archaeological Objects from County Fermanagh* (Northern Ireland Archaeological Monographs no. 5). Belfast: Blackstaff Press.

20

(Con)Fusion of Tradition? The Circle Henge in Ireland

William O'Brien

Introduction

The classification and interpretation of henges has given rise to considerable discussion ever since this monument type was first identified in Britain in the 1930s. The core definition, i.e. a circular area enclosed by a ditch and external bank, with one or opposing entrances and internal settings of stone or timber uprights, is sufficiently broad to include a range of sites having one or more of these characteristics. This morphological variability, when combined with a poor understanding of henge chronology and evolution, renders any classification imprecise in cultural terms. Yet, despite the many physical manifestations, it is widely accepted that there are certain traits common to henge monuments, which represent a radical shift from earlier beliefs and social values in the Neolithic.

The problems of classification are especially acute in Ireland where tens of thousands of circular earthwork enclosures are known and where research and excavation of henges is still in its infancy. The term 'hengiform' is increasingly used to describe almost any embanked enclosure with an internal ditch. This has given rise to some confusion as internally ditched enclosures are known from different periods, thus reducing the term 'henge' to a morphological label, rather than one having specific chronological and cultural associations. It also obscures the multi-period character of many monuments where henge features were fused with elements of older or more recent ritual traditions.

Derek Simpson addressed this broad definition of henges and related monuments in Ireland in their contribution to Aubrey Burl's Festschrift (Condit & Simpson 1998). The authors considered the Irish sites under seven headings, including earthen embanked enclosures, internally ditched enclosures, embanked stone circles, circle henges, timber circles, 'royal' enclosures and ritual ponds. Many would argue that this diverse range of monuments represents a *longue durée* of ritual tradition involving hengiform enclosures, which spanned three millennia or more from the Neolithic to the Later Iron Age (Clare 1987, 471; Newman 1997, 176 for further discussion).

The present paper examines one of these categories, the circle henge, reviewing the evidence for six possible sites in Ireland listed by Condit and Simpson. This category includes some of the most famous henge monuments in Britain, sites such as Stonehenge, Avebury, Arbor Low and Cairnpapple. The Irish evidence, as we shall see, is more equivocal and even calls into question the existence here of circle henges. This will be examined by first considering some sites in north-east Ireland that Derek believes may be circle henges. The focus of this paper is the south-west region where new dating and excavation evidence is presented for two sites long regarded as possible circle henges.

CIRCLE HENGES IN IRELAND

Like their British counterparts, Irish henges have a complex and poorly understood relationship to older and more recent monument traditions. This is evident in the first two circle henges listed by Condit and Simpson, namely Dun Ruadh, County Tyrone and Ballynoe, County Down. The former was first excavated by Oliver Davies who interpreted the monument as a multiple cist cairn with food vessel burials, surrounded by an earlier bank and ditch enclosure (Davies 1936). The henge connection was strengthened in 1987 when Derek excavated a section of the enclosure, obtaining a charcoal date of 2037–1940 cal BC from the basal ditch fill (Simpson *et al.* 1992; Simpson 1993). He subsequently drew attention to a pear-shaped arrangement of 17 stones with a south-west opening, interpreted by Davies as a revetment to the cist cairn. Derek argued that this could instead be viewed as a free-standing horseshoe setting of stones within the henge enclosure (Condit & Simpson 1998, 56).

The sequence at Ballynoe is equally problematic, as this monument incorporates a chambered long cairn, a subcircular mound with stone kerb and an enclosing stone circle (Groenman-van Waateringe & Butler 1976). There are several possible interpretations (see Bradley 1998, fig. 1.2), including Derek's suggestion of a possible henge ditch outside this stone circle (Condit & Simpson 1998, 56).

Neither Dun Ruadh nor Ballynoe is a convincing example of a circle henge, though both sites may incorporate elements of the henge tradition. Uncertainty also surrounds the destroyed site at Ballynahattin, County Louth, which is also listed as a circle henge by Condit and Simpson. An antiquarian plan of this extraordinary monument shows what is probably a circular bank and ditch enclosure, surrounded by a circle of massive stones with a double ring of smaller stones in the interior *(109)*. The British parallels argue for a henge connection, though this cannot be confirmed in the absence of archaeological excavation (see Buckley 1988 for possible site location in Carn Beg townland, County Louth).

Condit and Simpson listed three further possible circle henges, all located in the south-west region. They include the stone circle at Lissyviggeen near

Killarney, County Kerry and two sites in County Cork, Reanascreena South and Glantane East. This south–west region is well known for its concentration of Bronze Age megaliths. They include some 107 stone circles, 200 stone rows and 90 boulder-burials, as well as radial stone cairns and four-poster monuments (Ó Nualláin 1975; 1978; 1984; 1988). Many of the estimated 600 standing stones in this region may also be of Bronze Age date. These monuments, known as the 'stone circle complex', occur in close spatial association, raising the possibility that they '... are all manifestations of a single localised culture' (Ó Nualláin 1984, 102).

Stone circles in Cork and Kerry form a homogenous group in terms of their distribution and design concept. They are all of the axial stone variety, with consistent west to south–west orientations that probably emphasise the setting sun. The majority are circular arrangements of spaced upright stones, which typically reduce in height from tall portal stones forming an entrance on the eastern side to a low axial or recumbent stone on the western side. The two variants of this design are the five-stone circle and the multiple-stone circle, which have overlapping distributions in the Cork area. Some 55 examples of the former are known, diminutive monuments averaging only 2-4m in diameter. The 52 multiple stone circles range 4-17m in diameter and comprise 7-19 stones. These circles may have outlying standing stones, stone pairs or cairns, while boulder-burials and monoliths can also occur inside some of the multiple-stone circles.

The dating of these stone circles and related monuments has proved contentious and for a long time relied on an Early Bronze Age Coarse Ware association at Drombeg stone circle, County Cork (Fahy 1959). Revised dating of this pottery (Cleary 1993), and a recent radiocarbon result of 1125-793 BC (OxA-2683) for a central pit cremation at this site, points to a later Bronze Age date. This is consistent with pollen studies conducted by Ann Lynch and a date range of 1367-789 cal BC that she obtained for erection of

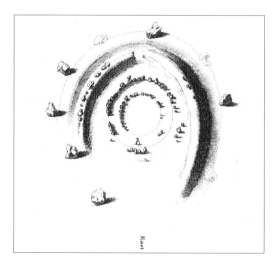

109 Antiquarian drawing of a destroyed circle henge at Ballynahattin, County Louth. *From Wright 1758*

the stone circle at Cashelkeelty, County Kerry (Lynch 1981). Radiocarbon dates for associated monuments such as rows and boulder-burials support the idea that stone circles in Cork and Kerry were mostly built during the Middle to Late Bronze Age, *c.*1600–800 BC (O'Brien 1993, fig. 7.5). A similar date range has been advanced for stone circles and rows in mid–Ulster (Pilcher 1969).

REANASCREENA SOUTH

This stone circle is one of 14 examples in the Rosscarbery area of coastal south-west Cork (Record of Monuments and Places CO134:32) The site was excavated in 1961 by Edward Fahy who had previously investigated stone circles at Drombeg (Fahy 1959) and Bohonagh (Fahy 1961) in this area. Reanascreena South comprises a circle of 13 upright stones surrounded by a shallow ditch with external bank *(110)*. The circle has an internal diameter of 9.35m, with the perimeter stones ranging 0.86–1.52m in height from the old ground surface. These grade down from the two tallest stones, which form entrance portals on the eastern side and are directly opposite the lowest stone lying recumbent to the west. This stone circle has a west–south–west/east–north-east orientation, represented by a line taken between the two portals across the centre of the recumbent or axial stone.

Excavation of the interior revealed a 0.3m depth of humus-peat overlying a grey layer representing an old ground surface (Fahy 1962). This sealed two pit features, one of which was lined along the sides and base by charcoal-rich sediment that contained fragments of burnt human bone. The enclosing ditch measured 3.75m in maximum width and up to 0.42m deep to a flat base *(111)*. The fill sequence consisted of surface humus overlying dark brown-black peat on a basal silt sediment. The fill was largely uniform, except on the eastern side near the portal stones where a deposit of large stones was found. These were mostly placed against the inner and outer sides of the ditch and compacted with soil. This was done to repair erosion caused by repeated movement in and out of the circle through the portal stone 'entrance'.

The outer bank measured 3.5m in maximum width, with an average height of only 0.2–0.3m. The bank was built using soil dug from the inner ditch. Some of this upcast overlay a group of four shallow pits on the eastern side, three of which contained broken rock chips. This probably represents tooling debris gathered from the preparation of monoliths for this stone circle, which was carefully buried as sacred stone. Similar pits have been identified in other Bronze Age monuments in west Cork, including Drombeg stone circle (Fahy 1959) and more recently at Altar wedge tomb (O'Brien 1999, 202). The fact that these pits were overlain by upcast sediment from the adjacent ditch suggests that very little time passed between the digging of the latter feature and the erection of the stone circle.

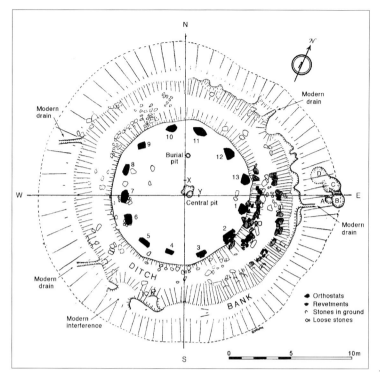

110 Left
Excavation plan of
Reanascreena
South stone circle.
From Fahy 1962

111 Below Section
from interior of
Reanascreena
South circle
through enclosing
ditch and external
bank, showing
burial pit and
radiocarbon sample
locations. *Modified
from Fahy 1962*

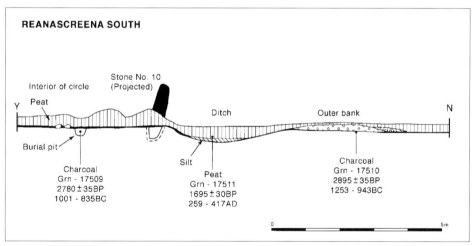

REANASCREENA SOUTH

The builders took care to leave a 0.45m wide strip of solid ground between the outside of the standing stones and the inner edge of the enclosing ditch. This was done so that the ditch would not undermine the foundation sockets of the standing stones. The ledge was reduced in width on the eastern portal side, where repeated movement led to erosion of the ditch sides. The fact that this was repaired with large stones and compacted soil convinced Fahy that those who dug the ditch were aware of the extent of the foundation sockets. This, he argued, points '... very securely to the fact that the circle, the enclosing ditch and the bank were planned, constructed and subsequently used by one and the same people' (Fahy 1962, 64). This argument is convincing, especially when combined with the stratigraphic position of the pits containing tooling debris in relation to the bank.

Fahy was unable to explore this further in the absence of datable artefacts or radiocarbon determinations. Fortunately, he anticipated the potential of the latter dating method by storing samples of charcoal and peat from this site in the Department of Archaeology, University College Cork. In 1989 the author submitted three samples for dating to Groningen, as part of a radiocarbon programme for Irish prehistory initiated by Anna Brindley and Jan Lanting. The following results were obtained (O'Brien 1992, 33-4):

> Charcoal (wood species unknown) from primary fill (Fahy fraction G) of pit containing cremated human bone, northern interior of stone circle.
> GrN-17509: 2780±35 BP.
> Calibrated to 973-841 cal BC (1σ) or 1001-835 cal BC (2σ).
> Dried peat sample from base of peat growth overlying primary silt in ditch.
> GrN-17511: 1695±30 BP.
> Calibrated to cal AD 263-401 (1σ) or cal AD 259-417 (2σ).
> Charcoal (wood species unknown) from grey layer representing old ground surface underneath bank.
> GrN-17510: 2895±35 BP.
> Calibrated to 1125-1015 cal BC (1σ) or 1253-943 cal BC (2σ).

The stratigraphic position of these samples is particularly useful, placing the construction of this monument within a 400-year period *(111)*. At two-sigma calibration, the first sample dates a burial event inside this stone circle to 1001–835 BC. The second sample provides a *terminus ante quem* of cal AD 259–417 for digging the surrounding ditch, with upcast sediment forming the external bank. The final sample provides a *terminus post quem* of 1253-943 cal BC for the bank construction. Together, these results indicate that the earthwork enclosure was built sometime between 1253 BC and AD 417. This can be narrowed to 1253-835 BC if we accept stratigraphic arguments (above) that the bank/ditch and stone circle were built around the same time and that the burial context inside the latter does not pre-date the monument.

LISSYVIGGEEN

This site in Killarney, County Kerry (RMP KE067-20), is another of the possible circle henges listed by Condit and Simpson. Certain features mark this site apart from other stone circles in the region and suggest parallels with British circle henges of the Arbor Low type (Burl 1976, 274-82). The monument consists of a small stone circle, surrounded by a low earthwork

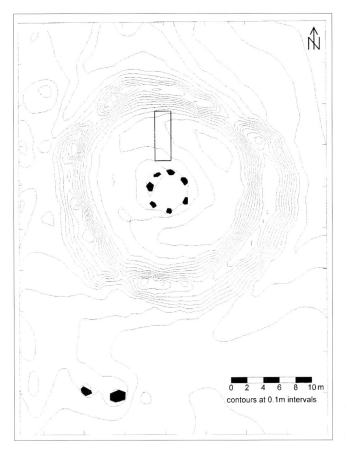

112 Lissyviggeen stone circle, Killarney, County Kerry. Excvation trench marked

0 2 4 6 8 10m

contours at 0.1m intervals

bank with traces of an inner ditch *(112)*. Two massive outlier stones, measuring 2.35m and 2.15m in height and 2.2m apart, are located 11.5m to the south of this enclosure. The stone circle is *c.*4m in diameter and comprises seven stones, ranging 0.9-1.2m in height. Ó Nualláin (1984, site 38) regarded this as typical of the Cork-Kerry series; however the identification of an axial stone and the associated orientation are open to question. The stone circle is set in the centre of a circular earthen bank enclosure, measuring some 20m in internal diameter, 1-2m in height and 3-5m in width. There are opposing depressions on the north-east and south-west sides of this bank; however, it is not known if these are original entrances.

The author carried out a keyhole excavation at this site in April 1998, to investigate the presence of a ditch inside the bank. It was hoped to obtain radiocarbon samples in the same way that Derek was able to date the Dun Ruadh enclosure. A 6m by 2m trench was excavated from the northern exterior of the stone circle to the inner base of the surrounding bank *(117)*. Excavation revealed soil horizons to a depth of 0.55m across the southern two-thirds of this trench. The brown podzolic profile comprised an A-horizon overlying an iron-enriched B-horizon on sandy-gravel subsoil. The only finds

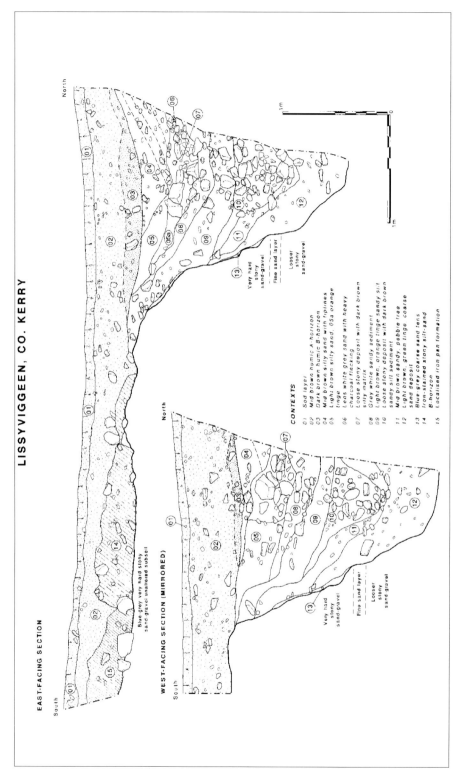

113 Stratification of ditch, Lissyviggeen

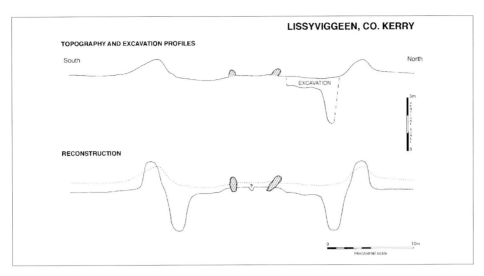

114 Surface profiles (modern and original) across Lissyviggeen stone circle

were modern china sherds from the A–horizon, where there were some indications of recent cultivation.

The presence of an internal ditch was suggested by a 0.2–0.3m deep depression extending 5m out from the bank base. Geophysical survey confirmed that this runs almost the entire circumference of the enclosure. Removal of 0.5m depth of A–horizon in the northern part of this trench revealed the outline of this ditch against the B–horizon. A total of ten sediment deposits were excavated within this ditch *(113)*.

The infilling of the ditch began with the deposition of a thick deposit of loose, light brown, sandy sediment, containing occasional small stones and cobbles (C12). This was overlain by a deposit of loose sandy sediment (C11) with a higher sand content. These basal sediments accumulated shortly after the ditch was dug, through slipping of the adjacent earthen bank. This was sealed by a deposit of rounded cobbles and small boulders with fine silt (C10) in the central ditch area. These may represent a collapsed stone revetment on the inner bank face; however this is not certain. The stones were overlain by a further influx of fine sandy sediment, which also contained rounded cobbles (C09). This sediment, in turn, was covered by another layer of sandy sediment (C08) with a coarse stone component. The presence of numerous cobbles and small boulders in the central ditch area made it difficult to differentiate these contexts (C08–10).

Context 08 was overlain by a stony deposit (C07), which incorporated a lens of white–grey sandy sediment with heavy charcoal flecking (C06). This averaged only 3–5cm in thickness and was similar in colour and texture to Context 08. A charcoal sample from Context 06 was submitted for radiocarbon dating (below). Context 07 was sealed by a further influx of fine sandy sediment (C05/05a) on the southern side of the ditch. This was followed by sedimentation from the bank in the form of a similar sandy layer (C04), which sealed the top of the Context 10 stones. Contexts 04 and 05 mark the final phase of ditch filling and are followed by the development of an A-horizon (C01–03) above this sequence.

This excavation confirms that the earthwork enclosure at Lissyviggeen consisted of a deep ditch cut into sandy-gravel soil, with upcast forming an external bank in a single-phase construction. The bank and ditch had a steep profile, which accounts for their rapid erosion after the monument was built *(114)*. When first dug, the ditch ranged in width from 3m (top) to 1m (base), with a central depth of 2.2–2.4m and had a narrow, slightly rounded base. The adjacent bank may have been *c.*1.5m high with a basal width of *c.*2.5m. There is no indication of an intervening berm between the bank and ditch features. The original entrance(s) to this enclosure cannot be identified with certainty, however a surveyed area of higher electrical resistivity inside the bank opening on the south-west side suggests a possible ditch causeway.

The ditch fill at Lissyviggeen was disappointing in terms of dating evidence, as no artefacts or bone were recovered. The basal sediment (C12) was particularly sterile with no charcoal available for radiocarbon analysis. The dry sandy fill may explain the absence of organic remains, but cannot account for a lack of charcoal or inorganic artefacts, which were also absent from the area excavated inside this ditch. This absence of finds and datable material was the reason why the adjacent bank was not sectioned during excavation.

The discovery of white china in Context 02 suggests that the top of the ditch was sealed by A-horizon by early modern times. The only dating

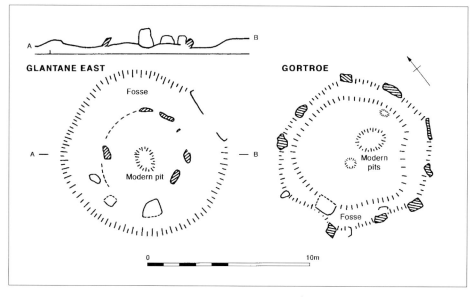

115 Glantane East and Gortroe stone circles, Co. Cork. *After* Ó *Nualláin 1984*

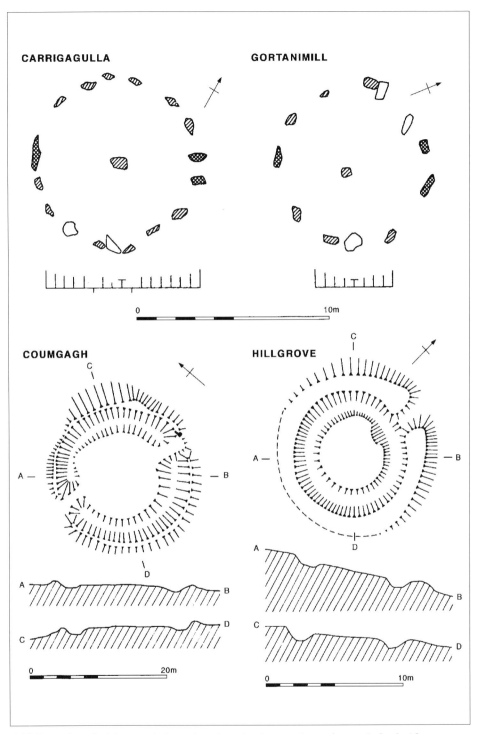

116 Examples of axial stone circles and earthen ring barrows in south-west Ireland. *After Ó Nualláin 1984; Cuppage 1986; O'Sullivan & Sheehan 1996*

evidence within the fill sequence is provided by a single radiocarbon date for charcoal from the upper ditch:

Charcoal (wood species unknown), Context 06.
Grn-23973: 1940±15BP
Calibrated to cal AD 31-76 (1σ calibration) or cal AD 27-117 (2σ).

This charcoal date provides a *terminus ante quem* of the first century AD for the accumulation of sediment (C08-13) in the lower part of the ditch. It is not possible to assess the interval of time between the digging of this ditch and the fire event that produced this charcoal. The latter raises interesting questions about the possible use of stone circles in religious practices of the Iron Age.

GLANTANE EAST

This axial stone circle in mid Cork is another site listed by Condit and Simpson (1998) as a possible circle henge *(115)*. This monument measures 4.5m in diameter and originally consisted of 11-13 stones, six of which are presently upright (Ó Nualláin 1984, 11). The stones are surrounded by a 2-2.5m wide ditch up to 0.6m deep, with indications of a possible external bank. Somewhat different is the stone circle at Gortroe in mid-west Cork *(115)*, where there is a 1-2m wide and 0.5m deep ditch directly inside a ring of 8-9 standing stones (*ibid.*, 17). While Glantane East and Gortroe have not been excavated, there are parallels with Reanascreena South in both cases.

DISCUSSION

Problems of dating and sequence are not unique to circle henges, as no doubt Derek will recall from Croft Moraig, Perth & Kinross, where he investigated a multi-phase monument with henge and stone circle associations (Piggott & Simpson 1971). By identifying these monuments as a separate category we are conflating a range of possibilities in terms of the dating and sequence of circle henges in Ireland. In some instances we may be looking at a stone circle built contemporaneously with an enclosing earthwork. Other circle henges may be hybrid in form, where elements of different contemporary ritual traditions come together in one monument. Then there are sites of multi-period construction, where older or younger ritual traditions are incorporated into henges. Finally, there are those sites with 'hengiform' characteristics that have no direct chronological or spiritual connection with the Neolithic henge tradition.

The identification of Reanascreena South as a circle henge (e.g. Evans 1966, 83; Clare 1986, 287) was based on the hengiform nature of its earthwork enclosure and the accepted Early Bronze Age date range for stone circles in Britain and Ireland. The site was regarded as a hybrid monument, with one

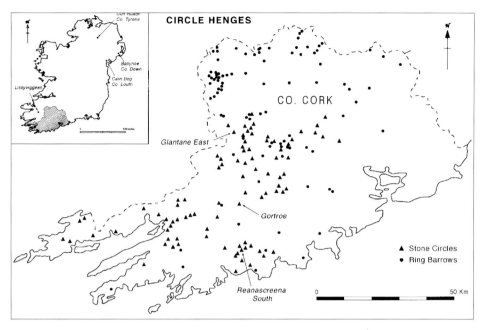

117 Distribution of stone circles and ring barrows in County Cork. *After Ó Nualláin 1984; Power 1992* et seq. Includes location of sites examined in text as possible circle henges

authority even suggesting a possible '… fusion of traits from chambered tombs, henges and recumbent stone circles' (Burl 1976, 220). The radiocarbon dates, however, indicate that this monument was built in the Later Bronze Age, probably around 1000 BC, ruling out any direct link with the Neolithic henge tradition. This is supported by a revised dating for stone circle complex monuments in south-west Ireland (O'Brien 1993).

The excavator, Edward Fahy, acknowledged that the site has henge characteristics, but raised the possibility that the builders were influenced by the ring barrow tradition (Fahy 1962, 68). Stone circles and ring barrows differ significantly in terms of the use of ritual space, but do share common elements of design and use *(116)*. These include the circular motif, the manner in which human remains are treated and the way artefacts are deposited. The differences in respect of orientation and ceremony are probably more signi-ficant that the similarities; nevertheless, it is possible to see fusion of these two ideas at Reanascreena South, Glantane East and possibly Gortroe. In this respect, these sites are more properly termed circle barrows than circle henges.

This can be explored further by looking at the distribution evidence for axial stone circles and earthen ring barrows in County Cork. A recent county survey identified 96 definite or possible ring barrows (Power 1992 *et seq*). These are small circular monuments, consisting of a level or raised central area that measures 5-15m in diameter. This is surrounded by a 1-4m wide ditch, usually less than 1m deep, with an external bank less than 1m high. A single causewayed entrance is often present, as are traces and records of internal cist burials (information from Power 1992 *et seq*).

The majority of ring barrows in County Cork occur in the north of the county, with a scattered distribution further south *(117)*. This contrasts with the distribution of an estimated 100 axial stone circles in Cork, which mostly occur in the central, southern and western parts of the county. There is an interesting overlap between the two monument types in the mid-Cork region, and also along the southern coastline where Reanascreena South is located.

The chronological position of ring barrows presents difficulties given the broad dating of this monument type in Ireland and the lack of excavation in the south-west region. Some of the Cork examples are likely to be of Middle-Late Bronze Age date, broadly contemporary with monuments of the 'stone circle complex'. This is supported by a ring barrow excavation at Leckaneen, which contained a cremation burial dated to 1523-1321 cal BC (O'Shaughnessy 1991). Investigations at Carriganimmy uncovered a pit cremation containing Coarse Ware similar to that found at Drombeg stone circle (in Power 1997, 150). Significantly, the Leckaneen and Carriganimmy barrows occur within the major distribution of stone circle complex monuments in mid-Cork. The latter site is located within 1km of Glantane East, pointing to contact between these monument traditions at a local level.

In contrast, the evidence from Lissyviggeen, with its large internal ditched enclosure, does suggest connections with the henge tradition. Comparisons might be made here with Sites 1 and 4 in the Curragh, County Kildare (Ó Ríordáin 1950). The interpretation of Lissyviggeen remains uncertain in the absence of secure dating evidence for its construction and use-history. There are several possibilities to be tested by future excavation. This may be a circle henge as defined by Burl (1976), namely a free-standing stone circle surrounded by a ditch with external bank, with a single construction phase in the Late Neolithic/Beaker period. Alternatively, an axial stone circle of Later Bronze Age date may have been inserted into an existing Neolithic henge. These two scenarios are considered more likely than the possibility that this is a Reanascreena-type monument of Later Bronze Age date or that the stone circle pre-dates the bank and ditch enclosure.

Support for a henge connection here may be found in the distribution of related monuments in County Kerry. There are few convincing examples of henges in south and west Kerry; however, four embanked enclosures in the northern part of the county may be linked with this tradition (Toal 1995, 69-73). These form part of a distribution that may extend south as far as the Killarney area, where a number of circular, internally ditched, enclosures in the 30-50m diameter range have been identified. These include Raheen (RMP KE059-017), Lisshaneraoughter (KE065-083) and Kilbreanbeg (KE067-002), the latter site located 2.5km north of Lissyvigeen. None of these sites has been excavated.

In conclusion, the evidence presented does not support the idea that the stone circles at Glantane East and Reanascreena South in south-west Ireland are '... diminutive versions of circle henges' (Condit & Simpson 1998, 57). This is a possibility for Lissyviggeen; however, the stone circle here may well be a later addition. Similar doubts hang over Dun Ruadh and Ballynoe, questioning the very existence of circle henges as a separate sub-class in Ireland. Ironically, the most convincing example here of a circle henge, Ballynahattin, was a totally unique monument and in that regard justifies the label 'Ireland's Stonehenge'.

Stone circles were probably linked to the henge tradition in Ireland, with Newgrange providing the most striking example. Those with the most likely henge connections may prove to be the embanked types, sites such as the Nymphsfield group near Cong, County Mayo, Boleycarrigeen in County Wicklow and Grange, Lough Gur, County Limerick. The latter is particularly significant given its Grooved Ware and Beaker pottery association, material culture that is noticeably absent from the 'circle henges' considered in this paper. Late stone circles, such as the Cork–Kerry and mid-Ulster groups, are unlikely to have any direct connection with Neolithic henges. Any hengiform element in these monuments may be regarded as an embellishment of the stone circle idea through contact with contemporary earthen barrow traditions.

The problems of henge chronology and classification raised in this paper emphasise the need for further excavation of these enigmatic monuments. We would do well to follow the example of Derek Simpson who, over four decades of inspiring research and incisive excavation, has contributed greatly to our understanding of death and ritual in the Bronze Age.

BIBLIOGRAPHY

Bradley, R., 1998 Stone circles and passage graves – a contested relationship. In Gibson & Simpson (eds), 1998, 2-13.

Buckley, V., 1988 'Ireland's Stonehenge' – a lost antiquarian monument rediscovered. *Archaeology Ireland,* 2 (2), 53-5.

Burl, A., 1976 *The Stone Circles of the British Isles.* London & Newhaven: Yale University Press.

Clare, T., 1986 Towards a reappraisal of henge monuments. *Proceedings of the Prehistoric Society,* 52, 281-316.

Clare, T., 1987 Towards a reappraisal of henge monuments: origins, evolution and hierarchies. *Proceedings of the Prehistoric Society,* 53, 457-77.

Cleary, R., 1993 The Later Bronze Age at Lough Gur; filling in the blanks. In Shee Twohig, E. & Ronayne, M. (eds), *Past Perceptions: The Prehistoric Archaeology of South-West Ireland,* 114-120. Cork: Cork University Press.

Condit, T. & Simpson, D., 1998 Irish hengiform enclosures and related monuments. In Gibson & Simpson (eds), 45-61.

Cuppage, J., 1986 *Archaeological Survey of the Dingle Peninsula.* Ballyferriter: Oidhreacht Chorca Dhuibhne.

Davies, O., 1936 Excavations at Dun Ruadh. *Proceedings of the Belfast Natural History and Philosophical Society*, 1, 50-75.

Evans, E., 1966 *Prehistoric and Early Christian Ireland*. London: Batsford.

Fahy, E., 1959 A recumbent stone circle at Drombeg, Co. Cork. *Journal of the Cork Historical and Archaeological Society*, 64, 1-27.

Fahy, E., 1961 A stone circle, hut and dolmen at Bohonagh, Co. Cork. *Journal of the Cork Historical and Archaeological Society*, 66, 93-104.

Fahy, E., 1962 A recumbent stone circle at Reanascreena South, Co. Cork. *Journal of the Cork Historical and Archaeological Society*, 67, 59-69.

Gibson, A. & Simpson, D. (eds), *Prehistoric Ritual and Religion. Essays in Honour of Aubrey Burl*. Stroud: Alan Sutton.

Groenman-van Waateringe, W. & Butler, J., 1976 The Ballynoe stone circle. *Palaeohistoria*, 18, 73-104.

Lynch, A., 1981 *Man and Environment in South-west Ireland*. BAR British Series 85. Oxford: British Archaeological Reports.

Newman, C., 1997 *Tara: an Archaeological Survey*. Dublin: the Royal Irish Academy and The Discovery Programme.

O' Brien, W., 1992 Boulder-burials: a Later Bronze Age megalith tradition in south-west Ireland. *Journal of the Cork Historical and Archaeological Society*, 97, 11-35.

O'Brien, W., 1993 Aspects of wedge tomb chronology. In Shee Twohig, E. & Ronayne, M. (eds), *Past Perceptions: the Prehistoric Archaeology of South-West Ireland*, 63-74. Cork: Cork University Press.

O'Brien, W., 1999 *Sacred Ground: Megalithic Tombs in Coastal South-west Ireland*. Bronze Age Studies 5, Galway: National University of Ireland, Galway.

Ó Nualláin, S., 1975 The stone circle complex of Cork and Kerry. *Journal of the Royal Society of Antiquaries of Ireland*, 105, 83-131.

Ó Nualláin, S., 1978 Boulder-burials. *Proceedings of the Royal Irish Academy*, 78C, 75-100.

Ó Nualláin, S., 1984 A survey of stone circles in Cork and Kerry. *Proceedings of the Royal Irish Academy*, 84C, 1-77.

Ó Nualláin, S., 1988 Stone rows in the south of Ireland. *Proceedings of the Royal Irish Academy*, 88C, 179–256.

Ó Ríordáin, S.P., 1950 Excavation of some earthworks on the Curragh, Co. Kildare. *Proceedings of the Royal Irish Academy*, 53C, 249-77.

O'Shaughnessy, J., 1991 Leckaneen. In Bennett, I. (ed.) *Excavations 1990*, 17-18, Dublin: Wordwell.

O'Sullivan, A. & Sheehan, J., 1996 *The Iveragh Peninsula, An Archaeological Survey of South Kerry*. Cork: Cork University Press.

Piggott, S. & Simpson, D., 1971 Excavation of a stone circle at Croft Moraig, Perthshire, Scotland. *Proceedings of the Prehistoric Society*, 37 (1), 1-15.

Pilcher, J.R., 1969 Archaeology, palaeoecology and radiocarbon dating of the Beaghmore stone circle site. *Ulster Journal of Archaeology*, 32, 73-91.

Power, D., 1992 *et seq. Archaeological Inventory of County Cork*, Vols I (1992), II (1994), III (1997) and IV (2000). Dublin: The Stationary Office.

Simpson, D.D.A., 1993 Dun Ruadh: a real Irish henge. *Archaeology Ireland*, 7 (2), 14-15.

Simpson, D.D.A., Weir, D.A. & Wilkinson, J.L., 1992 Excavations at Dun Ruadh, Crouck, Co. Tyrone. *Ulster Journal of Archaeology*, 54-5, 36-7.

Toal, C. 1995. *North Kerry Archaeological Survey*. Dingle: Brandon Press.

Wright, T., 1758 *Louthiana, a Collection of the Most Remarkable Remains of the Works of the Danes and Druids in the County of Louth*. Dublin (reprinted 2000 by Dundalgan Press).

21

FORTY-FIVE YEARS' RESEARCHES IN THE CHRONOLOGY AND ORDERING OF THE BRITISH BRONZE AGE: A PERSONAL MEMOIR

COLIN BURGESS

> The devolution of the Collared Urn… is some measure of the time taken by a wave of culture, or rather, of people, to spread over the British Isles… it survives in Ross-shire into La Tène times and in Co. Limerick perhaps later still. (Childe 1956, 150)

> Cordoned Urns represent one side of the Highland Zone Late Bronze Age tradition, and with them, too, other types with applied plastic ornament… (Piggott 1955, 134)

> In considering the Late Bronze Age… one is faced with the problem of what to include in this period (Annable & Simpson 1964, 31)

> What enables us to isolate the unities (epistemic entities) with which our research deals?… Can we investigate historical thresholds, ruptures, and transformations without resorting to meta-narratives concerning social progress or notions of teleological purpose in general? (Topics for discussion at a Theoretical Archaeology Group session on Time, Lampeter, 2003)

It was while digging in London in the late 1950s and pursuing bronzes in the London Museum that I got to know a charismatic polymath called Francis Celoria, then a keeper at the Museum. Francis had been organising for some years an archaeological survey of the Hebridean island of Islay. The project included some limited excavation, notably of a rich Bronze Age site at Kilellan Farm, and when in 1960 Francis lost his director of the excavations there, I rashly allowed myself to be talked into taking it over. Swiftly the excavation files were passed to me, and amongst the voluminous correspondence were numerous letters about the site's pottery from the site's finder and first explorer, a Glasgow businessman called James Whittaker, to a young specialist called Derek Simpson at Devizes Museum. I had the letters (now with the site archive in the National Monuments Record of Scotland in Edinburgh), but curiously it was to be many years before I actually met the man. Well, Derek, let this at least be a reminder of youthful sins – and a narrow escape, because all these years later Kilellan remains unpublished (Burgess 1976 for an interim), and has seen off everyone who has tried to take it in hand (though even as I finish this I gather the final report, by Anna Ritchie and others, has been completed).

My title, inspired of course by Mortimer's monumental work (Mortimer 1905), started out as *Forty Years' Researches…*, but after I began to write I came across one of the first undergraduate essays I produced for R.J.C. Atkinson at Cardiff, in late 1958, which asked me to discuss the evidence for Cinerary Urns continuing into the Late Bronze Age. At that time, as the first two quotations at the head of this essay make clear, it was received wisdom that Urns lasted right through the Bronze Age, with late forms, especially Cordoned and Encrusted Urns, belonging to the Late Bronze Age. It is instructive to look at chronological tables for the period then current, for example that of Grimes (1951, 94, fig. 30), in which the totality of Bronze Age material culture then available was divided up and spread neatly through the whole period. Thus Late Beakers and Food Vessels were Early Bronze Age, Enlarged Food Vessels and Collared Urns were Middle Bronze Age, followed by late Urns, Collared, Cordoned and Encrusted, and also Deverel-Rimbury, which carried the story through the Late Bronze Age to the Iron Age. The other assumption, evident in the first two quotations, is cultural retardation. It was received wisdom that it took millennia for things to spread from the East to the Atlantic West, and centuries for anything to spread from Europe to Britain, and then from the lowland south-east of England into the Highland Zone north and west.

What follows falls into two parts, though the two are linked and depend very much on each other. Firstly there is the general ordering of Bronze Age material, in effect the relative chronology. This has then to be given an absolute framework, and although today this is increasingly dependent on radiocarbon and other scientific dating methods, an understanding of metalwork remains crucial. This much is made clear by Needham's recent revision of Bronze Age chronology (Needham *et al.* 1997), never mind that, by and large, it is still the metalwork which relates the British sequence to what was happening in the outside world. Accordingly much of this paper will review the development of Bronze Age metalwork studies over the past few decades, a specialism that has become so unfashionable in Britain that it is in danger of dying out (Burgess 2001a).

When I wrote that essay in 1958 I had only recently started working on Bronze Age metalwork for an undergraduate dissertation, but even I could see that there were no associations which would put Urns even into the Middle Bronze Age, never mind the Late Bronze Age. On the contrary, their datable associations placed them entirely in the Early Bronze Age. But what seemed obvious to an undergraduate was to take years to get across to the world at large, and to this day I expect that there are museums up and down the country which still have Late Bronze Age labels on their Urns.

The other problem facing progress in the late '50s was terminological. Early, Middle and Late Bronze Age were in general use, but they did not mean the same thing to all people. To a certain extent the confusion has persisted ever since, exacerbated since the late '70s by the widespread use of the terms 'earlier' and 'later' Bronze Age alongside the traditional Early, Middle and Late. If Bronze Age specialists cannot always agree what these terms encompass, what hope is there for the rest? One surprise has been the persistence of this traditional Three Age terminology. As early as the mid-'50s attempts were being made to write prehistory without use of the Three Age system. Atkinson in his undergraduate lectures at Cardiff in the late '50s frequently remarked with pride that he had written *Stonehenge* (Atkinson 1956) without using the Three Ages. Decades later I tried to emulate him in writing the *Age of Stonehenge* (Burgess 1980), with no more success and causing a great deal of confusion which I recognised in the second edition (Burgess 2001b). Partly it is a problem of what to use instead, partly it is because of the terminological confusion referred to above. Atkinson (1960, 87), writing in an age when time-lag was received wisdom, muddled himself and everyone else: '... since... development does not take place uniformly, even in an area as small as Britain, it is inevitable that at one and the same time... a community, say, in Wessex... must be assigned to the Middle Bronze Age, while another in northern England, less advanced, belongs to the Early Bronze Age, and a third in northern Scotland, retarded through geographical isolation, will still be in the Late Stone Age.' Strictly speaking Atkinson was right: these are technological not time divisions. But once time-lag disappears, these become effectively time divisions, and the Early Bronze Age in Wessex is the Early Bronze Age in northern England and the Early Bronze Age in northern Scotland. And time-lag was soon to disappear, partly because of the growing contribution of C14 dates from the late '50s, and partly because of the increasing understanding of the metalwork, its chronology, and its relationships both within Britain and to the Continental material.

But in the '60s what constituted Early, Middle and Late Bronze Age was still a matter for dispute and confusion, not helped by the fact that two major pieces of research on the period in the late '50s were widely discussed but have never been published. One, a statistical examination of Wessex Culture graves by R.J.C. Atkinson, formed the basis of the undergraduate teaching I was given on the subject, and this approach I reworked and published 30 years later (Burgess 1996). The other, C.F.C. Hawkes' *Scheme for the British Bronze Age* (1960; see below), became one of the most widely circulated cyclostyled documents in archaeological history, and as its title implies it has provided a framework for the periodisation of the Bronze Age which essentially has lasted ever since. For all that dates and the content of the phases have changed dramatically, it is perhaps a sign of the *Scheme*'s lasting importance that it is finally to be published by Brendan O'Connor and Sabine Gerloff 44 years after it was circulated among a small group of people. Perhaps it will come at a good time, since there are no out-and-out Bronze Age specialists left in our universities to teach the period (Burgess 2001a), and it is left to generalists and those drafted in from other periods. The result inevitably is that when one reads of the excavation of a Middle Bronze Age barrow or Late Bronze Age settlement, goodness knows what is meant in chronological and cultural terms. 45 years ago, in the aftermath of Hawkes 1960, at least a student had some idea of what these terms involved.

In 1969, after a decade of intensive research on the metalwork, I felt ready to enter a plea for 'uniformity of phraseology, and to deplore persistent haphazard use of the terms "Middle Bronze Age" and "Late Bronze Age" in particular' (Burgess 1969, 22). I tried to show what went into the Early, Middle and Late divisions, and especially to demonstrate that all the forms of Urns could be assigned to the Early Bronze Age, with no evidence that any of them continued even into the Middle Bronze – as Bu'Lock (1961) had suggested some time before. Their place in the Middle Bronze Age was taken by Deverel-Rimbury pottery, as M.A. Smith (1959) had argued, following up the suggestions of Butler and I. Smith (1956). At this stage John Barrett's crucial studies on Deverel-Rimbury and post-Deverel-Rimbury developments were still several years in the future, but these would eventually show that Deverel-Rimbury was also present in the Early Bronze Age, and that a social difference was indicated vis-à-vis Urns. Alas, like all pleas for standardised terminology, mine fell on deaf ears, and as with so much that archaeologists do, became, as Woolley put it in another context, 'merely a bone of contention for the learned, and a source of confusion for the layman' (Woolley 1937, 17). As late as 1984 Longworth could still write of Collared Urns that 'the tradition may have persisted after 1000 BC' (Longworth 1984, 79). Radiocarbon had become king, and Bronze Age scholars had reached a point where they regularly tied themselves in knots trying to fit their material to a few potentially rogue C14 Dates (Burgess 1986, 342-4). That is why my named periods in the *Age of Stonehenge* (Burgess 1980) were such a disaster (Burgess 1986, 350; 2001b, 13-14).

Space allows only one other epoch-making development of the '60s to be mentioned. In 1966 J.G.D. Clark published his seminal *Invasion Hypothesis* paper (Clark 1966), and freed British scholars from the notion that cultural change had to be the result of invasion from outside. Suddenly we could have a largely indigenous Iron Age, for example, with Hallstatt and Marnian invasions banished, but paradoxically for Clark some invasions still seemed certain: 'There is no intention to question that the appearance of Beaker pottery in this country... indicates some intrusion of actual people' (*ibid.*, 180). But Clark had put everything up for scrutiny, and ten years later even the Beaker Folk had gone, to be replaced by some extra-cultural phenomenon which over much of Europe was absorbed by local cultures and adapted to their own needs (Burgess & Shennan 1976). Clark was careful to say that 'Invasions and minor intrusions' undoubtedly took place in British prehistory (*ibid.*, 188), and this has opened the door to other possibilities. What scale of movement is represented by the horseshoe-handled Urns of Southern England, Northern France and the Low Countries, and which way did it go? (Clark 1966, 184; Cruse *et al.* 1983; Burgess 1987a, 308-9; Blanchet 1984, 198-218; Blanchet *et al.* 1989, 494-8; Billard *et al.* 1996; O'Connor 1989, 519). Similarly, whether there is any foreign element in the Wessex Culture continues to be discussed (Piggott 1938; Clark 1966, 182-4; Burgess 1996). The problem, as Clark recognised, is to identify invasions unequivocally in the archaeological record. For example, there has been a major migration of Britons into France, and into other countries of the European Union, in the last dozen years. Probably no one knows just how many people have left Britain, but in France alone it is commonly accepted that hundreds of thousands have now settled. It is interesting to speculate just what changes these have wrought which would be identifiable in the archaeological record. I suspect that only in the rubbish dumps would there be any trace, of British furniture and fittings if conditions of preservation were exceptional, but otherwise only occasional fragments, of crockery, or of jars of Marmite or bottles of HP sauce or sherry; and right-hand drive cars that have escaped scrapping or repatriation to the UK. Of course the analogy is not exact, because these Britons live in French houses, eat French food, and are buried in French cemeteries if they do not return to Britain to die or be interred. But it shows how little trace even a significant incursion can leave.

Research and publication on the Bronze Age continued apace through the late '60s, the '70s and into the early '80s. Leaving aside the metal for the moment, corpora were undertaken of some of the major pottery types, notably Beakers (D.L. Clarke 1970) and Collared Urns (Longworth 1984; with suggested modifications by Burgess 1986). Of other forms of Urns we still await national surveys, and Food Vessels, long rumoured to be forthcoming in the '70s, have still not arrived. Scotland and some of the regions saw surveys of various ceramic types, for example by Cowie (1978: Food Vessel Urns), Simpson (1965: Food Vessels of south-west Scotland), and Gibson (1982: Beaker domestic material). Ireland has been a different story, with Bronze Age research continuing vigorously up to the present day. The pottery has been particularly well served, especially by Kavanagh (1973, 1976 and 1977), who dealt with all the Urns and Pygmy Cups, and Ó Ríordáin and Waddell (1993), who covered the Food Vessels, while Waddell (1990) has in addition given us a major survey of Bronze Age burials.

In many ways the most important ceramic work of the '70s was John Barrett's on Deverel-Rimbury, and especially post-Deverel-Rimbury, which revealed another Bronze Age. In 1974 I had produced a synthesis of what to me seemed the current state of knowledge on the Bronze Age, and metalwork apart I had been hard pressed to make much of the Late Bronze Age. One could talk of early hillforts, and speculate that simple plain vessels of ancient ancestry, sometimes shouldered and generally undecorated apart from fingertipping, might prove to be the intractable material that one had to deal with in the Late Bronze Age (Burgess 1974, 220-1). It is interesting to compare another synthesis from the end of the decade, in Megaw & Simpson, 1979, 178-343. Conveniently for present purposes, the period was divided into two, Simpson taking the early part, and Megaw the later Bronze Age, though chapter headings do not entirely agree with the division of labour claimed in the preface (*ibid.*, 4). What is remarkable is how little overall change there is in the treatment of the later Bronze Age from Burgess 1974: lots of metalwork and Deverel-Rimbury, some hillforts and enclosures, and a general scavenging in the highways and byways to show that the period still was not really understood. Mention is made of Barrett's work, but this survey came just too early for its full significance to be assimilated.

All was about to change. Barrett, in a series of crucial papers (Barrett 1975; 1976; 1979; 1980), dragged study of the period into the end of the twentieth century. What he showed was that 'much pottery always regarded as typically Iron Age is in fact Late Bronze Age' (Burgess 1988, 569). We were introduced to the concept of post-Deverel-Rimbury wares, and plain ware assemblages, and suddenly everything fell into place. We also heard increasingly of the 'earlier' and 'later' Bronze Age (Barrett & Bradley 1980), but exactly how these related to the traditional Early, Middle and Late divisions has been a source of confusion ever since (Selkirk 1979). Barrett and Bradley's original definition of the concept hardly helped matters. A re-reading of their words nearly 25 years later (Barrett & Bradley 1980b) suggests they themselves were not entirely clear what they intended. They remarked that their Later Bronze Age marked 'not too precisely' the period they wanted the contributors to their volume to discuss! Their imprecision certainly communicated itself to the contributors, whose papers reveal that no one then was at all clear what was intended by 'earlier' and 'later', because their papers range happily through the traditional Early, Middle and Late Bronze Age. I have railed against this uncertainty before (Burgess 1995a), and there should be no confusion, since Needham (1992) has set out the rules clearly enough. Whatever Barrett and Bradley intended, there is a natural break in the Bronze Age provided by the catastrophe in the twelfth century BC, and for me this has always been the obvious place to divide *Earlier* from *Later* Bronze Age. The continuum before the crisis, the traditional Early and Middle Bronze Age, is the earlier Bronze Age. It was followed after the dislocation by a later Bronze Age, the old Late Bronze Age, which was totally different in character (Burgess 1980, 157-9).

For me, the concept of a Bronze Age in two very different halves had arisen out of a hobbyhorse I had been riding for many years, the notion of catastrophic changes dividing abruptly one period from another, and giving each a very different character. In the late '70s, mainly as a result of all the settlement excavation that was taking place in many different parts of Britain, I became convinced that an environmental catastrophe in the late second millennium effectively divided the Bronze Age into two parts that bore very little resemblance to each other. I first published a note on the subject in *Current Archaeology* (Burgess 1979a), developed the theme at length in the *Age of Stonehenge* (Burgess 1980, 155-9), persisted with it through the '80s (e.g. Burgess 1985), but drew very little response until the theme was taken up by science. In 1989 both Mike Baillie and I contributed to a Catastrophe issue of *Current Archaeology* (Baillie 1989; Burgess 1989), and suddenly the notion became much more reputable. Subsequent work by Baillie (e.g. 1995a; 1995b) and others has emphasised that this twelfth century BC calamity was a global crisis. Its effects are visible throughout the Old World, from the collapse of the great Late Bronze Age civilisations of the East, Mycenaean, Hittite and Egyptian, to settlement and population disaster in the Atlantic margins (Burgess 1985; 1992; 2001c: Falkenstein 1997). For long it was thought to be the result simply of a volcanic event, the eruption of Hekla 3 on Iceland in 1159 BC, but more recently a wider variety of natural processes have been canvassed, and the causes of such downturns are deemed much less certain (Baillie 1995b; 1999 and pers. comm.).

One other crucial development in the '70s was the discovery of Bronze Age settlement and field systems, sometimes forming extensive relict Bronze Age landscapes. Even 40 years ago knowledge of Bronze Age settlement, outside Deverel-Rimbury sites in southern England and Trevisker sites in the South–West, was scrappy at best, and a total blank in many regions. Intensive fieldwork and large-scale excavations in the '70s changed all that, revealing how much of the second millennium landscape survives in lowland and upland alike. If I have to single out two remarkable pieces of pioneering work, they would be Pryor's uncovering of the fen-edge landscapes in eastern England (Pryor 2001), and Fleming's work on the Dartmoor reaves (Fleming 1988). This work of the '70s, as Barber (2003) has recently noted, marks a turning away from the artefact studies which had hitherto dominated Bronze Age research to an interest in settlement and landscape which characterised the '80s and beyond. Work on earlier Bronze Age landscapes continued apace, but also increasingly on Late Bronze Age settlements as their character became recognised. The work of Needham and others on Runnymede must be singled out (Needham 2000), of Bradley and his colleagues on the Kennet gravels (Bradley *et al.* 1980), the identification and excavation of Late Bronze Age ringworks (Burgess 1988, 565-6) such as Mucking (Bond 1988) and Springfield Lyons (Buckley & Hedges 1987) in Essex, and the Bronze Age elements of hillforts such as the Breiddin (Musson 1991).

I turn now to the second of my themes, the metalwork, familiarity with which remains crucial to understanding the Bronze Age. I hope I may be forgiven a personal aside at this point, but it does explain how different those days of archaeology nearly half a century ago were. In 1958 I was lucky to be given a unique opportunity to familiarise myself rapidly and intensively with one of the largest and most representative collections of metalwork in the country. I had come unexpectedly, late and unprepared, to my honours degree course, and Leslie Alcock (to whom I shall be eternally grateful) suggested for my undergraduate thesis *The Bronze Age Metalwork from the Thames at London*. Donald Harden, Keeper of the London Museum, was the new external examiner at Cardiff, and he and his staff at the Museum threw open their doors to me, and made available their extraordinary bronze collections. These had recently been dramatically swollen by the acquisition of the Layton Collection of material from the Thames, one of the largest and most important bronze collections ever assembled by an individual. Temporarily this resided in the basement of Lancaster House, and for weeks I laboured there alone in appalling light while international diplomatic conferences went on above my head. Security was less of a problem in those days, because I seemed able to come and go unchallenged. The vast room was lined with glass-fronted cabinets housing the bronzes, and almost filled by a great table on which I could spread out, sort and draw as representative a range of Bronze Age metalwork as could be found anywhere in the country. In particular it was possible to lay out and arrange the finest and most varied array of swords anywhere in Britain: everything from early Urnfield imports to Gündlingen weapons of Ha. C. It was there, with J.D. Cowen's publications at my elbow (Cowen 1951; 1955), that a typology of British swords took shape, later to form the basis of a *PBF* volume on the swords of Britain (Colquhoun & Burgess 1988).

The actual material was only one half of the equation; the other was the literature, and in the late '50s the publication of the metalwork was gathering pace. My 1958 essay on the dating of Urns had drawn heavily on a paper by Jay Butler and Isobel Smith (1956) that must be regarded as the starting point for the re-ordering and re-dating of the Bronze Age in modern times. It was they who pointed up the vital prerequisites necessary to understand and sort out the Bronze Age: thorough familiarity with the metalwork, the need to know something of what went before and came afterwards, the need always to look at the Continental evidence, and the fallacy of time-lag, whether within Britain and Ireland, or from the Continent to Britain and Ireland. With these tenets in mind they were able to show that Urns need not be distributed in penny packets through the whole Bronze Age, but that all were in use by the time of the Wessex Culture or not long after, including Biconical Urns. They then went on to think the unthinkable: that even Deverel-Rimbury, on the basis of the Dutch evidence, began in the Middle Bronze Age.

Butler and Smith were presenting revolutionary ideas, and necessarily could not be too bold in such conservative times. One of the problems evident in re-reading their paper is the vagueness in the period terminology of the time. Urns and Deverel-Rimbury could both be admitted in the Middle Bronze Age, but what was the Middle Bronze Age then, where was the Wessex Culture, what did the Early Bronze Age then comprise, and where did the Late Bronze Age begin and end? A new framework for the period was urgently needed to remind everyone where everything fitted. It might have come from Jay Butler, but he had taken himself off to the Netherlands in 1957 (Reinders 2001), and attention switched to C.F.C. Hawkes and to Oxford.

Between 1957 and 1970 a whole series of studies emanated from Christopher Hawkes and his pupils at Oxford: Margaret Smith (subsequently Brown), Dennis Britton, and, later, Sabine Gerloff. Their papers should be essential reading for anyone hoping to understand the Bronze Age. In the background were successive volumes of the international *Inventaria Archaeologica* series, begun by M.E. Mariën under the auspices of the ICPPS in 1950, the British contributions to which Hawkes began in 1955 (Hawkes 1955), with the collaboration of the CBA, drawing on the British Association metalwork Card Catalogue maintained at Oxford and the British Museum. The idea was wonderful: simple, good quality fully-illustrated and well-researched publications by the participating countries 'in uniform format, a series of cards of the finds essential to the understanding of each period in the region it covers'. With Hawkes in charge the British series was devoted entirely to the graves and hoards of the Bronze Age, eight issues appearing, all but one edited by Hawkes, Smith and Britton, between 1955 and 1960 (Britton 1960a). Alas, viability was sacrificed for quality, and in Britain at least the whole thing was impossibly expensive. The ninth and last, on the Heathery Burn finds, had to wait another eight years (Britton & Longworth 1968). Years later an attempt was made to revive the format under the auspices of the British Museum (Needham *et al.* 1985), but that, too, seems quietly to have faded away.

The *Inventaria* issues provided a background for a series of crucial papers emanating from this Oxford school. I fear the monumental first offering, Hawkes and Smith (1957) on buckets and cauldrons, was eventually to be proved fatally flawed, but is still worth reading simply as a showcase of Hawkes's encyclopaedic knowledge of the Continental material and sources. Alas, the thesis derived buckets and cauldrons from the wrong Aegean and central European prototypes, and was further led astray by the prevailing fashion of retardation. The result cast a shadow over Late Bronze Age metalwork studies for 20 years. On the other hand, Margaret Smith's (1959) paper on *Some Somerset Hoards* was one of the most illuminating Bronze Age studies of the post-War period. At a stroke it made sense of palstave typology and Middle Bronze Age metalwork generally, and showed the way forward for re-ordering the Middle and Late Bronze Age. It failed in only one major respect, in not recognising that there was a primary phase of the Middle Bronze Age that came between the Wessex Culture and the Ornament

Horizon. This was largely because of a failure to recognise two primary groups of palstaves, of which shield-pattern palstaves were the more important. Recognition of this Acton Park stage would come a little later, from Jay Butler working from the Dutch end (Butler, 1961; 1963), and myself by then working on the Welsh material (1962a; 1962b; 1964). But this anticipates events.

In the same volume of *Proceedings of the Prehistoric Society* as *Somerset Hoards* was a second paper by Margaret Smith, written with A.E. Blin-Stoyle. Confusingly it has her as M.A. Smith on the cover, and M.A. Brown, her new married name, inside (Brown & Blin-Stoyle 1959). This first mass analysis of Bronze Age metalwork showed how important metallurgical analysis could be in understanding the British Bronze Age. In 1960 it was Hawkes's turn again, with his monumental *Scheme for the British Bronze Age* presented at the December CBA Bronze Age Conference in London, but tragically never published. For the first time an overall classification of the Irish-British Bronze Age was presented, with the familiar Early, Middle and Late divisions set out much as they have continued to the present day. But it was a framework both forward-looking and anachronistic. The divisions and their dates were to last for decades, but retardation still ruled the day, and some of what went into each division was certainly not trend-setting. Metalwork throughout was dealt with by a series of lettered industries, starting with First A (in EBA 1, Migdale and Wessex I), and extending through to G, Carp's Tongue, all being allowed to overlap, and only successive in a broad sense. But he began by returning to the notion of a Copper Age, a concept which, alas, has never gained favour in Britain, and was to be ignored once more. At the risk of digressing, I must restate my belief (Burgess 1992, 37-8) that Hawkes was right: that Britain and Ireland need a Copper Age, not just to come into line with so many other parts of Europe, but in order to define that period immediately before the Bronze Age when society was still essentially Late Neolithic, but had been changed by the Beaker phenomenon and all that went with it, including copper metallurgy (and gold and silver). I shall discuss this in more detail below.

This is not the place to run through Hawkes's *Scheme* in detail, especially since, as previously noted, it is to be published at last after 45 years. While the phase divisions have provided a framework for the Irish-British Bronze Age ever since, their absolute dates have changed dramatically, as *Table 11* makes clear. What went into the phases has changed even more radically. Time-lag is still very much in evidence, and 'insular culture', as represented by Urns, continues right through to LBA1, and disappears only when we get to LBA2, after 750/700 BC. For Hawkes, like everyone at the time, regular incomings and invasions accounted for change, so that the scheme ends with LBA 3 (650/600-550/500 BC or later), and the arrival of 'groups of Continental Hallstatt people', bringing in distinctive Hallstatt I novelties. These opened the way for 'a hundred years or more of Late Hallstatt colonisation', which in the sixth and fifth centuries resulted in the Iron Age.

Much of this now seems quaint and no doubt extraordinarily turgid in an age of different preoccupations; but it achieved a widespread and long-lasting influence. No matter that it belongs to another era of research; familiarity with Hawkes, 1960, remains necessary for any would-be Bronze Age specialist. Its impact was immediate, starting with Coles's survey of the Scottish metalwork (Coles 1960, 17). Coles, however, eschewed Hawkes's numbered phases and named their Scottish equivalents after representative finds, a practice that was to become general among later writers. Much the same system was adopted by Eogan (1964; 1965) in considering the Irish material, though the framework of his chronological chart (Eogan 1964, 324, fig. 20) is very much that of Hawkes. The *Scheme* is also implicit in Butler's treatment of connections across the North Sea (Butler 1963). Butler, however, working from the Continental end, and with European chronologies in mind, realised that British and Continental chronologies were seriously out of sync, as the recent publication of Müller-Karpe's (1959) enormous Urnfield chronology tome had made clear for the Late Bronze Age. Butler began the process of whittling away at time-lag and backdating the Irish-British phases to bring them more into line with Europe. Thus he suggested Wilburton must begin in the tenth century, revolutionary indeed, and carp's tongue early in the eighth, but that was not much earlier than Hawkes. It appears strange now that his proposal for MBA 2, Taunton-Barton Bendish and Ornament Horizon, was so conservative in the light of Müller-Karpe: from the mid-twelfth into the eleventh century BC. He appears not to have taken on board Hawkes' concept of MBA 3 to take account of early Urnfield imports, especially first swords, and other novelties at the end of the MBA. In his time chart, indeed, he does have a box for the swords, in the eleventh century, but alongside Taunton-Barton Bendish.

Butler had one important advantage over his British colleagues, and that was his Continental base at a safe distance. It has to be remarked that in an age when several young researchers were beginning to work on Bronze Age problems, Hawkes exerted a fearsome grip on the period. Newcomers were very aware of what they could and could not say, especially about chronology, and this baneful influence was to last throughout the '60s and '70s. Accordingly, when in the mid-'60s, working from my new base in adult education in Newcastle, I attempted to tie all this new work together, it was necessary to be very cautious with dates. I had the advantage of a new awareness of French connections. I had been taught by R.J.C. Atkinson that France was *terra incognita*, and serious work there impossible, but the late and much-lamented Jacques Briard had changed all that. It was he who, in the '60s, made us suddenly aware how close was much of the north-west French to the British material. His lecture to the Prehistoric Society in London at the beginning of the '60s was a revelation for us all in Britain, and gave me the courage in 1963 to make my first visit to France. There I found not only that French colleagues made it easy to work, but also that French museums were not nearly as bad as I had been led to believe (and French hospitality, too, could be wonderful, especially as dispensed by Messrs Briard and Giot). Awareness of the relevance of the French material was confirmed by Briard's great volume on the Breton material (Briard 1965).

The synthesis of the British metalwork which took shape through the mid-'60s was thus able to take account of the French material. It was rejected for the *Proceedings of the Prehistoric Society* after a long delay, but the wonderful Jim Forde-Johnstone immediately seized on it for the *Archaeological Journal*. I had had to be very careful with the dates. Beginning Wilburton in the late tenth was as early as I dared go. The next stage, LBA 2, carp's tongue, Ewart Park, Heathery Burn, Dowris and the like, could not begin before the mid-eighth, because more than anything one dared not interfere with the dating of Hawkes's buckets and cauldrons. As yet this stage went without a general name: I introduced the Ewart Park phase only in 1972 (in Burgess *et al.* 1972, 214). But I did introduce a Penard stage to cover Hawkes's MBA 3, which I noted with surprise had not been taken up with any great enthusiasm (Burgess 1968a, 3). Other novelties were the Broadward tradition, characteristic principally of Wales and the Marches, later to be more fully explored in Burgess *et al.* 1972; and the Wallington tradition. This I had been working on alongside the *Archaeological Journal* paper, and it, too, was having difficulty finding a publisher. In this case it was David Smith, then Curator of the Joint Museum of Antiquities at Newcastle who came to the rescue and arranged for the Oriel Press to publish it (Burgess 1968b). The Wallington tradition was to the North and West of Britain, and Ireland, what Wilburton was to the South-East of England. It differed, however, in comprising a mix of old Middle Bronze Age ideas and new developments, and was only marginally touched by the lead-bronze Wilburton tradition. This interpretation and dating of Wallington would much later be disputed by Needham (1990); but the axes in the Wallington hoards are too sophisticated for the tradition to be entirely pre-Wilburton (Burgess 1995b), and I shall touch on this matter again at the end of this paper.

Dating changed little through the '70s. The chronology of Burgess 1974 was little different from Burgess 1968a, but there were hints that some of the Middle Bronze Age phases would have to go back a century or so (Burgess 1974, 203 and fig. 26). Licence for this had been given by Hawkes himself (Hawkes 1972, 115), and his remarks that the transition from Early to Middle Bronze Age would have to be set around 1500 BC, not 1400. Hawkes published little on the Bronze Age in the '70s, but in conversations, in lectures and at conferences, gave no hint that he was thinking of changing his ideas on LBA chronology in any major way. But the dam was waiting to burst, as more and more young Bronze Age specialists entered the field. It had been clear since the discovery of the Isleham hoard (Britton 1960b) that one day the Hawkes and Smith cauldron thesis would have to go, but somehow the words were never uttered. Coombs (1975, 72) went as far as referring to the fragments of cauldrons in the Isleham hoard, and as that was a late Wilburton assemblage (but see below), the implications were clear.

Throughout the '70s David Coombs and I were regular collaborators, and at the end of the decade edited a volume on hoards old and new (Burgess & Coombs 1979). We were only too aware that chronological changes were urgently needed, but it fell to my lot in that volume to publish what no one previously had dared utter aloud. In view of the Isleham association, I wrote, and of the need to bring the British LBA sequence into line with European chronologies, 'the Greek and Oriental cauldrons' must 'be irrelevant to the development of the western [cauldron] series'. We must 'set aside time-lag' concepts that for decades 'have displaced our chronologies by up to two centuries in relationship to Continental schemes' (Burgess, 1979b, 272). Accordingly Penard, correlating with Bz. D and Ha. A1-2, must be twelfth-eleventh centuries, Wilburton parallel with Ha. B1 must be tenth century, and Ewart Park, correlating with Ha. B2-3 must be ninth-eighth centuries. An overlong Ewart Park was a worry which even a prompt arrival of iron and first Hallstatt influence at 700 BC would not entirely allay. It was a worry that would not be resolved for another decade or so. The new dating did not finish there: MBA 1 was begun at 1500 BC, and Taunton was started in the fourteenth century, lasting into the thirteenth.

The fall-out was predictable. After worrying reports of Hawkes's reaction, eventually I wrote to clear the air. After months of silence, suddenly on 21 March, 1980, he replied at very great length, a letter full of intemperate language. Basically his response boiled down to me claiming innovations in dating that he and others had been working towards since the '50s and deceiving the reader for my own advantage. I was mystified, because neither then nor subsequently could I find anything in print or on the grapevine to suggest that either he or others had made, or were about to make, the sort of chronological changes I was proposing.

I thought that was that. But Hawkes was always a man of surprises, and after months of ominous silence, out of the blue I received another, much more normal and friendly letter, and it was as if the previous one had never been written. To my astonishment I was now taken to task for not being bold enough in my re-dating, especially of buckets and cauldrons. He had been working on them with Sabine Gerloff, and it was clear that their origins had to go back into early Urnfields, at least to 1200 BC! So, it is possible that he may have been thinking about major chronological changes, arising out of his work with Gerloff, and that I had stolen his thunder, but, alas, we may never know for sure exactly what had transpired. But meanwhile Brendan O'Connor, working in post-Hawkes Oxford, had come to very similar conclusions as David Coombs and I about cauldrons and buckets (O'Connor 1980, 147-8, 191-2, 272), and the new chronology became respectable.

Thus was a chronological framework established for the British Bronze Age that in essence was to last for the next 15 years. However, did we but know it, the metalwork bubble was about to burst. The various young workers who had been so assiduously pursuing bronzes through the '70s all disappeared in other directions. John Coles had gone already, into Palaeolithic, wetland and other studies; and Mike Rowlands, an anthropologist by vocation, who had been working on the Middle Bronze Age material (e.g. Rowlands 1976), Andy Lawson, whose contributions, particularly on the Ornament Horizon, promised much (e.g. Lawson 1979a; 1979b), Brendan O'Connor, who had produced his great tome on cross-Channel relations (O'Connor 1980), George Eogan, and David Coombs, all for reasons of career, necessity or inclination dropped wholly or partly out of intensive metalwork studies. And this writer, wearied by the effort of producing *The Age of Stonehenge* (Burgess 1980), and fed up after more than 20 years of unbroken research on British–Irish bronzes and Bronze Age problems, discovered foreign parts and other archaeologies.

By the early '80s Stuart Needham had the field effectively to himself, but in any case the incomprehensibility of the New and Newer archaeology had set in. My fourth quotation at the beginning of this essay epitomises for me why I think understanding of the Bronze Age, new sites and material apart, has changed comparatively little in the last 20 years; and why I felt little motivated to change much in the second edition of the *Age of Stonehenge* (Burgess 2001b). Metalwork, and indeed all material culture studies, became increasingly unfashionable as the '80s and '90s advanced, corpora disappeared (not, fortunately, in Ireland and on the Continent), and with rare exceptions – such as the Cranborne Chase study (Barrett, Bradley & Green 1991) – British universities effectively gave up on material culture, traditional archaeology, and the Bronze Age in particular. Many of the scholars from the '60s and '70s I have cited above have continued to publish from time to time, often major works (especially Eogan e.g. 1983; 1994); but the atmosphere has changed, and much of the work on the British Bronze Age has increasingly been done outside the universities. My own sporadic efforts in the last 20 years have appeared almost entirely in European publications, and formerly important subjects such as the Wessex Culture and cross-Channel relations have not been neglected (eg Burgess 1987a; 1988; 1990; 1991; 1992; 1996). In addition, French colleagues in particular have published a stream of important and often enormous compendia on aspects of the Bronze Age in Western Europe (e.g. Blanchet *et al.* 1987; Brun & Mordant 1988; Mordant & Richard 1992; Mordant & Gaiffe 1996). A small number of British and Irish colleagues have been regular contributors to these proceedings. But much of this is unfashionable stuff in Britain, and to judge from the frequency with which young researchers betray in their publications a need to re-invent the wheel, I doubt that very many in Britain ever read such things.

This regular participation of Irish–British researchers in major French programmes had arisen out of the formation of the Bronze Age Studies Group in 1976. This very informal gathering of European Bronze Age specialists had begun when I persuaded a dozen British and Irish friends to assemble at Alnwick Castle for a weekend that year. In subsequent years more and more Continental colleagues were enrolled, so that now membership extends to most countries of Western Europe, and members gather for a week of talk and field visits in a different region every year. The contrast with the lack of interchange between British and European colleagues just a few years before is remarkable, and the benefit not just to Bronze Age studies but to international friendship and co-operation has been remarkable.

One other aspect of metalwork research I must not forget, since it has occupied the efforts of many European researchers including myself since the late '60s. I refer, of course, to the German series *Prähistorische Bronzefunde*. Few archaeological enterprises have attracted so much flak over the years, but few, too, have made so much material available. Yes, it was annoying to say the least to discover from others that one's lovingly prepared *PBF* volume had been published months before, when one was still in course of writing the preface and adding the finishing touches! But however much one decries the production-line methods and often unfeeling drawings by ranks of artists unfamiliar with the material, the fact remains that we have available today many corpora of material that would not have existed otherwise. And are the drawings any worse than those executed by the unskilled who have had to illustrate their own publications; the illustrations that are put out as a matter of course these days by generalists with or without staff illustrators to hand? For since the early '80s we have come to live increasingly in an age without material culture specialists (Stoddart & Malone 2001).

The first British *PBF*, on the daggers and the Wessex Culture (Gerloff 1975), followed several years after the first Irish volumes (Harbison 1969a; 1969b). Only three more British volumes appeared, on the dirks and rapiers (Burgess & Gerloff 1981), on the axes of northern Britain (Schmidt & Burgess 1981), and on the British swords (Colquhoun & Burgess 1988). Ian Colquhoun was working on the spearheads in the late '80s when the Germans finally felt the financial squeeze and pulled the plug. Ian became a policeman, and still is. We look forward, however, to the publication as a *PBF* volume (hopefully soon) of Sabine Gerloff's habilitation thesis on buckets and cauldrons.

Inevitably absolute chronology has become more and more refined over the last two decades thanks to the contribution of the various scientific dating techniques. Dendrochronology, of course, has been the revelation (Baillie 1995a), but ever more sophisticated radiocarbon programmes also promise much, notably the work by Needham *et al.* (1997), dating wood associated with metalwork, and the programmes of Brindley and Lanting, especially on the Irish material (e.g. Brindley 1995). Radiocarbon dating of cremated bone means that increasing numbers of dates are appearing for the vessels with which they are associated (e.g. Sheridan 2003). But the same problems remain: to find appropriate samples and to avoid trying to squeeze the archaeology into a straightjacket suggested by rogue dates. The Bedd Branwen dates (Lynch 1971) illustrate this problem only too well. Having conceived a Bedd Branwen phase on the strength of these dates (Burgess 1980), I became increasingly convinced that they were much too late for the vessels they were supposed to date (Burgess 1986, 350). Happily a new series of dates has now confirmed these doubts (Lynch pers. comm.), fitting much more happily with the earlier dates suggested by the rest of the site evidence.

This brings me penultimately to Needham's recent and much-needed overhaul of British Bronze Age absolute chronology, bringing it into line with recent work on the European chronology (Needham 1996; Needham *et al.* 1997). It is a paradox that we have perhaps reached a point where the science-based chronology of the West is now more accurate than the history-based chronologies of the East; and the fact that so many eastern specialists are still resisting the chronological revisions suggested by science, creates extreme difficulties for anyone trying to relate West and East.

And finally: to end at the beginning. When and how did the Copper Age (Late Neolithic) end and the Bronze Age begin? Was there a long and drawn out process of transition or a big bang? If I incline to the latter it is because it seems to me that throughout Atlantic Europe at the end of the Copper Age people simply walked away from the past and into the wilderness. After all, there is nothing more final than people blocking up and concealing their ancestral tombs after centuries of use, and there is evidence of this happening from Britain, through France, in Portugal, Spain and even beyond. Not just that, they then abandoned their settlements, their diverse monuments of a rich cultural and spiritual heritage, and their traditional lands, and trekked out into the unknown. Sometimes they shifted only a few kilometres, but always it was to very different, poorer lands at the margins of their horizons. This all sounds melodramatic, but consider the evidence. In the archaeological record these events seem to a degree contemporary throughout the West, but how contemporary is contemporary (if that is not a solecism)? The common denominator everywhere is the Beaker and its accompaniments. Time and again the final use of chambered tombs is associated to a greater or lesser extent with a Beaker element, which may amount only to a sherd or two, or may include many complete Beakers and a range of typical Beaker artefacts. But they are always part of, and not a replacement for, the indigenous cultural material. The Beakers are always early, if not very early, and these episodes of final use appear often to have been sufficiently meaningful to deny that the Beakers in themselves could have been the direct cause of what came next – the blocking up and abandonment of the tombs, and the abandonment of associated long-settled lands.

It was a dramatic development that can be seen wherever Atlantic influence reached, even into the central Mediterranean. The island of Sardinia, for example, has 200-300 chambered tombs, originally perhaps many more (Moravetti 1998), but few of them have been excavated. Far more important, the repositories for the majority of Late Neolithic and Chalcolithic burials, were the tens of thousands of rock-cut tombs found all over the island. Modern excavations have been few, and published sections are even rarer, but astonishingly these rock-cut tombs, too, often show final phases of use in the local Copper Age in which classic Beakers and Beaker artefacts combine with local Copper Age material. And here, too, the end comes with a comprehensive blocking-up and concealment of the site. Published examples are rare, but the well-known cemetery of Anghelu Ruju (Taramelli 1909; Demartis 1989) makes the point.

Throughout Atlantic Europe domestic sites tell a similar story, most dramatically in the deeply-stratified sites of southern Spain. Typical is Los Castillejos at Montefrío, Granada (Arribas & Molina 1979), where more than 5m of deposits extend at least from the mid-Neolithic up to the Chalcolithic. In the uppermost levels, representing a lengthy period, local Chalcolithic is associated with classic Beaker and Beaker artefacts. Then – nothing; long abandonment of the site until it was re-occupied in the Iron Age. More often throughout Atlantic Europe it is the horizontal sequence that tells a similar story, of a long settlement history on the better, primary soils lasting from the Neolithic into the Chalcolithic, ending with local Chalcolithic and Beakers, and then abandonment. For the Bronze Age, if it can be found at all, one has to look to the much more inhospitable marginal lands. Consider Los Millares in its fertile valley setting, its final Copper Age phases, both in the settlement and the adjoining chambered tomb cemetery, associated with Beakers. For the Bronze Age one has to climb into the surrounding mountain desert, to find 10km away precipitous Bronze Age (Argaric) settlements such as Cerro del Enmedio and Cerro del Rayo (Schubart 1980).

All along the Atlantic lands, from Portugal northwards to Britain, the story is similar, except that all too often the Bronze Age is difficult or impossible to find. This contrast with the high-profiled Copper Age serves only to emphasise how different was the new Bronze Age world. Three regional surveys in which the writer has been concerned illustrate these points. At one end of the Atlantic margin, the Évora area of central Portugal (Burgess, 1987b) has a very rich and monumental Neolithic and Copper Age record. It is one of the great megalithic areas of Europe, with large numbers of chambered tombs, cromlechs (stone rings and settings in local parlance), standing stones, cup-marked rocks, stone-walled enclosures, and settlements. If no Beakers were found in any of these monuments in the 300sq.km surveyed, it may only be because of the lack of excavation. The sequence extends up to a mature phase of the local Copper Age, and then – nothing. Trying to find the Bronze

Age in this area is a problem never solved in seven seasons of fieldwork. After all that activity, the Bronze Age is represented putatively by a few cists and a few eroded surface scatters that may be Bronze Age but could equally be Copper Age. Substantial human activity only reappears in the archaeological record with Late Bronze Age hillforts of the early first millennium BC (Gibson *et al.* 1998; Burgess *et al.* 1999).

The point is made in a rather different way in the Milfield Basin in north Northumberland and the Lyne Basin in Peeblesshire. Unlike the Évora region, and indeed much of Portugal and western France, these are areas where abundant Bronze Age settlement has been identified – though not until the 1970s, and only after decades of field research. In both, Neolithic and Copper Age activity is concentrated on the valley bottom, and finishes with contexts which include a Beaker element. Then nothing for 1,000 years through much of the Bronze Age, apart from occasional burials (Burgess 1992; Speak & Burgess 1999). These lowlands were effectively abandoned, and to find Bronze Age settlement one has to look to the adjoining hills (Jobey 1980; Burgess 1984). And here it stayed for a millennium, until environmental catastrophe drove people back down to the lowlands in the twelfth century BC.

So the break between Copper Age and Bronze Age comes at a time when Beakers had been in use for some time, and so must have come despite the Beaker phenomenon, and not because of it. This still leaves the insoluble problem of how contemporary is contemporary. Irrespective of this, one thing that seems clear is that Atlantic society suffered a crisis at the end of the Copper Age, a complete rupture of settlement and social systems, and certainly a population collapse. This might be inferred by contrasting the nature of the settlements and the viability of the settlement areas, in which Copper Age and Bronze Age populations lived. It is not conceivable that the marginal environments to which Bronze Age populations retreated could have supported anything like the population levels of the plains and valleys of the Copper Age. Visit for yourself, reader, any Bronze Age settlement in the arid mountains of Almeria or the bleak hills of the Cheviots and this much will become clear. One might have come to the same conclusion from the sheer difficulty of finding the Bronze Age in so many parts of Atlantic Europe. So was there some common trigger which caused this break through so much of the West?

I have written so much about catastrophe in the Bronze Age that I cannot leave this without a catastrophic ending (or, rather, beginning). But I am not concerned here with the twelfth-century disaster which I and others have written so much about (e.g. Burgess 1980; 1985; 1989; 1992: Baillie 1989; 1995a; 1995b; 1999). The media these days are full of global environmental catastrophes, both those to come, and those that have been. The only things on which all agree is that one will come sooner rather than later, that they have happened regularly in the past, that they can empty whole regions and depopulate others, that they can completely change society, and that no one is yet sure in any particular case what the causes are. The worldwide crisis of the twelfth century BC I have already alluded to. Large parts of Britain, especially at the margins and possibly much of Scotland, had to be abandoned, and much-reduced (ultimately up to 50%?) populations concentrated in the more favourable niches, totally changed in their social, economic, technological and spiritual aspects. The cause seemed to be simple; the eruption in 1159 BC of the Icelandic volcano Hekla 3 (Baillie 1989; 1995a, 82-3; 1995b, 34-6: Falkenstein 1997: Burgess 2001c). But now, Hekla 3 seems not to be involved (Bogaard *et al.* 2002: Plunkett 1999), so a much wider range of causes has to be considered for such disasters, from comets, tectonic movements and seiches, to the failure of the Gulf Stream. So could such a disaster have separated Copper Age from Bronze Age?

It seems clear that the end of the western Copper Age was emphatic to say the least, to account for western populations walking away from a high-profiled past into an uncertain Bronze Age future. For once I am not the first to suggest that there may be a global environmental catastrophe involved. Baillie (1995b 32-3) has already speculated that there may be a connection with the major tree ring event which he sees at 2354-45 BC (Baillie 1995b & pers. comm.). Others, for a variety of reasons, have suggested an event around 2200 BC, perhaps because that is the traditional date for the end of Old Kingdom Egypt, supposedly amidst environmental crisis. But Baillie (1995b and pers. comm.) sees no specific tree-ring event in Irish oaks at this time, and in view of the notorious elasticity of Egyptian dates asks whether it could not be the same as his *c.*2354-45 BC event. For this he can pull together intriguing historical allusions to disaster from many parts of the world at very much this time. As with the 1159 crisis, the cause or causes have yet to be established. But as Baillie has hinted, could the dramatic end of the Copper Age and beginning of the Bronze Age throughout Atlantic Europe be linked to this event and date? Needham, in his latest Bronze Age chronology for Britain (Needham *et al.* 1997, 57, illus. 1) begins the Bronze Age at *c.*2100 BC, but apparently on no good evidence, and in a work which is mainly concerned with the Middle and Late Bronze Age. In a slightly earlier and more general work (Needham 1996), he ends his Period 1, what would be the Copper Age in many parts of western Europe, at *c.*2300 BC, and there follows from this date his Period 2, the Bronze Age. So, did the Copper Age end and the Bronze Age begin amidst disaster in 2354-45 BC?

Supposing that such an early date is possible, and freely adapting the Bronze Age dates in Needham, 1996 and Needham *et al.*, 1997, the following table can be offered to show how dates have changed over the last 44 years *(Table 11)*.

	Hawkes, 1960	Burgess, 2004
End Copper Age/beginning of Bronze Age	1650/1600	2354/ 2345
End of EBA/beginning MBA	1400	1700/1500
End of MBA1/beginning MBA2	1200	1400
End of MBA2/beginning LBA1 (old MBA3)	1000	1300/1250
End LBA1/beginning LBA2 (Wilburton)	900/850	1100
End LBA2/beginning LBA3 (Ewart Park)	750/700	950
End LBA3/beginning LBA4 (Llynfawr)	650/600	800

Table 11 Changes in Bronze Age chronology, 1960-2004

Well, Derek, that is how it seemed to me, this last half century, but how was it for you? I expect you saw it totally differently, because we have approached these problems from different ends. You have specialised, as your Belfast web entry reaffirms, in the Late Neolithic and Early Bronze Age, and that is a story of two very different halves. In a sense you have the best of both worlds, a period which seems to have had a monopoly on monuments, often big ones, and a period with so little of anything that one wonders whether people ever did anything apart from make bronzes and practise invisibility. Be that as it may, your choice was wise, because you will know how necessary it is to understand the Late Neolithic (and Copper Age, dare I say?) in order to appreciate how totally different was the Bronze Age. In the same way one has to know about the earlier Bronze Age to see that the Later Bronze Age bore it little resemblance.

Alas, space and coherence did not allow me to ride some favourite hobby horses. I did write about the notion of the episodic dumping of hoards, that is to say not irregularly and for all the familiar reasons, but at the interface between industrial phases (Burgess & Coombs 1979, v). This 'bunching' of hoards could account, for example, for the apparent discrepancies between the dates for the Wallington tradition and some of its hoards, and throw much light on the Wallington-Wilburton relationship (Needham 1990; Burgess 1995b). It could also explain apparent inconsistencies in the chronologies of the Wilburton and Saint-Brieuc-des-Iffs traditions (e.g. Needham *et al.* 1997, 90-2; Briard & Onnée 1972), when they have such a close relationship that they ought to be broadly contemporary. I would also have reaffirmed my conviction that Thames swords were Ewart Park swords influenced by Gündlingen swords and not Gündlingen progenitors as most Continental scholars believe (after all, there are Gündlingen fragments in Ewart Park/carp's tongue contexts, as at Boyton, Suffolk, and Graville-Sainte-Honorine, Seine-Maritime, but not any Thames swords (Burgess 1979; Verron 1976, 592-3, fig. 4.16). Alas all this had to go in the interest of 'flow'. Further, my brief did not allow me to write about anything too exotic, so, because I have spent so much of the last 20 years out of Britain and out of touch, I have been compelled to take this trip down memory lane. I should record that I have finished this amidst the catastrophe of moving house, surrounded by packing cases. Just before I wrote these last words I descended to my cellar for a last pilgrimage, and almost symbolically the stairs collapsed beneath me. Fate decreed that I broke neither bones nor glass, so there may yet be an opportunity to write up those discarded aspects of the Bronze Age touched on above.

ACKNOWLEDGEMENTS

This is perhaps an appropriate place to acknowledge the camaraderie and wise words over many decades of two dear, sorely-missed friends, Jacques Briard and David Coombs. All my friends in the Bronze Age Studies Group wittingly and unwittingly have played a part in the gestation of this paper. I owe a special debt, as so often, to Frances Lynch Llewellyn, who has tried to keep me right and up-to-date. Peter Northover kindly talked to me about metallurgical problems, and Sabine Gerloff discussed with me problems of finds both Irish-British and Continental. Warm thanks go to my wife, Norma, Stephen Briggs and Ian Shepherd, who all read and commented on various versions of the text. I must give special thanks to Mike Baillie for reading and improving parts of my text and sending me reams of stimulating material. Finally, I am particularly grateful to Brendan O'Connor for giving what I had written so much of his time, and making so many useful suggestions.

BIBLIOGRAPHY

Annable, F.K. & Simpson, D.D.A., 1964 *Guide Catalogue of the Neolithic and Bronze Age Collections in Devizes Museum*. Devizes: Wiltshire Natural History and Archaeological Society.

Arribas, A. & Molina, F., 1979 Nuevas aportaciones al inicio de la metallurgia en la peninsula Iberica. El poblado de Los Castillejos de Montefrio (Granada). In Ryan, M. (ed.) *The Origins of Metallurgy in Atlantic Europe, Proceedings of the Fifth Atlantic Colloquium, Dublin, 1978*, 7-34. Dublin: Stationery Office.

Atkinson R.J.C., 1956 & 1960 *Stonehenge*. London: Penguin Books.

Baillie, M.G.L., 1989 Do Irish bog oaks date the Shang dynasty? *Current Archaeology*, 117, 310-13.

Baillie, M.G.L., 1995a *A Slice Through Time*. London: Batsford.

Baillie, M.G.L., 1995b Dendrochronology and the chronology of the Irish Bronze Age. In Waddell, J. & Shee Twohig, E. (eds), *Ireland in the Bronze Age: Proceedings of the Dublin Conference, April, 1995*, 30-3. Dublin: Stationery Office.

Baillie, M.G.L., 1999 *Exodus to Arthur: Catastrophic Encounters with Comets*. London: Batsford.

Barber, M., 2003 *Bronze and the Bronze Age: Metalwork and Society in Britain c.2500-800 BC*. Stroud: Tempus.

Barrett, J., 1975 The later pottery: Types and affinities. In Bradley, R. & Ellison, A. *Rams Hill*. 101-18. BAR British Series 19. Oxford: British Archaeological Reports.

Barrett, J., 1976 Deverel-Rimbury: problems of chronology and interpretation. In Burgess, C. & Miket, R. (eds), 289-307.

Barrett, J., 1979 Later Bronze Age pottery in southern Britain. *Current Archaeology,* 67, 230-1.

Barrett, J., 1980 The pottery of the later Bronze Age in lowland England. *Proceedings of the Prehistoric Society,* 46, 297-319.

Barrett, J. & Bradley, R., (eds), 1980a *The British Later Bronze Age.* BAR British Series 83, Oxford: British Archaeological Reports (2 vols).

Barrett, J., & Bradley, R., 1980b Preface: The ploughshare and the sword. In Barrett, J. & Bradley, R. (eds), 9-13.

Barrett, J., Bradley, R., & Green, M., 1991 *Landscape, Monuments and Society: The Prehistory of Cranborne Chase.* Cambridge: Cambridge University Press.

Billard, C., Blanchet, J.-C. & Talon, M., 1996 Origine et composantes de l'Age du Bronze Ancien dans le Nord-Ouest de la France. In Mordant, C. & Gaiffe, O. (eds), 579-601.

Blanchet, J.-C., 1984 *Les Premièrs Métallurgistes En Picardie et Dans Le Nord de la France.* Mémoires Société Préhistorique Française, 17. Paris: Société Préhistorique Française.

Blanchet, J.-C. (ed.), 1987 *Les Relations Entre le Continent et les Iles Britanniques à L'Age du Bronze.* Actes du Colloque de Lille, 22 Congrès Préhistorique de France, 1984. Amiens: Révue Archéologique de Picardie.

Blanchet, J.-C., Brun, P. & Talon, M., 1989 Le Bronze Moyen en Picardie et dans le Nord Pas-de-Calais. In Mordant, C. (ed.) *Dynamique du Bronze Moyen en Europe Occidentale* 491-500. Actes du 113 Congrès National des Société des Savantes, Strasbourg, 1988. Paris, editions C.T.H.S.

Bogaard, C. van den, Dörfler, W., Glos, R., Nadeau, M.-J., Grootes, P.M. & Erlenkeuser, H., 2002 Two tephra layers bracketing Late Holocene paleoecological changes in northern Germany. *Quaternary Research,* 57, 314-24.

Bond, D., 1988 *Excavation at the North Ring, Mucking, Essex* East Anglian Archaeology Report 43. Chelmsford: Essex County Council.

Bradley, R., Lobb, S., Richards, J. & Robinson, M., 1980 Two Late Bronze Age settlements on the Kennet gravels: excavations at Aldermaston Wharf and Knights Farm, Burghfield, Berkshire. *Proceedings of the Prehistoric Society,* 46, 217-95.

Briard, J., 1965 *Les Dépôts Brétons et l'Age du Bronze Atlantique.* Rennes: Travaux du Laboratoire d' Anthropologie Préhistorique, Université de Rennes.

Briard, J. & Onnée, Y., 1972 *Le Dépôt du Bronze Finale de Saint-Brieuc-des-Iffs (I. et V.).* Rennes: Travaux du Laboratoire d'Anthropologie Préhistorique, Université de Rennes.

Brindley, A.L., 1995 Radiocarbon, chronology and the Bronze Age. In Waddell, J. & Shee Twohig, E. (eds), 4-13.

Britton, D., 1960a *Bronze Age Grave-groups and Hoards in the British Museum.* Inventaria Archaeologica GB 8. London: British Museum.

Britton, D., 1960b The Isleham hoard, Cambridgeshire, *Antiquity,* 34, 279-82.

Britton, D. & Longworth, I.H., 1968 *Late Bronze Age Finds in the Heathery Burn Cave, Co. Durham.* Inventaria Archaeologica GB 9. London: British Museum.

Brown, M.A. & Blin-Stoyle, A.E., 1959 A sample analysis of British Middle and Late Bronze Age materials using optical spectrometry. *Proceedings of the Prehistoric Society,* 25, 188-208.

Brun, P. & Mordant, C., 1988 *Le Groupe Rhin-Suisse-France Orientale et la Notion de Civilisation des* Champs *d'Urnes.* Actes Colloque International Nemours, 1986. Nemours: Mémoirs de Musée Préhistorique d'Ile de France.

Buckley, D.G. & Hedges, J.D., 1987 *The Bronze Age and Saxon Settlements at Springfield Lyons, Essex.* Essex County Council Occasional Paper 5. Chelmsford: Essex County Council.

Bu'lock, J.D., 1961 The Bronze Age in the North-West. *Transactions of the Lancashire and Cheshire Antiquarian Society,* 71, 1-42.

Burgess, C., 1962a The Bronze Age in Radnorshire: a re-appraisal. *Transactions of the Radnorshire Society,* 32, 7-24.

Burgess, C., 1962b A palstave from Buckley, Flintshire, with some notes on 'shield' pattern palstaves. *Flintshire Historical Society Publications,* 20, 92-5.

Burgess, C., 1964. A palstave from Chepstow: with some observations on the earliest palstaves of the British Isles. *Monmouthshire Antiquary*, 1(4), 117-24.

Burgess, C., 1968a The Later Bronze Age in the British Isles and north-western France. *Archaeological Journal*, 125, 1-45.

Burgess, C., 1968b *Bronze Age Metalwork in Northern England, c.1000-700 BC.* Oriel Press: Newcastle upon Tyne.

Burgess, C., 1969 Chronology and terminology in the British Bronze Age, *Antiquaries Journal*, 49, 22-9.

Burgess, C., 1974 The Bronze Age. In Renfrew, C. (ed.), *British Prehistory: a New Outline*. 165-232. London: Duckworth.

Burgess, C. 1976. An Early Bronze Age settlement at Kilellan Farm, Islay, Argyll. In C. Burgess & R. Miket (eds), 181-207.

Burgess, C., 1979a Catastrophe? *Current Archaeology*, 67, 251.

Burgess, C., 1979b A find from Boyton, Suffolk, and the end of the Bronze Age in Britain and Ireland. In Burgess, C. & Coombs, D. (eds), 1979, 269-83.

Burgess, C., 1980 *The Age of Stonehenge*. London, Toronto & Melbourne: Dent.

Burgess, C., 1984 The prehistoric settlement of Northumberland: a speculative survey. In Miket, R. & Burgess, C. (eds), *Between and Beyond the Walls: Essays on the Prehistory and History of North Britain in Honour of George Jobey,* 126-75. Edinburgh: John Donald.

Burgess, C., 1985. Population, climate and upland settlement. In Spratt, D. & Burgess, C. (eds), *Upland Settlement in Britain: the Second Millennium BC and After.* BAR British Series 143, 195-230. Oxford: British Archaeological Reports.

Burgess, C., 1986 'Urnes of no small variety': Collared Urns reviewed, *Proceedings of the Prehistoric Society*, 52, 339-51.

Burgess, C., 1987a Les rapports entre la France et la Grande-Bretagne: problèmes de poterie et d'habitats. In Blanchet, J.-C. (ed.), 307-18.

Burgess, C., 1987b Fieldwork in the Evora district, Alentejo, Portugal, 1986-1988: a preliminary report. *Northern Archaeology*, 8, 35-105.

Burgess, C., 1988 Britain at the time of the Rhine-Swiss Group. In Brun, P. & Mordant, C. (eds), 559-73.

Burgess, C. 1989, Volcanoes, catastrophe and the global crisis of the late Second Millennium BC. *Current Archaeology*, 117, 325-9.

Burgess, C., 1990 The chronology of cup- and cup-and-ring marks in Atlantic Europe. In Monnier, J.L. (ed.) *La Bretagne et l'Europe Préhistoriques: Mémoire en Hommage à Pierre-Roland Giot,* 157-71. Revue Archéologique de l''Ouest, Supplément 2, Rennes.

Burgess, C., 1991 The East and the West: Mediterranean influence in the Atlantic world in the Later Bronze Age, *c.*1500-700 BC. In Chevillot, C. & Coffyn, A. (eds) *L'Age du Bronze Atlantique,* 25-45. 1er Colloque de Beynac, Septembre 1990. Beynac: Association des Musées du Sarladais.

Burgess, C., 1992 Discontinuity and dislocation in later prehistoric settlement: some evidence from Atlantic Europe. In Mordant, C. & Richard, A. (eds), 1992, 21-40.

Burgess, C., 1995a Bronze Age settlements and domestic pottery in northern Britain: some suggestions. In Kinnes, I. & Varndell, G. (eds), *'Unbaked Urns of Rudely Shape': Essays on British and Irish Pottery for Ian Longworth,* 145-58. Oxford: Oxbow.

Burgess, C., 1995b A Bronze Age rapier from Catterick Bridge. *Yorkshire Archaeological Journal*, 67, 1-5.

Burgess, C., 1996 'Urns', Culture du Wessex et la transition Bronze Ancien-Bronze Moyen en Grande-Bretagne. In Mordant, C. & Gaffe, O. (eds), 605-21.

Burgess, C., 2001a Extended letter quoted in Stoddart, S. & Malone, C., 663-6.

Burgess, C., 2001b *The Age of Stonehenge* (2nd edition paperback). London: Phoenix Press.

Burgess, C., 2001c Swords, warfare and Sea Peoples: the end of the Late Bronze Age in the East Mediterranean. In Le Roux, C.-T. (ed.) *Du Monde des Chasseurs à Celui des Métallurgistes: Hommages à Jean L'Helgouach et Mélanges offerts a Jacqes Briard,* 277-87. Revue Archéologique de l'Ouest, Supplément 9. Rennes.

Burgess, C., 2001d Problems in the Bronze Age archaeology of Sardinia: seeing the nuragic wood for the trees. In W.H. Metz *et al.* (eds), 169-94.

Burgess C. & Coombs, D., 1979 *Bronze Age Hoards: Some Finds Old and New.* BAR British Series 67. Oxford: British Archaeological Reports.

Burgess, C., Coombs, D. & Davies, D.G., 1972 The Broadward Complex and barbed spearheads. In Lynch, F. & Burgess, C. (eds), *Prehistoric Man in Wales and the West,* 211-83. Bath: Adams & Dart.

Burgess, C. & Gerloff, S., 1981 *The Dirks and Rapiers of Great Britain and Ireland,* Prähistorische Bronzefunde, IV/7. München: Beck'sche.

Burgess, C., Gibson, C. & Correia, V., 1999 Hillforts, oppida and vitrification in the Évora area, central Portugal. In Frodsham, P., Topping, P. & Cowley, D. (eds), *We Were Always Chasing Time: Papers Presented to Keith Blood. Northern Archaeology* 17/18, 129-47.

Burgess, C. & Miket, R. (eds), 1976 *Settlement and Economy in the Third and Second Millennia BC.* BAR British Series 33. Oxford: British Archaeological Reports.

Burgess, C. & Shennan, S., 1976 The Beaker Phenomenon: some suggestions. In Burgess, C. & Miket, R. (eds), 309-31.

Butler, J.J., 1961 A Bronze Age concentration at Bargeroosterveld, with some notes on the axe trade across Northern Europe. *Palaeohistoria,* 8, 100-26.

Butler, J.J., 1963 Bronze Age Connections Across the North Sea. *Palaeohistoria,* 9.

Butler, J.J. & Smith, I.F., 1956 Razors, Urns and the British Middle Bronze Age, *Annual Report of the London Institute of Archaeology,* 12, 20-52.

Childe, V.G., 1956 *Prehistoric Communities of the British Isles,* London & Edinburgh: Chambers.

Clark, J.G.D., 1966 The Invasion Hypothesis in British Archaeology, *Antiquity,* 40, 172-89.

Clarke, D.L., 1970 *Beaker Pottery of Great Britain and Ireland.* Cambridge: Cambridge University Press.

Coles, J.M., 1960 Scottish Late Bronze Age metalwork: typology, distributions and chronology. *Proceedings of the Society of Antiquaries of Scotland,* 93 (1959-60), 16-134.

Colquhoun, I. & Burgess, C., 1988 *The Swords of Britain.* Prähistorische Bronzefunde, IV/5. München: Beck'sche.

Coombs, D., 1975 Bronze age weapon hoards in Britain. *Archaeologica Atlantica,* 1, 49-81.

Cowen, J.D., 1951 The earliest bronze swords in Britain and their origins on the Continent of Europe. *Proceedings of the Prehistoric Society,* 17, 195-213.

Cowen, J.D., 1955 Eine Einführung in die Geschichte der bronzenen Griffzungenschwerter in Süddeutschland und den angrenzenden Gebieten. *Bericht der Römisch-Germanischen Kommission,* 36, 52-155.

Cowie, T.G., 1978 *Bronze Age Food Vessel Urns.* BAR British Series 55. Oxford: British Archaeological Reports.

Cruse, R.J. & Harrison, A.C., 1983 Excavation at Hill Road, Wouldham, *Archaeologia Cantiana,* 99, 81-108.

Demartis, G.M., 1989 *The Necropolis of Anghelu Ruju.* Sassari: Delfino.

Eogan, G., 1964 The Later Bronze Age in Ireland in the light of recent research. *Proceedings of the Prehistoric Society,* 30, 268-351.

Eogan, G., 1965 *Catalogue of Irish Bronze Swords.* Dublin: National Museum of Ireland.

Eogan, G., 1983 *Hoards of the Irish Later Bronze Age.* Dublin: University College Dublin.

Eogan, G., 1994 *The Accomplished Art: Gold and Gold-Working in Britain and Ireland during the Bronze Age (c.2300-650 BC).* Oxford: Oxbow.

Falkenstein, F., 1997 Eine Katastrophen-Theorie zum Beginn der Urnenfelderkultur, in Becker, C. *et al.* (eds), *Beiträge zur Prähistorischen Archäologie zwischen Nord- und Südosteuropa* Leidorf: Espelkamp.

Fleming, A., 1988 *The Dartmoor Reaves: Investigating Prehistoric Land Divisions.* London: Batsford.

Gerloff, S., 1975 *The Early Bronze Age Daggers in Great Britain, and a Reconsideration of the Wessex Culture.* Prähistorische Bronzefunde VI/2. München: Beck'sche.

Gibson, A., 1982 *Beaker Domestic Sites: A Study of the Domestic Pottery of the Late Third and Early Second Millennia BC. in the British Isles.* BAR British Series 107. Oxford: British Archaeological Reports.

Gibson, C., Correia, V. & Burgess, C., 1998 Alto do Castelinho da Serra (Montemor-o-Novo, Évora, Portugal): a preliminary report on the excavations at the Late Bronze Age to Medieval site, 1990-1993. *Journal of Iberian Archaeology*, 0 [sic], 189-244.

Grimes, W.F., 1951 *The Prehistory of Wales.* Cardiff: National Museum of Wales.

Harbison, P., 1969a *The Axes of the Early Bronze Age in Ireland.* Prähistorische Bronzefunde IX/1. München: Beck'sche.

Harbison, P., 1969b *The Daggers and Halberds of the Early Bronze Age in Ireland.* Prähistorische Bronzefunde VI/1. München: Beck'sche.

Hawkes, C.F.C. (ed.), 1955 Grave Groups and Hoards of the British Bronze Age. *Inventaria Archaeologica*, GB 1st set (GB 1-8). London: British Museum.

Hawkes, C.F.C., 1960 *A Scheme for the British Bronze Age.* London: Council for British Archaeology, (unpublished typescript).

Hawkes, C.F.C., 1972 Europe and England: fact and fog. *Helinium*, 12/2, 105-16.

Hawkes, C.F.C. & Smith, M.A., 1957 On some buckets and cauldrons of the Bronze and Early Iron Ages. *Antiquaries Journal*, 37, 131-185.

Jobey, G., 1980 Green Knowe unenclosed platform settlement and Harehope Cairn, Peeblesshire. *Proceedings of the Society of Antiquaries of Scotland*, 110, 72-113.

Kavanagh, R., 1973 The encrusted urn in Ireland. *Proceedings of the Royal Irish Academy*, 73C, 507-617.

Kavanagh, R., 1976 Collared and Cordoned Cinerary urns in Ireland. *Proceedings of the Royal Irish Academy*, 76C, 293-403.

Kavanagh, R., 1977 Pygmy Cups in Ireland. *Journal of the Royal Society of Antiquaries of Ireland*, 107, 61-95.

Lawson, A., 1979a A late Middle Bronze Age hoard from Hunstanton, Norfolk. In Burgess, C. & Coombs, D. (eds), 43-71.

Lawson, A., 1979b Two quoit-headed pins in the British Museum. *Antiquaries Journal*, 59/i, 121-4.

Longworth, I.H., 1984 *Collared Urns of the Bronze Age in Great Britain and Ireland.* Cambridge: Cambridge University Press.

Lynch, F.M., 1971 Report on the re-excavation of two Bronze Age cairns in Anglesey: Bed Branwen and Treiorwerth. *Archaeologia Cambrensis*, 120, 11-83.

Megaw, J.V.S. & Simpson, D.D.A., 1979 *Introduction to British Prehistory.* Leicester: Leicester University Press.

Metz, W.H., van Beek, B.L. & Steegstra, H. (eds), 2001 *Patina: Essays Presented to Jay Jordan Butler.* Groningen & Amsterdam: privately published.

Moravetti, A., 1998 On the dolmens of pre-nuragic Sardinia. In Moravetti, A. (ed.) *Papers from the EAA Third Annual Meeting at Ravenna, 1997: III, Sardinia*, 25-45. BAR International Series 719, Oxford: British Archaeological Reports.

Mordant, C. & Gaffe, O. (eds), 1996 *Cultures et Sociétés du Bronze Ancien en Europe.* Actes du 117 Congrès National des Sociétés Savantes, Clermont -Ferrand, 1992. Paris: Éditions C.T.H.S.

Mordant, C. & Richard, A. (eds), 1992 *L'Habitat et L'Occupation du Sol a L'Age du Bronze en Europe.* Actes Colloque International de Lons-le-Saunier, 1990. Paris: Éditions C.T.H.S.

Mortimer, J.R., 1905 *Forty Years' Researches in British and Saxon Burial Mounds of East Yorkshire.* London: Brown & Sons.

Müller-Karpe, H., 1959 *Beiträge zur Chronologie der Urnenfelderzeit Nördlich und Südlich der Alpen.* Römisch -Germanische Forschungen XXII. Berlin: de Gruyter.

Musson, C.R., 1991 *The Breiddin Hillfort: A Later Prehistoric Settlement in the Welsh Marches.* Research Report 76. London: Council for British Archaeology.

Needham, S.P., 1990 The Penard–Wilburton succession: new metalwork finds from Croxton (Norfolk) and Thirsk (Yorkshire). *Antiquaries Journal*, 70, 253-70.

Needham, S.P., 1992 The structure of settlement and ritual in the Late Bronze Age of south-east Britain. In Mordant, C. & Richard, A. (eds), 49-69.

Needham, S.P. 1996. Chronology and periodisation in the British Bronze Age. In K. Randsborg (ed.) *Absolute Chronology – Archaeological Europe 2500–500 BC,* 121-140. *Acta Archaeologica* 67, Supplementa 1.

Needham, S.P., 2000 *Runnymede Bridge Research Excavations I: The Passage of the Thames: Holocene Environment and Settlement at Runnymede.* London: British Museum.

Needham, S.P., Lawson A.J. & Green, H.S., 1985 *British Bronze Age Metalwork.* London: British Museum.

Needham, S.P., Ramsey, C.B., Coombs, D., Cartwright, C. & Pettitt, P., 1997 An independent chronology for British Bronze Age metalwork: the results of the Oxford Radiocarbon Accelerator Programme. *Archaeological Journal*, 154, 1-53.

O'Connor, B., 1980 *Cross-Channel Relations in the Later Bronze Age.* BAR International Series 91. Oxford: British Archaeological Reports.

O'Connor, B., 1989 The Middle Bronze Age of southern England. In Mordant, C. (ed.) *Dynamique du Bronze Moyen en Europe Occidentale.* Actes du 113 Congrès National des Société des Savantes, Strasbourg, 1988, 515-21. Paris: Éditions C.T.H.S.

Ó'Ríordáin, B. & Waddell, J., 1993 *The Funerary Bowls and Vases of the Irish Bronze Age.* Galway: National University of Ireland.

Piggott, S., 1938 The Early Bronze Age in Wessex. *Proceedings of the Prehistoric Society*, 4, 52-106.

Piggott, S., 1955 *British Prehistory.* Oxford: Clarendon Press.

Plunkett, G.M., 1999 *Environmental Change in the Late Bronze Age in Ireland (1200–600 cal. BC).* Unpublished PhD thesis, Queen's University, Belfast.

Pryor, F., 2001 *The Flag Fen Basin: Archaeology and Environment of a Fenland Landscape.* Swindon: English Heritage.

Reinders, H.R., 2001 foreword. In W.H. Metz *et al.* (eds), 1-2.

Rowlands, M.J., 1976 *The Production and Distribution of Metalwork in the Middle Bronze Age in Southern Britain.* BAR British Series 31. Oxford: British Archaeological Reports.

Schmidt, P. & Burgess, C., 1981 *The Axes of Scotland and Northern England.* Prähistorische Bronzefunde IX/7. München: Beck'sche.

Schubart, H., 1980 Cerro de Enmedio: Bronzezeitliche Funde von einer Höhensiedlung am unteren Andarax (prov. Almeria). *Madrider Mitteilungen*, 21, 74-90.

Selkirk, A., 1979 The Later Bronze Age. *Current Archaeology*, 67, 229, 232-3, 237-9.

Sheridan, J.A., 2003 New dates for Scottish Bronze Age cinerary urns: results from the National Museums of Scotland *Dating Cremated Bones Project*. In Gibson, A. (ed.) *Prehistoric Pottery: People, Pattern and Purpose*, 201-26. BAR International Series 1156. Oxford: British Archaeological Reports.

Simpson, D.D.A., 1965 Food-vessels in South-West Scotland. *Transactions of the Dumfriesshire & Galloway Natural History & Antiquarian Society*, 3 ser. 42, 25-50.

Smith, M.A., 1959 Some Somerset hoards and their place in the Bronze Age of southern Britain. *Proceedings of the Prehistoric Society*, 25, 144-87.

Speak, S. & Burgess, C., 1999 Meldon Bridge: a centre of the Third Millennium BC in Peeblesshire. *Proceedings of the Society of Antiquaries of Scotland*, 129, 1-118.

Stoddart, S. & Malone, C., 2001 Editorial, *Antiquity*, 75, 659-74.

Taramelli, A., 1909 Nuovi scavi nella necropoli preistorica a grotte artificiali di Anghelu Ruju. *Monumenti Antichi dei Lincei*, 19, 397-540.

Verron, G., 1976 Les civilisations de l'Age du Bronze en Normandie. In Guilaine, J. (ed.) *La Préhistoire Française II: Les Civilisations Néolithiques et Protohistoriques de la France*, 585-600. Paris: C.N.R.S.

Waddell, J., 1990 *The Bronze Age Burials of Ireland*. Galway: Galway University Press.

Waddell, J. & Shee Twolig, E. (eds) 1995, *Ireland in the Bronze Age; Proceedings of the Dublin Conference, April, 1995*. Dublin: Stationary Office.

Woolley, L., 1937 *Digging Up the Past*. Harmondsworth: Penguin.

22

LAND SNAILS AS A GUIDE TO THE ENVIRONMENTS OF WIND-BLOWN SAND: THE CASE OF *LAURIA CYLINDRACEA* AND *PUPILLA MUSCORUM*

J.G. EVANS

INTRODUCTION

In the summer of 1963, I was sent by my PhD supervisor, F.E. Zeuner, to a site in Rainham, Essex, under the supervision of Derek Simpson and Isobel Smith to learn how to excavate. It was an auspicious choice because two significant strands of my PhD thesis on fossil snails were developed under these two archaeologists, the one on Neolithic chalk soils under Isobel and the other on wind-blown sand under Derek. I am glad to offer this paper to Derek in gratitude of his guidance in those earliest years. Apart from my work at Northton (Evans 1971), and a survey of sites where molluscan analysis had been done in Britain (1979), I did not in the end do a great deal on wind-blown sands myself. But the context was explored more widely by my students.

In this paper, I want to look at the behaviour of two species of snail which often occur in Holocene coastal blown sands in the British Isles, *Pupilla muscorum* and *Lauria cylindracea*. I have chosen these species because while they are similar in form and colour, both being small (between 3-4mm tall), cylindrical and dark-reddish brown, their behaviour and ecology is often erratic and diverse, both within sequences and from one region to another. This study has also been stimulated by the need to publish an interesting Beaker and Bronze Age sand and midden sequence from Ensay in the Sound of Harris which Derek and I visited in 1966 and sampled and which shows some of the relationships between the two species in question. The Northton sequence, while fully published long ago (Burleigh *et al.* 1973; Evans 1971), also shows some interesting aspects of the relationships between the two species, especially when compared regionally to other areas of the British Isles and locally in their ecology to other sites.

A significant point is that through a sequence or from site to site, any one species of snail often shows different ecologies. Some, like *Pupilla*, can be quite narrow in this way, although even this grassland and xerophile species can on occasion occur in wetland habitats. Others are much more eclectic and, as with *Lauria*, can occur in woodland or grassland or unstable sand-dune areas. As Ken Thomas (1985) noted, this is a problem in interpreting molluscan histograms because it means that the ecological signal of a particular species might change as one moves up the sequence. I tackled this through the use of diversity indexes (Evans 1991) and other forms of numerical analysis (Evans & Williams 1991), but in the end these lose out in generalising information and losing detail.

In this paper, I am not offering any further methodological refinements, such as plotting the same species in a single histogram more than once to take into account the different ecological modes. Instead, I want to draw attention to the problem with reference to the two species in question because they illustrate it well, and they do so in the blown-sand deposits of western Britain, and especially the Outer Hebrides, which have been such an important part of Derek's research.

THE SITES:

THE OUTER HEBRIDES

First, then, Ensay. This is a sequence of Beaker and Bronze Age middens on the northern end of Ensay in the Sound of Harris *(118-19)*. The samples were taken by me in a visit to the site with Derek in 1966 (during the second season of work at Northton in South Harris) and analysed but never published. The only record is in the undergraduate thesis of Penny Spencer (1974), while the archaeology is about to be published.

In the area sampled, the modern turf lay directly above the uppermost midden, but in other parts of the sequence there was blown sand with an abundance of two species introduced into the area in the Iron Age, *Helicella itala* and *Cochlicella acuta*. There were three shell middens, identified archaeologically by Derek by their pottery:

118 The Ensay sand mound showing the two main shell-midden layers

119 A close-up of the Ensay sand mound showing details of the sampled area. Metre scale

18-47cm – Bronze Age, with marine shells of mainly mussels and limpets.

70-78cm – Beaker, with marine shells of mainly winkles.

111-119cm – Beaker, with again mainly winkles.

Beneath the middens there was 25cm of sterile calcareous sand, devoid of land snails, and then a further 45cm of non-calcareous sand which overlay a buried soil on boulder clay.

In comparison to Northton, the molluscan sequence *(120)* is quite short, and does not show the marked changes of that site. However, there are some significant points to be made. The lower part of the sequence, faunal zone 1, reflects a diverse environment of grassland. Then, within the top part of the upper Beaker midden and the sand just above it there is a significant increase in faunal abundance and diversity, faunal zone 2, suggesting some quite dense vegetation, and with even a few hygrophiles indicative of local and seasonal ponding. It would be interesting to equate this with the upper Beaker occupation at Northton where there was an equally diverse fauna and an equally massive increase in *Lauria*, likely reflecting woodland. Faunal zone 3 at Ensay, the uppermost part of the sequence, sees a reduction in molluscan abundance. There is especially a drop in the three grassland species, *Vallonia excentrica*, *Vertigo pygmaea* and *Pupilla muscorum*, and sustained presence of a group of eclectic species, *Vallonia costata*, *Lauria cylindracea* and *Vitrina pellucida*, one habitat of which might be middens, another broken ground with actively accumulating sand. The presence of a number of large boulders in the upper part of the sequence *(118-19)*, possibly from collapsed buildings or walls, is another possible reason for the success of *Lauria* in these levels, for stone walls are another of its favoured habitats.

With reference now to *Lauria cylindracea* and *Pupilla muscorum*, both are significantly present throughout. More locally, *Pupilla* is most abundant in the lower half of the sequence (especially in faunal zone 1, less so in faunal zone 2) *(120)*, becoming considerably reduced in the upper half (faunal zone 3). *Lauria* shows a peak in the middle (faunal zone 2) which also sees a peak of *Vallonia costata* and several other species but, significantly, not *Pupilla*. On a percentage basis, too, there is a clear complementarity of behaviour, with *Pupilla* most abundant in the lower half of the sequence, *Lauria* in the upper. In terms of behaviour in relation to other species, *Pupilla* is behaving very similarly to the grassland species *Vallonia excentrica*, while *Lauria* is closest to the more eclectic species *Cochlicopa*, *Vallonia costata* and *Vitrina pellucida*, and

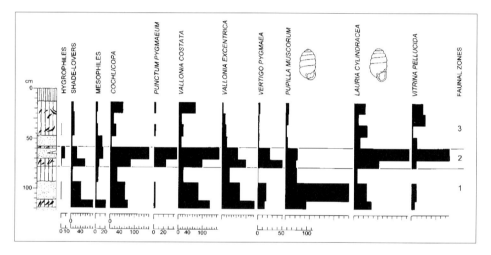

120 *Above* Ensay, the land molluscan sequence, presented as numbers of shells. Hygrophiles: *Carychium minimum, Lymnaea truncatula* and *Oxyloma pfeifferi.* Shade-lovers: *Carychium tridentatum, Vertigo pusilla, Vertigo substriata* and *Oxychilus alliarius.* Mesophiles: *Clausilia bidentata, Acanthinula aculeata, Cepaea hortensis, Euconulus fulvus* agg., *Vitrea contracta, Nesovitrea hammonis, Aegopinella pura* and *Aegopinella nitidula*

121 *Right* Comparison of the behaviour of *Pupilla muscorum* and *Lauria cylindracea* across the ramparts of Maiden Castle, Dorset (modern) and through the sand sequence at Northton, presented as numbers of shells

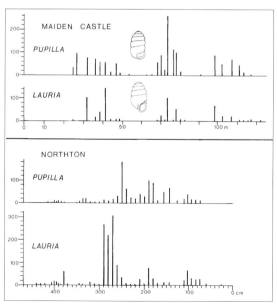

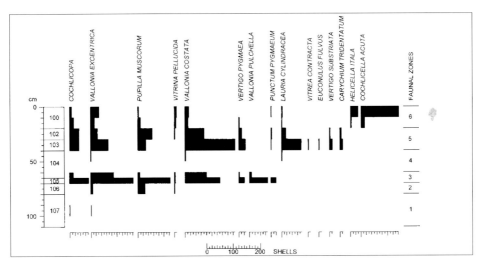

122 Sligenach, South Uist. Blown-sand sequence with Beaker horizon. Contexts: 107, grey-orange sand; 106, pale grey sand; 105, orange-yellow sand; 104, yellow sand, 103; Beaker ard-mark horizon; 102, brown sand; 100, modern turf

probably indicates more broken, unstable, ground or some other rather specialised habitat which here is likely to have been that of the midden itself.

Then there is Northton (Evans 1971). Here, both *Lauria* and *Pupilla* are present throughout, except for the absence of both in the upper Iron Age deposits and modern soil. On the whole, the distribution of the two species is a complementary one, brought out both in the percentage diagram (Evans 1971, fig. 11) and in absolute terms *(121)*. Mostly, *Lauria* is allying itself with the shade-loving species, seen especially in the Beaker II horizon (270-290cm), while *Pupilla* is more of an open-country form as seen in the clearance episode following on from the Beaker II phase (above 250cm). Ecologically, this is similar to Ensay. Yet the situation is not clear-cut, for there are episodes in the Northton sequence where the two species behave sympathetically, as in the Neolithic horizon (385-410cm) and in the sands between the two Iron Age levels (70-110cm).

The work of Nigel Thew in the Outer Hebrides (the Uists and Benbecula) shows the distribution of the two species as being often complementary (Thew 2003). This also comes out in my own work (unpublished) on Niall Sharples' site at Sligenach, Cill Donnain, in South Uist, one diagram from which he has kindly allowed me to include here. Here, in a Beaker deposit, *Pupilla* occurs more or less exclusively in the lower, grassland, zones *(122*, faunal zones 2 and 3) whereas *Lauria* only first appears in the upper part of the sequence, and especially in the more diverse assemblage of faunal zone 5. Thew notes *Lauria* as occurring significantly with *Oxychilus alliarius* in several occasions, for example at the Iron Age site of Hornish Point, also in South Uist, and at a later prehistoric (Later Bronze Age and Iron Age) site on the intertidal island of

Baleshare off North Uist, an association thought to be indicative of middens. But it is not an association of all middens; for example one of the Iron Age middens on Baleshare is virtually devoid of both *Lauria* and *Oxychilus*, having a very narrow grassland fauna of *Pupilla*, *Vallonia* and *Cochlicopa (ibid.).*

Thew also considers *Lauria* to be a species of woodland, or at least very diverse, habitats in prehistory in the islands: as well as *Oxychilus alliarius*, *Vallonia costata* is another close associate, while the narrow grassland species *Vallonia excentrica* and *Vertigo pygmaea* are not. Today, on the other hand, *Lauria* is more characteristic of grassland where it often occurs in abundance.

In other Outer Hebridean sites, both species are present, although at prehistoric Rosinish, Benbecula, their abundances are low and there is little obvious pattern (Vaughan 1976). In a Norse sequence from Udal, North Uist (Spencer 1974), the two species are common, especially in the middle part of the sequence, and appear to fluctuate in sympathy.

In summary, then, *Lauria* thrives best in the more diverse habitats in these islands, whether these are of broken and unstable ground (possibly Ensay), shade and middens (Northton) or middens (Ensay, Hornish Point and Baleshare). Today, and in the historical periods, there is an important additional habitat, namely coastal calcareous grassland, but this does not seem to have been the situation in prehistory. In comparison with other areas of the British Isles, the significant presence of both *Lauria* and *Pupilla* is a regional feature of the Outer Hebrides (at least from South Harris to South Uist). In Thew's work, *Pupilla* is a lot more common than *Lauria*, but in other sites like Northton and Ensay *Lauria* is by no means as scarce.

The Inner Hebrides

Turning to the Inner Hebrides, in the Mesolithic shell mound at Cnoc Coig, on Oronsay (Paul 1987), *Pupilla* is present in the lower part of the sequence in low numbers in a sparse open-country fauna, while *Lauria* occurs in the upper part in much greater abundance in a woodland fauna. At another such mound, Caisteal nan Gillean II, only the woodland fauna is present, with substantial *Lauria*, while *Pupilla* is present in very low numbers in the upper, open-country – and probably quite recent, judging by the *Helicella itala* and *Cochlicella acuta* – part of the sequence. Here, it is as if the complementary of these two species which is seen generally in the Outer Hebridean sites is resolved more or less completely, perhaps because of some other, more restricting, ecological factor.

The Orkney Islands

Sites in Orkney are: Birsay Bay, Mainland (Rackham *et al.* 1989); Buckquoy, Mainland (Evans & Spencer 1977; Spencer 1974); Knap of Howar, Papa Westray (Evans & Vaughan 1983; Spencer 1974; 1975; Vaughan 1976); Skara Brae, Mainland (Spencer 1974; 1975); Tofts Ness, Sanday (Milles 1991); and a study of some modern faunas (Evans & Vaughan 1983).

As in the Hebrides, *Lauria* and *Pupilla* are consistently present in most sections, and this is a part of a northern regional pattern. But there is a distinct feature of these Orcadian faunas which sets them aside from the Hebridean ones: *Lauria* is often very abundant and consistently far more so than *Pupilla*, while the latter is often virtually absent in whole sections, as at Tofts Ness. At the Knap of Howar and Birsay Bay it is the same story, with often huge numbers of *Lauria* and just a trickle of *Pupilla*. This may be partly due to local ecology, for some of these faunas have a much greater woodland facies in them than the Outer Hebridean ones. Yet there are suitable faunas of open-country and grassland type where one might expect *Pupilla*, and very occasionally it is abundant.

Locally in these sites, *Lauria* has several distinct ecologies, shade-loving (or at least very diverse) habitats, unstable open sandy soils, and middens or *plaggen* soils. Today, around Birsay Bay, *Lauria* occurs in 'superabundance', and along with *Pupilla* (although in much lesser numbers) is typical of the 'rabbit-grazed dune pasture' of the area (Rackham *et al.* 1989, 46). So in this respect the story is the same as that in the Outer Hebrides.

SOUTH WALES

Significant sites are: Flatholm (Young & Evans 1991), not a blown-sand site but a rocky coastal island in the Bristol Channel; Freshwater West, Pembrokeshire (Vaughan 1976); Kenfig Burrows, Mid Glamorgan (Martin 1989); and Stackpole Warren, Pembrokeshire (Evans & Hyde 1990). There are clear patterns here, such as the absence of *Pupilla* and presence, indeed abundance, of *Lauria* at Flatholm, the abundance of *Pupilla* and absence of *Lauria* at Freshwater West, and some clear complementarity at Kenfig Burrows. But the situation at Stackpole and some of the Kenfig sampling spots is less clear-cut. The two main subfossil sites, Freshwater West and Stackpole Warren, with their predominance of *Pupilla*, are significantly different from the Scottish sands and seem to be a link, rather, with the north Cornish sites.

SOUTH-WEST ENGLAND

At Brean Down, in the section studied by Spencer (1974), *Pupilla* is present in the upper half of the sequence, peaking between 60 and 70cm; there is no *Lauria*. In the section studied by Vaughan (1976), there is a similar general distribution of *Pupilla*, with a peak 50-62cm; there is one *Lauria* in the lowest shell-bearing sample, 350-360cm. In the more complete sequence of Bell (1990), *Pupilla* is present in low numbers from practically the base of the sequence (starting just above the Neolithic soil) but becomes more consistently present in the upper half with a peak between 48 and 60cm; *Lauria* is present in huge numbers in one sample, namely from a collapsed building, layer 6 alpha, low down in the sequence, and by a single shell towards the top. In regional terms, there is a clear similarity with some of the faunas in South Wales in the predominance of *Pupilla* and the sparseness, indeed virtual absence, of *Lauria*.

At Maiden Castle (Rouse & Evans 1994), although not a blown-sand site, the data make a useful comparison with Northton *(121)*. The assemblages are from modern grassland turves, analysed from across the ramparts of the Iron Age hillfort. Unlike the situation at Northton, there is a more or less completely sympathetic distribution of *Lauria* and *Pupilla*, with both species occurring on south-facing slopes where the soil is most calcareous and the turf not densely matted or with a closed thatch of dead vegetation. Here *Lauria* is occurring very much as a grassland species, with other species that occur quite narrowly in grasslands, especially *Vertigo pygmaea* and *Vallonia excentrica*. Both species avoid the shorter, trampled, grassland within the ramparts and the longer grass in the ditch bottoms. But *Lauria* is more tightly restricted than *Pupilla*, being confined to unstable, steep, areas where there are terracettes.

The occurrence of *Lauria* on the grassland ramparts of Maiden Castle represents one of its present-day habitats in this central part of the southern English chalklands while its confinement to the steep rubble areas is a reflection of its preference for broken and vertical surfaces. In prehistory, by contrast, the species lived in woodland. This is shown clearly in the sequence from the ditch at Stonehenge where it is confined exclusively to the lower levels, coming to an abrupt demise at the precise point where *Pupilla* begins its expansion in open country (Evans *et al.* 1984).

CORNWALL

Significant sites are: Daymer Bay (Milles 1991; Spencer 1974); Gunwalloe, Lizard Peninsula (Peters 1986; 1988); Gwithian (Milles 1991; Spencer 1974; 1975); Harlyn Bay (Spencer 1974); Perranporth (Spencer 1974; 1975); and Towan Head, Newquay (Milles 1991; Spencer 1974; 1975). Regionally, the Cornish sites are characterised by an extreme paucity or absence of *Lauria*, it occurring commonly only at Gunwalloe, as a grassland species (and then much more narrowly than *Pupilla*), and at Perranporth in a woodland assemblage. Its regional paucity or absence is not related to local ecology, for a range of conditions from woodland, through clearance to grassland and more unstable sandy soils is present. *Pupilla*, on the other hand, is behaving more strictly as a grassland and sand-dune species and is more generally and abundantly present. So in these respects, the behaviour of the two species is similar to that in the Welsh sites and at Brean Down.

With regard to present-day ecology, *Lauria* is present in abundance as a living species in the topsoil and amongst blown sand at Daymer Bay and Gunwalloe which is similar to the situation in other parts of Britain like Brean Down. *Pupilla*, by contrast, is not significantly abundant today, often showing a distinct decline in the topsoil.

BRITTANY

In four Breton coastal blown-sand localities (Haslett *et al.* 2000; Paul Davies, pers. comm.), *Pupilla* was present but *Lauria* absent. This continues the north-south trend seen in the British sites.

DISCUSSION

Changes in habitat preferences through time and regional differences of abundance are the main differences in the relationships of the two species, *Lauria cylindracea* and *Pupilla muscorum*, dealt with in this paper.

CHANGES IN HABITAT PREFERENCES THROUGH TIME

Today, in terms of their local ecologies, *Pupilla* is a lot narrower in its habitat preferences than *Lauria*. Where *Lauria* can occur in collapsed wall tumble (Bell 1990; Smith 1996), stable grassland, unstable broken soils of the foredunes, and woodland, *Pupilla* seems to be quite closely confined to grassland. Yet in any one habitat, *Lauria* can be quite narrowly distributed, as seen in its relation to *Pupilla* at Maiden Castle *(121)*. Inland, both species are widely present in southern central England, *Pupilla* as a grassland, and largely calcicole species, *Lauria* as a denizen of walls and more shaded habitats.

One of the factors in the ecology of *Lauria* may be its inability to co-exist with certain species in stable, long-lived, habitats such as managed grassland. In contrast, it often thrives best in places which are unstable and temporary. Its association with *Vitrina pellucida* which is another species of such behaviour may be significant in this respect. The precise nature of those habitats is not important: it is ephemerality and instability which is the key. To this extent, it is significant that large numbers of juveniles often make up the *Lauria* numbers, suggesting its abilities as a rapid coloniser. It may also be significant that *Lauria* is well adapted to survival on vertical surfaces, such as on stems and walls, through the flat flange of its aperture which allows it to appress the aperture closely to the surface and seal off its body from desiccation, something which is helped by the secretion of mucus which hardens and seals off any remaining gaps. Kerney (1999) contrasts its behaviour in this respect with *Pupilla* which 'rarely climbs vertical surfaces'. On the other hand, its occurrence in woodland, usually in quite low numbers in contrast to the enormous abundances in which it is often present in the more unstable situations, is allowed by the diversity of microhabitats and the very suitable nature of the environment for snails generally. It would be very interesting to do some detailed morphometric studies of *Lauria* apertures in populations from different habitats.

In subfossil prehistoric blown-sand sequences, *Lauria* was generally less eclectic than today in its habitats, favouring shaded or at least diverse habitats. It is only in the last 2,000 years or so that it has spread into more open grassland

and sand-dune habitats especially in western and northern Britain. This is essentially a broadening of the range of habitats it occupied in prehistory rather than a change in ecology. In the south and east, on the other hand, it has retained its woodland and rupestral preferences. This diversity is reflected in its widespread and virtually uniform distribution in terms of the 10km square mapping scheme in the British Isles today (Kerney 1999). Its seemingly anomalous occurrence in dry grassland at Maiden Castle may be due to the extreme suitability of the vertical and unstable faces of the chalk terracettes which serve *in lieu* of walls, a more normal habitat of the species in these central and eastern areas.

Pupilla is more narrowly a grassland species and this has been the situation through prehistory to the present day. There has, however, been a significant contraction of its distributions, with, for example, no records at all from the Outer Hebrides since 1965 and only one prior to that *(ibid)*.

REGIONAL DIFFERENCES OF ABUNDANCE

Present-day distributions in the British Isles *(ibid)* show *Lauria* present widely from the Shetlands to the south-west. *Pupilla*, in contrast, is much more sparsely represented being present in only three 10km mapping squares (out of a possible 27) in Orkney, totally absent from the Outer Hebrides (since the lone record prior to 1965), yet consistently present along the north Cornish coast.

In prehistory, there is a clear difference between the Scottish sites and those in southern Britain with regard to the two species. In the Scottish sites there is a consistent presence of *Lauria* while in south-west England, especially in Cornwall, it is really quite uncommon in spite of the range of habitats available for it. *Pupilla*, in contrast, occurs in a complementary fashion, being common in the south-western sites and extremely sparse or virtually absent in Orkney, a pattern continued into the present-day. Faunas in the Outer Hebrides occupy an intermediate position with both species moderately well represented, as seen in the Northton sequence *(121)*. Hints of an extension of this gradient (if that is what it is) are seen in the Orkneys themselves. Thus there is practically no *Pupilla* in one of the most outlying islands, Sanday, even though there is a range of deposits and habitats in the sequences, including blown sand and open-country, while the species is slightly more noticeable (although still sparse) on Papa Westray and Orkney Mainland.

These differences are difficult to explain. *Pupilla* is a climatically tolerant species and can occur in a variety of open-country habitats. Why is it so sparse in Orkney in prehistory and why has it declined so drastically in the Outer Hebrides since that time? The sparseness of *Lauria* in the south-west is equally mystifying especially as it is so common there today, although this is partly due to its spread in historical times into coastal blown-sand habitats. Again there is a suitable diversity of habitats for it in the sequences.

RELATIONS TO CLIMATE CHANGE

One possibility for explaining some of these patterns of distribution and change is climate. For example, the spread of *Lauria* into grasslands and dunes may have been aided by an increase in climatic wetness, higher precipitation and lower water loss from the surface, allowing it to spread into the more open habitats which were previously too dry for it to live in, especially in the more oceanic parts of western and northern Britain.

As a cause for the paucity of *Lauria* in the south-west and its abundance in the Scottish islands in prehistory, however, climate is more difficult to invoke. The problem is that susceptibility to winter cold seems to be the main constraint on the distribution of *Lauria*, it being a western and southern European species, a feature reflected in its late introduction (in the mid-Holocene) to Britain (Kerney 1968). If anything, therefore, one would expect this species to be *less* frequent in the northern islands (January mean temperature of 3-4°C in Orkney, 4-5°C in the Outer Hebrides) than in the south-west of Britain (January mean temperatures of above 6°C) (Kerney 1999).

RELATIONS WITH MIDDENING AND *PLAGGEN* SOILS

Another possibility for the abundance of *Lauria* in the Scottish sites, and especially in the Orkneys, may be land-use. The blown-sand areas may have been managed more intensively and in a more organised way, with manuring, tathing and regular rotation of crops and stock, than those in southern Britain. That is my suspicion. This would have had the effect of enriching the soils in the Scottish island sites and thus making them less harsh so that a wider diversity of species could colonise. There would be a greater diversity of refugia, and a greater instability and ephemerality of habitats, both of which could favour *Lauria*. Nigel Thew (2003) notes the presence of *Lauria* with *Oxychilus alliarius* as indicative of middens in South Uist and Benbecula, although not in all middens. Some of the Tofts Ness, Orkney, soils where *Lauria* is abundant are *plaggen* soils (Milles 1991). The concept of 'synanthropy' is attractive here, where a species, even though (and often *especially*) at and beyond the edge of its natural range, thrives in humanly-created habitats (Kerney 1966).

At the same time, the more calcicole and narrowly grassland *Pupilla* would be inhibited by such conditions and perhaps by competition from other species in these diverse habitats: we have already noted its complementary behaviour in relation to *Lauria* in the Outer Hebrides. However, this still does not explain the general paucity of *Pupilla* in Orkney, for surely it could thrive in some coastal grasslands.

Whether there have been such differences in land-use is a matter for further research, but I have the impression that areas of blown sand were a lot more important in human farming in the northern islands than they were in south-western Britain. This may be because the Cornish and Welsh blown sands are less extensive than those in Scotland and often a lot higher up. Today they appear as areas of hummocky dunes (towans, burrows or warrens) right across their extent, lacking the level surfaces of the machair. At a number of these sites in Cornwall, such as Gunwalloe and Towan Head, there are sequences of buried soils and occupation horizons, while at Gwithian there were extensive spreads of pottery and 'widespread scatters of domestic refuse' in some of the soils (Megaw *et al.* 1961) suggestive of manuring or middening. Jacky Nowakowski has informed me that the soils at Gwithian were probably artificially made up, and that similar soils were present at a site near Newquay, dating from the Iron Age and Roman periods. Yet in both the studies at Gwithian or indeed any of these sites there is hardly an inkling of *Lauria* (Spencer 1975; Milles 1991).

Perhaps, then, as well as involving specific farming conditions, management was about the creation of specific visual styles, and these were most strongly developed in the Scottish islands. The idea that Mesolithic shell mounds were created deliberately, not just in the disposal of shells but as visible monuments, is currently fashionable (e.g. Pollard 1996). The same may apply to later sites. Thus the blown-sand section on Ensay itself has a distinct mound form *(118-19)* which, equally, may have been created as a visual symbol in the land. At Northton, we do not know what the original form of the various land surfaces was like because we are left with only a vestige of the stratigraphy backed up against rock and boulder clay, but the repeated occupation of the same area over several millennia as the blown sand accumulated is highly reminiscent of another kind of monument, the tell, and may well have involved a similar construction of community identity. In later prehistory, mounded middens and farm-mounds are frequent in the western and northern isles (e.g. Davidson *et al.* 1986; Barber 2003). Perhaps the artificial creation of mounds through the build up of stones, midden material, *plaggen* soils and even the encouragement of some sand accumulation led to a diversity of habitats which were eagerly colonised by *Lauria*. In the Cornish sites, in contrast, this kind of management and monumentality did not occur, with means other than farming style being used in referencing social and community identity. Ultimately we could see these ideas as extending to entire landscapes, with the succession of blown sand and land surfaces as a way in which communities related to the cyclicity of their generations. Joanna Brück (2001) has explored such an idea in relation to settlements in the Bronze Age and I have suggested an active role for sedimentation in human agency in relation to loess and wind-blown sand (Evans 2003). The fact that ploughing takes place at a number of sites as blown sand is actively accumulating strongly supports such ideas. But they could be taken a lot further, and the blown-sand deposits discussed in this paper would provide a very suitable medium for such an exploration.

ACKNOWLEDGEMENTS

I am grateful to Niall Sharples for drawing my attention to the internet report of John Barber and for letting me publish one of the diagrams from the Sligenach site in advance of its publication. Paul Davies kindly supplied information about his Breton work. Jacky Nowakowski kindly discussed middening in prehistoric sites in Cornwall.

BIBLIOGRAPHY

Barber, J. (ed.), 2003 *Bronze Age Farms and Iron Age Farm Mounds of the Outer Hebrides*. Society of Antiquaries of Scotland/Council for British Archaeology/ Historic Scotland: Scottish Archaeological Internet Reports. http://www.sair.org.uk/sair3/index.html

Bell, M., 1990 *Brean Down Excavations 1983-1987*. London: English Heritage.

Brück, J., 2001 Body metaphors and technologies of transformation in the English Middle and Late Bronze Age. In Brück, J. (ed.) *Bronze Age Landscapes: Tradition and Transformation*, 149-60. Oxford: Oxbow.

Burleigh, R., Evans, J.G. & Simpson, D.D.A., 1973 Radiocarbon dates for Northton, Outer Hebrides. *Antiquity*, 47, 61-4.

Davidson, D.A., Harkness, D.D. & Simpson, I.A., 1986 The formation of farm mounds on the island of Sanday, Orkney. *Geoarchaeology*, 1, 45-60.

Evans, J.G., 1971 Habitat change on the calcareous soils of Britain: the impact of Neolithic man. In Simpson, D.D.A. (ed.) *Economy and Settlement in Neolithic and Early Bronze Age Britain and Europe*, 27-73. Leicester: Leicester University Press.

Evans, J.G., 1979 The palaeo-environment of coastal blown-sand deposits in western and northern Britain. *Scottish Archaeological Forum*, 9, 16-26.

Evans, J.G., 1991 An approach to the interpretation of dry-ground and wet-ground molluscan taxocenes from central-southern England. In Harris, D.R. & Thomas, K.D. (eds), *Modelling Ecological Change: Perspectives from Neoecology, Palaeoecology and Environmental Archaeology*, 75-89. London: Institute of Archaeology, University College London.

Evans, J.G., 2003 *Environmental Archaeology and the Social Order*. London & New York: Routledge.

Evans, J.G., Atkinson, R.J.C., O'Connor, T. & Green, H.S., 1984 Stonehenge – the environment in the Late Neolithic and Early Bronze Age *and* a Beaker-age burial. *Wiltshire Archaeological and Natural History Magazine*, 78, 7-30.

Evans, J.G. & Hyde, L.M., 1990 Land Mollusca. In Benson, D.G., Evans, J.G., Williams, G.H., Darvill, T. & David, A., Excavations at Stackpole Warren, Dyfed, 229-34. *Proceedings of the Prehistoric Society*, 56, 179-245.

Evans, J.G. & Spencer, P.J., 1977 Appendix 4: the Mollusca and environment, Buckquoy, Orkney. In Ritchie, A., Excavation of Pictish and Viking-age farmsteads at Buckquoy, Orkney, 215-19. *Proceedings of the Society of Antiquaries of Scotland*, 108, (1976-7), 174-227.

Evans, J.G. & Vaughan, M., 1983 Appendix 8: the Mollusca from Knap of Howar, Orkney. In Ritchie, A. Excavation of a Neolithic farmstead at Knap of Howar, Papa Westray, Orkney, 106-14. *Proceedings of the Society of Antiquaries of Scotland*, 113, 40-121.

Evans, J.G. & Williams, D., 1991 Land Mollusca from the M3 archaeological sites – a review. In Fasham, P.J. & Whinney, R.J.B. (eds), *Archaeology and the M3*, 113-42. Winchester: Hampshire Field Club and Archaeological Society.

Haslett, S.K., Davies, P. & Curr, R.H.F., 2000 Geomorphological and palaeoenvironmental development of Holocene perched coastal dune systems in Brittany, France. *Geografiska Annaler*, 82 A, 79-88.

Kerney, M.P., 1966 Snails and man in Britain. *Journal of Conchology*, 26, 3-14.

Kerney, M.P., 1968 Britain's fauna of land Mollusca and its relation to the Post-glacial thermal optimum. In Fretter, V. (ed.) *Studies in the Structure, Physiology and Ecology of Molluscs*. (Symposia of the Zoological Society of London, no. 22.), 273-91. London: Zoological Society of London.

Kerney, M., 1999 *Atlas of the Land and Freshwater Molluscs of Britain and Ireland*. Colchester: Harley Books and the Conchological Society of Great Britain and Ireland.

Martin, J., 1989 *A Study of Modern Molluscan Populations of the Kenfig Burrows Dune System, Mid Glamorgan*. Unpublished BA thesis, Cardiff University.

Megaw, J.V.S., Thomas, A.C. & Wailes, B., 1961 The Bronze Age settlement at Gwithian, Cornwall: preliminary report on the evidence for early agriculture. *Proceedings of the West Cornwall Field Club*, 2(5), 200-15.

Milles, A., 1991 *The Molluscan Biostratigraphy and Archaeology of Holocene Coastal Blown Sand in the British Isles*. Unpublished PhD thesis, Cardiff University.

Paul, C.R.C., 1987 Land-snail assemblages from the shell-midden sites. In Mellars, P. *Excavations on Oronsay: Prehistoric Human Ecology on a Small Island*, 91-107. Edinburgh: Edinburgh University Press.

Peters, C., 1986 *Gunwalloe: A Site and its Environment*. Cardiff:: Unpublished BA thesis, University of Cardiff

Peters, C., 1988 *The Past Environments of Gunwalloe, Cornwall*. Unpublished MSc thesis, University of Bradford.

Pollard, T., 1996 Time and tide: coastal environments, cosmology and ritual practice in early prehistoric Scotland. In Pollard, T. & Morrison, A. (eds), *The Early Prehistory of Scotland*, 198-210. Edinburgh: Edinburgh University Press.

Rackham, D.J., Spencer, P.J. & Cavanagh, L.M., 1989 Environmental survey. In Morris, C.D. *The Birsay Bay Project*. Vol. 1, *Coastal Sites Beside the Brough Road, Birsay, Orkney. Excavations 1976-1982*, 44-53. Durham: Durham University.

Rouse, A.J. & Evans, J.G., 1994 Modern land Mollusca from Maiden Castle, Dorset, and their relevance to the interpretation of subfossil archaeological assemblages. *Journal of Molluscan Studies*, 60, 315-29.

Smith, H., 1996 An investigation of site formation processes on a traditional Hebridean farmstead using environmental and geoarchaeological techniques. In Gilbertson, D., Kent, M. & Grattan, J. (eds), *The Outer Hebrides: The Last 14,000 Years*, 195-206. Sheffield: Sheffield Academic Press.

Spencer, P.J., 1974 *Environmental Change in the Coastal Sand-dune Belt of the British Isles*. Cardiff: Cardiff University, unpublished BA thesis.

Spencer, P.J., 1975 Habitat change in coastal sand-dunes areas: the molluscan evidence. In Evans, J.G. & Limbrey, S. (eds), *The Effect of Man on the Landscape: the Highland Zone*, 96-103. London: Council for British Archaeology.

Thew, N., 2003 Chapter 14: the molluscan assemblages. In Barber, J. (ed.) *Bronze Age Farms and Iron Age Farm Mounds of the Outer Hebrides*. Society of Antiquaries of Scotland/Council for British Archaeology/Historic Scotland: Scottish Archaeological Internet Reports. http://www.sair.org.uk/sair3/index.html; 163-177 & 280-325 (for the tables).

Thomas, K.D., 1985 Land-snail analysis in archaeology: theory and practice. In Fieller, N.J.R., Gilbertson, D.D. & Ralph, N.G.A. (eds), *Palaeobiological Investigations: Research Design, Methods and Data Analysis*, 131-56. BAR International Series 266. Oxford: British Archaeological Reports.

Vaughan, M.P., 1976 *Environmental Change in Areas of Blown Sand on the Western Coasts of the British Isles*. Unpublished BA thesis, University of Cardiff.

Young, M.S. & Evans, J.G., 1991 Modern land mollusc communities from Flat Holm, South Glamorgan. *Journal of Conchology*, 34, 63-70.

Index of
Principal Sites

If you are interested in purchasing
other books published by Tempus, or in case you have
difficulty finding any Tempus books in your local bookshop,
you can also place orders directly through our website

www.tempus-publishing.com